THE BRITISH A

SUPPLEMENTAL

I

The
Imperial Administrative System
in the Ninth Century

With a Revised Text of

The Kletorologion of Philotheos

By

J. B. Bury

Fellow of the Academy

London

Published for the British Academy
By Henry Frowde, Oxford University Press
Amen Corner, E.C.

1911

SUMMARY OF CONTENTS

PAGE

BIBLIOGRAPHY 3

A. PRELIMINARY 7
   (1) Sources for institutional history.
   (2) The text of Philotheos.
   (3) The contents and sources of the Klêtorologion. The Taktikon Uspenski.
   (4) Scope of the following investigation. General comparison of the Constantinian with the later Byzantine system.

B. DIGNITIES (αἱ διὰ βραβείων ἀξίαι) 20

C. OFFICES (αἱ διὰ λόγου ἀξίαι) 36
     I. στρατηγοί.
    II. δομέστικοι.
   III. κριταί.
   IV. σεκρετικοί.
    V. δημοκράται.
   VI. στρατάρχαι.
  VII. ἀξίαι εἰδικαί.

D. DIGNITIES AND OFFICES OF THE EUNUCHS 120
    I. ἀξίαι διὰ βραβείων.
   II. ἀξίαι διὰ λόγου.

TEXT OF THE KLÊTOROLOGION OF PHILOTHEOS 131

BIBLIOGRAPHY

SOURCES.

Saec. V.

[Not. Dig.]	*Notitia Dignitatum*, ed. Seeck, 1876.
[C. Th.]	*Codex Theodosianus*, ed Mommsen, 1905.
	Novellae Theodosii II, &c., ed. Meyer, 1905.
[C. I.]	*Codex Iustinianus* (see below).

Saec. VI.

[C. I.]	*Codex Iustinianus*, ed. Krüger, 1884.
	Iustiniani Novellae, ed. Zachariä von Lingenthal, 1881.
	Iustini II, Tiberii II, Mauricii Novellae, in Zachariä v. Lingenthal, *Ius Graeco-Romanum*, Pars III, 1857.
[Cass. *Var.*]	Cassiodorus Senator, *Variae*, ed. Mommsen, 1894.
[Lydus.]	Ioannes Lydus, *De Magistratibus*, ed. Wünsch, 1903.
[Pet. Patr.]	Petrus Patricius, *Catastasis*, fragments in Const. Porph. *De Cerimoniis* i, cc. 84–95 ; cp. also *ib.* pp. 497-8 (see below).
[(Maurice) *Strat.*]	Pseudo-Maurice, *Strategikon*, ed. Scheffer, 1664.

Saec. VII.

Descriptions of ceremonies in reign of Heraclius, in Const. Porph. *De Cerimoniis* ii, cc. 27–30 (see below).

' Diva iussio Iustiniani Augusti [II]. . . in confirmationem sextae synodi Constantinopolitanae ' [A. D. 687], Mansi, *Concilia*, xi. 737.

Saec. VIII.

Leo III and Constantine, *Ecloga*, ed. Monferratus, 1889.

Some descriptions of ceremonies, in Const. Porph. *De Cerimoniis*, esp. i. 43 and 44.

Saec. IX.

[Takt. Usp.]	Τακτικὸν ἐν ἐπιτόμῳ γενόμενον ἐπὶ Μιχαὴλ ... καὶ Θεοδώρας... ed. Th. Uspenski, in *Izviestiia russkago arkheologicheskago instituta v Konstantinopolie*, iii. 109, sqq. 1898.
[Ibn Khurd.]	Ibn Khurdâdhbah, *Kitâb al-Masâlik wa 'l-Mamâlik*, ed. De Goeje, in *Bibl. Geogr. Arab.* vi, 1889 (pp. 76–85).
[Kudâma]	Kudâma ibn Ja'far, ibid. (pp. 196-9).
[Bas.]	*Basilicorum libri lx*, vols. i–vi, ed. Heimbach, 1833–70 ; vol. vii, ed. Ferrini and Mercati, 1897.

[Epan.] — *Epanagoge legis Basilii et Leonis et Alexandri*, ed. Zachariä v. L., 1852.

[Prochiron] — ὁ πρόχειρος νόμος (of Basil I), ed. Zachariä v. L., 1837.
Leonis VI Novellae, in Zachariä v. L., *Ius Graeco-Romanum*, iii (see above).

[Leo, *Tact.*] — Leo VI, *Tactica*, in Migne, *P. G.*, vol. 107.

[Phil.] — Philotheos, *Klêtorologion*.
Ceremonies. Many of the ceremonies described in Const. Porph. *De Cer.*, date from the ninth century.
Description of Triumph of Theophilus, Const. Porph. περὶ τῶν βασιλικῶν ταξειδίων, 503 sqq. (see below).
Description of Triumph of Basil I, ibid. 498 sqq.
Leo VI. Τὸ ἐπαρχικὸν βιβλίον (le livre du Préfet), ed. Nicole, 1893.

Saec. X.

[Cer.] — Constantine Porphyrogennetos, *De Cerimoniis*, ed. Bekker [vol. i], Bonn, 1829.

[περὶ ταξ.] — — — περὶ τῶν βασιλικῶν ταξειδίων, ibid., 444–508.

[*De adm. imp.*] — — —, *De administrando imperio*, ed. Bekker [vol. iii], Bonn, 1840.

[*Them.*] — —, *De Thematibus*, ibid.
Romani I et Constantini VII Novellae; in Zachariä v. L., *Ius Graeco-Romanum*, iii (see above).

[Anon. Vári] — *Incerti scriptoris Byzantini saec. X liber de re militari*, ed. Vári, 1901.
Nicephorus Phocas, Στρατηγικὴ ἔκθεσις καὶ σύνταξις, ed. Kulakovski, in *Zapiski* of St. Petersburg Academy, viii⁰ sér. viii. 9, 1908.

To this list must be added the *Acta Conciliorum* (esp. of the 6th, 7th, and 8th General Councils), which are cited from Mansi's collection ; and the seals which begin in the sixth century and become more numerous and important afterwards.[1]

SEALS.

[*Sig.*] — Schlumberger, *Sigillographie de l'Empire byzantin*, 1884.

[*Mél.*] — Schlumberger, *Mélanges d'archéologie byzantine*, première série, 1895.

[Panchenko] — Panchenko, *Katalog molybdobullov* [in the collection of the Russian Arch. Institute at Cple.], in the *Izviestiia* of the Institute, viii. 199 sqq. (1903), ix. 342 sqq. (1904), xiii. 78 sqq. (1908).

[Konstantopulos] — Konstantopulos, Βυζαντιακὰ μολυβδόβουλλα [in the National Numismatic Museum of Athens], in the *Journal international d'archéologie numismatique*, vols. ix and x, 1906, 1907.

The chronicles and other literary sources need not be enumerated here. The historians and chroniclers are cited from the Bonn texts (Cont. Th. = Theophanes

---

[1] The collections of Egyptian Papyri (Pap. Brit. Mus., B. G. U., Oxyrhynchus, &c.) are occasionally useful for illustration.

Continuatus ; Gen. = Genesius), except Procopius, ed. Haury, Theophylactus Simocatta, ed. De Boor, Nicephorus Patriarcha, ed. De Boor, (Theoph. =) Theophanes, ed. De Boor, or where otherwise specified. Evagrius is cited from the ed. of Parmentier and Bidez ; the fragments of Menander, &c., from Müller, *F. H. G.* iv.

MODERN WORKS.

Godofredus, *Codex Theodosianus* (Commentary), 1736–45.
Böcking, *Notitia Dignitatum* (Commentary), 1839–53.
Karlowa, *Römische Rechtsgeschichte*, vol. i, 1885.
Schiller, *Geschichte der römischen Kaiserzeit*, vol. ii, Chap. I, 1887.

[Mommsen]   Mommsen, *Ostgotische Studien*, in *Neues Archiv*, xiv, 1888.
Mommsen, *Ephemeris Epigraphica*, v. 1884.
Aussaresses, *L'armée byzantine à la fin du vi⁰ siècle*, 1909.
Gelzer, (M.), *Studien zur byzantinischen Verwaltung Aegyptens*, 1909.
Bury, *Magistri scriniorum*, ἀντιγραφῆς and ῥεφερενδάριοι, in *Harvard Studies in Classical Philology*, 1910.
Diehl, *L'administration byzantine dans l'exarchat de Ravenne*, 1888.
Hartmann, *Untersuchungen zur Geschichte der byzantinischen Verwaltung in Italien*, 1889.
Diehl, *L'Afrique byzantine*, 1896.

[Ducange]   Ducange, *Glossarium ad scriptores mediae et infimae Graecitatis*, 2 vols., 1688. (Compare also his commentaries on works which he edited in the Paris Corpus.)
[Reiske]   Reiske, *Commentarii ad Const. Porph. de Cerimoniis* = Const. Porph., vol. ii, ed. Bonn.
[Rambaud]   Rambaud, *L'empire grec au dixième siècle*, 1870.
Zachariä von Lingenthal, *Geschichte des griechisch-römischen Rechts*, ed. 3, 1892.
[Bieliaev]   Bieliaev, *Byzantina : ocherki, materialy i zamietki po vizantiiskim drevnostiam*, i, 1891 ; ii, 1893.
[Uspenski, *Tabel*] Uspenski, *Vizantiiskaia tabel o rangakh*, in *Izv. russk. arkh. Instituta v Kplie*, iii, 1898.
Uspenski, *Konstantinopol'skii Eparkh*, ibid., iv, 2, 1899.
Uspenski, *Voennoe ustroistvo vizantiiskoi imperii*, ibid., vi, i, 1900.
Panchenko, Βασιλικὸς Πιστικός, ibid. vii, 1902.
Uspenski, *Partii tsirka i dimy v Kplie*, in *Vizantiiski Vremennik*, i, 1894.
Kulakovski, *Drung i drungarii*, ibid., ix, 1902.
Kulakovski, *Vizantiiskii lager kontsa*, *X vieka*, ibid., x, 1903.
Mitard, *Note sur la fonction d' ἐκ προσώπου τῶν θεμάτων*, in *Byzantinische Zeitschrift*, xii, 592–4, 1903.
Bury, *The Ceremonial Book of Constantine Porphyrogennetos*, in *English Historical Review*, xxii, April and July, 1907.
Vogt, *Basile I⁰ʳ*, 1908.

(On the organization, &c., of the Themes.)

Diehl, *L'origine du régime des Thèmes dans l'Empire byzantin*, 1896.

[Gelzer]   Gelzer, *Die Genesis der byzantinischen Themenverfassung*, in *Abhandlungen der kön. sächsischen Gesellschaft der Wissenschaften*, Phil.-Hist. Cl., xviii, 1899.

Brooks, *Arabic Lists of the Byzantine Themes*, in *Journal of Hellenic Studies*, xxi, 1901.

Kulakovski, *K voprosy ob imeni i istorii themy 'Opsikii'*, in *Vizantiiski Vremennik*, xi, 1904.

(On titles of honour.)

Hirschfeld, *Die Rangtitel der römischen Kaiserzeit*, in *Sitzungsberichte der Berliner Akademie*, 1901, 579 sqq.

Koch, *Die byzantinischen Beamtentitel von 400 bis 700*, 1903.

THE IMPERIAL ADMINISTRATIVE SYSTEM IN THE NINTH CENTURY

A. PRELIMINARY.

(1) *Sources for institutional history.*

FOR the history of the administrative institutions of the Roman Empire in the fourth, fifth, and sixth centuries A.D., we have material which is relatively ample. We have the lawbooks of Theodosius and Justinian, and the Notitia Dignitatum, of which the latest portions date from about A.D. 425. We have further the letters of Cassiodorus, written in his official capacity as quaestor in the palace of Ravenna, and, although he is concerned with the Imperial institutions as they were modified to suit the conditions of the Ostrogothic kingdom, the offices and functions were so little altered that the information supplied by Cassiodorus is, as Mommsen perceived, of the highest value not only for the administration of Ravenna but also of Constantinople. In addition to these authoritative documents, we have the mutilated treatise περὶ ἀρχῶν of John the Lydian, which, rambling though it is, furnishes precious material, the author having been himself an official in the reigns of Anastasius, Justin I, and Justinian. These sources—supplemented by inscriptions and the incidental notices to be found in literature—render it possible to obtain a sufficiently clear and fairly complete general view of the civil and military administration as it was organized by Diocletian and Constantine, and as it was modified in details down to the reign of Justinian. ⟨But after the death of Justinian we enter upon a period of about three hundred years which is absolutely destitute of documents bearing directly upon the administrative service⟩ We have no source in the form of a code; for the only lawbook that survives, the Ecloga of Leo III, does not deal with public law, and casts no light on the civil and military administration. We have nothing in the form of a Notitia of offices, no official correspondence like that of Cassiodorus, no treatise like that of John the Lydian. Moreover, in the seventh and eighth centuries there is very little literature, and inscriptions on stone are few and far between.[1] Our only compensation is a very small one ; we now begin to get inscribed lead seals of officials, which become numerous in the eighth and ninth centuries. At last, about the middle of the ninth century, a new series of sources relating to the official service of the Empire begins. The first of these is a notitia or τακτικόν, as it was called, of the chief dignitaries and officials in order of rank, dating from the early years of the reign of Michael III. It is a bare list, but about half a century later comes the Klêtorologion of Philotheos, which is by far the most important source for the organization of the Imperial civil service in the early Middle Ages. And then about half a century later still we have the Ceremonial book compiled by Constantine VII. This collection contains a great many older documents, some dating from the ninth century, and two or three even from the eighth. We have also other writings of Constantine VII, especially the περὶ τῶν βασιλικῶν ταξειδίων and some chapters of the De administrando imperio.

Now these documents of the ninth and tenth centuries show us an administrative system quite different from that which prevailed in the days of Justinian. It is probably due, at least in part, to the nature of the documents that this later system has never been thoroughly examined. For the documents, though of official origin, are not directly concerned with administration ; they are concerned with ceremonial and court precedence, and while they reveal a picture of the world of officialdom, they tell little of the serious duties of the officials. They have not therefore invited systematic investigation, like the Codex Theodosianus or the Notitia Dignitatum. One department indeed of the administration has, during the last twenty years, received particular attention, namely, the general administration of the provinces, the system of Themes. We have now a valuable study of the subject by the late Professor H. Gelzer, who has also partially examined the military organization. It must be added that the judicial machinery has been partly explored by Zachariä von Lingenthal. But the general civil administration and the great ministerial bureaux at Constantinople have not been studied at all. This neglect has been a serious drawback for students of the history

---

[1] For the administration of Egypt the papyri supply considerable material, even for the period from Justinian to the Saracen conquest. Particular attention may be called to the documents dating from the early Saracen period in *Papyri in the British Museum*, ed. Kenyon, vol. iv (accessible to me, before publication, through the editor's kindness). But the Egyptian material helps little for the general administrative changes with which we are here concerned.

of the Eastern Roman Empire. We can observe its effects in most of the works that are published on the subject. We can see that the writers do not attach clear and definite ideas to the official titles which are mentioned in their pages; they often confound distinct offices, and they confound offices with orders of rank. Schlumberger's magnificent work on Byzantine Seals may be cited in illustration; it is marred by many confusions between different officials and different departments.

It is therefore a task of urgent importance to reconstruct, so far as we can, the official organization of the later Empire at the earliest period for which we have sufficient evidence. It is true that at no period of Byzantine history have we documents that can be remotely compared with the Codes of Theodosius and Justinian or with the Notitia Dignitatum; but we must make the best of what we have.

Now the most important document we possess, the only one that gives us anything like a full notitia of the bureaux and officials, is the Klêtorologion of Philotheos, which was compiled in the reign of Leo VI, in the year A.D. 899. It is therefore the proper starting-point for an investigation of the subject. We may say that for the institutional history of the ninth and tenth centuries it holds the same position, in relative importance, which the Notitia Dignitatum occupies for the fourth and fifth.

Once the actual organization existing in the time of Leo VI has been worked out, a further problem presents itself, namely, to trace the steps by which it developed out of the organization existing in the time of Justinian. The evidence of our literary sources shows us that in all main essentials the later system existed in the eighth century. The transformations were effected between the end of the sixth century and the middle of the eighth, in the darkest period of Imperial history, for which we have little more than meagre second-hand chronicles and a few incidental notices in ecclesiastical documents.

In practice, however, it is impossible to separate the two investigations, namely, that of the institutions actually existing in the ninth century, and that of their history. The principal object of the present study is to determine the details of the ninth-century organization, but, as Philotheos, our main guide, only gives the names of the officials and does not indicate their functions, we are obliged to trace the offices, so far as we can, into the past, in order to discover what they were. In the case of many of the subordinate officials we have no data, and must leave their functions undetermined.

(2) *Text of Philotheos.*

As the foundation of these investigations, a critical text of Philotheos is indispensable. The Klêtorologion has come down to us as part of the second book (cc. 52–54) of the *De Cerimoniis* of Constantine Porphyrogennetos. But it was an independent treatise; it formed no part of Constantine's treatise, but was appended to it, along with other documents, probably by the Emperor's literary executors, shortly after his death, as I have shown in a study which I published on the Ceremonial Book in 1907.[1]

The treatise known as *De Cerimoniis* was first published by Leich and Reiske at Leipzig, in 1751–4, in two volumes. It was re-edited by Bekker for the Bonn edition of the Byzantine historians in 1829. Bekker consulted but did not make a complete collection of the MS.

The sole MS. in which this work of Constantine has come down to us is preserved in the Stadtbibliothek of Leipzig (Rep. i, 17). It is a fine large quarto parchment; the titles and lists of contents are in red ink, and the initials at the beginnings of chapters are coloured. It seems to have been written about the end of the eleventh century. It contains 265 folia, but ff. 1–212 are occupied by another treatise of Constantine, which in the Bonn edition curiously appears as an appendix to Book I of the *De Cerimoniis*. I have shown that it is an entirely distinct treatise.[2] It concerns military expeditions conducted by the Emperor in person, and I have designated it as περὶ τῶν βασιλικῶν ταξειδίων.

Until recently our only source for the text of the work of Philotheos was the Leipzig MS. But some years ago Theodor Uspenski, the Director of the Russian Archaeological Institute at Constantinople, found a portion of the text in a Greek codex in the Patriarchal library at Jerusalem. This MS. is numbered 39 in the Catalogue of Papadopoulos-Kerameus.[3] It was written in the twelfth or thirteenth century. The portion of the treatise which it contains (ff. 181–3, 192–4) is unfortunately small, corresponding to less than eleven pages of the Bonn edition. The fragment begins with τόμος β′ = p. 726,[4] and ends at κατὰ τάξιν τιμάσθωσαν = p. 736. Uspenski collated the fragment with the Bonn text and published his collation in Vol. III of the Izviestiia of the Russian Archaeological

---

[1] *English Historical Review*, April, 1907.

[2] *English Historical Review*, July, 1907, p. 439.

[3] Ἱεροσολυμιτικὴ Βιβλιοθήκη, p. 115.

[4] I refer throughout to the pages of Bekker's ed. which are entered in the margin of my text, and in most cases add the line for the convenience of those who care to refer to that ed.

Institute at Constantinople (pp. 98 *sqq.*   Sofia, 1898).   The occurrence of this fragment in the Jerusalem MS. illustrates the fact that the Klêtorologion circulated quite independently of the *De Cerimoniis*, with which it has been accidentally connected. Uspenski observes (p. 101) that ' it is impossible to doubt that as a practical manual the treatise of Philotheos must have been diffused in separate copies '.

But for the main bulk of the text we depend exclusively on the Leipzig MS. With a view to the text which I now publish, I had photographs made (by kind permission of the Oberbibliothekar) of the 27 folia which contain the treatise (cc. 52, 53).[1]   A comparison shows that the Bonn text is by no means trustworthy or accurate. The MS. itself is also a very careless copy of the original. It is full of errors, which were left undetected by Reiske and Bekker. Bekker did not study the subject at all, and Reiske, although he published a learned commentary, never made a methodical examination of the official organization, and therefore was not in a position to criticize and control the text, or to detect inconsistencies and mistakes.

The paucity of paragraphs and the absence of any tabular arrangement render the Bonn edition extremely inconvenient for practical use.   I have endeavoured to remedy this defect.   In introducing tabular arrangement I am only reverting to the form which the author undoubtedly adopted himself. For tabular arrangement is partly preserved in the Lipsiensis, and there can be hardly any doubt that Philotheos wrote his lists of offices in the form of a πίναξ or tabula.

(3) *Contents and sources of the Klêtorologion.   The Taktikon Uspenski.*

The superscription of the Klêtorologion states that it was compiled in September of Indiction 3 = A.M. 6408 (= September 1, 899–August 31, 900), i. e. September, A. D. 899.   The author describes himself as ' Imperial protospatharios and atriklines '. The duty of the atriklinai was to conduct the ceremonial of the Imperial banquets in the palace, to receive the guests and arrange them in order of precedence.   In the MS. we find the form ἀρτικλίνης as well as ἀτρικλίνης, but the latter is the true form of the word, which is evidently derived

---

[1] The ἔκθεσις of Epiphanios, which Philotheos appended to his treatise, and which appears as c. 54, does not concern my purpose, and I have omitted it. I may note here that (except in a few cases like σέκρετον, τοποτηρητής) I have not normalized the orthographical variations of the MS. but have retained the double forms καμίσια : καμήσια, ἀλλαξίματα : -ήματα, στράτορες : -ωρες, ἀτρικλίνης : ἀρτικλίνης (but not ἀρτοκλ.), &c.

from *a triclinio* (cp. ἀσηκρῆτις).[1] κλητόριον was a technical word for an Imperial banquet,[2] and the verb κλητορεύω was used both in the general sense of inviting,[3] and also in the special sense of receiving the guests and announcing their names in order of precedence,[4] a duty which devolved on the atriklines. To fulfil this duty, a list of the ministers, officials, and dignitaries, who had a right to be entertained in the palace, arranged in order of precedence, was indispensable to the atriklines, and such a list was called a κλητορολόγιον. These lists were revised from time to time ; for not only might new offices be instituted and old ones abolished, but changes might be made in the order of precedence.

That such changes were made is clear from the comparison of Philotheos with an earlier document which was published by Uspenski from the same MS., in which he found a portion of Philotheos.[5] This is a Τακτικόν, or table of ranks, which was compiled under Michael III and Theodora. The title is :—

Τακτικὸν ἐν ἐπιτόμῳ γενόμενον ἐπὶ Μιχαὴλ τοῦ φιλοχρίστου δεσπότου καὶ Θεοδώρας τῆς ὀρθοδοξοτάτης καὶ ἁγίας αὐτοῦ μητρός.

Uspenski has not touched upon the limits of the date of this document, but it can be fixed within fourteen years. The fall of Theodora occurred at the beginning of A.D. 856,[6] so that the Taktikon must have been compiled before that year and after A.D. 842, the year of the accession of Michael. Internal evidence bears out the date of the superscription. The Stratêgos of Cherson (στρατηγὸς τῶν κλιμάτων) is mentioned ; the first Stratêgos of Cherson [7] was appointed by Theophilus (c. A.D. 834). The Charsian province appears as a kleisura not a stratêgis [8]; this agrees with the Arabic lists which describe the themes as they existed in the period A.D. 838–845.[9] In

---

[1] It occurs in Gen. 31₁₁ τοῦ τὴν ἐπιστασίαν ἔχοντος τῶν εἰς τράπεζαν κεκλημένων ὃν ἀτρικλίνην φημίζουσι. The Latin version renders rightly *a triclinio*, and Sophocles gives the same explanation. The word does not appear in Ducange.

[2] Suidas explains κλητώριον as ἡ βασιλικὴ τράπεζα. Cp. Pseudo-Symeon 703, Leo VI crowned Anna, διὰ τὸ μὴ δύνασθαι ποιεῖν τὰ ἐκ τύπου κλητόρια μὴ οὔσης Αὐγούστης.

[3] Theoph. 375₁₉ (Justinian II) πρὸς ἀριστόδειπνον κλητορεύων.

[4] We meet it in this sense in Philotheos.

[5] loc. cit. 109 sqq. A notable example of changes in precedence is furnished by the different positions of the Domestic of the Excubiti and the Prefect of the City in the two lists.

[6] See the evidence in Hirsch, *Byzantinische Studien*, 60–1.

[7] Cont. Th. 123.

[8] P. 123, where we must read the singular ὁ κλεισουράρχης Χαρσιανοῦ.

[9] Of Ibn Khurdâdhbah, Ibn al-Fakih, and Kudáma, depending on a work of Al-Garmi, who had been a captive among the Romans and was redeemed in

A.D. 873 the Charsian theme was under a Stratêgos.[1] Kolonea, a theme in A.D. 863, is omitted, as in the Arabic lists.[2] The earliest mention hitherto known of the Stratêgos of Chaldia was in the Arabic lists ; he appears in the Taktikon.[3]

The Taktikon is an epitomized catalogue of officials and dignitaries, for the purpose of showing their order of precedence. It is therefore not arranged like the Notitia Dignitatum (of the fifth century) in which the subordinate officials are placed under their chiefs. It is arranged in classes, according to ranks (patricians, &c.). It is not a klêtorologion (or it would have been so named), but it must have served court ceremonials ; perhaps it was a handbook of the master of ceremonies (ὁ τῆς καταστάσεως). Τακτικὰ βιβλία are mentioned by the biographer of Theophilus (Cont. Th. 142), and evidently mean books which deal with court ceremonial. τάξις meant, among other things, a ' ceremony ',[4] and we might render τακτικόν as ' ceremonial list '.

A new list of this kind was naturally compiled with the help of older lists which it was intended to supersede. Philotheos tells us, as we shall see, that he made use of older klêtorologia. Now in the Taktikon we can detect certain inconsistencies which must have arisen in the process of bringing an older Taktikon up to date. (1) The governor of Chaldia appears both as stratêgos (113) and as archon (123). I infer that Chaldia had been an archontate till recently, when it had been made a stratêgis. The new dignity is duly inserted, but the compiler omitted to strike out the old title. (2) The same thing has happened in the case of Crete. We did not know before the position of Crete in the administrative organization, before the Saracen conquest. The Taktikon shows that it was

---

A.D. 845.   For these lists see Brooks, *J. H. S.*, xxi. 67 sqq. (1901) and Gelzer, 81 sqq.

[1] See Gen. 122.   But in A.D. 863 it was still a kleisurarchy, Cont. Th. 181.

[2] Cappadocia, which is still a kleisurarchy in the Arabic lists, is omitted altogether in the text. But this is probably a scribe's mistake. The text has (p. 123) :—

> οἱ κλεισουράρχαι
> οἱ κλεισουράρχαι Χαρσιανοῦ
> οἱ κλεισουράρχαι Σωζοπόλεως

In the second and third cases οἱ κλ. must clearly be errors for ὁ κλεισουράρχης. But the first οἱ κλ. cannot be right. ' The kleisurarchs ' would not be followed by a list of particular kleisurarchs. I have no doubt that we should read ὁ κλεισουράρχης ⟨Καππαδοκίας⟩.

[3] An ἄρχων Χαλδίας is also mentioned (123).

[4] Cp. e. g. *Cer.* 5₁₀, 516₁ ἡ τακτικὴ μέθοδος 517₁₂. Phil. (790₄) ἐκ τοῦδε τοῦ τακτικοῦ παραγγέλματος.

governed by an archon (123).   But a stratêgos of Crete also appears
(115), and it seems curious that this change should have been made
in the period immediately after the loss of the island.[1]   Perhaps we
may suppose that some small islands of the Aegean were included in
the circumscription of Crete, so that the Cretan commander was not
quite without a province.   It is possible that the appointment of
a stratêgos of Crete might have been made in connexion with the
expedition of Theoktistos in A.D. 843 (George Mon. ed. Bonn, 814),
in anticipation of the reduction of the island.   In that case the date
of the Taktikon would be 842–3.[2]   (3) The same explanation must
also apply to the duplication of ὁ πατρίκιος καὶ σακελλάριος (111
and 115).

The treatise of Philotheos is divided into four Sections, τόμοι.
The beginning of the first is not clearly marked, for τόμος a' has been
omitted in the MS.   The editors have inserted it before the list of
ἀξιώματα διὰ βραβείων (p. 708 B), without any indication that it is
an insertion of their own.   What led them to do this was, I have
little doubt, the occurrence in the margin of the words κεφάλαιον a'.
They took it for a heading corresponding to the subsequent τόμος β',
τ. γ', τ. δ', and silently substituted τόμος for κεφάλαιον.   But it is
clear that κεφάλαιον a' refers to the first of the eighteen classes of
dignities, each of which is marked by a numeral in the margin.   It is
not quite certain where τόμος a' originally stood.   The most probable
place seems to be at the end of the Preface, before the heading ἀρχὴ
τῆς ὑποθέσεως λόγου, and I have placed it here conjecturally, but it is
possible that it may have stood before the paragraph beginning Εἰσὶ
δὲ πᾶσαι ὁμοῦ.

Section I is introductory to the klêtorologion (ἐν εἰσαγωγῆς τάξει)
and consists of a πλινθίς or *laterculus* of the ranks and official dignities
of the Empire.   It falls into five parts : (1) orders of rank ; (2) great

---

[1] If the seal found at Gortyn, with the legend Σ[τ]εφανου στρατ' (published by
Xanthudides, *Byz. Zeitschrift*, 18, 177, 1909), belonged to a stratêgos of Crete
it must be referred to this period.

[2] I may call attention here to the fact that an archon of Dalmatia appears in Takt.
Usp. (124) and a stratêgos is not mentioned.   This bears on the date of a ninth-
century seal of Bryennios, stratêgos of Dalmatia : Βρυεν(ίῳ) β(ασιλικῷ) σπαθ(αρίῳ)
καὶ [στ]ρ⟨α⟩τ(ηγῷ) Δαλματία(ς), *Sig.* 205.   (There is another example in which Br. is
protospatharios.)   Schlumberger ascribes it to Theoktistos Bryennios and dates
it 'vers 840'.   But there seems to be no authority for this.   All we know of
Theoktistos Bryennios is that he was στρατηγός of Peloponnesus in the reign of
Michael III (*De adm. imp.* 221).   It is a mere guess that he is the Bryennios
of the seal.   In any case the Taktikon shows that the seal is later than
A. D. 842.

official posts; (3) minor offices in the staffs and bureaux of the great officials; (4) orders of rank of eunuchs; (5) great offices confined to eunuchs.

Section II and Section III contain lists of the officials in the order in which they are introduced by the atriklines, according as they belong to different orders of rank.   Section II deals with the highest ranks; Section III with the lower, beginning with the protospathars. These Sections ought to form one; the division is not logical or convenient.   To the end of III are appended explanations as to the treatment of ecclesiastics from Rome, Antioch, and Jerusalem, and of Saracen, Bulgarian, and German guests.

Section IV, which is the longer half of the treatise, contains directions for the conduct of the court banquets throughout the year: what guests are to be invited, how they are to be introduced, where they are to sit, what they are to wear, &c.   It is arranged in the order of the calendar, beginning with Christmas.   There follow two memoranda (which are marked off in the MS. as cap. 53 of *De Cerimoniis*, Bk. 2), (1) on the pious largesses (εὐσεβίαι) given by the Emperor to the officials on certain occasions, and (2) on the fees received by the atriklinai.   These memoranda might appropriately have formed a separate Section, but mediaeval compilers were so clumsy and careless in the arrangement of their books that it would be imprudent to guess the omission of a τόμος ε'.

Having concluded with a recommendation that his 'Order of Rank' (τακτικόν) should be adopted as canonical, Philotheos adds an appendix on ecclesiastical precedence and reproduces a list of episcopal sees by Epiphanios of Cyprus (= *De Cer*. ii. c. 54).   I have omitted this list, as it has no interest for the purpose of this study.

The author had before him older lists of dignities and descriptions of ceremonies, to which he refers in his preface as ἀρχαῖα συγγράμματα, αἱ τῶν ἀρχαίων ἐκθέσεις or συγγραφαί.   Some of these were doubtless Taktika or tables of rank, of which a specimen is extant in the τακτικόν of the reign of Michael III, described above; and others were κλητορολόγια which dealt especially with the arrangements at the Imperial table.   The title states that the work is compiled from old klêtorologia, and according to the first words of the preface this was the task imposed on the writer by his friends, men of his own calling.   But afterwards he says that he did not use lists which were out of date, so that ἀρχαίων is hardly an appropriate description of his sources.   For he writes : 'Since I have purposely passed over the expositions of the ancients, not all of them but those which time has rendered obsolete, I will subjoin in the form of a table, line by line, the expositions which are both recognized and practised in the time of our sovrans Leo and Alexander.'

Now we find in the paragraph on the functions of the eunuchs (725) a distinct proof that this was transcribed from an *ecthesis* published in the name of an emperor, whom we cannot hesitate to identify with Leo VI.

Ταῦτα δὲ πάντα φυλάττεσθαι, τηρεῖσθαί τε καὶ πράττεσθαι ἀπαρασάλευτα καὶ διαμένειν βέβαια καθὼς ἡ εὐσεβὴς καὶ ἔνθεος βασιλεία ἡμῶν ἐξέθετο, ὡς καὶ ἐξ ἀρχαίων τῶν χρόνων παρὰ τῶν πρὸ ἡμῶν εὐσεβῶς βασιλευσάντων δικαίως ἐξετέθη.

Here Leo is speaking, not Philotheos. The ecthesis of Leo can hardly have been concerned exclusively with the dignities of the eunuchs, and I think we may conjecture with great probability that one of the lists of offices contained in Section I was transcribed from the Emperor's official book. In this Section the high officials are enumerated three times : (1) a full list, in order of precedence ; (2) a full classified list ; (3) a list of the staffs, &c. (this is not complete, because only two stratêgoi are named as samples, and a few high officials who have no subordinates are omitted). Now of these three lists (1) and (3) are completely in agreement. But (2) exhibits one important difference. (1) enumerates 60 officials, while (2) enumerates 61. The additional dignitary is the ἑταιρειάρχης. This raises a presumption that (2) was derived from a different document, and the words which conclude the first list καὶ αὗται τὰ νῦν τιμηθεῖσαι ἀξίαι ἐπὶ Λέοντος δεσπότου are in accordance with the hypothesis that the transcriber at this point passed to a different source. The use of different sources here may be supported by the fact that, while (2) divides the officials into *seven* classes, this division is also mentioned at the beginning of the Section, where only *six* classes (ἐξ μέρη) are given (the stratarchai being omitted).

It might be thought that we have further evidence that the source of Philotheos for his first list dated from the early years of Leo VI. It does not mention the theme of Longobardia. Now this province was not, as is generally supposed (for instance by Gelzer, 133), organized as a theme by Basil I. The stratêgoi who command in South Italy during and immediately after the conquest are not yet stratêgoi of Longobardia. The first who bears that title is Symbatikios in 891, but even then Longobardia has not yet been established as a distinct theme ; for this commander is ' stratêgos of Macedonia, Thrace, Cephallenia, and Longobardia ',[1] and his successor George

---

[1] Trinchera, *Syllabus graecarum membranarum*, No. 3.

(A.D. 892) is 'stratêgos of Cephallenia and Longobardia'.[1] Hence Gay has rightly concluded that it is not till after this year that Longobardia became a separate theme.[2] But, on the other hand, there is no evidence that the separation was made before A.D. 900. Hence no inference can be drawn from the omission of Longobardia as to the date of the list.

The fact that the list includes the themes of Strymon and of Samos cannot be held to date it; for though the creation of these themes is often ascribed to Leo, this is by no means certain. The case of Thessalonica is a warning. Gelzer attributes the theme of Thessalonica to the *Neuordnung* of Leo VI (*op. cit.* 130); but this theme appears in the Taktikon of Michael III.[3] The themes of Strymon and Samos do not appear in that document,[4] but they may have been formed before the accession of Leo VI. The evidence, however, already adduced seems sufficient to date the source of the first list of Philotheos to the reign of Leo.

The lists of precedence in Sections II and III (cod. Lips.) agree with list 1 of Sect. I in omitting the hetaeriarch, but there are some variations in order. (*a*) In Section III the Drungarios of the Fleet follows, instead of preceding, the Logothete of the Course, and (*b*) the Logothete of the Flocks precedes, instead of following, the Protospathar of the Basilikoi (the latter does not occur in Section II); (*c*) in Section II the Comes Stabuli precedes ὁ ἐκ προσώπου τῶν θεμάτων, but Section III agrees here with the lists of Section I. The variations are common to both MSS.

Another point of difference to be noticed between Section I and Sections II, III, is the treatment of the Magistri. In Section II we have αἱ δὲ λοιπαὶ πᾶσαι τῆς δευτέρας ὑπάρχουσι τάξεως οἷον ὁ μάγιστρος, ὁ μάγιστρος, and in Section III (ad init.) simply ὁ μάγιστρος. In both cases we might expect οἱ μάγιστροι.

We may turn to the evidence of the Jerusalem MS. collated by Uspenski. (1) In this MS. in the lists of precedence, both in Section II and in Section III, we find the Hetaeriarch (μέγας ἑταιριάρχης) immediately after the Drungarios of the Watch. The fact that he occurs in both lists shows that the omission in the Leipzig MS. is not accidental. (2) The Stratêgos of Longobardia appears after the Stratêgos of Sicily in Section II. He is not mentioned in any of the lists in the Leipzig MS. On the other hand, the stratêgos of Nikopolis is omitted in the Jerusalem MS.; but this may be a mere scribe's error

---

[1] *Chron. Vulturnense* (Muratori, *R. I. S.* i. 2. 413).
[2] *L'Italie méridionale*, 171-4.
[3] Uspenski, 115.
[4] Phil. 713, 728.

(there are several other omissions in H which are clearly accidental). (3) Instead of ἀνθύπατος πατρίκιος the Jerusalem MS. has throughout simply ἀνθύπατος. (It also has in most cases σπαθάριοι instead of σπαθαροκανδιδάτοι, but probably this is merely a mistake of the scribe.) (4) In Section II where the Leipzig MS. has ὁ μάγιστρος ὁ μάγιστρος the Jerusalem MS. has ὁ μάγιστρος; but this may be due to parablepsia. (5) The precedence of the protospatharioi of the Chrysotriklinos is said in L to have been established πάλαι (Section III, p. 732), but in H it is attributed to Leo VI.

The probable inference seems to be that the Jerusalem fragment belonged to a slovenly copy of a later recension of Philotheos than that which is represented by the Leipzig text, which was copied from the original. The editor, whether Philotheos himself or another, brought the treatise up to date by inserting the Stratêgos of Langobardia, and repaired the error of omitting the Hetaeriarch. The discrepancies between Section II and Section III seem to be due to the circumstance that Philotheos was using old lists of different dates and he did not succeed in eliminating all the inconsistencies.[1]

(4) *Scope of the following investigation. General comparison of the Constantinian with the later Byzantine System.*

The following pages are not a complete commentary on Philotheos. The investigation is confined to the determination of the functions of the officials, and to the origin of the offices and of the orders of rank. I have not entered upon the subject of the fees (συνήθειαι) paid for dignities and offices, and the Imperial bounties (εὐσεβίαι, ἀποκόμβια, δῶρα) to which the dignitaries were entitled. The latter and main part of the book of Philotheos—Section IV—is important for my purpose, as it throws light on many difficulties which arise out of the earlier part; but a commentary on it belongs not to this inquiry, but to a treatise on the court ceremonies.

From Philotheos we derive no information as to the civil government of the provinces, except so far as finance is concerned. The provincial judges are not mentioned. We hear nothing of οἱ ἀνθύπατοι καὶ ἔπαρχοι τῶν θεμάτων or οἱ πραίτορες τῶν θεμάτων who appear in the Takt. Usp. (118, 119). A large question of considerable

---

[1] In Phil. 788₁₁ we meet the κατεπάνω of Paphlagonia. In the time of Philotheos, and since the early years of Michael III, the governor of Paphl. had been a στρατηγός (Phil. 713₉, Takt. Usp. 113). Under Theophilus he had been a Katepano (*De adm. imp.* 178₇), and perhaps Theophilus raised the dignity of the theme. It looks as if Philotheos were here using a document dating from more than sixty years back.

difficulty, touching the position and the districts of these officials, and their relations to the Stratêgoi, is involved, and I have not been able to discuss it in the present investigation.

A few remarks may be made here as to the general character of the organization of the ninth century as contrasted with the older system which it superseded.

If we compare the scheme of administration which was founded by Diocletian, and completed by his successors, and which remained intact, except in details, till the beginning of the seventh century, with the later Byzantine system, we find that while there is no break in continuity, and the changes seem to have been gradual, the result of these changes is the substitution of a new principle.

The older system has been described as a divine hierarchy. Gibbon designates its principle as 'a severe subordination in rank and office'.[1] There was a comparatively small number of great ministers and commanders-in-chief who were directly responsible to the Emperor alone. All the other administrators were ranged under these in a system of graded subordination. In the Notitia Dignitatum of the East we can count twenty-two high offices,[2] to some of which all the rest were in subordinate relations.

In the ninth century it is quite different. There is no hierarchy of this kind, so far as office is concerned.[3] The number of independent officials responsible only to the Emperor is enormously larger. Instead of twenty-two it is about sixty. And these numbers do not fully express the magnitude of the change. For in the fifth and sixth centuries the territory ruled from Constantinople was far more extensive than in the ninth. It included Syria and Egypt and extended to the Danube. Long before the ninth century, Syria and Egypt and a great portion of the Balkan peninsula were lost.

This change was brought about in two ways. (1) The whole provincial administration was reorganized. The provincial territory was divided into a number of military districts, or Themes, and the governor of each theme, who was primarily a military commander, had also a certain civil jurisdiction. He was independent, subject only to the Emperor. He was not under the orders of any Master of Soldiers or Praetorian Prefect. In fact the Masters of Soldiers and the Praetorian Prefects disappeared. (2) The great central

[1] *Decline and Fall*, c. xvii, p. 169, in Bury, new ed. vol. ii (1909).
[2] In the reckoning I omit the *castrensis*, and include the *Proconsul Asiae*, who was not under the *vicarius Asianae* or the *Praef. Praet. Orientis*.
[3] The hierarchy of rank remains and has been developed into a more elaborate scale.

ministries of the Master of Offices, the Count of the Sacred Largesses, and the Count of the Private Estate, each of which consisted of many different departments, and had an extensive range of functions, were broken up into a large number of offices with restricted competence.

These changes were not brought about at a stroke, by a single deliberative act of administrative reform. They came about by a gradual series of modifications, but they all tended in the same direction, to substitute the principle of co-ordination for that of subordination, and to multiply supreme offices instead of placing immense powers in the hands of a few. We cannot point to any single emperor as the Diocletian of the new system. It is probable that Leo the Isaurian did much to normalize it, but it was in the seventh century under the Heraclian dynasty that the older system had broken down and been irrevocably abandoned, and the chief principles of the newer had been introduced. Even in the sixth century we can discern some foreshadowings of the change.

B. Dignities (αἱ διὰ βραβείων ἀξίαι).

In the sixth century, apart from the exceptional titles of Caesar, nobilissimus, and curopalates, there were a number of dignities, unattached to office, which could be conferred by the Emperor. The highest of these was the Patriciate (introduced by Constantine), which was confined by a law of Zeno to men who had been consuls or prefects, but was opened by Justinian (*Nov.* 80) to all men of illustrious rank. There were also the titular offices of the consulship, the prefecture, and the stratêlasia (*magisterium militum*). The acting administrative officials were distinguished as *in actu positi* or ἔμπρακτοι [1] from the titular officials (ἄπρακτοι), who were of two kinds, (1) *illustres vacantes*, and (2) *illustres honorarii*.[2] The *vacantes* not only bore the title but wore the *cingulum*, the insigne of office; the *honorarii* had the title but not the *cingulum*. But in all cases the dignity was conferred by *codicilli*. In the case of most offices, the titular dignity was probably conferred only on those who had once held the office, but the consulship, the prefecture, and the stratêlasia were regularly conferred on others than officials. The

---

[1] In later texts we generally find the forms ἔμπρατος and ἄπρατος, e. g. *Cer.* 239₄ κἂν στρατηγὸς ἔμπρατος κἂν τε ἄπρατος. Cp. περὶ ταξ. 502₁₉ ἐν ταῖς ἐμπράτοις προελεύσεσιν. In *Cer.* 798 we find a curious third term μεσόπρατος. From this passage it would appear that ἔμπρατος was specially used of the Stratêgos, and μεσόπρατος πατρίκιος was applied to Patricians who held official posts in the capital (ὁ ἐμπολιτικὸς ὀφφικιάλιος).

[2] C. I. 12. 8. 2. Cp. Mommsen, *Eph. Epig.* v. 129.

comitiva, which was in principle an order of the same kind, had been appropriated with its three grades to particular offices, to which it belonged as a matter of course.

In the course of the seventh and eighth centuries, the number of these orders, or titular offices, was largely increased, and they were conferred by investiture with insignia. There were several schools of officers in the palace, who had various duties connected with the Imperial service : *silentiarii, vestitores, mandatores, candidati, stratores, spatharii.* All these titles came to be used as ranks of honour, and were conferred upon all the more important civil and military officials according to their degree. The chief of the school of spatharioi was entitled the *protospatharios*, and this term was adopted to designate a higher rank than *spatharios*—the rank next to Patrician itself. Between the *spatharioi* and *protospatharioi* was interpolated a new class of *spatharokandidatoi*. To the *hypatoi* (consuls) was added a new and higher class of *disypatoi* (*bis consules*).

The protospatharioi were probably not instituted as an order before the end of the seventh century. In the seventh century, the Patricians and Hypatoi were the two most eminent ranks, and the ἀποεπάρχων (*ex Praefectis*) and στρατηλάται were still very high dignitaries. In the course of the next two centuries these orders were re-arranged and multiplied. The Patricians were divided into two ranks : the ordinary Patricians (περίβλεπτοι), who retained as their insigne (βραβεῖον) the ivory tablets, and those to whom the dignity of Proconsul was added (ἀνθύπατοι καὶ πατρίκιοι) who had purple tablets. More important and interesting is the creation of a new and higher rank, that of μάγιστροι. This innovation was obviously connected with the abolition of the office of magister officiorum. At first it was intended that there should be only one *magister* (as there was only one *curopalates*); very soon we find more than one, but throughout the ninth century the dignity was sparingly conferred.

In this place it will be convenient to add a note on the use of the terms ἄπρατος, λιτός, and παγανός which occur in Philotheos. ἄπρατος (*vacans*), to which reference has already been made, is used of persons who bear the titles of *offices* of which they do not actually perform the duties (e.g. στρατηγοί, ἀσηκρῆται, &c., see Phil. 710₁₁, 737₃, ₆, ₇). λιτός is applied to persons who have orders (dignities διὰ βραβείων), but are not ministers or officials ; Phil. 729₁₅ οἱ λιτοὶ ἀνθύπατοι, ib.₂₂ λιτῶν πατρικίων (where there is question of an office being conferred on such), 730₁₅. παγανός[1] seems to be a less technical term, and to

---

[1] The nearest equivalent of παγανός is ‘ordinary’. Cp. *Cer.* 548₂₃ ἡμέραν π. ordinary day (not a s ecial feast), 234₂ κυριακὴν π. ordinary Sunday, 367 ἱππο-

be used in two senses, either as equivalent to λιτός, or to designate persons who were officials but had no rank διὰ βραβείων (these would naturally be functionaries in a very subordinate position).   In the first meaning we find it in Phil. 730₆ εἰ δὲ καὶ παγανοὶ τύχοιεν χωρὶς ὀφφικίων πατρίκιοι and 736₁₅ ὕπατοι παγανοὶ τῆς συγκλήτου (opp. to ὑπ. βασιλικοί, who had posts in the σέκρετα) ; in the second, Phil 739₁ εἰ δὲ παγανοὶ πέλοιεν, ἐν μόνοις τοῖς ὀφφικίοις τιμάσθωσαν.

Philotheos enumerates, in ascending scale, eighteen grades of dignity conferred by insignia, and as the lowest (προβάθμιος) grade includes two titles which are on a parity, we have nineteen titles altogether. They are as follows :—

List of Orders.

	Insigne (βραβεῖον) :		diploma
1 *(a) στρατηλάτης *(b) ἀπὸ ἐπάρχων			
*2 σιλεντιάριος	,,	,,	gold staff
*3 βεστήτωρ	,,	,,	fiblatorion
4 μανδάτωρ	,,	,,	red wand
5 κανδιδάτος	,,	,,	gold chain (of special kind)
6 στράτωρ	,,	,,	jewelled gold whip
*7 ὕπατος	,,	,,	diploma
8 σπαθάριος	,,	,,	gold-handled sword
9 σπαθαροκανδιδάτος	,,	,,	gold chain (of special kind)
*10 δισύπατος	,,	,,	diploma
11 πρωτοσπαθάριος	,,	,,	jewelled gold collar
12 πατρίκιος	,,	,,	ivory inscribed tablets
13 (πατρίκιος καὶ) ἀνθύπατος	,,	,,	purple inscribed tablets
14 μάγιστρος	,,	,,	white gold-embroidered tunic, mantle, and belt
15 ζωστὴ πατρικία	,,	,,	ivory tablets (like Patrician)
16 κουροπαλάτης	,,	,,	red tunic, mantle, and belt
17 νωβελήσιμος	,,	,,	purple tunic, mantle, and belt
18 Καῖσαρ	,,	,,	crown without cross

δρόμον ordinary horse race, Phil. 769₁₆ π. προέλευσις ordinary ceremony (opp. to ἔμπρατος προέλ., see above).   The use of παγανός for ' without office' originated the verb παγανοῦν, to deprive of office, which we find in Leo Diac. 37₂₂ τῶν ἀξιωμάτων παγανοῖ, 96₁₁.

Five (six) of these dignities (marked by asterisks) are designated by Philotheos as senatorial (707_{11} εἰς συγκλητικούς, 712_{14} τῇ συγκλήτῳ ἁρμόζονται$), the rest as προελευσιμαῖοι [1] or βασιλικαί (707_{12} εἰς προελευσιμαίους, 712_{17} ἐν τοῖς βασιλικοῖς κατατάττονται κώδιξιν). Apparently there were two *cursus dignitatum*, one a senatorial (ἀπὸ ἐπάρχων, σιλ., βεστ., ὑπ., δισυπ.), the other of a military character (μανδ., κανδ., στρατ., σπαθ., σπαθαροκανδ., πρωτοσπ.); while the higher orders from Patrician upwards might be conferred on members of either class. Compare *Cer.* 242_{23} where the case is contemplated of the elevation to patrician rank of a person who οὐκ ἔστι συγκλητικὸς ἀλλ' ἔστιν ἀπὸ σπαθίου.[2] But this question demands a special investigation, for which the seals furnish a good deal of material. It is noteworthy that in the seventh century we often find the titles of spathar and hypatos combined.

ἀξίαι προελευσιμαῖοι means dignities which gave a right to take part in the προελεύσεις or Imperial processions (cf. Reiske 160). The holders of these titles formed in a general sense the Imperial retinue. Holders of the synklêtic titles took part in some ceremonies, but not generally in the προελεύσεις (πομπαί, πρόκενσα). All the βασιλικοί resident in the capital formed in a wide sense the προέλευσις or cortège of the Emperor; so that σπαθάριοι ἐξωτικοί (i.e. not resident in the capital) are designated in Takt. Usp. 123 as ἔξω τῆς προελεύσεως.

All those who held ἀξίαι προελ., from the magistri down to the candidati, were grouped together for some ceremonial purposes as ἄρχοντες τοῦ Λαυσιακοῦ (a building in the Palace), a category which also included eunuchs who were praepositi or protospathars. See Phil. 787_{3-7}.

(1) ἀπὸ ἐπάρχων and στρατηλάται.

We know that the honorary ἐπαρχότης existed before the sixth century from a law of Justinian, *Nov.* 90 (ed. Zach. i. 500), which refers to it as ancient. ἴσμεν γὰρ ὡς τὸ ἀρχαῖον ἦν τινὸς ἐπαρχότητος σχῆμα ἣν ὀνοραρίαν ἐκάλουν, κωδικίλλων ἐκ τῆς βασιλείας ἐπ' αὐτῇ παρεχομένων κτλ. Menander (fr. 46, p. 255) mentions that Tiberius II honoured the physician Zacharias τῇ λεγομένῃ ἀπὸ ἐπάρχων ἀξίᾳ. The historian Evagrius was an ἀπὸ ἐπάρχων (p. 4, l. 1; p. 241, l. 6). The importance of the rank in this earlier period is illustrated by *Cer.* 306 (an old ceremony, not later than seventh century, since the praetorian

---

[1] So I correct for the προσελευσιμαῖοι of the MS. The same correction should be made, I think, in Miklosich and Müller, *Acta et Diplomata*, vi. 23. It seems probable that Philotheos intended to include the στρατηλάται among the Senatorials.

[2] Cp. 243_{21}.

prefect appears ; cp. 343$_{12}$), and by early seals. Most of those published in *Sig.* 508–11 are of the sixth and seventh centuries; some of them are of men who had actually filled the office of Praet. Praef. or Praef. Urbis.[1] The dignity had been degraded to be the lowest in the scale, perhaps in the eighth century, at all events by the reign of Michael III (see *Cer.* 633$_{10}$).

The association of the στρατηλασία with the ἀποεπαρχότης is illustrated by the same Novel of Justinian (p. 501), καὶ γὰρ δὴ καὶ στρατηλασίας *praefectorias* εἶναι οἱ ἡμέτεροι λέγουσι νόμοι, and the στρατηλασία could be conferred without a post, οἱ δὲ ψιλοὶ τῆς στρατηλασίας κωδίκιλλοι μόνην παρέχουσιν ἀξίαν τύχης (sc. βουλευτικῆς) οὐκ ἐλευθεροῦντες. The few seals of στρατηλάται belong to the sixth or seventh century, *Sig.* 366–7. Schlumberger, ib. 337, refers the seal of Tatas στρατηλ(άτου) καὶ κανδ(ιδάτου) συνδρουγγαρίου to seventh or eighth century. I suspect it belongs to the eighth century, and illustrates the degradation of the dignity below that of κανδιδάτος. Theopemptos, described as πρωτοστρατηλάτης (seventh century, *Sig.* 367), may have been the senior or doyen of the class of στρατηλάται (cp. πρωτοπατρίκιος). These στρατ. must not be confused with the local στρατ. whom we find in Egypt in the sixth century (M. Gelzer, *Studien zur byz. Verw.*, 30).

The ἀπὸ ἐπάρχων (cp. *Cer.* 99, 247) and the στρατηλάται are associated in *Cer.* 202, 235, 237.

It is to be noted that in the case of these dignitaries, the order is conferred (as in early times) by a codicil (χάρτης), which, however, is now regarded as a βραβεῖον. So too in the case of the hypatoi and patricians.

(2) σιλεντιάριοι.

The silentiaries originally belonged to the class of the *cubicularii* ; they were in the *officium* of the Praepositus and under the jurisdiction of the Mag. Off. Cp. C. I. 12, 16, 4. They were *clarissimi*, ib. 5. The ceremony of their investiture by the Emperor with the insigne of

---

[1] The seal of Eugenios ἀποεπάρχων καὶ δρουγγαρίου is interesting. Schlumberger, *Sig.* 336, refers it to Eugenios mentioned by Theophanes A. M. 6053 (A.D. 560). Here the title is evidently honorary. It is not unlikely that the seal of Theodore ἀποεπάρχων καὶ ἐξάρχου 'Ιταλίας (*Sig.* 211) belonged to Theodore Kalliopas, who was exarch in the seventh century (Lib. Pont. 126, 133), and is described in a papyrus (Marini, Pap. Dipl. 132) as *gloriosus praefecturius.* I believe that *praefecturius* is used as the equivalent of ἀποεπάρχων (Diehl, *Études sur l'adm. byz. dans l'ex. de Ravenne*, 166, n. 2, suggests *praefectus*). L. Hartmann, note to Gregory I, Epp. ix. 115, vol. ii. p. 120 (*Eutychum—inlustrem praefecturium*) is undecided.—Note that ἀπὸ ἐπάρχων is often treated as declinable : plur. ἀποεπάρχοντες or written ἀπὸ ἐπάρχοντες.

their office, the golden band, is described by Peter Patr. (*Cer.* 389) ;
four silentiaries were appropriated to the service of the Empress (ib.).
Their chief duty, from which they derived their name, was to act as
marshals at Imperial audiences ; *silentium nuntiare* was the technical
phrase for calling a meeting of the consistorium (Justinian, *Nov.* 80,
p. 463 ; cp. Mommsen, 482).[1]   (For ὁ ἀδμηνσιονάλιος see below under
C. VII. 6.)

The origin of the *silentiarii* as a senatorial rank is explained by
a constitution of Theodosius II (C. Th. 6, 23, 4): *cum optatam
quietem acceperint* (after their retirement from service) *et inter sena-
tores coeperint numerari, honore curiae sine aliqua functione laetentur,*
&c.   They were freed from senatorial burdens ; but this privilege was
to be confined to thirty.   The institution of a special senatorial class
of ex-silentiaries naturally led to the creation of honorary silentiaries.

There are several seals in which the silentiariate appears as an
order.   Panchenko viii. 240 (eighth or ninth century) σιλ. καὶ βασιλικὸς
νοτάριος, *Sig.* 603 Michael, Chartularios of the Vestiarion is ὕπατος
and σιλεντιάριος, ib. 604 Σεργίῳ σιλεντιαρίῳ καὶ βασιλικῷ βεστίτωιρ, cp.
the earlier seal 602 (3) σελεντιαρίω καὶ βεστίτωρη.

(3) βεστήτορες.

The *vestitores,* or officers of the wardrobe, were, like the silentiaries,
cubicularii, and the origin of the βεστήτορες as a senatorial order was
doubtless similar.   Their creation by a *petitorium,* signed by the
Emperor, is mentioned in Peter Patr., *Cer.* 390.   For their duties
cp. *Cer.* 305, 342, 129, Theoph. 226$_{20}$.   For seals of officers who had
the rank of βεστήτωρ see *Sig.* 180 (5), 194 (3).   Cp. ib. 602 (3, 4),
603 (6), 604 (15).[2]   Compare Bieliaev, i. 172 *sq.*

(4) μανδάτορες, (5) κανδιδάτοι.

See below under the office of the πρωτοσπαθάριος τῶν βασιλικῶν.

(6) στράτορες.

See below under the office of the Protostrator.

(7) ὕπατοι.

After the abolition of the consulate by Justinian and the deaths
of those who had been consuls before that date, the consular order of
the Senate was composed entirely of honorary ὕπατοι (who *consulatus*

---

[1] In illustration of their duties cp. Peter (*Cer.* 426), *Cer.* 233, 247, 306.
[2] Schlumberger has confounded in the same category *vestétores, vestarchai,* &c.

insignibus decorantur, Justinian, *Nov.* 80, p. 464).[1] The honorary consulate can be amply illustrated from seals (ὕπατος and ἀπὸ ὑπάτων), of sixth, seventh, and eighth centuries, of which a selection is published in *Sig.* 476 sqq. A seal of Sisinnios ἀπὸ ὑπάτων, who was Count of Opsikion in the eighth century, and prominent at the time of the revolt of Artavasdos, may specially be mentioned (*Mél.* 250). The title may also be illustrated from the addresses of letters of Theodore of Studion (cp. I, 44; II, 148, 218, 149, 173, also p. 1678, ed. Migne). It is to be remembered that the ὕπατοι were a senatorial order; compare the formula in the ceremonies ἵστανται οἱ ὕπατοι κονσιστώριον (καὶ οἱ λοιποὶ συγκλητικοί), *Cer.* 192$_9$, 209$_{19}$, 232$_{15}$, &c. ὑπατικοί (*consulares*) means the same thing: οἱ συγκλητικοὶ ὑπατικοί 303$_6$; cp. 288$_3$, 289$_{21}$, 291$_1$, $_{24}$.

(8) σπαθάριοι.

See below under the office of the Πρωτοσπαθάριος τῶν βασιλικῶν.

(9) σπαθαροκανδιδάτοι.

The earliest mention of a σπαθαροκανδιδάτος seems to occur in Sebaeos (ed. Patkanian, 114) in reference to A.D. 645; the next in the First Letter of Gregory II to the Emperor Leo III διὰ αὐγουσταλίου τοῦ σπαθαροκανδιδάτου, Mansi, xii. 959, and the officer who pulled down the Image ' in the Chalkoprateia' is described as a spatharo-candidatus, ib. 970. This letter indeed is almost certainly a fabrication of much later date than the age of Leo III,[2] but the insignificant detail of the rank of these officers may rest on older and genuine evidence. In any case, the institution of the order of spatharo-candidates seems to belong to the first half of the seventh century. Panchenko has published a seal (13, 85), Κωνσταντίνῳ [ὑπ]άτῳ καὶ σπαθαροκανδιδάτῳ which he attributes to the seventh or eighth century. A text in *Chron. Pasch.* 696, sub A.D. 605 Ἰωάννης καὶ Τζίττας σπαθάριοι καὶ κανδιδᾶτοι suggests that σπαθάριοι, who were also candidati, may have been set apart as a special class of σπαθάριοι and were afterwards elevated into a new and separate order. It is remarkable that spatharocandidates are not mentioned in the Taktikon Uspenski.

---

[1] In Procop. *H. A.* c. 2 (p. 14 Haury) ἔς τε ὑπάτων ἀξίωμα ἥκεις the honorary consulship is meant, as Photios to whom the words refer was never an acting consul. The honorary consulate was conferred by Anastasius on Chlodwig, Greg. Tur. ii. 38 *ab Anast. imp. codecillos de consolato accepit . . . ab ea die tamquam consul . . . est vocitatus* (where *tamquam consul = ex consule,* the official expression for the honorary consulate). *Proconsul* in the Lex Salica (125 ed. Behrend) is due to misunderstanding.

[2] Cp. Bury, in Gibbon, vol. v, Appendix 14.

In the reign of Theophilus, Petronas was a spatharocandidate before he was raised to the rank of protospatharios (Cont. Th. 123). Among the seals published by Schlumberger may be mentioned those of Martin, Logothete of the Course (*Sig.* 529) [βασι]λικῷ σπαθαροκανδιδάτῳ καὶ λογοθέτῃ τοῦ ὀξέως δρόμου, of Kosmas protonotary of Thessalonica (ib. 103),[1] and of Clement, commerciarius of Hellas (ib. 167). These and the seal of Thomas (ὑπάτῳ βασ. σπ. καὶ τουρμάρχῃ, Panchenko, xiii. 106) are not later than ninth century. Spatharocandidates will also be found in the correspondence of Photios.

The spatharocandidates were not, like the spathars, under the Protospatharios τῶν βασιλικῶν; they did not form a taxis in any officium; and in this they resembled the order of the protospatharioi.

(10) δισύπατοι.

The senatorial order of δισύπατοι seems to have been a late institution, perhaps of the eighth century, and we seldom hear of it. Theodore of Studion addresses a letter (i. 12, ed. Migne, p. 949) Θωμᾷ δισυπάτῳ, and in the reign of Leo V we meet Θωμᾶς πατρίκιος ἀπὸ δισυπάτων γενόμενος (Scr. Incert. 358₁₂), who may be the same person. The *disupatoi* seem to have been a very small class; seals are rare. Of the five published by Schlumberger, only one (*Sig.* 215) is as early as the ninth century: Θεοδώτῳ δισυπάτ(ῳ) πατρ(ικίῳ) β(ασιλικῷ) (πρωτο)σπ(αθαρίῳ) καὶ διοικ(ήτῃ) Σικελ(ίας).

(11) πρωτοσπαθάριοι.

The protospatharios was originally the chief of the *taxis* of Imperial spatharioi. Narses, the eunuch and cubicularius, held this post under Justinian (Theoph. 243₃₁). The order of protospatharioi was probably differentiated from the spatharioi under the Heraclian dynasty. In A.D. 717-8 we meet Sergios ὁ πρωτοσπαθάριος καὶ στρατηγὸς Σικελίας. Numerous seals of protospatharioi of the eighth and ninth centuries will be found in Schlumberger, *Sig.*

(12) πατρίκιοι.

The order of patricians founded by Constantine survived till the latest period of the Empire. In the fourth and fifth centuries it was a very high dignity, sparingly bestowed. Theodosius II made an enactment disqualifying eunuchs (Theoph. 96₂₁), but in the sixth century this was a dead letter. Justinian (as we saw above) opened the patriciate to all *illustres,* and in his time the number of patricians increased considerably. The same law of Justinian (*Nov.* 80) enacts

---

[1] I question whether the seal of Constantine Kontomytes (ib. 109) is as early.

that consuls should have precedence among patricians. In the reign of Justinian II (A.D. 711) we find Barisbakurios, the Count of the Opsikian Theme, designated as πρωτοπατρίκιος (Theoph. 380$_{29}$), which appears to mean that he was the senior or doyen of the ἱερὰ τάξις τῶν ἐντίμων πατρικίων (*Cer.* 37$_4$). A seal of this patrician is published by Schlumberger (*Sig.* 249): Βαρασβα[κ]ουρίῳ πατρικίῳ καὶ κόμ[ιτ]ι τοῦ θεοφυλάκτου βασιλικοῦ ὀψικίου. For the patricians as an order in the Senate cp. John of Epiphania, *F. H. G.* iv. 274 (οἱ π. τῆς συγκλήτου βουλῆς).

(13) ἀνθύπατοι.

This order seems to have been of comparatively late institution. Schlumberger (*Sig.* 438) has published some seals of ἀνθύπατοι (who are not patricians) mostly later than the ninth century. One (No. 6), with Κωνσταντίνου ἀνθυπάτου, is of the sixth or seventh century, and probably belonged to a provincial governor with the proconsular title. We may suspect that No. 5 (Δαυιδα ανθυπατω) is also earlier than the Isaurian epoch. The first occasion on which we hear of a πατρίκιος καὶ ἀνθύπατος is when the Emperor Theophilus raised Alexius Musele to be patrician and anthypatos (Cont. Th. 108). There seems good reason to think that at this time there was no order of ἀνθύπατοι, and that the title conferred on Alexius (who was presently elevated to the rank of magister) was singular.[1] For in the Taktikon Uspenski, which was drawn up soon after the death of Theophilus, we find no mention of πατρ. καὶ ἀνθ. distinguished from simple πατρίκιοι (as we find in the work of Philotheos), but we find ὁ πατρίκιος καὶ ἀνθύπατος enumerated as a singular office or dignity (p. 111, between the Domestic of the Schools and the Strategos of the Armeniacs). It is legitimate to infer that under Theophilus, and in the first part of the reign of Michael III, there was only one ἀνθύπατος, and we may guess that the office was created for Alexius Musele. In that case the description of the ceremony for the creation of ἀνθύπατοι in *Cer.* i. 49 may date from the reign of Theophilus.

In the reign of Michael III, Antigonos, Domestic of the Schools, is described as ἀνθύπατος καὶ πατρίκιος (Cont. Th. 236). We may conjecture that it was in the latter part of the reign of Michael III that the rank of ἀνθύπατος was extended, so as to constitute a class higher than patricians, to which only patricians could be raised. In the time of Leo VI it seems to have been conferred on not a few, as he contemplates the possibility of almost any of the chief administra-

---

[1] It is perhaps significant that according to Stephen Asolik, ii. 6, p. 171 transl. Dulaurier, Theophilus conferred the proconsular patriciate on Ashod, an Iberian prince. Cp. Marquart, *Osteuropäische und ostasiatische Streifzüge,* 421.

tive officials being invested with this order. The ἀνθύπατοι are usually designated as ἀνθύπατοι καὶ πατρίκιοι (regularly in Philotheos and constantly in the Ceremonies); cp. ἀνθυπατοπατρικίους, in περὶ ταξ. 485₁₇.

(14) μάγιστροι.

In A.D. 718–19 Nicetas Xylinites was the μάγιστρος of the deposed Emperor Artemios (Theoph. 400₂₅ μαγίστρου αὐτοῦ)[1]; in A.D. 741 the patrician Theophanes was μάγιστρος ἐκ προσώπου of Artavasdos (ib. 415₃). Under Constantine V and his successors (A.D. 767–89) a certain Peter is μάγιστρος (ib. 442₂₆, 456₁₆, 464₂₃), and in A.D. 792 Michael Lachanodrakon (ib. 468₁).

In Cer. i. 43 a document is preserved dating from A.D. 768, and describing the ceremony of investing the sons of Constantine V with the rank of Caesar.[2] There we find ὁ μάγιστρος playing a part in the ceremony (219₉, 220₄), but he is also designated as ὁ πρῶτος μ. (224₅, ₁₃), while at certain stages of the solemnity οἱ μάγιστροι appear as a velum (218₁₁, 221₁₀). At this time, then, μάγιστρος was a dignity which could be conferred on more than one person, but among the μάγιστροι there was one, ὁ μ. or ὁ πρῶτος μ., who had certain high functions in the court. Evidently this office is to be identified with that held by Xylinites in A.D. 718 and Theophanes in A.D. 741.

The μάγιστρος of the eighth century is the magister officiorum shorn of most of his old functions. This is not only clear from the name (the magistri militum and the magistri scriniorum were not termed μάγιστροι in Greek), but can be proved by several facts. (1) The part which the μάγιστρος plays in the eighth-century ceremony, just referred to, is appropriate to the position occupied by the mag. off. as master of ceremonies. (2) In ceremonies which are of older date (Cer. i. 68 and 70)[3] the μάγιστρος acts as master of ceremonies; and these seem to supply a link between the eighth and seventh centuries. (3) In the ceremony for the creation of a μάγιστρος (i. 46) he is described as κεφαλὴ τοῦ σεκρέτου (233₁₃), which seems to mean that he was the highest in rank at an imperial audience (σέκρετον = κονσιστώριον, see below under the σεκρετικοί). This ceremony (231–3) dates from a time when there was only one μάγιστρος, for no other μάγιστροι are mentioned, whereas in the second ceremony described in the same chapter (234–6) the μάγιστροι appear.[4] (4) Stylianos, the father-in-

---

[1] See further below under the λογοθέτης τοῦ δρόμου, p. 91, where the evidence for the mag. off. in the seventh century is given.

[2] This was shown by Diehl. Cp. Bury, Ceremonial Book, 431.

[3] See Bury, ib. 433.

[4] Contrast 232₁₉ with 235₇; in the second case the μαγ. must be already a patrician.

law and minister of Leo VI, was a μάγιστρος, and he (quite exceptionally) bore the full title of μ. τῶν ὀφφικίων, by which he is designated in Leo's Novels.

In the ninth century the chief evidence for the μάγιστροι is as follows :—

Theoktistos was μ. under Nicephorus I and Michael I : Theodore Stud. Ep. i. 24, ed. Migne, Theoph. 492₆, 500.

Under Michael II we hear of τὰς τῶν μαγίστρων τιμάς : Cont. Th. 72₃.

In the same reign Christophoros was made μ. : Gen. 35₂.

Theodore of Studion addressed a letter of consolation to Stephen, magister, apparently in A. D. 821, in which he is described (ad fin.) as τῆς συγκλήτου πρωτόβαθρον (Ep. ii. 76, ed. Migne).

Under Theophilus, Alexios Musele was raised to the rank of μ. before he became Caesar : Cont. Th. 108₃.

During the absence of Theophilus on a military expedition in A. D. 831, special responsibility devolved upon ὁ μάγιστρος for the security of the city : περὶ ταξ. 504₄.

Manuel was μ. in and after A. D. 842 : Cont. Th. 148₁₃.

In the Taktikon Uspenski μάγιστροι do not appear.

Under Theophilus or Michael III, Arsaber (brother-in-law of the Empress Theodora) became μ., and it was perhaps in Michael's reign that Theodora's nephews-in-law, Stephen and Bardas, became μ. : Cont. Th. 175.

Under Michael III his uncle Petronas was made μ. : Gen. 97₈ ; and Basil received ἡ τῶν μ. τιμή, ib. 111₁₉.

In the same reign (Leo) Theodatakes was made a μ. : Nicetas, Vit. Ignatii apud Mansi, xvi. 237.

In Cer. 631₁₂, however, in a document of the same reign, we read ἀναμεταξὺ τῶν δύο μαγίστρων.

In several ceremonies, which probably date from the reign of Michael III, the μάγιστροι appear as an order like the patricians, and in Cer. i. 26 of the same period we meet the text εἰ μὲν κελεύει ὁ βασιλεὺς ποιῆσαι μαγίστρους κτλ. (p. 143).

Under Basil I Manuel ὁ μ. is mentioned, Cont. Th. 307₂₀.

In the Acts of the Fourth Council of Constantinople (A. D. 869–70) we meet Theodore πατρικίου καὶ μαγίστρου (Mansi, xvi. 309), and in the same Acts we hear of οἱ μ. καὶ πατρίκιοι πάντες (ib. 409).

In the same reign we hear of τοῖς δυσὶ τῆς πολιτείας μαγίστροις, Cont. Th. 347₆ (οἱ λαμπρότατοι μ. 347₂₀).

During Basil's campaign against Tephrike ὁ μ. shared the responsibility for the government at Constantinople : περὶ ταξ. 503₉, and here it is said that, in the case of such imperial absences, it was the custom of old (τὸ παλαιόν) for the emperor παρεᾶν τὴν ἑαυτοῦ ἀρχῆς ἐπικράτειαν καὶ τῷ μ. καὶ τῷ ἐπάρχῳ (of the city) τὴν τῆς πολιτείας καὶ τοῦ κοινοῦ [τὴν] διοίκησιν.

At the beginning of the reign of Leo VI Stephen (nephew-in-law of Theodora) was a μάγιστρος (Cont. Th. 354_{18}), and Stylianos was created μ. and Logothete of the Course : ib. 354_9.

In the same reign, while Stylianos was in power, Katakalon, who became Domestic of the Schools, was a μ.: Cont. Th. 359_{23} ; and at the same period the μ. Leo Theodatakes was still alive : ib. 361_{11}.

In the Vita Euthymii (3_6) Stylianos is designated as πρωτομάγιστρος.

A number of the Novellae of Leo VI (1, 18, &c.) are addressed Στυλιανῷ τῷ περιφανεστάτῳ (or ὑπερφυεστάτῳ) μαγίστρῳ τῶν θείων ὀφφικίων.

A seal of Stylianos has been preserved (Sig. 533) : Στυλιαν(ῷ) μαγ(ίστρῳ) ἀν(θυπάτῳ) πατρ(ικίῳ) β(ασιλικῷ) (πρωτο)σπ(αθαρίῳ) καὶ λογ(οθέτῃ) τοῦ δρόμ(ου). Clearly he was not yet Basileopator, so the date of the seal can be fixed to A. D. 886–8.

From this evidence we may infer that at some time in the eighth century the title μάγιστρος was first conferred on eminent patricians for life, but involving certain duties. Not more than two bore this title at the same time. One of these was the leading member of the Senate ; he was designated as protomagistros, or ὁ μάγιστρος ; he was the κεφαλὴ τοῦ σεκρέτου ; and he shared with the Praepositus and the Prefect the cares of government during imperial absences. Although he descends from the mag. off., his position is higher, as well as less onerous, and corresponds rather to that of a curopalates. The πρωτομάγιστρος is also mentioned in Philotheos, 781_{11}.

The second μάγιστρος shares in the ceremonial duties of the first (Cont. Th. 347_6, cited above). This is illustrated by the document cited above from Cer. 631, and by the description of the creation of patricians, Cer. i. c. 48, which probably dates also from the reign of Michael III. There (143) ὁ πρῶτος μ. stands on the right of the new patrician, and afterwards another μ. stands on his left (cp. below, 144_7 ὁ ἐκ δεξιῶν μ. καὶ ὁ ἐξ ἀριστερῶν). There is nothing to show that before the reign of Michael III there were as many as three bearing the title at the same time. We may conclude that in the eighth and the first half of the ninth century there were not more than two magistri—οἱ δύο τῆς πολιτείας μ., and that the practice of creating more than two was introduced under Michael III. In the minority of Constantine we find three—Stephen, John Eladas, and Leo Phocas (Cont.

Th. 380, 385, 388, 390). In the later period of Constantine's reign we meet four—John Kurkuas, Kosmas, Romanos Saronites, and Romanos Musele (*ib.* 443). It seems to follow from *Cer.* 24 that in that period the number of μ. was less than twelve. The text is τῇ τάξει τῶν τε μαγίστρων καὶ ἀνθυπάτων ἤγουν τῶν φορούντων τοὺς δώδεκα χρυσοϋφάντους λώρους. This shows that there were not enough magistri to wear the twelve lôroi, and that some of the anthypatoi were chosen to make up the number (the other anthypatoi appeared with the patricians as a second velum).

There is another piece of evidence which may tell in favour of the conclusion that there was a period in which the magistri were two in number. The repetition ὁ μάγιστρος, ὁ μάγιστρος in the text of Philotheos, 727₂, would be explained if we may assume that it was taken from an older klêtorologion compiled at a time when there were two magistri.

Two seals published by Schlumberger call for notice. One, of Isaac, πατρ]ίκιον καὶ μάγιστρον, he ascribes to sixth–seventh century (*Sig.* 563); the other of John, πατρικίῳ καὶ μαγίσ]τρῳ, to eighth–ninth century. It seems probable that both seals date from the period when μ. still désignated an office and not an order of rank, and that Isaac was simply magister officiorum. John, if his seal is as late as Schlumberger thinks—not earlier I suppose than the middle of the eighth century—belongs to the period when there were only two magistri, and when the dignity had not yet been made an order of rank like the patriciate.

To sum up. Before the end of the reign of Leo III the office of magister officiorum had been transformed; his special functions had been transferred to the Logothete of the Course, and other ministers ; and he was elevated to the position of head of the Senate and the ministerial world, representative of the emperor in his absence, &c. The dignity was conferred διὰ βραβείου, for life. He was called simply ὁ μάγιστρος (as the μ. τῶν θείων ὄφφ. is usually termed by Theophanes). Perhaps at the same time, or perhaps soon afterwards, a second μάγιστρος was instituted, and the first was distinguished from him as ὁ πρωτομάγιστρος. This innovation was introduced before A. D. 768. I conjecture that the institution of the second μ. is to be connected with the imperial absences from the city. On such occasions the presence of the μ. in Constantinople was necessary, but the emperor may have found it inconvenient not to have a μ. in his moving court. (Observe that in the περὶ ταξ. the emperor is accompanied by μάγιστροι, 485₁₆.) This second μ. would be on such occasions μ. ἐκ προσώπου—the expression which Theophanes uses of the μ. of

Artavasdos (415$_3$). In the reign, probably, of Michael III, the dignity of μ. began to be conferred on more than two ; and thus the μάγιστροι came to form a small order of rank. Within that grade the two μάγιστροι (τῆς πολιτείας) continued to function ; and in the case of Stylianos Leo VI revived the original title μάγιστρος τῶν ὀφφικίων. In the middle of the tenth century, if we can trust Liutprand (*Antapodosis*, vi. 10)[1]—I am not quite confident that we can—there were as many as twenty-four magistri.

(15) ζωστὴ πατρικία.

We have no material for determining the date of the origin of this title. The earliest ζωστὴ πατρικία,[2] of whom we hear on good authority, is Theoktiste, the mother of the Empress Theodora (Cont. Th. 90$_1$). Antonina, according to the author of the Πάτρια (ed. Preger, p. 254), was ζωστή of Theodora (sixth century) ; but there does not seem to be any contemporary confirmation of this statement. The ζωστὴ πατρικία was the only lady who was πατρικία in her own right, and the title might be translated, ' mistress of the robes.' The elaborate ceremony for conferring the dignity is described in *Cer.* i. 50 : it probably dates from the ninth century, and possibly from the joint reigns of Michael II and Theophilus, when, we may suppose, Theoktiste was invested.

(16) κουροπαλάτης.

In the early part of the fifth century *curapalati* was the title of officials of *spectabilis* rank, who were subordinate to the Castrensis, and whose duties seem to have concerned the material condition of the imperial palace. See Not. Dig., *Or.* 17. 5 ; C. Th. xi. 18. 1 (probably A. D. 412, see ed. Mommsen). At the court of Theodoric we find a curapalati of *spectabilis* rank, but apparently not in the officium of a castrensis (there seems to have been no castrensis at Ravenna) : Cass., *Var.* 7. 5. There is some reason for supposing that in the course of the fifth century at Constantinople a new *cura-palati* was instituted, independent of the castrensis, and at least equal in importance to him. For in the reign of Justin I the grand-daughter of a certain Nomos (or Oninos), a patrician, married the king of the Lazi, and Nomos is described as ἀπὸ κουροπαλατῶν.[3] It

---

[1] Four magistri are mentioned under Constantine VII in Cont. Th. 443. Some of them were stratêgoi.

[2] ζωστή must mean *cingulo donata* (Combefis, and Reiske, ii. 166), not *ornatrix* as Ducange thought. One seal of a ζωστή (Maria Melissene), of the Commenian epoch, is published by Schlumberger, *Sig.* 607 ; she is simply ζ., not ζ. π.

[3] Chron. Pasch. 613, Theoph. 168$_{21}$; cp. John Mal. 413.

is not at all probable that an ordinary curapalati would have been created a patrician unless he had risen to some higher office, and in that case he would have been designated by that higher office. I infer that in the time of Anastasius, at latest, there existed a high official, entitled Curapalati, to be distinguished from the earlier subordinate curapalati (who was one of several). If this conclusion is right we can the more easily understand the action of Justinian, who, towards the end of his reign, exalted the dignity and gave it a new significance by conferring the title upon his nephew Justin.[1] The title was taken to mean that Justin was marked out to be the successor to the throne, and the dignity evidently did not involve any of the functions connoted by the name. Through jealousy, perhaps, Justinian did not care to create his nephew a Caesar, but κουροπαλάτης was interpreted as equivalent. This is expressly said by Corippus (in laud. Just. i. 134 sqq.) :

> par extans curis, solo diademate dispar,
> ordine pro rerum vocitatus curapalati,
> dispositu nam Caesar eras.

After this, and till the tenth century, the title curapalati, κουροπαλάτης, was only bestowed on a relative of the emperor : and the patriarch Nicephorus (7_3) describes the post as τὴν μετὰ βασιλέα πρώτην ἀρχήν (i. e. of course, when there was no Caesar). From the nature of the case it was, like Caesar, only occasionally conferred. The following is a list of the κουροπαλάται till A.D. 900 :—

Emperor.	Kuropalates.
Justinian I	Justin (nephew): Corippus, loc. cit., Evagrius, 5, 1.
Maurice	Peter (brother): Chron. Pasch. 694_6.
Phocas	Domentziolos (nephew): Theoph. 292_{25}.
Heraclius	Theodore (brother) : Niceph. 7_3.
Leo III	Artavasdos(son-in-law): Theoph. 395_{12}.[2]
Nicephorus I	Michael (son-in-law) : Theoph. 492_9.
Michael III	Bardas (uncle) : Cont. Th. 176_3.

Leo VI conferred the title on the Iberian king Adranases (De adm. imp. 199); it had been more than once in earlier times bestowed on Iberian princes. In the tenth century Nicephorus II created his brother Leo a κουροπάλατης; in the eleventh the title was no

---

[1] May the idea of this dignity have been derived from Persia? Cp. Theoph. Sim. 3. 18. 12.

[2] A seal of Artavasdos is extant, Sig. 249 Ἀρτανάσδη πατρ[ικίῳ] κουρ[οπαλάτῃ] καὶ κόμ[ιτι] τοῦ Ϲεοφ[υλάκτου] β[ασιλικοῦ ὀψικίου].

longer confined to relatives of the Emperor (cp. the seals in Schlumberger, *Sig.* 490 *sqq.*).

A ceremony for the creation of a kuropalates is described in *Cer.* i. 45, p. 229 *sqq.* When this description was first written down there were two emperors, one of whom was still a boy (ὁ μικρός). It may be conjectured that it refers to the creation of Michael by Nicephorus I and Stauracius. At the end of the chapter there is a notice to the effect that a kuropalates can be created ἐν τῷ ἰδίῳ by the Basileus, without a public ceremony. I conjecture that Bardas was thus invested, and that this additional notice dates from the reign of Michael III.

(17) νωβελήσιμος.

In the third century *nobilissimus* was the standing epithet of the title Caesar which the emperors conferred on natural or adopted sons (Mommsen, *Staatsrecht,* ii.[3] 1141 and note). In the fourth century we find Jovian creating his child-son Valerian a νωβελίσιμος, but not Caesar; the epithet becomes an independent title (Philostorgius 8. 8). In the fifth century Constantine, the 'tyrant' of Britain and Gaul in the reign of Honorius, creates his eldest son, Constans, *Caesar,* and his second, Julian, νωβελίσσιμος (Olympiodorus, fr. 12). Honorius created his child-nephew, Valentinian, nobilissimus (*ib.* 34), and afterwards V. was invested as Caesar at Thessalonica before he was crowned Augustus at Ravenna (*ib.* 46). Nobilissimus is thus a title lower than Caesar, but confined to the emperor's family. Justinian [1] introduced the new title of kuropalates to do duty for nobilissimus or Caesar, but in the eighth century Constantine V revived the dignity of νωβελήσιμος. In A.D. 768 he created his second and third sons Caesars, and his fourth νοβελίσιμος (Theoph. 444): afterwards also his fifth son (*ib.* 450₂): and the sixth received the same dignity from Leo IV (*ib.*).

A description of the ceremony performed on the first of these occasions is described in *Cer.* i. 44 (the mention of two Caesars proves this, as Diehl has shown). As to the insignia there is a discrepancy between *Cer.* and Theoph. The latter says that the νοβ. was invested with a χλαῖνα χρυσῆ and ὁ στέφανος. In *Cer.* 229 we read that his χλαμύς is not purple like that of the Caesar but κόκκινος, and στέφανον οὐ περιτίθεται. Philotheos says that the insignia are χιτὼν ἐξ ἀλουργίδος χρυσόθετος καὶ χλαμὺς καὶ ζώνη. It is clear, then, that Theoph. has made two mistakes; he has confounded the χλαῖνα

---

[1] He seems himself to have borne the title under his uncle; cp. Marcellinu *sub* A.D. 527. Women sometimes received the dignity, e.g. Galla Placida, C. I. L. 15, 7153.

or χλαμύς with the tunic which was χρυσόθετος, and he erroneously supposed that the νωβελήσιμος was crowned like the Caesar.

(18) Καῖσαρ.

For the Caesar title, as a promise of succession under the Principate, see Mommsen, *Staatsrecht*, ii.[3] 1140. After Justinian's reign we find it conferred on Tiberius by Justin II ; on Germanus and Maurice by Tiberius II ; on Constantine junior by Heraclius ; on David and Marinus by Heraclius ; on Christophorus and Nicephorus by Constantine V ; on Alexios Musele by Theophilus ; on Bardas by Michael III.   The only case I know (later than the third century) of the elevation to this rank of one who was not a near relative (by birth, adoption, or marriage) of the emperor is that of Patricius, son of Aspar, who was created Caesar by Leo I.

From Theodosius I it was the invariable practice of the emperor, if he had a son, to create him a colleague (Basileus and Augustus). Hence the title Caesar was rarely conferred.   Justin II and Tiberius II conferred it to mark out their successors, but after Maurice it was only conferred on persons who might, in certain events, succeed.   Heraclius and Constantine V bestowed it on younger sons ; Theophilus on a son-in-law ; Michael III, who was childless, on an uncle.

The ceremony which accompanied the elevation of the sons of Constantine V is described in *Cer.* i. 43.

C. Offices (αἱ διὰ λόγου ἀξίαι).

The administrative officials are grouped by Philotheos in seven classes : I. στρατηγοί, II. δομέστικοι, III. κριταί, IV. σεκρετικοί, V. δημοκράται, VI. στρατάρχαι, VII. various (ἀξίαι εἰδικαί) ; and it will be convenient to take them in his order.

The use of the term ὀφφικιάλιοι, which frequently occurs in his pages, has not, so far as I know, been precisely explained.   But he supplies the material for determining its denotation.   In early times *officiales* seems to have been applied only to the members of the *officium* of a minister, but not to the minister himself.   The Master of Offices, or the Count of the Sacred Largesses, would not have been called an *officialis*.   In the time of Philotheos, it was applied to the ministers as well as to their subordinates.[1]   And it was applied to all the functionaries holding office or command, with the exception of the στρατηγοί.   This can be proved from the following passages.

---

[1] Speaking of the posts in the staffs and bureaux of the high officials, Philotheos (716₈) says that these dignities καὶ αὐτὰ ὀφφίκια ὀνομάζονται.

(1) The author expressly states that the Domestici (notwithstanding their military character) were counted as ὀφφικιάλιοι (715$_{12}$). (2) In 742$_{18}$, 742$_{2}$, $_3$ the στρατ. and ὀφφ. are distinguished: 6 στρατ., 2 ὀφφ. Cp. also 767$_{29}$. (3) Equally clearly they are contrasted in 766$_{17}$ and 767$_{1-3}$. (4) So too in 710$_{10}$.[1] In 784$_{15}$ and 767$_9$ σεκρετικοὶ ὀφφικιάλιοι are mentioned, meaning all those comprised in class IV.

While ὀφφίκιον in later documents is more often used in our sense of office, than in its earlier meaning of the whole staff of subordinate officials, the term τάξις is employed for the staffs of the Stratêgoi, Domestics, Kritai, &c., and σέκρετον for the officials of class IV.[2] For this distinction cp. Cer. 6$_{8}$, $_9$ πάσαις ταῖς τάξεσι καὶ πᾶσι τοῖς σεκρέτοις.[3] On σέκρετον see below in section IV on σεκρετικοί, p. 83.

The high officials themselves are thus divided into seven classes, but their subordinates are grouped in three classes (716$_9$): A. ταγματικοί, B. θεματικοί, C. συγκλητικοί. Obviously A comprises the subordinate ὀφφίκια of the Domestics (class II), and B those of the στρατηγοί (class I); it follows that the subordinate officials of classes III–VII were all designated as συγκλητικοί.

The use of συγκλητικοί, which constantly occurs in Philotheos and the Ceremonies of Constantine, is confusing, and demands some observations. We must first of all distinguish the Synklêtos in the narrow sense of the Council of high officials who assisted the Emperor in business of state from the whole body of συγκλητικοί, or persons of senatorial rank, who had the right of being received at court, and were expected to take part in the ceremonies and processions.[4] But there are other variations in its meaning. It seems sometimes to be

---

[1] In 784$_{11}$, however, στρατηγοί are loosely included under ὀφφ.

[2] But σέκρετον was doubtless also commonly used of the bureaux of subordinate officials belonging to the other classes.

[3] A. Vogt, in his Basile Ier, p. 75, gives προέλευσις as the term for suite or bureau. Its ordinary meaning is ceremonial procession (cp. προέρχεσθαι), and it is used for the suite of a strategos (comitatus, cp. the προελευσιμαῖοι of κριταί in Const. Porph. Nov. 9, p. 268$_1$), but not for a bureau. The passage in Phil. 716$_7$ is difficult: εἴδη ἀξιωμάτων διάφορα, κατὰ ἀναλογίαν καὶ τάξιν καὶ τῆς ἑκάστου προελεύσεως (the text seems doubtful: I think we must read καὶ τῆς τάξεως). The meaning seems to be that these subordinate offices differ according to the kind of staff to which each belongs. τάξις is used generally (including the σέκρετα), προέλευσις especially of the military staffs. See above, p. 23.

[4] It seems probable that in such passages as Cer. 87$_3$ οἱ πατρίκιοι καὶ στρατηγοὶ ἐκεῖσε καὶ ἡ λοιπὴ σύγκλητος, or 150$_{18}$ οἱ πατρίκιοι καὶ ἡ σύγκλητος, the senate in its narrower sense is meant; the contexts suggest that only officials of very high rank are contemplated. For the two senses of σύγκλητος cp. Ellissen, Der Senat im oströmischen Reiche, 27 sqq. (1881).

opposed to βασιλικοί,[1] yet in its application to the officials of classes III–VII (see above), it embraces many officials who were distinctly βασιλικοί. The fact is that persons holding ἀξίαι διὰ βραβείων βασιλικαί might be συγκλητικοί, if they held offices under classes III–VII, and we are thus able to explain the passage in *Cer.* 61₂₂ δισυπάτους, σπαθαρίους συγκλητικούς, καὶ ὑπάτους, where I remove the comma which appears in the Bonn edition after σπαθαρίους; only those spathars, who are also συγκλητικοί by virtue of an ὀφφίκιον, are designated. The eunuch officials are not described as Synklêtic, but some of them certainly were.[2]

It appears that in its widest sense συγκλητικοί included (1) high dignitaries, magistri and patricians,[3] whether they held office or not; (2) all the high officials who obtained their office διὰ λόγου (except perhaps some of the eunuchs), and including Stratêgoi[4] and Domestics; (3) the officials subordinate to the ministers of classes III–VII; (4) the Synklêtic dignitaries διὰ βραβείων, namely disypatoi, hypatoi, &c.; and possibly (5) an obscure class who had no such dignities (but see below VII (6) under ὁ ἐπὶ τῆς καταστάσεως). The term was also used in a restricted sense to designate the fourth (or fifth) of these categories.

In this connexion must be noticed a phrase which often occurs in the latter part of Philotheos, οἱ ὑπὸ καμπάγιον (those who wear the kampagion, some kind of footgear,[5] cp. Ducange s. v.). Compare :—

(1) 742₁₈ τὴν ὑπὸ καμπάγιν σύγκλητον πᾶσαν, οἷον ἀσηκρῆτας κτλ. (various members of the Sekretic officia) οἷον ἀπό τε σπαθαροκανδιδάτων καὶ κατώτερω, ὑπάτων, δισυπάτων, and some of the tagmatic officials.

(2) 752₁ τοὺς ὑπὸ κ. συγκλητικοὺς ἅπαντας, οἷον ἀσηκρῆτας κτλ. (various officials under classes III–VII, and also some of the tagmatic officials).

(3) 757₁₉ φίλους τοὺς ὑπὸ κ. ἅπαντας, ἄρχοντας τῆς συγκλήτου, ἀπό τε μαγίστρων, ἀνθυπάτων, πατρικίων, ὀφφικιαλίων, βασιλικῶν πρωτοσπαθαρίων, ἀσηκρητῶν κτλ. (including some tagmatic officials).

(4) 759₉ φίλους ἐκ τῶν συγκλητικῶν, τοὺς ὑπὸ κ. πάντας, οἷον μαγίστρους, ἀνθυπάτους, πραιποσίτους, πατρικίους, ὀφφικιαλίους, βασ. πρωτοσπαθαρίους, συγκλητικούς, τὸν πρωτοασήκρητις κτλ. (including tagmatics).

(5) 769₁₉— ἀπὸ τῆς τάξεως τῶν μαγίστρων, πατρικίων καὶ λοιπῶν σὺν

---

[1] Cp. *Cer.* 516₁; 3₂₃–4₁.

[2] The Praepositus, e. g. was a member of the Senate. Cp. Mansi, xvi. 392 (A. D. 869) ὁ μεγαλοπρεπέστατος πραιπόσιτος ὡς ἐκ προσώπου τῆς ἱερᾶς συγκλήτου. *Ib.* 329 Gregory, a Spatharocubicularius, is described as ἀπὸ τῶν τῆς συγκλήτου.

[3] Also praepositi, cp. Phil. 741₁₇.

[4] Cp. *ib.* the στρατ. belong to the βασιλικὴ σύγκλητος.

[5] For the καμπ. as ceremonial footgear cp. John Mal. 322₁₁ (A. D. 330).

τῷ δομεστίκῳ τῶν σχολῶν καὶ βασιλικῶν ἀνθρώπων ἀπὸ τῆς τάξεως τῶν σπαθαροκανδιδάτων μέχρι τῆς τάξεως τῶν στρατώρων—τοὺς μὲν ὑπὸ καμπάγιν πάντας μετὰ τῶν οἰκείων ἀλλαξημάτων—τοὺς δὲ πρωτοσπαθαρίους μετὰ σπεκίων—τοὺς δὲ βασιλικοὺς μετὰ τῶν σκαραμαγγίων καὶ μόνον.

(6) 774_{15}.

(7) 777_{22} ἀπὸ τῶν σεκρετικῶν τῶν ὑπὸ καμπάγιν πάντων.

(8) 779_{10} τῶν μαγ., ἀνθ., πατρ., ὀφφικιαλίων, πρωτοσπ. καὶ λοιπῶν συγκλητικῶν τῶν ὑπὸ καμπάγιν ὄντων.

(9) 780_2 οἱ μὲν μαγ., πραιπ., πατρ. ὀφφικιάλιοι καὶ οἱ ὑπὸ καμπάγιν πάντες—οἱ δὲ λοιποὶ βασιλικοί.

(10) 781_4 ἀπὸ τῆς τάξεως τῶν μαγ., πραιπ., ἀνθ., πατρ., ὀφφικιαλίων, πλὴν τῶν εὐνούχων—καὶ ἀπὸ τῆς τάξεως τῆς ὑπὸ καμπάγιν συγκλήτου, καὶ τῶν ταγματικῶν ἀλλαξιμάτων.

Of these passages, 3, 4, and 5 make it clear that the kampagion was worn by the highest officials. 1 and 2 refer only to subordinates, and in 10 the high dignitaries are contrasted with ἡ ὑπὸ καμπάγιν σύγκλητος. There is no real contradiction in this; in 8 and 9 the magistri, &c., are specially singled out of the kampagion category, and the rest are grouped together as οἱ ὑπὸ καμπάγιν. What dignitaries and officials did not belong to οἱ ὑπὸ καμπάγιν? First of all, probably the eunuchs, except patricians and praepositi (cp. 4 and 9). Secondly, the Stratêgoi and their staffs, who are never mentioned in these passages. Thirdly, protospatharioi, &c., who were not Synklêtic by virtue of office. Fourthly, some lower subordinates (cp. 7), such as δρομεῖς (Phil. 752_{12}). It is remarkable that tagmatic officers, subordinates of the Domestics, are enumerated among οἱ ὑπὸ κ. συγκλητικοί (cp. 1–4). Is this loose language?

I. στρατηγοί.

(1) to (26). Stratêgoi.

This class includes, along with twenty-five stratêgoi of themes (including the Count of Opsikion), the official known as ὁ ἐκ προσώπου τῶν θεμάτων (al. σχολῶν).

The origin of the themes, and their history up to the ninth century, has been so fully treated by Gelzer [1] that I need only call attention to a few general points before considering the staff of the stratêgos.

The precedence of the Eastern over the Western themes is fundamental. This order of rank is not explained by the precedence of the

---

[1] Gelzer's conclusions, for the ninth century, have indeed to be supplemented by the Arabic evidence produced by Brooks (see Bibliography) and by the Taktikon Uspenski.

Prefecture of the East over the Prefecture of Illyricum, as many of the provinces in the latter had a higher rank than the provinces of the former.   It is due to the fact that the Illyric provinces were almost a lost position in the seventh century, and that the strength of the Empire lay entirely in Asia Minor with Thrace at the time when the theme system was developed and normalized under Leo III. The naval circumscriptions, which were equally important when that emperor came to the throne, and which may truly be said to have saved the Empire under the Heraclian dynasty, were included by him among the Western themes, because recent experience had shown that they might prove a dangerous element of opposition, and his own power was based on the Asiatic armies.[1]   On the other hand, when at a later time Macedonia became a theme, it was included in the Eastern class (while Thessalonica and Strymon remained in the Western).   The Stratêgoi of the Eastern themes all received a fixed salary from the treasury, whereas those of the Western raised their pay in their own provinces; but the naval themes were for this purpose included in the Eastern class.[2]   The number of twenty-five stratêgiai corresponds of course only to the situation at the moment when this particular list was drawn up, in the early years of Leo VI. Before the end of his reign there was a new stratêgia of Mesopotamia, and the Kleisurarchies of Sebasteia, Lykandos, Seleukeia, and Leontopolis had been raised to the rank of themes.[3]

The Stratêgos of the Anatolic theme [4] holds the highest rank among the stratêgoi, and his is the highest office of those not confined to eunuchs, with the exception of those of Basileopator and Rector and the ecclesiastical post of Synkellos.   At a court reception, only the magistri, and these three dignitaries, the Praepositus (if a patrician), and eunuchs of patrician rank, preceded the Stratêgos of the Anatolics, provided he was a patrician.   But so long as he was a patrician, although not an anthypatos, he sat among the anthypatoi.   If he was

---

[1] Cp. Gelzer, 34–5.

[2] The salaries of the Eastern Stratêgoi were graded as follows : class 1, Anatolic, Armeniac, Thrakesian, 40 litrai (about £1752); class 2, Opsikian, Bukellarian, Macedonian, 30 l. (about £1314) ; class 3, Cappadocian, Charsian, Paphlagonian, Thracian, Kolonean, 20 l. (about £876), and to this class must be added the Chaldian strat., who received only 10 l., in consideration of the income he derived from custom-dues, and the Mesopotamian, who derived all his pay from customs.   The naval themes formed a class 4, Kibyrrhaeot, Samian, and Aegean, 10 l. (about £438) ; and, class 5, the Kleisurarchs (Lykandos, &c.) received 5 l. (about £219).   See the salaries as paid under Leo VI in Cer. 696–7.

[3] Cer. ii. 50.

[4] It is called τὸ αʹ θέμα in Gen. 5$_{17}$.

only a protospatharios, he was first in that order, unless the Praepositus happened to be also a protospatharios. At one time the Sakellarios seems to have been superior in rank to the Stratêgos Anat.; this question will be considered below in connexion with the Sakellarios. But the exalted position of the Strat. Anat. in the imperial service corresponds to what, as I pointed out long ago, was the origin of the post; he took the place of the magister militum per Orientem. Next to him in rank, among the officials, was the Domesticus Scholarum, who in the later Empire corresponds most nearly to the old magister militum in praesenti (though he does not descend from him); and after the Domesticus comes the Stratêgos of the Armeniac theme, who represents the magister militum per Armeniam, instituted by Justinian.

The officium of a stratêgos is as follows :—)

(1) Turmarchae, (2) merarches, (3) comes τῆς κόρτης, (4) chartularius, (5) domesticus, (6) drungarii bandorum, (7) comites bandorum, (8) centarchus spathariorum, (9) comes τῆς ἑταιρείας, (10) protocancellarius, (11) protomandator (and in the case of the maritime themes, (12) protocarabi, (13) centarchi).

(1, 2) The turmarchs commanded the τοῦρμαι, or divisions of the | military θέμα or corps, and governed the turms or districts of the geographical theme. The military unit was the βάνδον, of which \ the commander was entitled (7) *comes*. According to Leo, *Tact.* iv. | 42, the βάνδα were grouped in higher units, called μοῖραι or δροῦγγοι, and these regiments were commanded by μοιράρχαι or δρουγγάριοι. The turm or brigade consisted of three such μοῖραι, *ib.* 9. The turm) was also called μέρος, and the τουρμάρχης a μεράρχης.[1] There were three turmarchs under the stratêgos.[2] This account differs from that of Ibn Khurdâdhbah, who wrote his description of the administrative organization of the Roman Empire, c. A.D. 840-5 (ed. De Goeje, see Bibliography). According to him, there were two turmarchs under the command of the stratêgos of one of the larger themes. Under the turmarch were five drungarioi, and under the drungarios five comites.[3] The discrepancy arises from the fact that the number of turms and turmarchs differed in the different themes. We have tenth-century documents (A.D. 935 and 949) showing that there were three turms in the Thracesian theme.[4] Ibn Khurdâdhbah generalized

[1] *Ib.* 8, 9.   [2] *Ib.* 44.
[3] Gelzer has tabulated the subdivision, pp. 116, 118.
[4] *Cer.* 663₃ and 666₁₇. The text of the former passage requires correction. It stands ὁ τουρμάρχης τῶν Θεοδοσιακῶν, οἱ τουρμάρχαι τῶν βικτόρων, οἱ τουρμάρχαι τῆς παραλίου. Read ὁ τουρμάρχης for the plural in both cases (cp. 663₂₀ ὁ τ. τῶν βικτόρων).

from one theme. We can prove this by the fact that he represents the numbers of troops in the (larger) themes as uniform—10,000 men.[1] Now we know from another Arabic writer, Kudâma (who copied Ibn Khurdâdhbah, but added new facts), that the number of the troops in the various themes both larger and smaller varied considerably.

Leo VI speaks of μεράρχης as an (older) equivalent of τουρμάρχης (*Tact.* iv. 8, 9). In Philotheos they are distinguished, and other texts prove that μεράρχαι is not a gloss on τουρμάρχαι. In the official description of the troops sent to Italy in A. D. 935 by Romanus I, ὁ μεριάρχης[2] of the theme of Charpezikion, and ὁ μεριάρχης of the Thracesian, are mentioned as well as the turmarchs.[3] Moreover, we find ὁ μεράρχης in the treatise περὶ ταξειδίων.[4] These passages entitle us to correct the text of Philotheos, and read μεράρχης for μεριάρχαι.

These divisions of the army τοῦρμαι, μοῖραι, βάνδα correspond to the sixth-century divisions, μέρη, μοῖραι, τάγματα. Turmarchs replace merarchs, the drungarioi correspond to the moerarchs (see below), and the κόμητες (see below) to the ἄρχοντες (also called κόμητες). See (Maurice) *Strat. passim*, and Aussaresses, *L'armée byzantine*, 19 *sqq.* Who then is the later merarch? I suggest that in most themes there were *two* geographical turms in the ninth century and two turmarchs, while the army consisted (as in the sixth century) of *three* brigades, and that the third brigade was under a commander who bore the old title μεράρχης and had no geographical district.

(6, 7) We must also correct δρουγγάριος τῶν βάνδων to δρουγγάριοι τ. β.[5] The drungarios, as we have seen, was the commander of a μοῖρα, and there were probably three μοῖραι in each turm. With δρουγγάριος, τῶν βάνδων has a collective sense—the (ten) banda which compose his μοῖρα; with κόμητες (ὁμοίως = τῶν βάνδων) it is distributive, each comes commands a βάνδον. For the drungarioi compare *Cer.* 666_{19} (οἱ δρ. καὶ κόμητες), 667_{10}, $662_{15, 21}$. They are also called

---

[1] From the Armeniac, if Gelzer is right in his probable correction of Kudâma (p. 98).

[2] The MS. of *Cer.* varies between μεριάρχης and the right form μεράρχης (663_{18}). Compare the seal published by Schlumberger (*Sig.* 201) σφραγὶς μερεάρχ(ου) τῆς Κνώσσ(ου) Κωνσταντίνου. This belongs to the later period after the reconquest of Crete by Nicephorus II. In Genesios we meet the merarch of the Charsian theme in A. D. 863 (97_2).

[3] *Cor.* 662_{19}, 663_4, and 663_{18} (ἀπὸ τοῦ βάνδου τοῦ μεράρχου, which is obscure).— In the theme of Charpezikion we find great and minor turmarchs distinguished, $662_{18, 20}$, $667_{8, 9}$, $669_{6, 8}$.

[4] *Cer.* 482_{19}.

[5] This was not apprehended by Kulakovski, *Drung i drungarii*. To this article I may refer for the history of the terms drungos and drungarios.

δρουγγαροκόμητες, 482₁₉, 663₆. In Takt. Uspenski, 129, ὁ δρουγγάριος τῶν θεμάτων must be corrected οἱ δρουγγάριοι τ. θ.

(3) On the duties of the comes τῆς κόρτης (count of the tent) [1] the chief source is the treatise περὶ τῶν βασιλικῶν ταξειδίων. When the emperor leads a military expedition, the comites τῆς κόρτης of the various themes attend the emperor to pitch the imperial tent, along with the *cortinarii* who are under their command, and accompany the Drungarios of the Watch in his nightly circuit round the camp. They supply posthorses to the Drungarios of the Watch for imperial business, *Cer.* 489–90. They might also be sent on special missions. For instance, the stratêgos of the Anatolic theme sent his comes τῆς κόρτης to examine Theodore of Studion in prison at Smyrna (A. D. 819, Theod. Stud., *Epist.* ii. 38, p. 1233, ed. Migne). In Leo, *Tact.* iv. 30, the comes τῆς κόρτης is described as a member of the general's staff (προέλευσις). These officials might be spatharioi, see Philotheos, 735₇, where the text must be corrected ὁ σπαθάριος καὶ κόμης τῆς κόρτης τῶν Ἀνατολικῶν. The Theophylactus, count of the tent in the theme of Chaldia, whose name is preserved on a seal in Schlumberger's collection (*Sig.* 289, 331), was a *candidatus*.[2] The emperor sometimes had a comes τῆς κόρτης of his own ; e.g. Michael the Amorian filled the post for Nicephorus I (Genes. 10₁₃, Cont. Th. 9, 12).[3] The seal of a κ. τῆς κόρτης (ninth–tenth century) is published by Schlumberger, *Mél.* 245.

(5) The δομέστικος is mentioned as a member of the general's staff in Leo, *Tact.* iv. 30. Compare *Cer.* 482₂₀, 662₂₀, and 663₅ (ὁ δομέστικος τοῦ θέματος) ; Takt. Usp. 128. These officers have the rank of strator in Phil. 737₁. See also Alexius Comnenus, Nov. 30, p. 374, ed. Zach.

(8) The κένταρχος τῶν σπαθαρίων must be distinguished from the κένταρχοι mentioned in Leo, *Tact.* iv. 11, who commanded each 100

---

[1] κόρτη was the tent, especially of the emperor, but also of the stratêgos. See Ducange, *s. v.* Cp. Cont. Th. 236₂ ; George Mon. (Bonn) 830₁₈ = Pseudo-Simeon, 678₂₁.

[2] The legend is θεοτόκε βοήθει τῷ σῷ δούλῳ + Θεοφιλάκτῳ β(ασιλικῷ) Κανδ(ιδάτῳ) καὶ κόμ(ητι) τῆς κόρτ(ης) Χαλδ(ίας). The seal belongs to the ninth century. Chaldia seems to have become a separate government towards the end of the eighth century (Gelzer, 95–6), and it was raised to the rank of a stratêgia before the middle of the ninth century. Gelzer thought that it was a κλεισοῦρα till the reign of Leo VI. But the Taktikon Uspenski mentions ὁ πατρίκιος καὶ στρατηγὸς Χαλδίας (p. 113) and also ὁ δοὺξ Χαλδίας (p. 119). We may infer that it had been at first a Ducatus and had been recently made a στρατηγία ; ὁ δοὺξ X. was taken over from an older list.

[3] In Alexius Comnenus, Nov. 30, p. 374 (foot of page) κομήτων . . . δομεστίκων τῶν θεμάτων, we should, I conjecture, read κομήτων τῆς κόρτης.

men, and were subject to the comes.[1] This distinction seems to correspond to the distinction in Phil. 738₁₈, ₂₀ between the κένταρχοι τῶν στρατηγῶν τῶν θεματικῶν and the κένταρχος τῶν βάνδων. Are we to identify the κένταρχος τῶν σπ. with the πρωτοκένταρχος who is recorded on seals (Schlumberger, Sig. 166 Σησηνήω πρωτωκ(εν)τάρ(χω) 'Ελ(λ)άδ(ος) 357 Στρατιγ(ω) ἀκενταρκ(ω)))? But there were more than one πρωτοκένταρχος in a theme. Six are mentioned in the staff of the general of the Thrakesians (Cer. 663₁₀).[2] It seems possible that κένταρχος in the text of Phil. is an error for κένταρχοι. The spatharioi whom the centarch commanded were probably a guard attached to the immediate service of the general.[3]

(9) The κόμης τῆς ἑταιρείας is, I conjecture, referred to in Cer. ii. 44, p. 659₁₅ ἵνα ἀποσταλεῖ τῆς ἑταιρείας μετὰ κελεύσεως πρὸς τὸν κατεπάνω, where perhaps τὸν κόμητα has fallen out after ἀποσταλεῖ.

(4) The χαρτουλάριος of the theme was in the officium of the stratêgos, but his duties connected him with the department of the Logothete τῶν στρατιωτικῶν, so that he also belonged to his officium and was responsible to him. This is explained in Leo, Tact. iv. 31, where the function of the chartularius is described as πρὸς τὴν τοῦ στρατοῦ (MS. στρατηγοῦ) καταγραφήν τε καὶ ἀναζήτησιν (he kept the military rolls), and it is said that while he and the protonotary and the praetor were in some respects (ἔν τισιν) subject to the stratêgos, they were also directly responsible to the central government: τοὺς λόγους τῶν ἰδικῶν αὐτῶν διοικήσεων πρὸς τὴν βασίλειαν ἡμῶν ἀφορᾶν ὥστε δι' αὐτῶν μανθάνειν τάς τε τῶν πολιτικῶν καὶ τῶν στρατιωτικῶν πραγμάτων καταστάσεις καὶ διοικήσεις ἀσφαλέστερον ἡγούμεθα.

From the relation of the chartularius to the Logothete τ.στρατιωτικῶν, and from the functions of the χαρτουλάριοι τῶν δήμων referred to in the edict of Cer. ii. 56,[4] we can see that he had financial duties, and that the pay of the officers and soldiers came into his department. He might have the rank of a spatharios (Phil. 735₁₆) or a strator (736₂₀). Nicephorus, chartularius of Sicily (eighth–ninth century),

---

[1] It is to be noted that Ibn Khurdádhbah speaks of Kontarhīn who command each forty men and are identified by De Goeje with kentarchs (hekatontarchs), but by Gelzer (115) are explained as (pente)kontarchs, on the basis of a passage in the Acta S. Demetrii, 181 C. Leo does not mention pentekontarchs.

[2] πρωτοκένταρχοι occurs in a doubtful passage in Basil II, Nov. 29 (p. 311), and in the list of the stratêgic officials (A. D. 1079) in Miklosich and Müller, Acta et Diplomata, vi. 21.

[3] At the beginning of the eighth century the stratêgos had also stratores, for in A. D. 718 (Theoph. 388₂₂) we meet a δομέστικος τῶν στρατόρων of the strat. of the Anatolic theme.

[4] Cp. Rambaud, 204.

whose seal is preserved (Panchenko, 9. 384), was a spatharios. Drosos, chartularius of Thrace (eighth or ninth century) (Schlumberger, *Sig.* 122), was a candidatus. Orestes, chartularius of the theme of the Aegean Sea (tenth century), had the higher rank of a spatharocandidatus (*Sig.* 194).[1]

(10) The πρωτοκαγκελλάριος was the chief of what would in earlier times have been called a *schola* of cancellarii. There was such a schola under the mag. off. of the West in the fifth century (Not. Dig. Occ. ix. 5). There was probably a cancellarius in all bureaux of the first and second class ; we find a cancellarius of the Prefect of the City in the time of Julian (*C.I.L.* 6. 1780), and one attached to the bureau of the Dux Pentapoleos in the reign of Anastasius I. His duty was to keep the public from entering the secretum of the minister,[2] and to carry communications between him and the general officium. He was outside the officium (see Cass. *Var.* xi. 6), and this may explain why he is not mentioned in the Not. Dig. When John Lydus wrote, the Praet. Praef. of the East had two cancellarii, but this may have been exceptional and temporary ; the Praet. Pref. selected his cancellarii from the *schola Augustalium* ; the post was not filled by ordinary advancement within the officium.[3] Cancellarii and a protocancellarius are found in most of the officia (except in the domesticates) enumerated by Philotheos, but they occupy a low position in the matricula. There are no seals of protocancellarii. The protocancellarius of the theme is mentioned in *Cer.* 659$_{17}$.

(11) Mandatores, with a πρωτομανδάτωρ at their head, occur not only in the officia of the Stratêgoi, but also in those of the Domestics, of some of the Logothetes, and others. They were properly adjutants, or bearers of commands (μανδατοφόροι). The mandatores of the Stratêgos are defined in Leo, *Tact.* iv. 16, as οἱ τὰ μανδάτα ἀπὸ τῶν ἀρχόντων πρὸς τοὺς στρατιώτας ὀξέως διακομίζοντες (cp. *ib.* 49).[4] The protomandator of a theme was an official of some importance. For a seal of a protomandator of Dalmatia see Schlumberger, *Sig.* 206. Carbeas was protom. of the Strat. Anatol. under Michael III (Cont. Th. 166$_2$).

---

[1] The seal of a ὕπατος καὶ χ. of Cephallenia (eighth–ninth century), and another of a βασ. σπαθαροκανδιδάτος καὶ χ. of the Cibyrrhaeot Theme, are published by Schlumberger, *Mél.* 205, 208. The chartularies of the themes are mentioned in Alex. Comn., *Nov.* 30, p. 374.

[2] See Agathias, i. 19, p. 55. On the cancellarii see esp. Krüger, *Kritik des Justinianischen Codex*, 163 *sqq.* (1867).

[3] See Mommsen, 478 *sqq.*

[4] See (Maurice) *Strat.* iii. 5, vii. 16. Cp. Aussaresses, *op. cit.* 23.

(27) Οἱ ἐκ προσώπου τῶν θεμάτων.

The functions of the ἐκ προσώπου have been discussed by Reiske,[1] Rambaud,[2] Schlumberger,[3] and most recently by Mitard.[4] I need not consider Reiske's view, which is palpably wrong. Rambaud rightly saw that these functionaries were representatives of the emperor, and that the temporary government of a province or district was delegated to them ; they were temporary stratêgoi, distinguished from the Stratêgoi proper. This has been more clearly and fully set out by Mitard. That ἐκ προσώπου means ἐκ προσώπου τοῦ βασιλέως is proved by the passage in *De adm. imp.* 228 *sqq.*, which Rambaud and Mitard consider,[5] and is illustrated by Leo VI's idea that the stratêgos himself is an ἐκ προσώπου of the emperor, who is the supreme stratêgos (*Tact.* 4. 7, cited by Mitard). We might further cite a late seal (*Sig.* 577) Παναγ(ιωτη) ανθ(υπατω) πατρ(ικιω) και εκ προσ(ωπου) τ(ου) φιλ(οχριστου) δεσπ(οτου).

These writers have not called attention to the difficulty which lies in the alternation of the plural with the singular in Philotheos, to whose notices we have to add the evidence of Takt. Usp.

Singular : (1) Takt. Usp. 120 ὁ ἐκ προσώπου τῶν θεμάτων (a proto-
             spatharios).
       (2) Phil. 714$_5$ ἡ τοῦ ἐκ π. τῶν θ.
       (3) *ib.* 729$_6$ ὁ ἀνθ. πατρ. καὶ ἐκ π. τῶν θ.
Plural : (4) Phil. 715$_7$ οἱ ἐκ προσώπου τῶν θεμάτων (cod. σχολῶν).
       (5) *ib.* 732$_1$ οἱ πρωτοσπαθάριοι ἐκ προσώπου τῶν θεμάτων
            κατὰ τὸ ἴδιον ἔκαστον θέμα.

We must interpret the singular as equivalent to a plural ; as these officials were appointed for temporary needs, it is clear that there might sometimes be one, sometimes more than one, sometimes none. It is, however, quite possible, seeing the constant confusions of sing. with plur. both in the Taktikon and in Philotheos, that the plural should be read in 1, 2, and 3. From the nature of the case, an ἐκ προσώπου had no permanent ὀφφίκιον, he would use the existing ὀφφίκιον of the Stratêgos in the theme to which he was sent ; and

---

[1] 837 'puto eum fuisse qui legiones integras repraesentaret, eorum loco et nomine ad imperatorem peroraret', &c. He is followed by Schlumberger.
[2] 197-8.   [3] *Sig.* 576.
[4] See Bibliography. Uspenski, *Tabel*, 135 quotes from Kekaumenos, *Stratêgikon*, 40 (ed. Jernstedt) ἐγχειρίσθητι κἂν ἐκπροσωπικὴν ἢ τὴν ἀρχοντίαν ἢ τὸ βασιλικὸν τῆς πολιτείας ἡμῶν, where ἐκπροσωπικὴ (ἀρχή) is probably the office of a locum tenens for a stratêgos. But Uspenski throws no light on the subject.
[5] τοῦ γὰρ πρωτοσπαθαρίου Εὐσταθίου καὶ ἀσηκρῆτις ἐν τῷ τῶν Κιβυρραιωτῶν θέματι ἐκ προσώπου ἀποσταλέντος.

therefore these officers are passed over by Philotheos in his list of the ὀφφίκια.

Philotheos 'mentions (788₁₀) the fees paid by the ἐκ πρ. to the atriklinai, and here he uses the phrase ἐκ προσώπου στρατηγοῦ, which illustrates the construction of the genitive τῶν θεμάτων, in the title ἐκ πρ. τῶν θ., as dependent not on ἐκ πρ. but on στρατηγῶν or a word of the kind.

Schlumberger has published a seal (Sig. 245) of eleventh or twelfth century of an ἐκ προσώπου in the Theme of the Optimati : Μιχαηλ εκ προσωπου των οπτε(ματων).[1] An earlier seal of the eighth or ninth century (ib. 577, No. 6) records a πρωτοσπαθάριος καὶ ἐκ προσώπου. The ἐκ προσώπου τοῦ δρόμου (Sig. 123) must be kept apart from the τῶν θεμάτων. An earlier seal of Theodotos, ἐκ προσώπου Μεθώνης, will be found in Mél. 204.

II. δομέστικοι.

The Domestici fall into two groups, the four Domestici of the Tagmata,[2] and the rest. Before treating them separately, some general words of explanation seem required concerning the Tagmata, as to which vague and incorrect opinions have been held.[3]

The Byzantine army consisted of two great divisions, the θέματα and the τάγματα, and troops were designated as thematic or tagmatic according to the division to which they belonged.[4] The themata were the troops of the provinces, and the tagmata were the troops stationed in or about the capital. The themata were commanded by stratêgoi, the tagmata by domestici, and there were differences in the organization.

The tagmata are frequently mentioned by Theophanes in the history of the eighth century, e. g. σχολάριοί τε καὶ τῶν λοιπῶν ταγμάτων (437₂, A.D. 764),[5] and he opposes them to the themes (τὰ ἔξω θέματα 442₂₈, cp. τὰ ἔσω τάγματα 449₂₇). In the ninth century there were four Tagmata proper, namely (1) the Scholarii, (2) the Excubitores or

---

[1] Cp. also 577, No. 4.

[2] οἱ μεγάλοι δομέστικοι τῶν τ. in Cer. 287₂₀, 299₁₄ seem to mean these four, cp. 291₁₇.

[3] The subject has been treated by Uspenski, Voennoe ustroistvo (see Bibliography). Reiske (837) enumerates the four tagmata incorrectly, and it is clear that Gelzer (17 sqq.) did not realize what they were.

[4] Cp. e. g. Nov. Nicephori Phocae xviii, p. 290 ταγματικοὶ καὶ θεματικοί.

[5] Also 461₂₀, 468₇, 471₁₄, &c. It may be noted that τάγματα is used of the Scholarians by Agathias, 5, 15 (310₁, ₁₃). Cp. Menander, fr. 11 τῶν κατὰ τὴν αὐλὴν ταγμάτων commanded by the Mag. Off. In the sixth century τάγμα was used for βάνδον, see above, p. 42.

Excubiti, (3) the Arithmos, (4) the Hikanatoi. The evidence [1] for the four Tagmata is abundant in documents of the ninth and tenth centuries. For the eighth century there is no explicit evidence as to their number, but, as the Hikanatoi seem to have been instituted by Nicephorus I (see below), we may assume that there were three.[2] They consisted of cavalry.[3] But tagmata was also used in a looser sense to include two other bodies, the Numeri and the Imperial fleet.[4] The Numeri were infantry[5] and did not leave Constantinople, and this applies also to the troops who were under the command of the Count of the Walls.[6]

The term σχολάριοι, though strictly used of the troops of one tagma, the Σχολαί, was also used for the rank and file of all four Tagmata.[7]

It appears from a document of the tenth century that detachments of the four Tagmata were stationed in Thrace, in Macedonia, and in the 'Peratic' region on the Asiatic side of the Bosphorus.[8]

---

[1] Phil. 758₄ λοιπῶν ἀρχόντων τῶν δ' ταγμάτων, 763₅ οἱ δ' δομέστικοι τῶν δ' ταγμάτων. *Cer.* 598₁₈ (ii. 16) οἱ τῶν δ' τ. ἄρχοντες, καὶ ὁ μὲν δομέστικος τῶν σχολῶν καὶ ὁ ἐξκούβιτος καὶ ὁ ἱκανάτος εἰσέρχονται . . . χαιρετίζουσιν τὸν δρουγγάριον τῆς βίγλας.   Cp. 605₁₈₋₂₁. Περὶ ταξ. 484·₃ τὰ τάγματα . . . αἱ σχολαὶ . . . τὰ ἐξκούβιτα . . . ὁ ἀριθμός . . . ὁ ἱκανάτος (leg. οἱ ἱκανάτοι). *Cer.* 666₃,₇, &c. Cont. Th. 181₁₆ (A. D. 863) μετὰ τῶν βασιλικῶν τεσσάρων ταγμάτων.   The earliest enumeration is in Kudâma (depending on Al Garmi and relating to A.D. 838–45), De Goeje, 196 *sq.* (Gelzer, 17 *sqq.*). Some of the names are mutilated.   (1) Scholarii ; (2) Excubiti—so Gelzer, and Uspenski, *op. cit.* 169 ; (3) ''wkws, under the command of a trungar' (*drungarios*) : Gelzer thinks the Hikanatoi are meant, but (*a*) the title *drungarios* points to the Arithmos, and (*b*) the Arithmos is third in precedence ; Uspenski also believes that the Arithmos is meant ; (4) *fidaratiyin* = φοιδεράτοι ; De Goeje indiscreetly suggested σκουτάριοι : it is very unlikely that the Hikanatoi are designated under the name φοιδεράτοι, but emendation is out of place.   See below, p. 64.

[2] We cannot press Theoph. 461₂₀ τῶν σχολαρίων τε καὶ ἐκσκουβιτόρων καὶ τῶν λοιπῶν ταγμάτων, esp. as ' the remaining tagmata ' may include the Numeri and Teichistai. The Arithmos (Vigla) is included 491₁₁, where however the Hikanatoi are not mentioned (A. D. 811).

[3] Kudâma says they were each 4,000 strong ; but Ibn Khurdâdhbah (81) seems to suggest that they were 6,000.

[4] *Cer.* 604₇ οἱ τῶν ταγμάτων ἄρχοντες· τῶν σχολῶν, τοῦ ἀριθμοῦ, τῶν νουμέρων ἐν μιᾷ τάξει· οἱ δὲ τῶν ἐξσκουβίτων, οἱ ἱκανάτοι καὶ οἱ τοῦ βασιλικοῦ πλοίμου ἐν ἑτέρᾳ τάξει.

[5] Kudâma, *ib.*   [6] Cp. *Cer.* 524₂₂–525₂.

[7] The text (which can be dated A. D. 949) in *Cer.* ii. 45, 666₃₋₁₃ proves this quite clearly. The ἄρχοντες τῶν δ' τ. are opposed to the σχολάριοι τῶν δ' τ., and the ἄρχοντες and σχολάριοι of the Excubiti and Hikanatoi are mentioned. So too *Cer.* 619₉ οἱ ἄρχ. τῶν τ. μετὰ τῶν σχολαρίων.   This ought to have been recognized by Uspenski (cp. *loc. cit.* 171).

[8] *Cer.* 666.   This passage will be discussed below in connexion with the topotêrêtês of the Schools.

As to the title Domesticus. In the fourth, fifth, and sixth centuries it constantly occurs in the sense of *princeps officii*, as the designation (primicerius is used in the same way [1]) of the chief subaltern of a general, minister, or governor of a province.[2] In the fifth and sixth centuries the domestici of the magistri militum were important persons. It will be shown below (p. 50) that the elevation of the title to designate the commanders of the guard troops was probably due to the withdrawal of the Schools from the control of the Master of Offices.

(1) ὁ δομέστικος τῶν σχολῶν.

At the beginning of the fifth century there were seven scholae of palace guards at Constantinople.[3] Some of these scholae were composed of foreigners (*gentiles*),[4] and during that century up to the reign of Zeno the foreign element seems to have been chiefly Armenian.[5] Zeno introduced Isaurians.[6] The total number of the scholarian troops was 3,500,[7] and we may infer that each schola was 500 strong. As palace guards they were under the orders of the magister officiorum. Justinian at the beginning of his reign increased the number to 5,500, adding four new 'supernumerary' scholae.[8] The number might seem to have been afterwards reduced to the original seven by Justinian himself. For Theophanes records that in A. D. 562 that emperor transferred to Thrace (Heraclea and the adjacent cities) the scholarians who were settled in Nicomedia, Prusa, and other Bithynian towns. The text (p. 237) gives τῶν ἑπτὰ σχολαρίων τοὺς καθεζομένους κτλ., where σχολαρίων should be corrected to σχολῶν. Again in the περὶ ταξειδίων of Constantine Porph. an account of a ceremony in the reign of Justinian is preserved, and αἱ ἑπτὰ σχολαί are mentioned (497₂₁). But it seems more probable that the original seven scholae were distinguished from the four new supernumerary regiments. Further there is indirect evidence that the number of scholae was afterwards increased to fifteen, for in the

---

[1] Cp. Cass. *Var.* 10, 11 *primiceriatus qui et domesticatus nominatur.*
[2] See Mommsen 508, and *Eph. Epigr.* v. 139–41, where the material will be found. Marcian was a dom. of Aspar, Theoph. 104₂₁.
[3] *Not. Dig. Or.* xi. 4–10.
[4] *Ib. Scola gentilium seniorum,* and *sc. gent. iuniorum.* Amm. Marc. 14. 7, 9; 20. 2, 5; 27. 10, 12, &c.
[5] Proc. *H. A.* 24. 16.   [6] (*Ib.* 17 and) Agath. 5. 15, p. 310.
[7] Proc. *ib.* 15.
[8] *Ib.* 19 (ὑπεράριθμοι). *C. I.* 4. 65. 35 (A. D. 530) *in undecim deuotissimis scholis.*

tenth century there were fifteen counts, and the count was the commander of the schola [1] (see below).

The Domestic of the Schools is first mentioned in the eighth century (Theoph. 442, A. D. 767). The abolition of the Magister Officiorum led to the distribution of the various duties which he performed to a number of independent functionaries, and the Domestic of the Schools was his successor in the command of the scholarian guards. As we have no formal evidence as to the date or mode of the change, it must be left an open question whether the Magister was relieved of this command before his final disappearance from the scene. But we may ask whether the Domestic was a new creation, whose title was invented at the time when the Magister was superseded, or was he an already existing subordinate who was raised to the supreme command. [2] Now there is an important text in the *Chron. Pasch.* (724) which throws light, I believe, on this question. The chronicle tells that when Heraclius went to the East in A.D. 624 he was accompanied by Anianus, the Domesticus of the Magister (δομεστίκου τοῦ μαγίστρου). [3] The Magister, standing alone, means the Magister Officiorum. The obvious inference is that the Scholarians went with the emperor, and were under the command of the Domesticus of the Magister, while the Magister remained at Constantinople. The Domesticus of the Magister is mentioned in the fourth century (Ammianus Marc. 30. 2, 11), and is perhaps the same official who is called the *adiutor* in the *Not. Dig. (Or.* xi. 41). The text connecting the Domesticus with the scholarian guards seems to supply the explanation of the origin of the Domestic of the Schools. The supersession of the Magister meant, so far as the Schools were concerned, the transference of the command to his Domestic, who retained the title. To this change we may probably attribute the exaltation of the title δομέστικος. [4]

When we meet δομέστικος without any qualification, it means the

---

[1] For a place in the Palace called πρώτη σχολή see schol. on *Cer.* 8₁₁.

[2] We must eliminate a passage of Theophanes, which, as the text stands, might seem to point to a κόμης over the scholae. He records a mutiny of the scholae in A. D. 562 (p. 237): ἐπανέστησαν αἱ σχολαὶ τῷ κόμητι αὐτῶν—καὶ ἐπῆλθον αὐτῷ. We should expect τοῖς κόμησι and αὐτοῖς. It is not a case for emendation; the chronographer misunderstood his source.   [?]

[3] The Parisinus has μεγίστου.

[4] It may be noted that in late times domesticus was used as an ecclesiastical title. Referring to a precentor at Thessalonica, Philotheos, in an Encomium on Gregory Palamas, says δομέστικον ἡ συνήθεια τοῦτόν φησιν (Migne, *P. G.* 151, 638). I notice this passage only because Uspenski strangely cites it as if it were important, B. Z. 3. 186.

δ. τῶν σχολῶν (as in Theoph. 456₁₀).[1]   The Domestici Schol. in the eighth century mentioned by Theophanes had the Patrician rank. From the Taktikon Uspenski (111) we learn that in the reign of Michael III they came in order of precedence above all military commanders except the stratêgos of the Anatolics, and they hold the same place in the list of Philotheos.   The Domesticate was held in the ninth century by such men as Manuel and Bardas, and for military expeditions the Domestic was sometimes appointed Commander-in-Chief of the whole army.[2]   But it was not till the tenth century that it became the habit to appoint him to this supreme command. The biographer of Basil I says that he sent the Domestic of the Schools against Chrysocheir συνήθως (Const. Th. 272₃). This συνήθως seems to be an inference of the writer from the practice of his own time.[3]   In the second half of the tenth century the δομέστικος τῶν σχολῶν has become the δομέστικος ἀνατολῆς, and has his counterpart in a new creation, the δομέστικος δύσεως [4]; but this lies outside our present scope. The ceremony of creating the Domestic of the Schools was the same as that for other domestics (Cer. ii. 3).

There are but few extant seals of these Domestici. Four, none of which seems to be earlier than the tenth century, will be found in Sig. 360.   In two of these the Domestic holds also the post of λογοθέτης τῶν ἀγελῶν.

(1) The first official in the bureaux of all the Domestics is the τοποτηρητής, which represents the Latin vicarius. We find the name used officially in this sense in the sixth century in laws of Justinian [5]: Nov. 152, § 19 (p. 284) τοποτηρητὴν τῶν ἐνδοξοτάτων ἐπάρχων ἢ στρατηγίδος ἀρχῆς, 16, § 4 ἐκπέμπειν ἐν ταῖς πόλεσι τῆς ἐπαρχίας ἧς ἄρχει τοὺς καλουμένους τοποτηρητάς. Nov. 166 (p. 375), topoteretai of praet. praef., com. larg., com. r. priv. Chron. Pasch. (A. D. 532), p. 876

---

[1] Artavasdos, the Domestic of the tyrant Artavasdos (Theoph. 419₁₅), must have been Dom. Schol. Cp. Takt. Usp. 111.

[2] The appointment did not depend on the post, but on the man. Thus Petronas, to whom the command of all the forces (both τάγματα and θέματα) was entrusted in A.D. 863, was stratêgos of the Thrakesian theme at the time. In Cont. Th. 167 it is suggested that Bardas should have led an expedition, as being Dom. Schol., but that he deputed his brother Petronas to take his place. I imagine that the statement is coloured by the later practice.

[3] Kestas Styppiotes is another instance of a Dom. Schol. appointed Commander-in-Chief under Basil : George Mon. 847, Cont. Th. 286.

[4] Cont. Th. 415, 479₁₅ ; Leo Diac. 7₁₁, 49₆, 18₁₂. Cp. Cer. 610₁₆, 613₁₅.

[5] See also Nov. 16. 4, p. 99 ; Nov. 21. 10, p. 144—of sending τοποτ. to provincial cities. Cp. also B. G. U. ii. no. 669 μεγαλοπρεπεστάτῳ καὶ περιβλέπτῳ Φλαυίῳ Μαρκέλλῳ καγκ(ελλαρίῳ) καὶ τοποτηρ(ητῇ).

ὁ τόπον ποιῶν τοῦ μαγίστρου = *ibid.* τὸν τοποτηροῦντα τὸν μάγιστρον. It is often used of ecclesiastical deputies.

The τοποτηρηταί of the Domestics must not be confused with the provincial τοποτηρηταί, whom we find in charge of districts and forts. The topotêrêsia or geographical bandon was a subdivision of the turma : see Const. Porph., *Them.* i. 16; *De adm. imp.* 50. Some seals of such officers have been preserved (*Sig.* 370₂-1). Schlumberger cites one seal which might be that of a topotêrêtês of one of the Domesticates (633) [+ ΘΕΟΔ]ΩΡΩ [ΤΟΠ]ΟΤΗΡΙΤ[Η ΤΩ] ΚΑΤΑΚ[ΑΛΩΝΙ]. He ascribes it to the ninth century.

The official document on the Cretan expedition of A.D. 949 (in *Cer.* ii. 45) contains an important passage (666) bearing on the tagmata and the topotêrêtai, the significance of which has not been appreciated. It must be given in full :—

(1) ἀπὸ τοῦ θέματος Θράκης, ὁ τοποτηρητὴς καὶ ἀπὸ τῶν δ΄ ταγμάτων ἄρχοντες, ἄνδρες ρλθ΄, σχολάριοι τῶν δ΄ ταγμάτων ἄνδρες τνδ΄· ὁμοῦ ἄρχοντες καὶ σχολάριοι τῶν δ΄ ταγμάτων, ἄνδρες υςγ΄ [139 + 354 = 493].

(2) ἀπὸ τοῦ θέματος Μακεδονίας, ὁ τοποτηρητὴς καὶ ἀπὸ τῶν δ΄ ταγμάτων ἄρχοντες, ἄνδρες πγ΄. σχολάριοι τῶν δ΄ ταγμάτων ἄνδρες σςγ΄· ὁμοῦ ἄρχοντες καὶ σχολάριοι τῶν δ΄ ταγμάτων ἄνδρες ωξθ΄ [83 + 293 = 376, + 493 = 869].

(3, 4) ἀπὸ τῶν περατικῶν θεμάτων.

(3) ὁ ἐξσκουβίτωρ μετὰ τοῦ τοποτηρητοῦ αὐτοῦ καὶ παντὸς τοῦ τάγματος αὐτοῦ, ἀρχόντων καὶ σχολαρίων ὁμοῦ ἀνδρῶν ψ΄ [700].

(4) ὁ ἱκανάτος μετὰ τοῦ τοποτηρητοῦ αὐτοῦ καὶ παντὸς τοῦ τάγματος αὐτοῦ, ἀρχόντων καὶ σχολαρίων, ὁμοῦ ἀνδρῶν υνς΄ [456].

Here we have the four τοποτηρηταί of the four tagmata. Those of the Excubiti and Hikanatoi are expressly designated. The order suggests that (1) is the topotêrêtês of the Schools ; (2) would then be the topotêrêtês of the Arithmos. The passage proves [1] that detachments of all the tagmata had their quarters in Thrace and Macedonia, and detachments at least of the Excubiti and Hikanatoi had quarters in Bithynia. (Under Justinian II, Scholarians stationed in Bithynia were transferred to Thrace, Theoph. 236₁₇.) So too in the Cretan expedition of A.D. 902, we find Thracian and Macedonian Scholarians (*Cer.* 652₄), and in the Italian expedition of A.D. 935 (*ib.* 660₁₉). We may reasonably conjecture that it was a special function of the topotêrêtai to command the provincial detachments of the tagmata.

In military expeditions (Anon. Vári, 6₁₉) we find the topotêrêtês and the chartularius of the Schools each in charge of half the tagma. For the τοπ. τῶν σχολῶν see further *Cer.* 599₂, 256₇. The topotêrêtai

---

[1] The inferences of Uspenski (*loc. cit.* 186-7) are very perverse.

are spathars in Takt. Usp. 127; in Phil. (734) they may be spatharocandidati. For their participation in ceremonies see *Cer.* 524₁₉.

(2) The κόμητες τῶν σχολῶν belong to the not large number of
officers who have retained the title which they bore in the fifth century.
In the fourth century the commander of the schola was a *tribunus*
(Amm. Marc. 20. 2, 5; *C. Th.* 7. 4, 23 *scholarum tribunos*, A.D.
396), but before A.D. 441 he has become a (*vir spectabilis*) *comes
scholarum*, *Nov. Theod.* ii. 21 = *C. I.* 1. 31. 3). κόμητες σχολῶν are
mentioned in the reigns of Leo I (document in *Cer.* 416₁₆) and of
Anastasius I (Theoph. 138₁₀), and in the sixth century we meet τὸν κόμητα τῆς ἕκτης ἢ ἑβδόμης σχολῆς in a fragment of Peter Patr. (*Cer.* 391₁₂,
392₁). A seal (eighth or ninth century, according to Schlumberger)
of the count of the fifth schola is preserved (*Sig.* 359 κόμη[τη] τῶν
σχολῶν σχολῆς πέμπτης).

The text of Philotheos gives δύο κόμητες. This is plainly an error,
but can easily be corrected to β', which corresponded to the following
γ' and δ' and meant that the κόμητες were the second item in the
officium. We have seen already that there were seven scholae in the
fifth century and that Justinian raised the number to eleven. How
many were there in later times? For the end of the tenth century
we have evidence in Anon. Vári, where we find thirty counts, κόμητες
ἀνὰ ὀκτώ . . . κόμητες ἀνὰ ἑπτά (6₂₂, ₂₈). From the same context we
learn that there were thirty banda, so that each count was
captain of a bandon,[1] but we are not told by this writer the size
of a bandon. Was the schola a bandon, considered tactically?
In that case there would have been thirty scholae. But if so,
the schola cannot have retained its old number of 500 men (cp.
above, p. 49), for 15,000 is much too high for the total number of
the scholarii. If we assume the bandon to have been 200 the total
would be 6,000, a figure which might be defended by a statement of
Ibn Khurdâdhbah that 'the emperor's camp, in his residence or in
the field, consists of four divisions of cavalry commanded by a patrician, under whom are 6,000 soldiers and 6,000 servants' (81, cp.
Gelzer, 125).[2] But this statement does not agree with the statement
of Kudâma, which comes from the same source as Ibn Khurdâdhbah's
information. According to Kudâma the total number of the scholarians
was 4,000 (157). It may, however, be shown that the data of Anon.
Vári (even assuming that no change had been made in the organization of the scholae in the intervening century and a half) cannot be
combined with the data of the Arabic writers. For the anonymous

---

[1] Cp. Kulakovski, *Vizantiiski Lager*, 71.
[2] This is observed by Vogt, *Basile Ier*, 348.

military writer cannot possibly have contemplated as present in the camp which he describes a force of scholarians numbering anything like 4,000. In c. viii (p. 17) he says that the minimum number of cavalry with which an emperor can march in person is 8,200, which includes a thousand guards (i. e. the Hetairoi and Athanatoi). Ordinarily he would have more ; let us say, with Kulakovski,[1] 10,000 or even 12,000. If we consider that not only the other three tagmata, but also cavalry of the themes have to be included in this total, it is clear that the scholarii alone cannot have numbered anything like 4,000, much less 6,000. The bandon therefore must have been much smaller than 200 men. As a matter of fact, we learn what the bandon of cavalry in the latter half of the tenth century was from the Στρατηγικὴ ἔκθεσις of Nicephorus II (see Bibliography) : τῶν καβαλαρικῶν διατάξεων οἱ ἀρχηγοὶ ἐχέτωσαν βάνδα. τὰ δὲ βάνδα αὐτῶν εἶναι ἀνὰ ἄνδρας πεντήκοντα (p. 12). Thirty such banda give a total of 1,500, which is a reasonable proportion.

We might attempt to reconcile this result with the number of Kudâma by supposing that only a part of the tagma of Scholarii is contemplated by Anon. Vári.[2] But the figures of the Arabic writer seem to be very doubtful in view of the numbers given for the Excubiti and the Hikanatoi. Kudâma gives 4,000 for each of these corps ; but in the document of A. D. 949 cited above (*Cer.* 666) we find that the *whole* tagma of the Excubiti, including officers, numbered 700, and the *whole* tagma of the Hikanatoi, including officers, 456. There are two alternatives : either the tagmata suffered an immense reduction in numbers between the middle of the ninth and the middle of the tenth century, or the figures of Kudâma are utterly erroneous. I have little doubt that the latter inference is the correct one.

The data point to a complete reorganization of the Scholae since the sixth century. Under Justinian, there were the seven old Scholae, and four ' supernumerary' scholae, each 500 strong, so that the whole number was 5,500. In the tenth century there are thirty banda, each fifty strong : in all 1,500. Whether the bandon was a schola, so that there were thirty scholae, or whether each schola had several banda, is a difficult question. For the first alternative it may be argued (1) that the seal of a count of the fifth schola, belonging to the eighth or ninth century (see above), points to the continued connexion of the count with the schola ; to which it may be replied that the thirty counts of the banda may have been instituted subsequently to the date of the seal ; (2) that a passage in the περὶ ταξ. of Con-

---

[1] *Loc. cit.* 70.

[2] But the writer speaks as if the whole τάγμα were present 6₁₇₋₂₀.

stantine VII points to the comites being still assigned each a schola
(494₁₆), ἵνα καὶ οἱ κόμητες κατὰ μίαν σχολὴν τὴν αὐτὴν ἀκολουθίαν ἔχωσιν.
The κόμητες τῶν σχολῶν are of spathar rank in Philotheos (735₈), of
lower rank in Takt. Usp. 127.

(3) The functions of the chartularius (spathar, Phil. 735₁₇, lower,
Takt. Usp. 127 *leg.* ὁ χαρτουλάριος, 129) must have corresponded,
mutatis mutandis, to those of the chartularius of the theme (see above,
p. 44). He, the topotêrêtês, and the comites are distinguished as
μεγάλοι ἄρχοντες from the lower members of the officium, *Cer.* 524₁₉.
His rank next, and near to, the τοποτηρητής, is also illustrated by the
position his tent occupied in a camp, Anon. Vári, 6₂₁.

(4) The domestici (stratores, Phil. 736₂₁, candidati, Takt. Usp. 128)
were officers under the comites. *Cer.* 599₄ οἱ πρῶτοι καὶ δεύτεροι
ἄρχοντες τῶν σχολῶν ἤγουν κόμητες καὶ δομέστικοι. Anon. Vári, 6₂₃
κἀκεῖθεν κόμητες—σὺν τοῖς ὑπ' αὐτοὺς δομεστίκοις. If the comes commanded a bandon of fifty, it may be conjectured the domesticus
commanded a subdivision of ten, so that there would be five domestici
under each comes, and 150 domestici in all.

(5) The προέξημος or πρόξιμος (so Takt. Usp. 129) was of lower
than spathar rank. We meet him in the reign of Constantine V
described as an ἀνὴρ ξιφήρης : in the *Vita S. Stephani iunioris* (Migne,
P. G. 100, 1169, 1172) he removes Stephen from the prison of the
Praetorium). The position of his tent in the camp (on an expedition
led by the emperor) is noted in Anon. Vári, 5₆.[1] From a comparison
with the officium of the Domesticus Excubitorum we might surmise
that he performed the same kind of duties as the protomandator of
that officium, and this is confirmed by *Cer.* 599₁₁, ₁₈, where these two
officers play corresponding parts in the ceremony there described.

In early times *proximus* was the title of the chief in certain bureaux
(*scrinia*), e. g. in the *sacra scrinia* (*memoriae,* &c., C. Th. 6. 26. 10),
in the scrinium ammissionum (Peter Patr., in *Cer.* 394 ὁ πρώξιμος
τῶν ἀδμηνσιόνων). We must suppose that the proximus of the Schools
was chief of a scrinium (not mentioned in *Not. Dig.*), which performed
for the Scholae the same functions that the *scriniarii* of the *magister
militum* performed for them (*Not. Dig. Or.* v. 72, 73, &c.).

(6) The προτίκτορες can hardly be dissociated from the *protectores*
of the earlier empire. These guards, who were instituted in the third
century, and the Domestici, have been fully studied by Mommsen,
Eph. Epig. 5. 121 *sqq.* They were closely associated and were under
the two comites domesticorum (*equitum* and *peditum*). In the latter
half of the sixth century Menander, the historian, was a protector.

[1] ὁ δὲ πρώξιμος καὶ ὁ κόμης τῶν βουκίνων σὺν τοῖς μαγκλαβίταις ἔστωσαν κτλ.

In a Novel of Justinian (158, A. D. 548) mention is made of domestici and protectores, deputed on service in Pontus.[1] In A. D. 559 the protectores are mentioned with the Schools as guarding the walls against the Huns and Slavs (Theoph. 233₁₈). By the eighth century these guards and their counts have disappeared. The προτίκτορες under the Domesticus of the Schools point to the conclusion that they were merged in the Scholarian guards.

(7, 8, 9) The εὐτυχοφόροι (? εὐτυχιοφόροι) were so called because they carried εὐτύχια (vulgo πτυχία), images of Fortune or Victory (see Reiske, 668 sqq., and Bieliaev, ii. 70–71, note). Cp. Cer. 576₁₆ ἔστησαν τὰ Ῥωμαϊκὰ σκῆπτρα καὶ πτυχία καὶ λοιπὰ χρυσᾶ σκῆπτρα. This passage does not support Reiske in holding that they were vexilla. Rather they were σκῆπτρα, staves, with images at the top. See Cer. 11₁₈ τά τε Ῥωμαϊκὰ σκῆπτρα τὰ λεγόμενα βῆλα, ὁμοίως καὶ τὰ εὐτύχια καὶ τὰ ἕτερα σκῆπτρα, πρὸς τούτοις τὰ σκεύη τῶν προτικτόρων καὶ σινατόρων, καὶ τὰ σκεύη τῶν δρακοναρίων; λάβουρά τε καὶ καμπηδηκτόρια, μετὰ καὶ τῶν βάνδων. The σκῆπτρα called vela may have been the σκῆπτρα of the σκηπτροφόροι. σκεύη is used as a general word for all such insignia or emblems.[2] We are not told what the σκεύη of the protectores were. It is probable that the ἀξιωματικοί also had σκεύη. Each of the four tagmata had four (the Hik. alone, three) classes of this kind, and they may be placed here side by side.

Scholae.	Excubiti.
προτίκτορες	δρακονάριοι
εὐτυχιοφόροι	σκευοφόροι
σκηπτροφόροι	σιγνοφόροι
ἀξιωματικοί	σινάτορες

Arithmos.	Hikanatoi.
βανδοφόροι	βανδοφόροι
λαβουρίσιοι	
σημειοφόροι	σημειοφόροι
δουκινιάτορες	δουκινιάτορες [3]

We may conjecture that the καμπηδηκτόρια (Cer. 11 and 575), whatever they were,[4] may have been the emblems of the ἀξιωματικοί. These groups are arranged in strict order of precedence.

[1] Cp. C. Th. 7. 4. 27, and Not. Dig. Or. xv. 8 et deputati eorum.
[2] Cp. Cer. 640₁₆–641₃.
[3] The text of Philotheos transposes, but in another place (738₂₋₄) he shows the true order.
[4] In connexion with this, it is relevant, I think, to note the part played by campiductores at the elevations of Leo I and Anastasius (Cer. 411, 423).

The ἀξιωματικοί seem to be referred to in *Cer.* 250, where they are
mentioned with the σκευοφόροι of the Excubiti ; but in 251_{23}, 230_{22},
236_8, 239_{17} the word can hardly have this narrow sense ; it means
dignitaries, as generally elsewhere.

(10) Of the μανδάτορες it need only be said that they were a part of
the officium of all military chiefs. The place of protomandator seems
to have been taken by the proximos.

(2) ὁ δομέστικος τῶν ἐξκουβίτων.

The Excubitores (ἐξκουβίτορες or ἐξκούβιτοι) were a body of palace
guards, as the name denotes, organized probably by Leo I.[1] They
were under the command of a comes, a post which was held by
Justin I at the time of his elevation (*Cer.* 426, John Mal. 410).
We can trace this title down to A. D. 680.[2] In the eighth century we
first meet the δομέστικος τῶν ἐκσκουβίτων instead of the κόμης (Theoph.
438_{11}, A.D. 765). This was more than a simple change of title.
There must have been a general reorganization of the guards (perhaps
by Leo III), and the style of the commander of the Excubiti was
assimilated to the title of the commander of the Scholae, the origin of
which was discussed above. The high importance of the post in the
sixth and seventh centuries is shown by the fact that it was held by
Tiberius, afterwards emperor, by Philippicus, the brother-in-law of
Maurice, and by such an important person as Priscus (under Maurice
and Phocas) ; and by the fact that a subordinate of the Count had
patrician rank in A. D. 680 (see below under τοποτηρητής). In the
eighth century we meet Domestici Excubitorum who have only
spathar rank (Theoph. 438_{11}, 454_{18}). This degradation in rank shows
that the old comes was not renamed but abolished, and that the Excubitors were placed under an officer of inferior rank and title. The
policy of Leo III, to whom we may most probably ascribe the change,
was to make the guards more dependent on himself by decreasing the
dignity of their chiefs. But the inferior position of the commanders
of such important troops did not endure. Their very position raised
the title of Domesticus to high honour. In the case of the Schools
we meet a Domestic who is a patrician in the reign of Constantine V
(Theoph. 442. 25). In the case of the Excubiti the rise seems to have
been slower. Michael the Amorian was created Patrician and Dom.

---

[1] They first definitely appear in the reign of Leo I, John Mal. 371_{23}, but we
meet an Excubitor at an earlier period, in a letter of St. Nilus (Migne, *P. G.* 79,
Epp. ii. 322) ; then A.D. 490, Chron. Pasch. 606, cp. 608.

[2] Theoph. 272_{21} (reign of Maurice), 294_{12} (reign of Phocas) ; Chron. Pasch. 703,
sub a. 612 ; Mansi, xi. 209 (A. D. 680).

Exc. by Leo V (*Gen.* 12₁₆). In the Takt. Usp. the δομέστικος τῶν ἐξσκουβίτων is a patrician, inferior in precedence to all the στρατηγοί and to the Prefect of the City [1]; in the time of Philotheos he immediately precedes the Prefect, and both of them are superior to the stratêgoi of the western themes. He is often called, for brevity, ὁ ἐξκούβιτος, according to a common Byzantine fashion (cp. ὁ γενικός, ὁ ἱκανάτος), cp. e. g. περὶ ταξ. 460₁₃, Cont. Th. 142₁₀.

The Excubitors are often called as a body τὸ ἐξκούβιτον [2] or τὰ ἐξκούβιτα.[3] They were divided into eighteen or more bands.[4] In A. D. 949, according to the official text quoted above, p. 52, the total number of the body, including officers, was 700. Possibly there were 100 officers, and 600 guardsmen. But the organization seems to have been different from that of the Schools. The σκρίβονες (see below) correspond to the κόμητες τῶν σχολῶν, but no officers are mentioned corresponding to the δομέστικοι.

Schlumberger has published a seal, which he does not date, of a Domesticus of the Excubitors (*Sig.* 346): πατρικ(ιω) β(ασιλικω) ασπαθ(αριω) καὶ δομεστ(ικω) τ(ων) β(ασιλικων) εξκουβ(ιτων).

(1) In the list of this officium the MS. has falsely the plurals τοποτηρηταί, χαρτουλάριοι, πρωτομανδάτορες for the corresponding singulars.[5] The topotêrêtês of the Excubitors first appears in the Acts of the Sixth Ecum. Council (A. D. 680 : see Mansi, xi. 209), and curiously has the rank of Patrician : 'Αναστασίου τοῦ ἐνδοξοτάτου ἀπὸ ὑπάτων πατρικίου καὶ τοποτηρητοῦ τοῦ κόμητος τοῦ βασιλικοῦ ἐξκουβίτου.

(2) χαρτουλάριος.

(3) In the sixth century we find σκρίβωνες as a company of imperial guards. The word first occurs, so far as I know, in the beginning of the fifth century in the address of a letter of St. Nilus, Οὐάλεντι σκρίβωνι (ii. 204). Agathias (3. 14, p. 171) mentions (A. D. 554) Metrianus, a scribon, explaining that he was one of τῶν ἀμφὶ τὰ βασίλεια δορυφόρων. Eustratios (*Vita Eutychii, P. G.* 86 A, 2353) describes the persons who were sent to bring Eutychius back to Constantinople (A. D. 574-8)

----

[1] In the Acts of the Fourth Council of Constantinople (A. D. 869), Leo dom. exc. is mentioned before the Prefect, but after the Logothete of the course ; his rank is not given (Mansi, xvi. 310).

[2] Theoph. 491₁₁, Mansi, xi. 209 τοῦ βασιλικοῦ ἐξκουβίτου.

[3] Theoph. 279₁₈ τὰ ἐκσκούβιτα. This plural also meant the quarters of the Excubitors in the palace, as in Cont. Th. 383₈, &c.

[4] Sabas, *Vita Ioannicii*, in *AA. SS.* Nov. 4 (1894) *ad init.* Ioannikios, at the age of 19, in A. D. 773 εἰς τὴν τῶν ἐξσκουβιτόρων στρατιὰν καὶ ἐν βάνδῳ ὀκτοκαιδεκάτῳ κατ' ἐκλογὴν ἀκριβῆ ἐντάττεται.

[5] But elsewhere the text has the singular correctly : 734₇ τοποτηρητής, 735₁₉, 759₁₃ χαρτουλάριος, 737₁₉ πρωτομανδάτωρ (738₁₀ however οἱ πρωτομανδάτορες, read οἱ μανδάτορες).

as τοὺς γενναιοτάτους σκρίβωνας. Comentiolus, the well-known general of Maurice, had been a σκρίβων, and Theophylactus Simocatta explains it to mean one of the emperor's σωματοφύλακες (see 1. 4, 7; also 7. 3, 8). Bonosus whom Phocas made comes orientis (Theoph. 296₂₂) had been a scribon (Theoph. Sim. 8, 9, 10), as also Theodore, who was Patriarch of Alexandria at beginning of seventh century (List of Patriarchs at end of Nicephorus, Chron. 129). Schlumberger (*Sig.* 361) has published a seal Στεφάνου σκρίβονος which he ascribes to the sixth or seventh century, and Panchenko another of the same period (Ἰωάννου σ., xiii. 148). These data point to the existence of a taxis of scribones, perhaps connected with the Excubitors, and supplying officers to that body. Even in later times we find σκρίβωνες taking part in ceremonies separately from the rest of the Excubiton. Thus *Cer.* 81₂₀ κανδιδάτοι δὲ καὶ σκρίβονες καὶ μανδάτορες βασιλικοί, 99₆ οἱ δὲ κανδιδάτοι καὶ μανδάτορες, ὡσαύτως καὶ οἱ σκρίβωνες, 99₂₆ σκρίβωνες καὶ μανδάτορες βαστάζοντες τὰ βεργία αὐτῶν. These σκρίβωνες can hardly be the regular officers of the divisions of the Excubiton (cp. 99₁₃), but they may have been under the control of the Dom. Exc. The candidati and mandatores associated with them were under the protospatharios τῶν βασιλικῶν, and were at the emperor's disposal for special service. The scribones seem to have been employed in the same way. Scribones were regularly attached to the regiments of the themes, as *deputati* to remove and look after the wounded in battle.[1] They had the rank of stratores, Phil. 736₂₀. The ceremony of creating a scribon was performed in the hall of the Excubiti (*Cer.* 130–1), and is described along with that of a κόμης τῶν σχολῶν (132). In the ceremony described in *Cer.* ii. 16 (599₁₅) they play a similar part to that of the κόμητες.

(4) The πρωτομανδάτωρ corresponded to the proximus of the Schools (see above). His rank was low (Phil. 737₁₉). Both he and the scribones are omitted in Takt. Usp.

(5) The δρακονάριοι seem to correspond on one hand with the domestici of the Schools (see *Cer.* 599₁₅, where they are associated with the scribones, as the domestici are associated with the comites), but in rank they were lower, being inferior to the προτίκτορες (Phil. 737₁₉), to whom they also seem to correspond, as bearers of insignia (δράκοντες).[2]

(6, 7, 8) The σκευοφόροι in the Excubiton corresponded to the eutychophoroi in the Schools (Phil. 737₂₃), the σιγνοφόροι to the

---

[1] Leo, *Tact.* 4. 15 δεποτάτοι (*sic leg. pro* δεσποτάτοι). Cp. *ib.* 4. 6.
[2] Cp. Ducange, s. v. δρακονάριος.

skeptrophoroi (Phil. 738$_1$), the σινάτορες (i. e. *signatores*) to the axio-matikoi (Phil. 738$_3$). See above, p. 56.

(9) μανδάτορες. There were also λεγατάριοι in the Excubiton, though not mentioned here ; but see Phil. 738$_{10}$ οἱ μανδάτορες (see above) καὶ λεγατάριοι τῶν ἐξκουβίτων.

(3) ὁ δρουγγάριος τοῦ ἀριθμοῦ.

The third tagma had two designations, ὁ ἀριθμός [1] (also οἱ ἀριθμοί) [2] and ἡ βίγλα [3] (ἡ βασιλικὴ βίγλα) [4]. The earliest δρουγγάριος τῆς βίγλας mentioned in our sources seems to be Alexius (of spathar rank) in A.D. 791 (Theoph. 466$_4$). The designation βίγλα is more frequent than ἀριθμός in the sources, and appears on two seals of drungarioi pub-lished by Schlumberger.[5] The βίγλα (*vigiliae*) and its commandant had special duties, which differentiated it from the other tagmata and are indicated by the name. On Imperial expeditions they had sentinel duty to perform, and the drungarios was responsible for the safety of the camp and received and conveyed the orders of the emperor (see the section περὶ κερκέτων in περὶ ταξ., 481 *sqq.*). [6] The exceptional posi-tion of the drungarios is also reflected in the ceremony in the Hippo-drome in *Cer.* 598–9, cp. 605$_{20}$.[7] He had also duties connected with prisoners of war, see *Cer.* 614$_{18}$, Cont. Th. 303.[8]

From (1) their duties, from (2) the double name of the tagma, and (3) the title of the commander, it may be inferred that the βίγλα existed before the tagmata were reorganized on a symmetrical plan. If it had only been instituted when the Scholae and Excubitors were reorganized, the commander would almost certainly have been entitled Domesticus. Now there is some evidence which suggests that the ἀριθμός descends from a body which existed in the sixth century. In the barbarian invasion of A.D. 559, the scholae, the protectores, καὶ οἱ ἀριθμοί, and all the senate, were set to defend the Theodosian Wall

---

[1] e. g. Phil. 715$_{10}$, 718$_6$; *Cer.* 611$_{12}$, &c.   [2] Takt. Usp. 115, 119.

[3] Phil. 713$_{23}$, 728$_{17}$, &c.   [4] Theoph. 491 ; see next note.

[5] *Sig.* 340–1 (1) Αετιω βασιλικω πρωτοσπαθαριω και δρογγαριω της βιγλης, (2) Λεοντι βασιλικ(ω) σπαθαρι(ω) και δρουγγαρι(ω) τη[ς] θεοφυ(λάκτου) βασιλικης β[ιγλη]ς. Both may be of the ninth century. Schlumberger suggests that Aetios may be the same as the patrician who was stratēgos of the East and in charge of Amorion when it was destroyed by Mamun (A. D. 838, not, as Schl. says, A. D. 846).

[6] The drungarios was one of the ministers who had the duty and privilege of attending the emperor in his private yacht, *De adm. imp.* 234.

[7] Cp. also *Cer.* 546$_5$ οἱ τοῦ ἀρ. where the other tagmata are not associated.

[8] Leo, ὁ καλούμενος Κατάκαλος, who was τῆς β. δρουγγάριος under Basil I (Niketas, *Vit. Ign.*, Mansi xvi. 288), seems to be the same as Katakalon who was dom. schol. under Leo VI. Others who held the post in the ninth century are Petronas, Constantine Maniakes and Joannes (George Mon. 793, 822, 835, 842).

(Theoph. 233₁₈). The ἀριθμοί are clearly residential troops like the scholarians. If we observe that the ἀριθμός appears in the plural, τῶν ἀριθμῶν, in Takt. Usp. (*loc. cit.*), there is evidently a case for the connexion of the later with the earlier body. The ἀριθμοί mentioned in A. D. 540 by Theophanes, who records that Bulgarian captives κατετάγησαν, in Armenia ἐν τοῖς νουμερίοις ἀριθμοῖς (219₁₆), are *numeri* in the wide sense of the word, but there is some corruption in the phrase, and De Boor may be right in his conjecture ἐν τοῖς νουμέροις (ἀριθμοῖς being a gloss). *Numeri* meant generally the regiments, &c., of the army (cp. *in numeris militant*, frequent in the *Not. Dig.*).[1] ἀριθμός is a translation of *numerus*, but was used (as *numerus* also) in a more restricted sense of certain troops stationed in the capital. It is tempting to connect their origin with a regiment instituted by Arcadius. John Malalas, who has devoted only half a dozen lines to that emperor's reign, singles out for mention the institution of the Arcadiaci (349₅) ἐποίησε καὶ ἴδιον ἀριθμὸν οὓς ἐκάλεσεν Ἀρκαδιακούς. These are, doubtless, to be identified with the Comites Arcadiaci, a vexillatio palatina, under the general command of the mag. mil. per Thracias (*Not. Dig. Or.* viii. 25). There were two other associated vexillationes palatinae, the Comites Honoriaci and the Equites Theodosiaci iuniores (*ib.*), established evidently about the same time. My conjecture is that these troops, as distinguished from the vex. pal. under the two magg. mil. in praesenti, had special garrison duties in the capital and came to be designated as οἱ ἀριθμοί. I put it forward merely as a guess, founded on the probability that the special mention of the Arcadiaci by Malalas points to their having an exceptional position, as well as the title *comites*.

The title of δρουγγάριος occurs on a seal which Schlumberger (*Sig.* 336) attributes to the sixth century : Ευ[γε]νιω αποεπαρχων και δρουγγαριου (*sic*). He plausibly identifies Eugenios with Εὐγ. ὁ ἀπὸ ἐπάρχων mentioned by Theophanes, A.D. 560 (235₁). Now the Emperor Heraclius, in his letter of A. D. 628, of which the text is given in the contemporary Chron. Pasch. (p. 731) relates that he sent to conduct Siroes Ἡλίαν τὸν ἐνδοξότατον στρατηλάτην τὸν ἐπίκλην Βαρσοκὰ καὶ Θεόδοτον τὸν μεγαλοπρεπέστατον δρουγγάριον. It seems possible that Theodotus was commander of the ἀριθμοί, and if so it would be natural to suppose that Eugenios held the same post. But we have no material for a conclusion. We do not know at what date δροῦγγος, which originally had a tactical meaning (=*globus*)[2], came to be used for

---

[1] This is so familiar that it requires no illustration. Cp. *C. I.* 12. 35. 14.

[2] In the sixth century [(Maurice), *Strat.*] it had a general meaning, and could be applied either to the μοῖρα or the μέρος (= 3 μοῖραι) or to other groups. Cp, Kulakovski, *Drung i drungarii*, 6.

a definite subdivision of the army, or whether in A. D. 628 all the officers commanding subdivisions (μοῖραι) of a particular size would have been known as drungarioi.

(1) Here, as in all the domesticates (except the Schools), the MS. has the false reading τοποτηρηταί for τοποτηρητής (cp. Phil. 746$_{18}$, 734$_9$). See Cer. 82$_{16}$.

(2) The χαρτουλάριος, the chief of the office, was below spathar rank, Phil. 737$_7$, Takt. Usp. 129. A seal of Nikolaos βασιλικὸς σπαθαροκανδιδάτος καὶ χαρτουλάριος τοῦ ἀριθμοῦ (ninth or tenth century) has been published by Panchenko (viii. 246): the rank suggests a date later than Philotheos.

(3) The ἀκόλουθος (Phil. 737$_{19}$) corresponds to the proximus of the Schools, and to the protomandator of the Excubiton. He is mentioned in Ceremonies in Cer. 523$_{14}$, 442$_6$. He is omitted in Phil. 746$_{18}$, where we should expect to find him—no doubt accidentally. In later times ἀκόλουθος was the title of the chief of the Varangian guard.

(4, 5) The κόμητες correspond in position in the officium to the κόμητες of the Schools and the scribones of the Excubiton (Cer. 494$_{20}$). In Cer. 599 they and the κένταρχος accompany the topotêrêtês; in Phil. 753$_{23}$, 772$_2$, they are also bracketed with the κένταρχοι. In Takt. Usp. 129 ὁ κόμης τοῦ ἀριθμοῦ is an error for οἱ κόμητες. In Cer. 230$_{22}$ (οἱ ἀξιωματικοὶ καὶ κόμητες τοῦ ἀριθμοῦ) ἀξιωματικοί means (not the ἀξ. of the Schools, but) the officials of the ἀριθμός superior in rank to the κόμητες. These officers, like the κόμητες of the Theme, evidently commanded the banda of the Arithmos, and the divisions of the bandon were commanded, as in the Theme, by κένταρχοι. It is strange that in the list of precedence in Phil. 737$_{16}$ the κένταρχοι should have the rank of stratores, and the Akoluthos, who was superior to the κόμητες in the officium, should have a lower rank (737$_{19}$).

(6, 7, 8, 9) The βανδοφόροι, λαβουρίσιοι, σημειοφόροι, and δουκινιάτορες correspond (Phil. 737$_{22}$–738$_4$) to the drakonarioi, skeuophoroi, signophoroi, and sinatores of the Excubiton respectively. Λαβαρήσιοι are mentioned in the sixth century (Peter Patr., Cer. 404$_4$), when they seem to have been under the magister officiorum.

(10) The μανδάτορες appear Cer. 578$_9$ μετὰ σπαθίων καὶ σκουταρίων. There were also λεγατάριοι (Phil. 738$_{11}$), σκουτάριοι[1] (Cer. 236$_9$), θυρωροί and διατρέχοντες (Phil. 746$_{20}$) attached to the Arithmos.

---

[1] Pseudo-Symeon (719$_{17}$) has μέχρι τῶν σκουταρίων, evidently a mistake for ἐξκουβίτων; see the corresponding passage in George Mon. (ed. Bonn.) 875$_{21}$ (ed. Muralt, p. 800), Leo Gramm. 289$_{23}$.

(4) ὁ δομέστικος τῶν ἱκανάτων.

The tagma of the Hikanatoi is not mentioned in our sources till the ninth century, and it was said to have been first organized by Nicephorus I. Our authority for this is a passage in the *Vita Ignatii*, ascribed to Niketas the Paphlagonian (in Mansi, xvi. 213):

Νικήταν δὲ πρῶτον μὲν δεκαέτη τυγχάνοντα τῶν λεγομένων ἱκανάτων παρὰ Νικηφόρου φασὶ τοῦ πάππου προβεβλῆσθαι, δι' ὃν ἐκεῖνο τὸ πρᾶγμα πρῶτον καταστῆναι.

That is, Nicephorus created his grandson Nicetas (afterwards the Patriarch Ignatius), domesticus of the Hikanatoi at the age of ten years, on whose account that body (for πρᾶγμα read τάγμα) was first instituted. The biographer does not commit himself to either statement; he records both the appointment of Nicetas[1] and the institution of the tagma as resting on report (φασί). It would therefore be rash to say that this date for the origin of the Hikanatoi is certain. Schlumberger has published two seals (*Sig.* 351)[2] which *might* belong to the eighth century, but he has not demonstrated that they could not belong to the ninth; the chronology of the types is not at all clearly enough defined to justify his observation that the type of these seals 'vient démentir cette hypothèse' (namely, of the origin under Nicephorus I). A very large number of seals which he has published he ascribes to the 'eighth or ninth century' without being able to define the date more precisely.

The Domestic of the Hikanatoi appears in Takt. Usp., with the rank of protospatharios (119).[3] In the Arabic list of Kudâma —which, as we saw, represents roughly the same period as Takt. Usp.— the fourth body of cavalry guarding the capital are termed *fidaratiyin.* Uspenski holds that the Hikanatoi are meant,[4] and apparently suggests that the text should be amended. But it is clear that the writer meant to say φοιδεράτοι. Now, as Gelzer points out, a body of φοιδεράτοι is mentioned in our sources as existing in the early years of the ninth century. Leo the Armenian (afterwards Leo V) was rewarded by Nicephorus I, for abandoning the cause of Bardanes, by the post of commander of the φοιδεράτοι (Gen. 10_{12} = Cont. Th. 9_{18}). The revolt of Bardanes was in A.D. 803. Gelzer does not notice that

---

[1] This statement is borne out by Cont. Th. 20_5.

[2] Ιω(αννη) β(ασιλικω) α' σπ[αθ]αριω και δομεστικ(ω) των [ι]κανατ(ων), and [...] καὶ Δο[μεστι]κω τ(ων) [ικανα]τω(ν). Is it possible that the first of these might be Ioannes Krokoas who was Dom. Hik. under Basil I (George Mon. 847_{16})?

[3] Orestes, dom. τῶν ἰκ., present at the Council of Constantinople A.D. 869, was a protospathar, Mansi, xvi. 309.

[4] See above, p. 48.

ten years later, after the accession of Leo, A.D. 813, Thomas was made a captain of the φοιδεράτοι : Gen. 12_{14} τουρμάρχην εἰς φοιδεράτους ἐπέστησεν, and he seems to have held this post at the time of Leo's death (Cont. Th. 52). Then, in Takt. Usp., we find among the spatharii (123) οἱ τουρμάρχαι τῶν φιβεράτων.[1] In view of this evidence we cannot hesitate to connect the *foederati* of Kudâma with these φοιδεράτοι who existed under that name as late, at least, as A.D. 813–14.

The possibility then might be entertained that the Hikanatoi are the foederati under a new name, and that Kudâma's authority (Al-Garmi) used an old notitia in which they were called by the old name. Such a view, I think, must be rejected. For in the first place, there is no evidence whatever that the Hikanatoi were foreigners, as the φοιδεράτοι certainly were. In the second place, as our only evidence for the origin of the Hikanatoi refers their creation to the reign of Nicephorus I, and as φοιδεράτοι still existed three years after his death, a conversion of the one body into the other is excluded. And that the φοιδεράτοι in A.D. 813–14 were differently organized from the Hikanatoi is proved by the title 'turmarch of the foederati' which Thomas bore, and which is guaranteed by the Takt. Usp. ; the Hikanatoi had no turmarchs.

In the reigns of Basil I and Leo VI we find the foreign soldiers in the service of the Empire organized as the ἑταιρεῖαι, under the ἑταιρειάρχαι or ἑταιρειάρχης (in connexion with which post they will be considered below, p. 106). We may therefore safely identify the φοιδεράτοι of Kudâma and the Takt. Usp. with the later ἑταιρεῖαι, and conclude that the Hikanatoi are not mentioned by Kudâma. It is possible that Al-Garmi used a notitia which was anterior to the creation of the Hikanatoi.

The corps of Hikanatoi seems to be called ὁ ἱκανάτος in περὶ ταξ. 484_{15} (cp. τοῦ ἱκανάτου Cont. Th. 389_5) : one would rather expect τὸ ἱκανάτον, for ὁ ἱκανάτος usually means the Domestic (περὶ ταξ. 460_{13}, 489_6, Cer. 598_{19}). The number of the Hikanatoi in the official document of A.D. 949 (Cer. 666_{13}) is given as 456, including officers (possibly eight banda of fifty men, and fifty-six officers).

All the officials of the Hikanatoi, except the topotêrêtês,[2] are below spathar rank. The officium, as observed above, is identical with that of the Arithmos, except that a protomandator corresponds to the akoluthos, and he is placed after, instead of before, the κόμητες.[3] In Phil. 738_{12} the mandatores are omitted accidentally.

---

[1] The same corruption appears in the MS. of Genesios, 10_{12}, 12_{14}.
[2] He is a spathar in Takt. Usp. 124, where for οἱ τ–αί read ὁ τ–ῆς.
[3] Takt. Usp. 129 ὁ κόμης τῶν ἱκ., read οἱ κόμητες.

(5) ὁ δομέστικος τῶν νουμέρων.

In our literary sources, the troops known as τὰ νούμερα are first
mentioned as such in Takt. Usp. 119 and Kudâma. It is at least
generally agreed (so Gelzer and Uspenski) that De Goeje's emendation of *mwnrh* to *nwmrh* = nûmera, in Kudâma's text, is certain.
The importance of this text is that it describes the Numeri as a body
of infantry.[1] The Numeri and their Domestic are mentioned in
other texts relating to the reign of Michael: Nicetas, *Vit. Ignat.*
apud Mansi, xvi. 233 (Leo Lalakon = Dom. Num.)[2]; Cont. Th.
$175_{18, 20}$.[3] Both these passages mention the Numera, a barracks in the
palace which was used as a prison (like the Chalke), and is frequently
referred to in the Book of Ceremonies (cp. also Cont. Th. 430_{16}). The
Domestic is often called, *more Byzantino*, ὁ νούμερος (Cont. Th. 175_{18},
Cer. 293_{16}, περὶ ταξ. 460_{14}).

We have, however, a piece of evidence for the Numeri which
seems to be older, in the form of a seal which Schlumberger ascribes
to the seventh or eighth century[4]: Νηκηφορω β(ασιλικω) κανδιδατ(ω)
και δρουνγαριω [το]ν νου[μερου]. The corps is here called by a
collective singular τὸ νούμερον and the officer is a drungarios. Now
there were no drungarioi under the Domestic of the ninth century,
and it is permissible to infer that in older times the commander bore the
title of Drungarios. The titles of some of the subordinate officers
prove to a certainty that these troops were not a comparatively new
institution like the Hikanatoi. The survival of the names τριβοῦνοι
and βικάριοι is a guarantee of antiquity (cp. also πορτάριοι). Now
in the sixth-century document (probably from the Κατάστασις of
Peter the Patrician) describing the accession of Justin I, we have
the following passage: ἐδήλωσεν δὲ καὶ ὁ τῆς θείας λήξεως Ἰουστῖνος
τοῖς στρατιώταις καὶ τριβούνοις καὶ βικαρίοις ἀπαντῆσαι καὶ τοὺς πρώτους
(*sic*) τῶν ἐξκουβιτόρων (*Cer.* 426). Justin was Comes Excubitorum.
This suggests that the tribuni and vicarii were officers of a *numerus*,
which then was subordinate to the comes excubitorum, and from which
the later tagma of the Numeri descends. It may have been under
a drungarios in the seventh century, and perhaps still subordinate to
the comes excubitorum; it was probably organized under a Domestic

---

[1] Kudâma says that it was 4,000 strong. But we have seen that we can attach
no weight to these numbers.

[2] Cp. Pseudo-Symeon 668_{12}.

[3] The Domesticus is mentioned in *Cer.* 109_{11} in a ceremony of which the
description probably dates from the reign of Michael III.

[4] *Sig.* 355. Schlumberger confuses (after Reiske) the Numeri with the
Arithmos.

in the eighth century.   Observe that the Drungarios had only the rank of a candidatus.   In Takt. Usp. the Domestic is a proto-spathar (119).

It is obvious that the first three items in the officium are (1) τοποτηρητής, (2) χαρτουλάριος, (3) τριβοῦνοι, and this correction of the text is demonstrated by another passage in Philotheos (753$_1$), τοὺς δύο τοποτηρητὰς καὶ χαρτουλαρίους τῶν νουμέρων καὶ τειχέων, τριβούνους, βικαρίους, &c.[1]   In 737$_{12}$ the tribuni precede the chartularius; and while (5) βικάριοι may be stratores (737$_{17}$), the (4) πρωτομανδάτωρ is of lower rank (738$_8$).   The tribuni [2] and vicarii are commonly mentioned together, Phil. 789$_{21}$, Cer. 293$_{17}$, 294$_{12}$, $_{14}$, 295$_{22}$.   The tribuni evidently correspond to the κόμητες of the other tagmata, the vicarii to the κένταρχοι.   In the Procheiron, xi. 20, p. 21, we read τοὺς χαρτουλαρίους καὶ ληγαταρίους καὶ τριβούνους τοῦ ἀριθμοῦ.   As Phil. mentions no tribunes in the Arithmos, ἀριθμοῦ is probably an error for νουμέρου.   The occurrence of λεγατάριοι here makes it probable that the λεγατάριοι mentioned immediately after the βικάριοι in Phil. 753$_2$ were λεγ. τῶν νουμέρων καὶ τῶν τειχέων.   (6) μανδάτορες.   (7) πορτάριοι = θυρωροί.

(6) ὁ δομέστικος τῶν ὀπτιμάτων.

Although entitled a Domestic, and counted as such, the Domestic of the Optimati held the position of a stratêgos, as governor of a geographical circumscription, the θέμα τῶν ὀπτιμάτων, and resided at Nicomedia.   But these commanders occasionally adopted the title of stratêgos, as on a seal (not later than ninth century) published by Schlumberger (Sig. 244): β(ασιλικω) στρ(ατηγω) καὶ δομ(εστικω) του ὀπτιματ(ων).   Their order of rank, considerably below that of all the stratêgoi, corresponds to the inferiority of the optimatoi as a branch of the army.[3]   The observations of Constantine Porphyrogennetos

---

[1] Takt. Usp. 124 (under the spatharioi) οἱ τοπ. τῶν νουμ.   Phil. enumerates the items of the officium as six (so also in the case of the κόμης τ. τειχ.); they are really seven.

[2] Ducange, sub τριβοῦνος, cites Martyrium S. Mauricii num. 3 τριβοῦνος ἐχρημάτισεν ἐπισημοτάτου νουμέρου.   I can find no trace of this document.   It is not mentioned in his Index Auctorum.   But the passage is irrelevant; νούμερος is used in its wide sense.

[3] The treatise περὶ ταξ. furnishes information as to duties, connected with the baggage mules, to which Optimati were deputed, during imperial progresses through Asia Minor (476, 477, 487).   But in the sixth century the Optimati had a privileged position, belonging to the select troops (ἐπίλεκτα), among which they acted as a reserve.   They were under a taxiarch.   See (Maurice) Strat. i. 3, 28, cp. Aussaresses, op. cit. 16, who thinks they may have been about 2,000 strong.

(*Them.* 26) show how they were looked down upon by the scholarians, &c.   They were exclusively infantry, and Ibn Khurdâdhbah says that they numbered 4,000 (Gelzer, 18).

The Optimati were not divided into turms or drungoi (*Them.*, *loc. cit.*), and so there was no turmarch or drungary in the officium of the Domestic.   His officium was similar to that of the other Domestics, though he seems to have had no protomandator; on the other hand, like the stratêgoi, he had a protocancellarius.   The chartulary and the κόμητες are enumerated among the strators, Phil. 737₁₂₋₁₃.

In περὶ ταξ. 477₁₂, ₁₅ we find διὰ τοῦ κόμητος τῶν ὀπτιμάτων.   The question therefore arises whether κόμητες in Philotheos is a mistake for κόμης.

(7) ὁ κόμης τῶν τειχέων.

This dignitary is called by Philotheos ὁ δομέστικος τῶν τειχέων twice (715₂₂, 772₁₂), but elsewhere κόμης (714₂, 728₄, 731₂₁, 752₂₀), which was evidently the official title.   So Takt. Uspenski 119, *Cer.* 6₇. He was also called briefly ὁ τειχεώτης, Cont. Th. 175, 398, *Cer.* 295₂₁, περὶ ταξ. 460₁₄.

The post is mentioned by Genesios (5), where the reference is to the reign of Michael I.   But it is of much older date.   In A.D. 718–19 we meet an ἄρχων τοῦ τειχίου (Theoph. 401, τειχῶν Niceph. Patr. 56₅).[1]   The question arises whether the τείχη, with the care and defence of which he was charged, are the walls of the city, or the Long Wall of Anastasius.   The title would apply to either, though in the latter case we might expect μακρῶν, but the singular τὸ τειχίον, which comes no doubt from the common source of Theophanes and Nicephorus, would apply to the Long Wall, but not to the city walls. The Long Wall was called both τὸ μακρὸν τεῖχος and τὰ μακρὰ τείχη (cp. De Boor, Index to Theoph., p. 655).   The walls of the city were plural (including the τ. Θεοδοσιακόν or χερσαῖον and the τείχη παράλια). Other considerations also point to the connexion of the κόμης τ. τειχέων with the Long Wall.

Among the troops stationed in the capital, Kudâma does not include those of the Count of the Walls.   But among the themes, he designates, under the name of Tafla, a district, including Constantinople, and extending to a wall, two days' march from Constantinople (De Goeje 77).   Masûdî in a parallel passage (Gelzer, 86) names the wall *Makrun Tihos*.   Gelzer cites a passage

---

[1] Anastasius has in his version of Theophanes *comitem Titichei* (ed. de Boor, 259).

from the Acta of S. Demetrius (seventh century) to show that μακρὸν
τεῖχος was used to denote the whole district between the Long Wall
and Constantinople.[1]   But he is undoubtedly wrong in his theory that
both the military and civil administration of this district were in the
hands of the Prefect of the City until the reign of Leo VI.   For this
there is no evidence.   Uspenski has suggested that Kudâma's
province of Tafla should be connected with the κόμης τῶν τειχέων.[2]
But neither Uspenski nor Gelzer have noticed the important texts in
the laws of Justinian bearing on the subject.   In *Nov.* 16 (p. 114)
we meet an official named ὁ βικάριος τοῦ Μακροῦ τείχους (March A.D.
535).   In *Nov.* 25 (published a couple of months later) we learn that
there were two βικάριοι τοῦ μ. τ., one military, the other civil (p. 170).
Justinian, by this ordinance, combines the two offices in one, and
gives to the new governor the title of πραίτωρ Ἰουστινιανὸς ἐπὶ Θρᾴκης
(p. 171).   These texts permit us to infer that the district between
the Long Wall and the capital had been segregated as a special
circumscription by Anastasius when he built the Wall.   The civil and
military governors whom he set over it were vicarii respectively of the
Praet. Prefect of the East and the Mag. Mil. per Thracias.   We may
take it, then, that the ἄρχων τοῦ τειχίου descends from the Justinianean
praetor, who would certainly have been a *comes primi ordinis.*   Though
Kudâma is wrong in co-ordinating the province of the Long Wall with
the Themes, he is right in designating it as a district distinct from
Thrace.[3]   De Goeje's view (accepted by Gelzer) that Tafla should be
corrected to Tafra = ἡ τάφρος is not very convincing.   It is to be
noted that the Wall of Anastasius had no ditch.[4]

We have no evidence to show whether the Count of the Walls
retained the civil powers entrusted to the praetor Justinianus.   It
is not inconceivable, for another of the group of Domestics, the
Dom. of the Optimati, had civil powers, like the stratêgoi, in his
province.   In Takt. Usp. the Count of the Walls is a protospatharios.

The officium τῶν τειχέων was *modelled* precisely on the officium
τῶν νουμέρων, or vice versa.

---

[1] *AA. SS.* Oct. 8, iv. 179 C ἔτι μὴν καὶ Θρᾴκης καὶ τοῦ πρὸς Βυζαντίου Μακροῦ
Τείχους. See also Theoph. 455₁₂ where, as Gelzer says (88), ἐν τοῖς μακροῖς τείχεσι
τῆς Θρᾴκης means the district.

[2] *Op. cit.* 181.

[3] The Justinianean texts seem to me to dispose of the doubts of Vasil'ev (in
his review of Gelzer's work, *Viz. Vrem.* 10, 201 (1903)), as to the existence of the
circumscription.

[4] Cp. Schuchhardt, in the *Jahrbuch des deutschen arch. Instituts*, 16, 107 *sqq.*,
1901.

III. κριταί.

(1) ὁ ἔπαρχος τῆς πόλεως.

The Prefect of the City [1] is one of the few high officials of the Empire who retained both his name and, for the most part, his functions unchanged throughout successive ages. In the capital his authority was supreme, next to the Emperor's.[2] His functions were both administrative and judicial. He was the head of the police administration and was responsible for preserving order in the City; and all the trades were organized in colleges under his control. Cp. the Ἐπαρχικὸν Βιβλίον (see Bibliography), which is supposed to date from the reign of Leo VI. For his judicial functions see Zachariä von Lingenthal, *Griech.-röm. Recht* 366. His official quarters were the Praetorium (in the Mese, between the Augusteum and the Forum of Constantine), where was the chief prison of the city.[3]

In Takt. Usp. (115) the Prefect ranks after all the stratêgoi and immediately before the Domestic of the Excubitors. In Philotheos his place is higher. He ranks above all the stratêgoi of the western Themes, but on the other hand the Domestic of the Excubitors is placed immediately before him. This change in precedence was probably due to Basil I or Leo VI. The ceremony of the Prefect's investiture is described in *Cer.* i. 52. He was officially termed πατὴρ τῆς πόλεως (*ib.* 264$_{12}$, 528$_2$; Cont. Th. 461), and his office was one of the few which could not be held by a eunuch.

It has been held by Zachariä (*op. cit.* 365) that on the abolition of the Praetorian Prefect some of that minister's functions were transferred to the Prefect of the City. Zachariä puts it much too strongly when he says that 'die letztere Dignität [Praef. Praet.] in damaliger Zeit mit der ersteren [Praef. Urbi] verschmolzen war.' The fact that both offices are treated together in *Bas.* vi. 4 does not prove this. The only evidence we have is *Epan.* xi. 9, where the ἔπαρχος is named as a judge of appeal; but it is not quite clear from this that appeals from provincial courts could come before his court, and the comparison of *Bas.* ix. 2. 7, to which Zachariä refers, does not prove it. The question must be left open.[4]

It seems probable, however, that another office was transferred to

---

[1] ἔπαρχος in the lawbooks, in the Ἐπαρχικὸν Βιβλίον, and in the first list of Philotheos; ὕπαρχος elsewhere in Philotheos and in Takt. Usp.

[2] Cp. *Epan.* iv. 11.

[3] Cp. *Chron. Pasch.* ad ann. 532. The principal modern study of the functions of the Prefect is Uspenski's *Konstantinopol'skii Eparkh* (see Bibliography). It is probably he who is designated by Ibn Khurdâdhbah as Great Judge (p. 84).

[4] Uspenski accepts Zachariä's view without discussion, *op. cit.*, 80, cp. 88.

the Prefect of the City. Justinian (A.D. 535) abolished the old *Praefectus vigilum* or νυκτέπαρχος, who was subordinate to the Praef. Urbis, and instituted instead the *Praetor plebis*[1] or πραίτωρ δήμων (*Nov.* 38) who had a court, an assessor, twenty soldiers, and thirty firemen (ματρικάριοι)[2] under him (*ib.* § ε΄).[3] One of his most important duties was to put out fires. This Novel is reproduced in *Bas.* vi. 5, and Zachariä (*op. cit.* 372) infers that the office existed in the ninth century, notwithstanding the fact that it is not mentioned in the Epanagoge, or the Peira.[4] But the silence of the Taktikon Uspenski and Philotheos seems to be decisive against this supposition. It is not conceivable that such an important official could have been passed over in these *notitiae* if he had existed ; and there is no reference to him in the Ceremonial Book of Constantine. We must infer that the title in the Basilica has, like so many in that compilation, only antiquarian significance; that the praetor plebis and his court had been abolished, and that his duties devolved upon the Prefect and his officium.

(1, 2) The σύμπονος and the λογοθέτης τοῦ πραιτωρίου were co-equal in rank (*Cer.* 274₃). In Takt. Usp. 127–8 they precede the chartularii of the military themes and domesticates, but are below spathar rank. In Phil. 735₁₀ they are included among the possible spathars. They appear together at court ceremonials 750₄, 752₄, 772₁₄. The procedure of their investiture is described in *Cer.* i. c. 57. Both officials are described as σύμπονοι in Cont. Th. 470. Cp. also *Cer.* 13₆.

The title σύμπονος is equated with *assessor* in the Glosses to the

---

[1] The Novel speaks throughout of *praetores plebis* in the plural. But it also refers to νυκτέπαρχοι in the plural. Only one praetor seems to be contemplated. See Procopius, *H. A.* 20, p. 125 πραίτωρα δήμων. Cp. Zachariä, *op. cit.*, 372, n. 1336.

[2] This seems to be the meaning of ματρικάριοι, cp. Ducange, *s. v.* Fire-engines are mentioned in the older *Vita Theodori Stud.* (Migne, 99, 312), τὴν τῶν σιφώνων κατὰ τόπους παρασκευήν.

[3] Cp. also *Nov.* 98, p. 10.

[4] Zachariä refers to the fact that the office is mentioned by Codinus, *De off.*, p. 60, but the list of Codinus is full of obsolete titles. He also refers to Cantacuzenus, iv. 9, p. 53 Σιγηρὸν τὸν πραίτωρα δήμου (selected as an envoy to the Pope). I suspect that the office which Sigeros held was that of Prefect of the City. Leo Diaconus, there can be little doubt, used πραίτωρ in this sense, 65₆, 95₂₂. The latter passage runs ταῖς μεγίσταις τῆς πολιτείας ἀρχαῖς οἰκείους ἄνδρας ἀποκαθίστησι, πραίτωρα καὶ τοῦ πλωίμου δρουγγάριον τῆς τε βίγλης καὶ ὃν καλοῦσι νυκτέπαρχον. There was no distinct great officer entitled νυκτέπαρχος. We must read τῆς τε βίγλης ὃν καλοῦσι νυκτέπαρχον, 'the drungarios of the Vigla who is known as νυκτέπαρχος', viz. on account of his sentinel duties in keeping watch over the emperor's tent.

Basilica. It seems impossible to identify this official with any of the subordinates of the Praefectus Urbis, who appear in *Not. Dig. Occ.* We may conjecture that he was the successor of the *consiliarius* or *adsessor* of the Prefect, who is found in a constitution of Theodosius II A.D. 444 (*C. I.* i. 51. 11), 'non parum adsessoribus magistratuum maiorum . . . ideoque consiliarios virorum illustrium praefectorum tam praetorio quam huius inclitae urbis,' &c. This may perhaps be borne out by a constitution of Zeno, in which such coadjutors (*consiliarii, adsessores*) are described by the term σύμπονοι (*C. I.* i. 51. 13 = *Bas.* 6. 1. 71), though it is possible that σύμπονοι may have been substituted for some other word by the compilers of the Basilica. We learn something about one branch of his duties from the ἐπαρχικὸν βιβλίον, where he appears as acting for the Prefect in overseeing the guilds of the λωροτόμοι, ἀρτοποιοί and κάπηλοι. Thus xviii. § 4 προσερχέσθωσαν τῷ ἐπάρχῳ, ἵνα διὰ τοῦ συμπόνου οἱ σταθμοὶ τῶν ἄρτων πρὸς τὴν ἐξώνησιν γίνωνται, also xiv. § 2, xix. § 1. Nicole is quite in error (p. 90) in supposing that the corporations, or most of them, had each a σύμπονος of its own. It is quite clear that in all three texts the reference is to the σύμπονος of the Prefect.[1]

There is no direct evidence for the functions of the logothete of the praetorium. His equality with the σύμπονος makes it virtually certain that the sphere of the Prefect's administrative functions was divided into two complex departments, in one of which he was represented and assisted by the σύμπονος, in the other by the logothete. In the former was included the administration of the guilds; while from the title of the latter (associating him with the Praetorium, which was the Prefect's courthouse, and the chief prison of the city) we may infer that his functions were specially connected with the administration of justice. λογοθέτης points to the descent of this official from an accountant in the Prefect's bureau, possibly from the chief of the *numerarii* (*Not. Dig. Occ.* iv. 24).

(3) The κριταὶ τῶν ῥεγεώνων (who were, in the phraseology of the Notitia Dignitatum, *sub dispositione* but not in *officio praefecti*). See Zachariä v. Lingenthal, *Gr.-Röm. Recht*, 373. (He thinks that they correspond to the old *curatores regionum* of the *Descr. Urbis Cplanae.* I would rather identify the latter with the γειτονιάρχαι, see below.) They might have had the rank of protospathars, Phil. 732₁₈.[2]

---

[1] It may be doubted whether the σύμπονοι of seals published by Panchenko, ix. 345, and Schlumberger, *Sig.* 598, belong here. For a seal of a λογ. τοῦ πραιτ. see Konstantopulos, no. 407 β.

[2] For a seal with the inscription Πολυδώρω ῥεγεωναριω (6th–7th cent.) see Schlumberger, *Mél.*, 210.

(4) For the ἐπισκεπτῆται or inspectors we have no evidence to distinguish their functions from those of the similarly named ἐπόπται.

(5) There were two πρωτοκαγκελλάριοι, or chiefs of the bureau (Phil. 772₁₉). This exceptional arrangement suggests that a second officium was at some time or other combined with the officium proper of the Prefect, and that the πρωτοκαγκελλάριοι or principes of both were retained in the amalgamated office. We saw above that the praefectus vigilum, who used to be subordinate to the Prefect of the City, was replaced by the πραίτωρ τῶν δήμων under Justinian. This praetor existed under Maurice (Theoph. Sim. 6. 10. 6), but afterwards disappears. I conjecture that his functions were handed over to the Prefect, and the second πρωτοκαγκελλάριος descends from the *princeps* of the praetor. In Cont. Th. 442 only one protocancellarius seems to be contemplated.

(6) The name of the κεντυρίων points to the office being relatively ancient. We may conjecture that he commanded the στρατιῶται who were under the Prefect. See *Epan.* iv. 8 ἔχει στρατιώτας ἐπὶ τῇ εἰρήνῃ καὶ ἐπὶ τὸ ἀναφέρειν αὐτῷ τὰ πανταχοῦ κινούμενα.

(7) The ἐπόπται τῆς πόλεως (Phil. 750₇) were four in number (Phil. 772₁₉).

(8) The ἔξαρχοι were heads of guilds. In the ἐπαρχικὸν βιβλίον we find an ἔξαρχος of the πρανδιοπράται (v. §§ 1, 3), and ἔξαρχοι of the μεταξοπράται. The presidents of other guilds were προστάται (mentioned below). The Book of the Prefect does not refer to the heads of all the guilds; some of them it describes by the general term ὁ προεστώς. Probably in these cases the president was either an ἔξαρχος (Nicole thinks in the case of the most important) or a προστάτης.

(9) The twelve γειτονιάρχαι (Phil. 772₁₉) correspond to the *curatores regionum* of the *Descriptio Urb. Const.*, who however were thirteen (p. 243 in Seeck's ed. of *Not. Dig.*), the fourteenth region having none. Uspenski (*op. cit.* 100) would identify them with the old Vicomagistri, but these were far more numerous, sixty-five in all (*Descr. ib.*).

(10) For the college of the νομικοί or notaries[1] (cp. *Cer.* 12. 4) see the ἐπαρχικὸν βιβλίον i. (περὶ ταβουλλαρίων), §§ 13, 15, 16; cp. Nicole, pp. 82 *sqq.*, who has not noticed the Glossa nomica cited by Zachariä (*Gr.-Röm. Recht*, 297, n. 99) ταβελλίων (that is, *tabularius*) ὁ τὰ τῆς πόλεως γράφων συμβόλαια, ὁ παρὰ τοῖς πολλοῖς νομικὸς λεγόμενος, ἅπαντα ἐπιτελῶν τὰ τῶν πολιτῶν γραμματεῖα, ἕκαστον αὐτῶν οἰκείους ἐπισφραγίζων γράμμασι.

---

[1] The γέρων νομικὸς εἰς τὰ Σφορακίου in *Scr. Incert.* (Leo Gramm., ed. Bonn, p. 350) was one of these.

(11) The duty of the βουλλωταί was to mark with the bull or seal of the Prefect the weights, scales, measures, and sometimes the goods of the merchants and tradesmen. See ἐπαρχικὸν βιβλίον, viii. § 3.

(12) προστάται, heads of trade corporations; cp. above under (8). From the ἐπαρχικὸν βιβλίον we learn that the presidents of the σαπωνοπράται, λωροτόμοι, χοιρέμποροι, ἰχθυοπράται, ἐργολάβοι, &c., had this title.

(13) καγκελλάριοι. See above under (5).

(14) For the παραθαλασσίτης, whose name connects his duties with the policing of the seashore, see Peira, li. 29 (οἱ δὲ πλέουσι τὴν θάλασσαν καὶ ὑπόκεινται τῷ παραθαλασσίτῃ). His position here argues that in the time of Philotheos he was not an important official; but half a century later Liutprand (Ant. 3. 7) speaks of him as if he were one of the high dignitaries of the court. He is mentioned in περὶ ταξ. 461₄. On the occasion of the Cretan expedition A.D. 902 he was directed to arm 1,200 men (Cer. 660₆).[1] Uspenski compares the comes riparum and the comes portus who were under the Prefect of Rome.[2]

Another member of the officium, not included in this list, is mentioned by Philotheos 750₈ (as a guest in the Palace) ὁ λεγατάριος τοῦ πραιτωρίου. The ἐπαρχικὸν βιβλίον, c. xx, treats of this functionary and explains his duties, which consisted in supervising foreign merchants and inspecting their merchandise.[3]

(2) ὁ κυαίστωρ.

The Quaestor sacri palatii survived the changes of time, but the range of his functions was altered and his official rank was lowered. In early times his chief duties were leges dictandae and preces. He had to draft the Imperial laws and deal with the petitions addressed to the Emperor. He was the chief legal authority in the state and the legal adviser of the government. Cp. Cass. Var. vi. 5 (formula quaesturae).[4] The quaestor of the ninth century had a court of his own and extensive judicial functions.

[1] ἀπὸ συνδόσεως τῶν αὐτῶν, Reiske ἀστῶν, from a contribution by the citizens.

[2] Op. cit. 100. (See Not. Dig. Occ., iv. 6, 7.) Cp. Zachariä, op. cit. 373. See also M. Goudas, ἡ καταμέτρησις τῶν ἐμπορικῶν πλοίων, in Βυζαντίς, I. 35 sqq. 1909. In the twelfth century there was a σέκρετον τῆς θαλάσσης, and two parathalassitai are mentioned along with the notaries of this bureau, Miklosich-Müller Acta et Dipl. vi. 3, 124. (In Manuel Comnenus, Nov. 54, p. 537 eparcho parathalassite, should we not read eparchi?) Was Addaeus in Proc. H. A. c. 25 a parathalassites?

[3] Cp. Uspenski, op. cit. 97. There is no reason whatever for the suggestions that the λεγατάριος is identical with the σύμπονος (Nicole) or with the λογ. τοῦ πραιτ. (Vogt, Basile Iᵉʳ, 142).

[4] He used to assist in the appeal court of the Praetorian Prefect. Cp. Justinian, Nov. 46.

This change arose from the fact that the Quaestor of the Sacred Palace had taken over the duties of the new quaestor or quaesitor (ἐρευνητής) who had been created by Justinian. The law which created the new office is *Nov.* 99.[1] Here the official is called *quaestor*, but Procopius, *H. A.* 20 (p. 125), and Lydus, 2. 29 (p. 85), call him *quaesitor* (κυαισίτωρ); Lydus however also speaks of him and the Quaestor together as οἱ ἄμφω κυαίστορες (3. 20, p. 109). In *Bas.* vi. 6 they are treated as the same office; the compilers evidently did not realize that they were originally two. The section of the *Epanagoge* (5) on the quaestor merely reproduces Justinian's *Novel*. But it would be erroneous to draw the conclusion that the later Quaestor is simply the Quaesitor and that this old Quaestor was abolished. This is disproved by the Quaestor's officium, in which we find the ἀντιγραφῆς, that is the old *magistri s. scriniorum* (see below), whose functions were closely associated with those of the Quaestor of the Sacred Palace. This proves the continuity, which is borne out by the fact that a eunuch could not hold the post of Quaestor, a circumstance pointing to its ancient associations and prestige.

For the functions of the Quaestor, derived from those of the Quaesitor, see Zachariä v. Lingenthal, *op. cit.* 368. They were of an administrative as well as judicial order: supervision of travellers and provincials visiting the capital; supervision of beggars; decision in the case of complaints of coloni or tenants against their landlords who resided in the capital; duty of punishing injustice in such cases; duty of reporting misconduct of magistrates to the Emperor; judging all cases of forgery. Besides these duties (imposed on the Quaesitor by Justinian) the Quaestor had others connected with wills and inheritances. All wills were sealed with his seal and opened in his presence;[2] he had powers of supervision over the execution of wills, and especially over the administration of the property of minors.[3]

The Quaestor ranks after the General Logothete both in the

---

[1] It is entitled περὶ τάξεως καταίστωρος καὶ τῶν βοηθῶν αὐτοῦ καὶ τῶν ἀντιγραφέων. This title is obviously late. The law has nothing to do with the ἀντιγραφῆς, who are not mentioned in the text.

[2] These formalities formerly devolved on the *magister census* (for whom see Böcking, *Occ.* 193-4). See *Nov.* 44 of Leo VI (cp. Peira, xiv. 11), *Nov.* 7 of Constantine VII (αἱ διαθῆκαι παρὰ τῷ κοιαίστωρι ἀνοίγονται, p. 258). The motive of transferring the duty to the quaestor (or quaesitor), after Justinian, may have been the competence of this minister in cases of forgery. See Zachariä, *op. cit.* 157.   For the μάγιστρος τῶν κήνσων (in connexion with orphans) cp. Justinian, *Nov.* 151, p. 275.

[3] Cp. Peira, xvi. 5. 13.

Taktikon Uspenski and in Philotheos.[1] For the ceremony of his creation see *Cer.* i. 54.

(1) The ἀντιγραφῆς (spathars, Phil. 752₄; of inferior rank, Takt. Usp. 127, 128; in both texts, precede the σύμπονος and λογ. πραιτ.) are the old *magistri scriniorum*.[2] In the fifth century they were four in number (memoriae, epistolarum, libellorum, graecarum: *Not. Dig. Or.* xi and xix).[3] Their *scrinia* were *sub dispositione* of the Master of the Offices, not of the Quaestor, but the quaestor who had in former times no officium of his own made use of *adiutores* from the bureaux of the magistri (*Not. Or.* xii). In John Malalas 494₈ the ἀντιγραφῆς are mentioned along with the quaestor.[4] Their transference to the officium of the quaestor was probably connected with the abolition of the post of magister officiorum. In the Proem to the *Ecloga* of Leo III (τοὺς ἐνδοξοτάτους ὑπάτους καὶ ἀντιγραφεῖς, p. 3) they are associated with the quaestor [A.D. 740]. Cp. also George Mon. ed. Bonn. 749₉.

The magister memoriae dealt with decisions made in the form of *annotationes* by the emperor on the margins or backs of documents presented to him; he also replied to petitions (*preces*). The magister epistolarum drew up the answers to communications from foreign powers and from the *civitates* of the empire; examined the questions propounded by officials (*consultationes*); and dealt with such petitions as were connected with his other duties. The magister libellorum dealt with the appeals to the emperor from lower courts and with petitions from parties to suits in such courts. The magister epistolarum Graecarum 'eas epistolas quae graece solent emitti aut ipse dictat aut latine dictatas transfert in graecum' (*Not. Dig. Or.*, xix. 13).[5]

It is clear that the duties of the magistri epistolarum connected them more closely with the magister officiorum, while those of the two other magistri associated them with the quaestor. All four had the right of direct access to the emperor, but the functions of the

---

[1] He comes last among the officials who have Patrician rank in the Acta of the 6th General Council, A. D. 680, Mansi, xi. 209 Ἰωάννου τοῦ ἐνδοξοτάτου ἀπὸ ὑπάτων πατρικίου καὶ κοιαίστωρος.

[2] Mommsen, 482. Peter Patr. fr. 14 ἀντιγραφεὺς τῆς μνήμης. Suidas *sub* Ἀδριανός, ἀντ. τῶν ἐπιστολῶν (see also Procop., *B. P.* 2. 23, *H. A.* 14; Justinian, Nov. 10, 113, 124, 133, 1). Cp. Bury, *Magistri scriniorum* (see Bibliography).

[3] I do not include the *comes dispositionum* who was under the Master of Offices; he was not one of the magistri scriniorum. He superintended the programme of the emperor's daily movements.

[4] We meet an ἀντιγραφεύς in *Chron. Pasch.*, s. a. 605, p. 973. Cp. also Menander, fr. 6, p. 248 εἰς τῶν βασιλείων διαιτητῶν οὓς δὴ ἀντιγραφέας ἀποκαλέσαις.

[5] For fuller explanation see Karlowa, i. 834 *sq.*

magister memoriae would naturally bring him into most frequent contact with the sovran.

As Greek became the official language of the empire, the necessity of a second magister epistolarum was less cogent, though so long as Africa (throughout the seventh century) and the Exarchate of Italy (till the middle of the eighth) were held, there must have been some provision for Latin.

The abolition of the Master of Offices involved a change in the position of the *scrinia.* What seems to have happened was this. The magister memoriae remained an independent minister under the Greek name ὁ ἐπὶ τῶν δεήσεων (see below), while the magister libellorum and the magister epistolarum (now Greek) along with their scrinia were subordinated to the quaestor. That one of the quaestor's ἀντιγραφῆς was the mag. lib. is supported by the occurrence of the λιβελίσιος (see below) in his officium. That there were two ἀντιγραφῆς in the ninth and tenth centuries seems a probable inference from a passage in the ceremony of their investiture, Cer. 274$_{14}$ κἂν τε εἶς ἐστι κἂν τε δύο.[1]

(2) The σκρίβας of the quaestor is mentioned in a constitution of Constantine VII (*Nov.* vii, p. 259). We may conjecture that he descends from the *scriba* of the magister census, who in the fifth century was subordinate to the Prefect of the City (*Not. Dig. Occ.* iv). This official, whom Lydus describes as ἄρχοντα τῶν ἀρχετύπων συμβολαίων, had a scriba, instead of a notarius, in his scrinium (σκρίβαν μὲν ἐκείνῳ ἀντὶ τοῦ ὑπογραφέα ὑπηρετεῖσθαι, Lydus, 2. 30). This identification is borne out by the circumstance that the functions of the *magister census* in connexion with the sealing and opening of wills were transferred to the quaestor (see above), and we know the σκρίβας represented the quaestor in looking after the interests of minors (*Nov.* 7, c. 3, of Constantine, vii, p. 259).

(3) The σκέπτωρ, evidently = *exceptor*, must descend from the *exceptores*[2] of the sacra scrinia. In these scrinia the officials were (1) proximus, (2) melloproximus, (3) exceptores, (4) memoriales or epistolares or libellenses (respectively). The σκέπτωρ had doubtless a number of clerks under him who performed duties similar to those of the *exceptores*, copying documents and writing from dictation. In Const. Porph., *Nov.* vii, c. 2 the quaestor is said to have two νοτάριοι[3] : Zachariä (*op. cit.* 368) suggests that they are the σκέπτωρ and λιβελίσιος.

---

[1] In *Vita Steph. iun.* Migne P. G. 100, 1140 we meet Κομβοκόνωνα τὸν ἀντιγραφέα.

[2] Cp. Grenfell and Hunt, *Oxyrhynchus Papyri*, i, p. 91 (A.D. 295) ἐκσκέπ(τορσι).

[3] Peira, xiv. 11 οἱ νοτάριοι τοῦ κοιαιστώριου, li. 21 τοῦ νοταρίου αὐτοῦ (sc. quaestoris).

(4) The λιβελίσιος descends from the *libellenses* of the *scrinium libellorum* as the σκέπτωρ from the *exceptores* (cp. Justinian, *Nov.* 46, c. 9, p. 286).

(5, 6) The πρωτοκαγκελλάριος was under spathar rank, Phil. 738₇. The καγκελλάριοι are mentioned in the above-cited Novel of Constantine VII, where, as in *Cer.* 269₃ (τοὺς ἀντιγραφέας καὶ καγκελλαρίους), the πρωτοκαγκελλάριος is obviously included. The domesticus of the quaestor's cancellarii is once mentioned, *Cer.* 11₂₅. The cancellarii used to recite Latin chants at the procession of the emperors to St. Sophia (*ib.* and c. 74, p. 369), perhaps because they were supposed to have some acquaintance with Latin.

. The seal in Schlumberger, *Sig.* 578, of a chartularius and protonotarius of the quaestorium is of later date than our period.

(3) ὁ ἐπὶ τῶν δεήσεων.

The functionary known as ἐπὶ τῶν δεήσεων, of which the Latin would be *a precibus*, must be regarded as the successor of the *magister memoriae*, one of whose functions was *precibus respondere* (*Not. Dig.*, Or. xix. 7). It is true that on the *magister libellorum* and the *magister epistolarum* it also devolved *preces tractare* (*ib.* 9. 11) ; but the *scrinium memoriae* was the chief of the *sacra scrinia* (it is always mentioned first), and was therefore the most likely to have been made an independent office, and we have seen that there is reason for thinking that the *magister libellorum* was one of the ἀντιγραφῆς subordinated to the quaestor. The *mag. epist.* need hardly be considered, as *preces tractare* can only have been a minor and incidental part of his business. While the ἀπὸ δεήσεων belonged to the judicial class, it does not appear that he had a court of his own ; he seems to have only examined and prepared petitions to be presented to the Emperor. Cp. Zachariä, *Gr.-röm. Recht*,³ 356.

In Takt. Usp. 123 he is of spathar rank ; in Phil. 729, 732 he may be ἀνθύπατος, πατρίκιος or πρωτοσπαθάριος.[1] It was obligatory for him (κατὰ τύπον) to accompany the Emperor when he made excursions by sea in the neighbourhood of Constantinople (*De adm. imp.* 234).

It may only be an accident, whether of his own or of a copyist, that the officium of the ἐπὶ τῶν δεήσεων is omitted in the list of Philotheos ; but it may well be that he had no officium (except clerks). If he had one, we have no materials for reconstructing it. Philotheos twice mentions an official whose name appears in the MS. as

---

[1] Cp. Nicephorus Phocas, *Nov.* 22, p. 299 ὁ πρωτοσπαθάριος Βασίλειος ὁ ἐπὶ τῶν δεήσεων.

δεκσογράφῳ, 758₂₀, and δεκσωγράφῳ, 774₄. Reiske proposed to read δεησογράφῳ. This form seems impossible; we should have to go further and write δεησιγράφῳ. But even if an emendation of this kind were accepted, it is not probable that the official in question was connected with the ἐπὶ τῶν δεήσεων. He is quite mysterious. In both passages he is named next the aktuarios and οἱ τοῦ ἡλιακοῦ παραστάται.

In the provinces there were officials subordinate to the minister for petitions. Schlumberger (*Sig.* 493) has published the seal (eighth or ninth century) of an ἐπὶ τῶν δεήσεων Σικελίας. There are some other seals which probably belong to the minister himself. Schlumberger, *Mél.* 265 (eighth or ninth century), of Basil, βασ. σπαθ. and ἐπὶ τῶν δεησέων (cp. also *Mél.* 269); Panchenko, 8. 220 (tenth or ninth century) Κωνσ[ταν]τίνῳ [β(ασιλικῷ)] α'[σπ]αθαρίῳ καὶ [ἐπ]ὶ τ(ῶ)ν δεή[σε]ων, 9. 394 (ninth or eighth century) Βασιλήῳ τῶν δεήσεω(ν) κεφ., where Panchenko proposes κεφαλῇ; but we should obviously read Κεφαλᾷ; Basileios Kephalas was the name of the person.

IV. σεκρετικοί.

As all the officials of this section, except the Logothete of the Course (4) and the Chief Secretary (7), are connected with financial administration, it will be convenient to discuss here as a whole the troublesome but important question of the origin and nature of the financial bureaux which existed in the ninth century. One of our greatest difficulties in understanding and estimating the policy of the later Roman Emperors lies in our ignorance of the machinery of the financial administration. The chroniclers notice financial measures rarely and briefly, but do not explain the details in such a way as to let us see how they operated and how they were carried out. Official documents are few. Even for the earlier period, from Constantine to Justinian, though we have much information about the raising of the revenue and the methods of taxation, we have very little about the expenditure and how it was divided among the several treasuries.

Under the system of Constantine there were two great financial ministries, unconnected and independent. These were the fisc, under the comes sacrarum largitionum (κόμης τῶν θείων θησαυρῶν), and the *res privata* under the comes rei privatae (κ. τῶν θείων πριβάτων or τοῦ θείου ταμείου). Besides these two principal and independent treasuries there were also the chests of the Praetorian Prefects, to which part of the fiscal revenue was diverted and from which the army was paid.[1]

---

[1] For the *praefectoria arca* in the fifth century cp. C. Th., 11. 9. 17 (where it is distinguished from *utrumque nostrum aerarium = s. larg.* and *res priv.*). For the

In the sixth century, if not earlier, the Praetorian Prefect *of the East* had two distinct chests, or at least two distinct accounts, which are designated as the γενική and the ἰδικὴ τράπεζα in laws of Justinian and Justin II.[1]   We do not know the nature of the distinction.

Besides the *res privata* there was another administration of the same kind, the *divina domus per Cappadociam*, which was under the control of the praepositus sacri cubiculi, and was administered through his subordinate, entitled comes domorum per Cappadociam [2] (κόμης τῶν οἰκιῶν, Justinian, *Nov.* 46. 2).   We meet in Novels of Justinian [3] ὁ θεῖος οἶκος distinguished from τὰ θεῖα πριβάτα and τὸ θεῖον πατριμώνιον, and as these laws do not refer to Cappadocia but to the provinces of Arabia and Phoenicia Libanensis, it would seem that the *domus divinae*, which were under the comes r. priv. (*Not. Dig., Or.* xiv. 3), had been detached from the *res privata* and joined with the *dom. div. per Capp.* as a separate administration.   Now in A. D. 566 we find, instead of the περίβλεπτος κόμης τῶν οἰκιῶν, a μεγαλοπρεπέστατος κουράτωρ τῶν οἰκιῶν.[4]   This is more than a change of name.   We can infer that the *div. dom. per Capp.* has been withdrawn from the praepositus (otherwise he must have been mentioned in the context, in which all the ministers who had financial charges are enumerated) and, with the other *domus divinae*, placed under a Curator.

Another financial administration, named the *sacrum patrimonium* (τὸ θεῖον πατριμώνιον), was instituted by Anastasius I about the end of the fifth century.[5]   We may doubt whether there was any distinction in principle between this *sacrum patrimonium*, which was called ἡ ἰδικὴ κτῆσις, and the *res privata*, which was called ἡ ἰδικὴ περιουσία.   The word κτῆσις (not κτήματα) might suggest that the *res privata* had become so large, through landed property falling to the state, that Anastasius placed under the control of a new minister recent acquisitions and all that should be acquired in the future.   It is doubtful whether the expressions of Lydus really signalize an important principle of distinction between the two offices.[6]   It is to be observed that the organization of the office of

[1] Justinian, *ib.* 96. 9,' p. 536 προνοεῖν τῆς εἰσπράξεως τῶν δημοσίων φόρων τῶν εἰς ἑκατέραν τράπεζαν εἰσφερομένων τοῦ δικαστηρίου τῆς σῆς ὑπεροχῆς, τῇ τε ἰδικῇ τῇ τε γενικῇ, also 11, 12, &c.   Justin II, *Nov.* 1, p. 4.   Cp. Lydus, 3. 36.

chest of the Pref. of Illyricum cp. Justinian, *Nov.* 163, p. 351 ; Justin II, *Nov.* 1, p. 4.   The officials of the Prefect's *arca* are called ἀρκάριοι, Justinian, *ib.*, 96, p. 542 ; 163, p. 353.

[2] *C. I.*, 12. 24. 3 ; 3. 26. 11 ; 12. 5. 2.

[3] 53, p. 357 ; 55, pp. 366-7.   Also ἡ ἡμετέρα οἰκία, 158. 2.

[4] Justin II, *Nov.* 1, p. 4.

[5] *C. I.*, 1. 34. 1 ; Lydus, 2. 27.

[6] *Ib.* κόμιτα πριβάτων ἀντὶ τοῦ τῶν ἰδίᾳ πως τοῖς βασιλεῦσι προσηκόντων, and ὁ

the Patrimony was an exact copy of the office of the *res privata* (κατὰ μίμησιν—αὐτὴν διοικῶν, *C. I.*, 1. 34. 1, where it is also enacted that the officials of both shall have the same privileges).

In the sixth century, then, there were (omitting Africa and Italy from consideration) seven independent treasuries. (1) The fisc (*largitiones*); (2) the two τράπεζαι of the Praetorian Prefect of the East; (3) the chest of the Praetorian Prefect of Illyricum; to which must be added (4) the chest of the Justinianean quaestor of Moesia and Scythia (Justin II, *Nov.* 1, p. 4). These four coffers were replenished by the general taxation of the Empire. (5) *Res privata*; (6) *sacrum patrimonium*; (7) *domus divinae*; three treasuries deriving their revenue from the Imperial estates.

When we come down to the ninth century we find a variety of bureaux with a new nomenclature: the γενικόν, σακέλλιον, στρατιωτικόν, βεστιάριον, μεγάλη κουρατωρεία, ἀγέλαι, στάβλον, εἰδικόν. Of these the γενικόν corresponds to the *sacrae largitiones*. The στρατιωτικόν fulfils the functions of the arcae of the Praet. Prefects so far as military finance is concerned. The μέγας κουράτωρ is the descendant of the κουράτωρ τῶν οἰκιῶν of the sixth century. The βεστιάριον is the old *vestiarium sacrum* which used to be under the control of the comes s. larg. (*Not. Dig.*, *Or.* xiii. 28), and has become an independent office. The ἀγέλαι and στάβλον are the *greges* and *stabula* which used to be under the comes r. priv. The εἰδικόν is concerned with the state-factories which used to be under the magister officiorum and the comes s. larg. All these offices will be discussed in detail below.

More may be said here about the σακέλλιον, because an important change is involved. σάκελλα or σακέλλιον means purse, and σακελλάριος keeper of a purse. The Patriarch had a sakellarios (cp. e.g. *Chron. Pasch.* 697, *sub* A. D. 607), and we hear of the sakellarios of a ' strategos ' of Numidia (*Acta Maximi*, Migne, *P. G.*, 90. 112).[1] Now the Emperors, manifestly, must always have had a private purse (apart from the treasuries of the *res privata* and *s. largitiones*), and an official in charge of it. Such an official, if he were mentioned in

λεγόμενος πατριμώνιος ἀιτὶ τοῦ φύλαξ τῆς ἰδίᾳ πως ἀνηκούσης τῷ βασιλεῖ καὶ τυχὸν ἐκ προγόνων περιουσίας. The last clause does suggest a distinction, and also perhaps the use of τοῖς βασιλεῦσι in one case, and τῷ βασιλεῖ in the other. Pamphronios in Menander, fr. 8 (A. D. 561) προεστῶτα τῆς αὐτοῦ βασιλέως περιουσίας, was presumably *com. r. priv.*

[1] A σακκελλάριος is mentioned in a papyrus of seventh century, published in Wessely's *Griechische Papyrusurkunden kleineren Formats*, no. 992, p. 174 (1908) and in the early Arab period σάκελλα is used apparently for the central treasury of that province; e.g. Pap. Brit. Mus. iv, no. 1336 (A. D. 709) ἀπὸ τῆς σ., no. 1412 (A. D. 710) εἰς τὴν σ.

the Notitia Dignitatum at all, would have appeared in the officium of the Praepositus—where there is an unfortunate lacuna in our texts. The Sakellarios first appears as a prominent official, under this name, at the beginning of the seventh century; but he seems to be mentioned in the sixth under the periphrasis ταμίας τῶν βασιλικῶν χρημάτων (see below under σακελλάριος). I infer that the σακέλλιον and σακελλάριος had long existed, but that in the sixth and seventh centuries they begin to emerge from comparative obscurity into administrative importance.

Now it is to be observed that in the seventh century, while the Sakellarios is ascending in rank and prominence, we cease to hear of the comes rei privatae. In the ninth century we find no single department which can be pointed to as simply the old res privata with a new name. The management of the res priv. and the θεῖοι οἶκοι seems to be divided between two departments, that of the σακέλλιον and that of the Great Curator—the general administration of the estates being presumably under the latter, and the revenue being dealt with by the σακέλλιον. We may conjecture that this new arrangement, which led to the disappearance of the comes r. p., and also of the comes s. patrimonii, came about in the seventh century. The administrative importance which the Sakellarios possessed in the reign of Justinian II, when he must have had a bureau of officials under him, points to this conclusion. The imperial estates—res priv., s. patr., and θεῖοι οἶκοι—were placed under the control of the Sakellarios and the Curator (κουράτωρ τῶν οἰκιῶν), the former acting as Receiver, the latter as High Steward. We may suspect that this change may have been partly due to the loss of the Imperial estates in Syria and Egypt.

This development was an intelligible consequence of the connexion which we may reasonably assume to have existed between the sakellion and the revenue of the Imperial estates in the fifth and sixth centuries. We may take it that the sakellion was the receptacle of the net profit arising from the Imperial estates. The treasuries of the s. largitiones and the Praetorian Prefects provided for the standing expenses of the government—army, civil service, &c.—and it is highly improbable that any money was diverted from these sources into the Emperor's sakellion. We may assume that, when the treasuries of the Private Estate, the Patrimony, and the Divine Houses had paid the expenses of administration, and perhaps certain standing charges which were allocated to them, the net annual profits were deposited in the sakellion, which not only supplied the Emperor with money for his personal expenses, but also provided for extraordinary and irregular outlay, such as on wars, buildings, &c. The large accumulations which were made by the parsimony of Anastasius I were doubtless stored in the sakellion.

It is to be noticed that the *res privata* was itself a spending department. Its expenditure was known as the *largitiones privatae,* for which there was a special scrinium.[1] This bureau must have been incorporated in the new organization of the Sakellion in the seventh century.

Another change of great importance was subsequently made in the financial administration. In the ninth century the head of the Sakellion is no longer the Sakellarios, but the χαρτουλάριος τοῦ σακελλίου. It is evident that this functionary was originally one of the chief subordinates of the Sakellarios, but he has become the minister in charge of the department. The Sakellarios himself has not disappeared; he has been exalted to a new position. He has no special officium of his own, but he exercises a general control over all the financial bureaux and is superior to all the financial ministers. In the words of Philotheos, ' he supervises what is done in each bureau (σέκρετον) by the written reports of his own notary.' This is a fact of the highest importance, which has escaped notice. It places the later financial system in a new light. There was in the ninth century a general and methodical control exercised over all the offices which dealt with finance or administered the sources of revenue, and this control, which was not only a check on malversation but helped to mitigate the disadvantage of not having a single central exchequer, was an innovation and improvement on the Constantinian system. We cannot determine whether this arrangement was due to the Heraclians or to the Isaurians. Under the Heraclians, considerable changes were made in financial administration. The sakellarios first becomes prominent in the reign of Heraclius himself. Under his dynasty the comes s. larg. disappears and his place is taken by the Logothete of the Genikon. The Logothete of the Stratiotikon appears under Constantine IV, and was probably created either by Heraclius or by Constantine II. But it seems not unlikely that the Sakellarios under the Heraclians remained simply the minister of the Sakellion, and that his later office, as General Comptroller, was an innovation of the Isaurian period when the various administrative changes which had come about in the previous century were systematized and developed. It may be added that on general grounds it seems probable that the Sakellion, as a treasury, not as a department, was in the keeping of the sakellarios.

---

[1] *Not. Dig., Occ.* xii. 4.

The heads of most of the later financial bureaux were entitled logothetes, or chartularies. λογοθέτης is the word which in early times was used to render *rationalis*, and in the Constantinian system the *rationales* were all financial subordinates of the great financial ministers.[1] The chartularies were much lower in the scale ; they were clerks in the various *scrinia*, and so we hear little about them. The Notitia Dignitatum does not enumerate the members of the *scrinia*. At that time, however, the head of a *scrinium* under the Castrensis bore the title of Chartularius (*Not. Dig., Or.* xvii. 10 ; *Occ.* xv. 11). The rise of the chartularii to importance is a subject which deserves a special investigation, but it lies outside my present scope. I will only note the *schola chartulariorum* in the officium of the Praetorian Prefect of Africa, as organized by Justinian (*C. I.* 1. 27.1)[2] ; the importance of the three Chartularies of the Cubiculum (Justinian, *Nov.* 16)[3]; the distinction drawn between ἄρχοντες χαρτουλαρικοί and στρατιωτικοί by Peter the Patrician (*Cer.* 92, p. 418)[4] ; the evidence of Lydus (iii. 17, 18, 20, 27) ; and the Italian material in the letters of Gregory the Great and the Liber Pontificalis (reviewed by Diehl).[5] The original function of the chartularii, from which they derived their name, was probably to keep and register *chartae*—receipts, dockets, &c., connected with the financial business of the bureau to which they belonged. The registers, e.g. containing the debts to the fisc were called *chartae*, cp. *C. Th.* 11. 28. 2 ; 6 (*chartis quibus debita publica continentur*), 12, &c.

A word may be said about the term σέκρετον = *sēcrētum* (the long vowels are preserved in ἀσηκρῆτις). Hesychius (*s. v.*) explains it as κονσιστώριον, and in *C. Th.* 6. 35. 7, we find *intra consistorii secreta* of notaries. Cp. Cass. *Var.* 6, 16 *principis secretum et consilium.* Also in Theoph. Sim. 8, 8, 9, the Emperor Maurice, having given an audience to Germanos, μεθίσταται τοῦ παρὰ Ῥωμαίοις λεγομένου σεκρέτου. It appears from these passages that originally σέκρετον meant the Imperial Consistorium or Council, and the precincts in which it met.

[1] Andreas, ὁ ἀπὸ λογοθετῶν, became Prefect of the City in A. D. 563, Theoph. 239₈.

[2] Cp. also the *chartularii numerorum militarium*, *C. I.* 12. 37. 19. Cp. too Justinian, *Nov.* 141, p. 221.

[3] Cp. also *ib.*, p. 404₁₅, τοὺς χ. τῶν βαρβάρων, and 405₁₈. For chart. in the *scrin. fabr.* of the mag. off. see Justinian, *Nov.* 108, p. 61.

[4] L'exarchat de Ravenne, 154-5.   Cp. also the chartarii in Cass. *Var.* 7. 43 (apparently of the *comes patrimonii*, cp. 8. 23).

[5] Cp. *Chron. Pasch.* 703, *sub* A. D. 612 : Philaretos was one of these chartularii.   For a seal of a σπαθάριος καὶ χαρτουλάριος, seventh or eighth century, see Panchenko, 8. 225.

In these precincts the *notarii* (who were under the primicerius not., *Not. Dig., Or.* xvii) discharged their duties. This early meaning of the term explains the usage in the Ceremonial Book of Constantine, in describing some of the court solemnities: e.g. *Cer.* 218_{10} καὶ καθεσθέντων τῶν δεσποτῶν, δέχονται τὸ σέκρετον, viz. magistri, patricians, &c., successively according to rank. When the reception is over ἐξέρχεται τὸ σέκρετον, except the patricians who ἵστανται κονσιστώριον. (This latter phrase is frequent in the ceremonies: since the Consistorium had coalesced with the Synkletos, κονσιστώριον ceased to be used except in a ceremonial sense[1] with ἵστασθαι, 'stand in attendance'.) Again 226_{12} τὸ σέκρετον ὅλον, 212_{6} τὸ σ. τῶν ὑπάτων, 616_{10} τὸ σ. τῶν συγκλητικῶν (and 618_{18} of official ladies received by the Empress).

In *C. Th.* 6. 35. 7, the officials of the scrinia (sacra), of the finance bureaux, of the castrensis, &c., are distinguished from the notaries of the *secreta*. But the term σέκρετον in time became extended to all or most of the bureaux in which the work was chiefly secretarial and clerical, and all their officials were called σεκρετικοί. Philotheos confines the term to a certain number of such offices, but it was also used in a wider sense, covering most of the offices in classes III, V–VII, as appears from *Cer.* 527, cp. esp. l. 21, where the ὕπαρχος is distinctly classed as a σεκρετικός. (Compare also $575_{10, \ 12}$, 608_{10}, 698_{18}, 524_{14}.)

The offices (σέκρετα) of the σεκρετικοί in the restricted meaning were in the Palace.

(1) ὁ σακελλάριος.

In the reign of Heraclius we meet Theodore, a financial functionary termed βασιλικὸς σακελλάριος by Theophanes (A. D. 635; 337_{23}, 338_{3}). In the reign of Constans II a sakellarios conducted the examination of the Abbot Maximus (τῷ σακελλαρίῳ πρώτῳ τὴν ἀξίαν τυγχάνοντι, *Acta Maximi*, Migne, *P. G.* 90, 88, 112, 113).[2] Under Justinian II the office was held by the notorious and influential Stephen (Theoph. 367_{15}).

This functionary also appears in our records under another description, ταμίας τῶν βασιλικῶν χρημάτων. The equation of this expression with σακελλάριος results from three data. Nicephorus in his Chronicle

---

[1] Also, of course, τὸ μέγα κ., a hall in the palace.

[2] The Abbot Maximus addressed a letter (c. A.D. 629) πρὸς Κωνσταντίνον σακελλάριον (*Ep.* 24, Migne, 91, 608), but he may have been an ecclesiastical, or a local, sakellarios.

applies it (1) to Theodore (23_{12}) and (2) to Stephen (37_{13}), whom, as we have seen, Theophanes designates as sakellarioi.   He also (3) applies it to Leontios (5_6, A.D. 609), who is described as ὁ ἀπὸ σακελλαρίων in *Chron. Pasch.* 701, *sub* A.D. 610. Hence we can infer that Philagrios, to whom he applies the same title (28_{12}), was Sakellarios in A.D. 640.

The equation also enables us to trace the Sakellarios in the sixth century. For Agathias (3. 2, p. 140) designates Rusticus (who was sent by Justinian with money to the army in Lazica) as ταμίας τῶν βασιλικῶν χρημάτων, and explains οὐ μὴν τῶν ἐκ τῆς δασμοφορίας ἐρανιζο- μένων (i. e. he was not comes s. larg.), ἀλλὰ τῶν ὅσα ἐκ τῶν βασιλείων θησαυρῶν ἐπεπόμφει. Rusticus was Sakellarios.

The history of the Sakellarios, so far as our meagre records enable us to discern it, has been traced above. At first he was simply the keeper of the Emperor's sakellion or treasury which received the surplus derived from the Imperial estates. In the seventh century, he took over the more specially financial functions of the ministers who managed the estates, and the Sakellion became an important ministry. As a treasury it was no longer merely the receptacle of a reserve fund for extraordinary expenses, but bore some of the regular state expenses. The Proem to the *Ecloga* of Leo III orders payments to be made ἐκ τοῦ εὐσεβοῦς ἡμῶν σακκελλίου to the quaestor, the ἀντιγραφῆς, &c.   The third stage is reached when, probably in the eighth century, the Sakellarios (doubtless retaining the charge of the treasury) becomes a sort of Comptroller, with authority over all the financial ministries, while his place as head of the bureau of the Sakellion is taken by the χαρτουλάριος τοῦ σακελλίου.[1]

The Taktikon Uspenski (p. 111) attests the importance [2] of the office of Sakellarios in the reign of Michael III by placing him at the head of all the officials of the Empire, not only the civil but also the military. But this position in the hierarchy depended on the order of rank of the man who held it, and the Sakellarios appears again in this document immediately after the Domestic of the Excubitors and before the General Logothete. In the list of Philotheos, he comes immediately after the stratêgoi of the western themes and before the General Logothete. However his place might vary in the scale as a whole, he had precedence over all the other

---

[1] In George Mon. 842_{22} (ed. Bonn), τοῦ σακελλίου doubtless means χαρτ. τοῦ σακ.

[2] Leo, who was sakellarios with Patrician rank under Michael II, was em- ployed by him to negotiate with Theodore of Studion and the Image worshippers in A.D. 824, Theod. Stud. *Ep.* ii. 129 (Migne, *P. G.* 99).   He may have been chosen because he was on friendly terms with Theodore.

cabinet officials (σεκρετικοί). Under Basil I the office was held by Baanes, patrician and praepositus (περὶ ταξ. 503).[1]

The importance of the Sakellarios as General Comptroller of the bureaux dealing with finance has been emphasized already (p. 82). The expression of Philotheos ὑποτέτακται τὰ ὀφφίκια is perhaps to be confined to the financial offices; it may not have extended e. g. to the σέκρετον of the protoasecretis. Philotheos mentions his notary, which obviously implies notaries,[2] and he had also mandatores at his special disposal (Cer. 698₁₈).[3]

See further Cer. 525, 572, 606, περὶ ταξ. 471 (where he acts with the εἰδικός).

On the few extant seals of Sakellarioi, the office is generally combined with the rank of protospatharios. See Panchenko, 9. 385 (No. 269: ninth–tenth century); Schlumberger, Sig. 580.[4]

(2) ὁ λογοθέτης τοῦ γενικοῦ.

The title comes sacrarum largitionum vanishes in the seventh century. The latest ministers whom we meet bearing the title are Theodore, under Tiberius II (Menander, fr. 46), Athanasius in A.D. 605 (Chr. Pasch. 973), Anastasius in A.D. 608-9 (Theoph. 297₂₀). The title λογοθέτης τοῦ γενικοῦ (often briefly designated ὁ γενικός) first occurs in the reign of Justinian II (Theodotos, Niceph. Patr. 37₁₉; Sergius, Theoph. 365₂₄, A.D. 692). It is possible, however, that it had come in long before, for in A.D. 626 (Chr. Pasch. 721) we meet Theodosius ὁ ἐνδοξότατος πατρίκιος καὶ λογοθέτης (evidently a high post).[5] The γενικὸν λογοθέσιον had generally the same functions

---

[1] ὁ Λυδὸς σακ. in Niketas, Vit. Ign., Mansi, xvi. 281, was sac. of the Patriarch.

[2] In a charter of A. D. 1088 (Miklosich-Müller, Acta et Dipl., vi. 57), we meet a βασιλικὸς νοτάριος τοῦ σεκρέτου τοῦ σακελλαρίου, κριτῆς καὶ ἀναγραφεὺς τῶν Κυκλάδων νήσων. Cp. ib. 120 (A. D. 1186) τὸ σέκρετον τοῦ μεγάλου σακελλαρίου.

[3] In later times (twelfth century) the Sakellarios was called ὁ μέγας σ.: Miklosich-Müller, Acta et diplomata, vi. 120 (A. D. 1186), τὸ σέκρετον τοῦ μεγαλοῦ σ. Cp. 57 (A. D. 1088) βασιλικὸς νοτάριος τοῦ σεκρέτου τοῦ σακ. This volume of Miklosich-Müller contains important material for the financial offices in the eleventh and twelfth centuries.

[4] A seal of Ioannes πρωτοσπαθαρίῳ ἐπὶ τοῦ θεοφυλάκτου κοιτῶνος καὶ βασιλικ.˙ σακελλαρίῳ is published by Schlumberger, Sig. 526. He ascribes it to the time of the Comneni, and at the same time attributes it to Ioannes, a eunuch who was sakellarios under Irene in the eighth century.

[5] The patrician Constantine Lardys is described as λογοθέτης, and ex-Praetorian-Prefect in Chron. Pasch. 694 (A. D. 602). Theophylactus Simocatta (8. 9. 6) says: τὴν ἡγεμονίαν τῶν φόρων τῆς ἑῴας πρό τινος καιροῦ ὑπὸ τοῦ αὐτοκράτορος ἀπειλήφει, ὃν ἔπαρχον πραιτωρίων εἰώθασιν ὀνομάζειν Ῥωμαῖοι. But for the statement in Chron. Pasch., these words would naturally be taken to mean that he was still Praet. Pref. It looks as if λογοθέτης must mean here com. s. larg.

as the ministry of the *sacrae largitiones*; it surveyed and collected the taxation of the Empire. Some departments indeed were withdrawn from the Logothete's control, especially the *vestiarium* which became an independent bureau. For early seals of λογοθέται γενικοί see Schlumberger, *Sig.* 530 No. 1, 531 No. 10.[1]

(1) The χαρτουλάριοι μεγάλοι τοῦ σεκρέτου (below spathar rank Takt. Usp. 127; spathars Phil. 735₁₃) probably were the heads of a number of different departments or scrinia. Many of the same scrinia which existed in the officium of the comes largitionum must have continued down to later times. They are enumerated in the *Not. Dig.*, *Or.* xiii (canonum, aureae massae, &c.). Their chiefs were then called *primicerii*.[2]

(2) χαρτουλάριοι τῶν ἀρκλῶν, also called οἱ ἔξω χαρτουλάριοι τοῦ γενικοῦ (*Cer.* 694₁₈), where ἔξω shows that they functioned in the provinces. τῶν ἀρκλῶν suggests that they may have taken the place of the *praepositi thesaurorum* of the *Notitia*. This, however, is by no means certain. But they cannot be identified with the *chartularii de cohortalibus officiis uniusque provinciae*, mentioned in a constitution of Leo I (*C. I.* 10. 23. 3, A.D. 468) as revising taxes, for these are evidently mere clerks. There is an interesting seal (of a later period, tenth–eleventh century) in Panchenko, 13, 129, of Eustathios, spatharocandidatus, who was (at the same time, apparently) βασιλικὸς τοῦ γενικοῦ λογοθεσίου χαρτουλάριος and πρωτονοτάριος τῶν Ἀνατολικῶν. In the latter capacity he was subordinate to the Chartulary of the Sakellion (see below).

(3) The ἐπόπται τῶν θεμάτων were the provincial tax-controllers. Cp. Cont. Th. 346, Schlumberger, *Sig.* 513. The ἐξισωταί seem to have been different from the ἐπόπται. The two names are closely associated in Cont. Th., *loc. cit.*, but they are enumerated distinctly in Alexius Comn., *Nov.* 30 (Zach., p. 374). [The seal of Michael Kamateros, ἐξισωτὴς τῆς Δύσεως (end of twelfth century, *Sig.* 516) is hardly relevant.]

(4) The functions of the κόμητες ὑδάτων must have been connected with the aqueducts, probably not in Constantinople but in all parts of the Empire. Cp. the *comes formarum*, under the Prefect of Rome in *Not. Dig.*, *Occ.* iv. 4.

---

[1] The curious seal, published by Panchenko 13. 124, is too uncertain to build on. He ascribes it to the first half of the seventh century, and restores ['Ι]ωάννου ἐνδόξο[τ(άτου)? ἀπ]ὸ ὑπ(άτων) πατρικ(ί)[ου λο]γοθέ(του) βασιλ(ικῶν) [ἀ ?]ρκα[ρίω]ν. If ἀρκαρίων is right, J. was a *rationalis* under the Praetorian Prefect.

[2] For the σέκρετον of the Log. Gen. in the eleventh century see Miklosich-Müller, *op. cit.* vi. 50, 54–5, where μεγάλοι χαρτουλάριοι and λογαριασταί are mentioned; cp. his λογαριαστής and νοτάριοι in Alex. Comn. *Nov.* 34, p. 398.

(5) ὁ οἰκιστικός. The name of this official is rightly given in Phil. 789₂, but appears as ὁ κιστικός in the list of officia and in 736₇. The true form is shown by two seals of the Comnenian period (*Sig.* 559) : (1) Ιωαννη β(ασιλικω) σπαθ(αριω) και χαρτουλαριω του οικιστινου (*sic*); (2) Δᾱδ [= Δαυιδ] [α′]νοταριω του οικιστικου; also a seal (3) in Konstantopulos, No. 435 *a νοτ. τοῦ οἰκιστικοῦ*. It is impossible to admit Panchenko's theory that οἰκιστικός is a mistake for πιστικός (xiii. 116). The βασιλικὸς πιστικός of the three seals which he has published and who, as he has shown (*ib.* vii. 40 *sqq.*),[1] had functions connected with maritime commerce, must be accepted ; but there can be no doubt that οἰκιστικός was also an official title. Besides the seals cited above, cp. οἰκιστικῶν in the Donation of Alex. Comn. A.D. 1087, Miklosich-Müller, *Acta et Dipl.* vi. 28. The meaning is quite obscure.

(6) The κουμερκιάριοι were the officers who collected duties and customs throughout the Empire. They represent the comites commerciorum of *Not. Dig.*, *Or.* xiii. 6, and are thus evidence of the continuity between the spheres of the comes s. larg. and the General Logothete. The term κομμερκιάριος is officially used in the sixth century. Schlumberger publishes a seal (*Mél.* 237, κομμ᾽ Τυρου) which he ascribes to that period, and another dates from the reign of Justin II (*Sig.* 317). In *Chron. Pasch.* 721 (A.D. 626) we meet Θεόδωρος ὁ ἐνδοξότατος κομμερκιάριος ὁ τὴν ἰσάτιν (?),[2] evidently a comes commerciorum.

A seal [τῶν β]ασιλικῶν κομμερκίων στρατιγίας Ἑλλάδο[ς] is dated to A.D. 708 (*Mél.* 221, and cp. 200). Early seals of κομμερκιάριοι are comparatively numerous, cp. *Sig.* 471 *sqq.*; Panchenko, viii. 18 *sqq.* I may note those of Constantine (*Sig.* 165) ἀποεπάρχων καὶ γενικοῦ κομμερκιαρίου ἀποθήκης Ἑλλάδος (ἀποθήκη = customs depôt), and of Kosmas (Panchenko, xiii. 115) κομμερκιαρίου ἀποθήκης Ἀγκύρας (?), both belonging to the reign of Constans II, and the latter dated apparently to A.D. 644. These officials might have the rank of hypatos or spathar : cp. Panchenko, *ib.* 147 No. 489, 149 No. 495.

(7) ὁ τῆς κουρατωρίας, fuller title 736₂ ὁ(σπαθ. καὶ) ἐπὶ τῆς κουρατωρίας τῶν βασιλικῶν οἴκων. This functionary presided over a special department dealing with the fiscal revenue derived from the taxation of the Imperial estates (*res privata*). I believe that this was the function of the *magistri privatae* who are under the com. s. larg. in *Not. Dig.* (*Or.* xiii. 15). For we find that before Justinian's innovation in the

---

[1] Cp. Ashburner, *The Rhodian Sealaw* (1909), cxxxii. 93 ; Leontios, *Vita Iohannis*, ed. Gelzer, xxvii, xxviii ; Pap. Brit. Mus. iv. No. 1341, p. 13.

[2] Rendered in the Latin version of Ducange, *commerciarius Glasti.*

government of Cappadocia in A. D. 536, the collection of the fiscal revenue in the Imperial estates was in the hands of μαγίστερες (*Nov.* 44. 2, 4, p. 266), who are evidently the magistri privatae. Justinian replaced them, for Cappadocia, by πράκτορες. At some subsequent period, these πράκτορες were either replaced by, or placed under, a single controller ὁ ἐπὶ τῆς κουρατωρίας. This title is explained by the concrete use of κουρατωρία = *res privata*. Cp. Theoph. 487₂ τὰ δὲ κρείττονα τῶν κτημάτων εἰς τὴν βασιλικὴν κουρατορίαν αἱρεσθαι.

(8) It may be conjectured with probability that ὁ κόμης τῆς λαμίας (cp. *lamna*, see Reiske, *ad loc.*) had to do with bullion and mines, and it is tempting to identify him with the comes metallorum per Illyricum who appears under the comes s. larg., in the *Not. Dig.*, *Or.* xiii. 11. For a seal of a κ. τῆς λ. see Konstantopulos, No. 206.

(9) The διοικηταί were the officers who presided over the collection of taxes. (Cp. Leo VI, *Nov.* 61, p. 157 τοὺς ἐπὶ συλλογὴν τῶν δημοσίων φόρων καθισταμένους, διοικητὰς δ' αὐτοὺς ἡ συνήθως ὁμιλία καλεῖν οἶδε.) Paulos ὁ ἐνδοξότατος ἀπὸ ὑπάτων καὶ διοικητὴς τῶν ἀνατολικῶν ἐπαρχιῶν, in the Acts of the Sixth Ecum. Council A. D. 680 (Mansi, xi. p. 209) probably represents the 'comes largitionum per dioecesim Asianam' (*Not. Dig. Or.* xiii. 5). The abolition of the diocesan divisions led to the replacement of the ' comites largitionum per omnes dioceses ' by διοικηταί of themes and districts. See the seals of διοικηταί in *Sig.* 496-7 (cp. *Mél.* 205 διοικητῇ τῆς Ἄνδρου, saec. ix); Panchenko, xiii. 131 διοικητῇ Σάμου καὶ τῆς Χίου, saec. viii-ix; Mansi, xii. 837 *dioecete quod Latine dispositor Siciliae dicitur*).[1] They were responsible to the General Logothete for the fiscal revenue from their districts, and liable to punishment if it fell short (cp. Theoph. 367₂₇, from which it appears that Theodotos, the Logothete under Justinian II, was unreasonably strict in calling the διοικηταί to account). It appears from Theoph. 412₁₈ that there were διοικηταί at Constantinople as well as in the provinces. The πράκτορες, who are often mentioned in our sources, must not be confounded with the διοικηταί. The πράκτορες were the officials who actually went round and collected the taxes (φορολόγοι), and every διοικητής must have had a number of πράκτορες under him.

(10) κομεντιανός (κοβεντιανός ?)[2] seems to be equivalent to κομβεντιανός from κομβέντος = *conventus* (e. g. *Chron. Pasch.* 596₂₀, John Mal. 438₂₃, 494₁₂), cp. *Cer.* 422₁₁, 433₅ σιλέντιον καὶ κομέντον (κοβέντον ?) ;

---

[1] The office of δ. might be united with that of κομμερκιάριος, cp. the seal (saec. viii-ix) published by Panchenko, xiii. 87.

[2] The letters μ and β were easily confused.

but the meaning is obscure.   Can it have anything to do with
market dues?

(11, 12) πρωτοκαγκελλάριος, καγκελλάριοι.

(3) ὁ λογοθέτης τοῦ στρατιωτικοῦ.

In the fifth and sixth centuries one of the most important functions
of the *arca* of the Praetorian Prefect was to furnish the pay of the
army (cp. *C. I.* 12. 37).   Difficulty has been felt as to the duties
of the *schola chartulariorum* in the officium of the Pr. Pr. of Africa
(*C. I.* 1. 27. 1 (38)).[1]   I conjecture that some of their duties were
connected with the *annonae militares*.   In the Prefecture of the East
we find *scriniarii* of the Pr. Pr. administering military expenditure
(στρατιωτικὰ διοικεῖν), and in Egypt such a scriniarius was called
στρατιωτός; see Justinian, *Nov.* 96. 13, p. 544.

In the seventh century we find that a separate military chest, \
called τὸ στρατιωτικόν, has been formed, at least for the eastern
portion of the Empire, and removed from the control of the Praetorian Prefect.   In A. D. 680 we meet Julian ὁ ἐνδοξότατος ἀπὸ ὑπάτων
πατρίκιος καὶ στρατιωτικοῦ λογοθέτης, as one of the ministers who,
along with the Emperor, are present at the Sixth General Council
(Mansi, xi. 209).   Schlumberger has published (*Mél.* 242) a seal
Εὐσταθίου STRAT̄ LOGOTHETOȲ which seem to belong to the seventh
century.[2]

Under Irene we meet Ioannes λογοθέτης τοῦ στρατιωτικοῦ λογοθεσίου,
holding the rank of (βασιλικὸς) ὁστιάριος (therefore a eunuch) in
A.D. 787 (Mansi, xii. 999, 1051) and attending the sessions of the
Seventh Council; two years later he is Sakellarios as well as λογ.
στρατ.

(1) χαρτουλάριοι τοῦ σεκρέτου.   Takt. Usp. οἱ χαρτ. τοῦ στρατιωτικοῦ
127 (ὁ χαρτ. 129); *Cer.* 524$_{15}$, 694$_{19}$, Phil. 752$_3$ (τοῦ στρ. λογοθέτου);
Sig. 353 seal of Constantine β' σπαθαροκανδιδατω και χαρτ' τ' στρατηοτ'
(eighth-ninth century) and of John υπατω μεγαλω χαρτουλαριω του
στρατιωτικου λογοθεσιου (perhaps tenth century).

(2, 3) χαρτουλάριοι τῶν θεμάτων and τῶν ταγμάτων.   The chartularius
of a theme or a tagma was subordinate to the Log. Strat. as well as
to the Stratêgos or Domestic.   He performed similar duties to those
which used to be performed by scriniarii (στρατιωτός, &c., see above)
of the Praetorian Prefect.

[1] Cp. Karlowa, i. 887.
[2] For other seals see *Sig.* 352.   Panchenko, ix. 372 Ἰω(άννῃ) ὑπ(άτῳ)[λ]ογοθ[έτ]ι
[σ]τρ[α]τιο[τ]ικ[οῦ] (eighth-ninth century).

(4) We met λεγατάριοι also in the office of the Excubiton and the Arithmos.

(5) ὀπτίονες, the officers who distributed pay to the soldiers (οἱ ὀπτίονες τῶν ταγμάτων Phil. 738₆). This was their function in the sixth century, Procopius, B. V. i. 17, ii. 20; Justinian, Nov. 150. 1, p. 262. (Cp. Nov. 141. 11, p. 221 in case of foederati.)

(6) πρωτοκαγκέλλαριος, implying καγκελλάριοι.

(7) μανδάτορες.

The νοτάριοι τοῦ στρατιωτικοῦ, not mentioned in this list, appear in Cer. 694₂₀ (they received half the honorarium of the chartularii).

(4) ὁ λογοθέτης τοῦ δρόμου.

This title should correspond to rationalis cursus publici. There was no such official, and we may conclude that the Logothete of the Course descends from the Curiosus cursus publici praesentalis who was in the officium of the magister officiorum (Not. Dig., Or. xi. 50, cp. Lydus, 2. 10).

The magister officiorum can be traced in the seventh century to the reign of Constantine IV. In the reign of Heraclius the post was held by Bonus (Chron. Pasch. 718, 726), by Anianus and Theodorus (Niceph. Patr. 24₆, 25₁₈).[1] In A.D. 680 it was held by Niketas (τοῦ ἐνδοξοτάτου ἀπὸ ὑπάτων πατρικίου καὶ μαγίστρου τῶν βασιλικῶν ὀφφικίων, Acta Conc. Const. III, Mansi, xi. 209, 217). For the break-up of the office and for the μάγιστροι of the eighth century see above B (14) p. 29.

The magister had performed multifarious duties, and he was the functionary who most nearly corresponded to a minister of foreign affairs. This important part of his work was transferred to the curiosus who presided over the state post. It seems not unlikely that before the time of Leo III the magister had been deprived of some of his functions, and, for instance, that the state post may have been raised to a separate and independent office. In any case the official who derived his title from the state post and was named λογοθέτης τοῦ δρόμου, a name which does not appear till the eighth century, took over also from the mag. off. the duties connected with diplomacy, correspondence with foreign powers, and the reception of ambassadors.

When λογοθέτης is used without qualification, in Byzantine writers, the Logothete of the Course is generally meant (e. g. Cont. Th. 122₃,

---

[1] In Chron. Pasch. 696, A.D. 605, the subadiuva of the magister is mentioned.

198_{16}, *Cer.* 520_3).[1] The office was sometimes united with others, e. g. in the reign of Theophilus, Theoktistos was Logothete and also ἐπὶ τοῦ κανικλείου (Gen. 83_{17}). This must also, I think, have been the case with Gregory Bardas under Leo IV, of whom Schlumberger has published a seal (*Sig.* 528) which he reads [βασι]λικ(ω) ασικριτ' και λογοθετ(η) του δρομου. I suspect that ασικριτ' is intended for a' ασικριτ' = πρωτοασηκρήτῃ, though it is of course possible that an ἀσηκρήτης on becoming logothete might retain his position in the τάξις ἀσηκρητῶν.[2]

The logothete was received in audience every morning by the Emperor (*Cer.* 520) in the Chrysotriklinos. It was his duty to present ministers and officers (stratēgoi, domestici, &c.) to be invested by the Emperor (*ib.* 525 *sqq.*). At the silention in the Magnaura, at which the Emperor makes a public speech, the logothete is associated with the protoasecretes and the chief of the Imperial notaries (*ib.* 546_9). He naturally played the most important part at the reception of foreign envoys or potentates (*ib.* 568, 138) ; also at the exhibition of captives ($610_{7, 15}$).

(1) The πρωτονοτάριος τοῦ δρόμου (spathar Phil. 735_5, and Takt. Usp. 124, or inferior *ib.* 127) appears in some of the ceremonies (conducting captives at a triumph, *Cer.* 609_{21}, 613_3 ; bearing the sportula of the archon of Taro, 138_{22}, 569_5). He is mentioned in Cont. Th. 198_{19}.

(2) χαρτουλάριοι τοῦ δρόμου (spathars Takt. Usp. 125 ; omitted accidentally in the list of spathars in Phil.), in full οἱ χ. τοῦ ὀξέου δρόμου Phil. 788_{22}, and so *De adm. imp.* 184 (Sinartes, a eunuch) χ. τ. ὀξέος δ. They are probably to be identified partly with the *curiosi per omnes provincias* [3] (*Not. Dig., Or.* xi. 51), and partly with the χαρτουλάριοι τῶν βαρβάρων who play a part in the reception of the Persian ambassador, as described by Peter the Patrician (*Cer.* 404_{15}, 405_{14}) and belonged to the *scrinium barbarorum* (see below). For νοτάριοι in the scrinium of the (provincial ?) χαρτουλάριος we have the evidence of a seal (tenth or eleventh century) : Λεον(τι) νοτ' του χαρτ' του δρομ' (*Mél.* 240).

---

[1] We may, I think, assume that Thomas the logothete, in *Vita Euthymii* (ed. De Boor) 16. 9, was Log. of the Course. Probably Χασανις στ[ρ]άτο(ρι) τοῦ λογ(οθεσίου), *Mél.* 260 (ninth–tenth century), belonged to this officium.

[2] We have also a seal of Martin, Imperial spatharocandidatus and λογοθετη του. οξεως δρομου (*Sig.* 529) and one of Stylianos (533)?

After the eighth century the Logothete would hardly have as low as spatharo-candidate rank. Theoktistos was a patrician. Under Leo VI the office was held by his father-in-law Stylianos, with the rank of magister (Cont. Th. 354_9) ; in the tenth century Leo Rhabduchos was μάγιστρος καὶ λογοθέτης τ. δρ. (*De adm. imp.* 156).

[3] Cp. *C. Th.* 6. 29, *De curiosis.*

(3) ἐπισκεπτῆται. There are some late seals of ἐπισκεπτῆται who possibly belong here, e.g. that of Epiphanios, βασιλικοῦ ἐπισκεπτίτου Ποδάντου (*Sig.* 315). They probably had to report on matters connected with the safety of the provinces and frontiers.[1]

(4) ἑρμηνευταί are the *interpretes diversarum gentium* in the officium of the mag. off. in *Not. Dig., Or.* xi. 52. Cp. Peter Patr., in *Cer.* 404$_{16}$. (On this subject cp. Bury, *Byzantinische Zeitschrift*, xv. 540–1.[2]) The body of *interpretes* must have belonged to the *scrinium barbarorum* which is mentioned in A.D. 441 in a constitution of Theodosius II, addressed to the mag. off. (*Nov.* 21), and is referred to in the text of Peter (*Cer.* 400$_8$), from which we learn that, besides the chartularii an optio (ὁ ὀπτίων τῶν β., 401$_6$), was attached to it, who was sent to Chalcedon to supply the Persian envoy with money.

(5) ὁ κουράτωρ τοῦ ἀποκρισιαριείου. The ἀποκρισιαριείου was (as the title κουράτωρ shows) a building ; and we may readily conjecture that it was a hostel for the entertainment of foreign envoys (ἀποκρισιάριοι).[3]

(6, 7) διατρέχοντες (= *cursores*) and μανδάτορες, cp. Phil. 786$_{18, 19}$.

The *scrinium barbarorum*, though not mentioned by Philotheos in connexion with the Logothete, seems to have been still in existence. Phil. 725$_5$ mentions ὁ βάρβαρος (see also περὶ ταξ. 461$_4$), who is evidently identical with ὁ ἐπὶ τῶν βαρβάρων, who is recorded by several seals. Schlumberger has published six seals of Staurakios, a protospathar, who held this office. A seal of Peter β. α´ σπαθαριος και επη των βαρβαρων he ascribes to the ninth century. *Sig.* 448 *sqq.* See also Panchenko, ix. 357, xiii. 142 ; Konstantopulos, No. 307. Rambaud thinks that the function of the scr. barb. was to defray the expenses of foreign ambassadors. It seems to me more probable that the βάρβαρος exercised supervision over all foreigners visiting Constantinople.

(5) ὁ χαρτουλάριος τοῦ σακελλίου.

The Sakellion has been already dealt with. The Chartulary is sometimes called briefly ὁ τοῦ σακελλίου (Phil. 777, *Cer.* 115$_{20}$). We also find σακέλλης instead of σακελλίου (e.g. Takt. Usp. 127, Phil.

---

[1] There were ἐπισκεπτῆται under (1) the Prefect of the City, (2) the Logothete of the Course, (3) the Great Curator, (4) the Logothete of the Flocks. Seals of officers with this title are generally ambiguous, e.g. that of an ἐπισκ. and κουβουκλίσιος published by Panchenko, xiii. 113.

[2] A ἑρμηνεύς for Arabic, in the army, is mentioned by Theoph. Sim. 2. 10. 6.

[3] This word was applied to foreign as well as Imperial envoys ; cp. Theoph. 392$_{13, 15}$, 429$_{27}$, 475$_{27}$.

735₂₂, 750₁₈, 763₆. Schlumberger (*Sig.* 580) has published a seal of uncertain date (' VIIIᵉ–XIᵉ siècle ') of a Chartulary :

λ' καὶ χαρ[τουλ]αρ' τοῦ β[ασ(ιλικοῦ) σ]ακελ[λί]ου.

(1) νοτάριοι βασιλικοὶ τοῦ σεκρέτου (Takt. Usp. ὁ νοτάριος σακέλλης, read οἱ —οι, under spathar rank), Phil. 735₂₁ οἱ σπαθάριοι καὶ βασιλικοὶ νοτάριοι τῆς σακέλλης, 752₅ v. τοῦ σακελλίου, Cer. 694₂₀ οἱ v. τῆς σακέλλης, 594₇. They correspond to the *primiscrinii* of the comes rei priv. (*Not. Dig. Or.* xiv).

(2) πρωτονοτάριοι θεμάτων.[1] The duties of a πρωτονοτάριος of a theme are illustrated in the schedule of the preparations for the Cretan Expedition of A.D. 902, *Cer.* ii. c. 44. There we find the proto-notary of the Thrakesian theme arranging for the purchase of the provisions required by the soldiers, for a supply of flax for caulking the vessels and for the use of the Greek fire-guns, and for a supply of nails (p. 658). The protonotary of the Cibyrrhaeot theme is to buy 60,000 nails for fastening hides to the vessels (p. 659). For duties connected with moving the Imperial baggage, which the Emperor left behind when he crossed the Saracen frontiers, see περὶ ταξ. (see further 464₃, 466₂, 477₉, 479₁₈, 489₂.) The protonotaries had it in their power to oppress the provincials, Cont. Th. 443₁₅. Their seals are common.[2]

(3, 6, 7) The ξενοδόχοι and γηροκόμοι (spathars Phil. 736₄, ₆ ; inferior Takt. Usp. 127) were heads of ξενῶνες [3] and γηροκομεῖα supported by the state. They appear in the company of ὁ τοῦ σακελλίου (sc. χαρτ.), *Cer.* 115₂₀, Phil. 777₁. The χαρτουλάριοι τῶν οἴκων, i. e. τῶν εὐαγῶν οἴκων, dealt with the accounts and expenditure of these establishments. Possibly εὐαγῶν should be restored here : Takt Usp. has οἱ χαρτουλλάριοι τῶν εὐαγῶν οἴκων 127, and so Phil. 753₄. εὐαγής was technical, in this connexion, from an early period : cp. *C. I.* 1. 3. 41 (11), A. D. 528 τῶν τε εὐαγῶν ξενώνων καὶ νοσοκομείων κτλ. 'the pious hostelries, hospitals,' &c. ; Justinian, *Nov.* 60, p. 388.

(4, 5) The ζυγοστάτης (spathar Phil. 736₄, inferior Takt. Usp. 127) examined and weighed the nomismata which came into the treasury.

---

[1] Cont. Th. 447₁₇.

[2] Cp. *Sig.* 103, 112, 122, 298–9, 345, &c., &c. See also *Mél.* 208 Στέφανω β' καυδ' και άνοτ. Σικελ', saec. ix ; 223 β' σπαθαρ' κανδ' και ανοταρ' Πελοπον', saec. xi ; 236 Λεοντι υπατω και ανοταρ Χαλδιας saec. viii–ix.

[3] e. g. those of Sampson, Theophilus, Eubulus, Narses, St. Irene. There was a ξενοδοχεῖον at Nicaea, cp. Panchenko, ix. 352 Μανουὴλ βασιλικῷ πρωτοσπαθαρίῳ καὶ ξενοδόχῳ Νικαίας (see Schlumberger, *Sig.* 381, *Mél.* 300) ; at Lopadion in Bithynia (*Sig.* 381), &c., &c. Cp. Panchenko, ix. 387–9. See also below under the Great Curator.

Cp. the constitution in *C. Th.* 12. 7.   Julian refers to ζυγοστατaί in the various cities (*ib.* 2 : *quem sermo graecus appellat per singulas civitates constitui zygostaten*), who decided if there was any dispute *de qualitate solidorum.*   The μετρηταί had similar duties connected with weights and measures.[1]

(8, 9) πρωτοκαγκελλάριος and καγκελλάριοι.

(10) ὁ δομέστικος τῆς θυμέλης (ὁ ἄρχων τῆς θ. *Cer.* 382₂) had for his province expenditure on public amusements.   We may regard him as the successor of the *tribunus voluptatum* of the fifth century (*C. Th.* 15. 7. 13).   For θυμέλη in this technical sense cp. the edicts of A. D. 426, *C. Th.* 8. 7. 21, 22 (*actuarios thymelae et equorum currulium*) ; Justinian's edict περὶ τῶν ὑπάτων, addressed to the comes s. largitionum, *Nov.* 81, p. 468 τὰς ἐπὶ τῆς σκηνῆς τε καὶ θυμέλης ἡδυπαθείας.   There seems to have been a theatrical treasury controlled by the Prefect of the City in the sixth century (τῇ θεατραλίᾳ, *Nov.* 84, p. 480).

(6) ὁ χαρτουλάριος τοῦ βεστιαρίου.

In the fifth century (as stated above) the *vestiarium sacrum* was a *scrinium* in the *officium* of the comes s. larg., and its chief was, as usual, entitled *primicerius.*   The officials at the head of the department were in the East the magistri lineae vestis (*Not. Dig., Or.* xiii. 14), in the West the comes vestiarii (*ib., Occ.* xi. 5).   We may conjecture that the elevation of the *vestiarium* into an independent office, under a chartularius, was coincident with the transformation of the *s. largitiones* into the γενικόν, was in fact part of that transformation. But when the *vestiarium* branched off from the fisc, the new office was increased in compass.   In fact, three of the scrinia, which used to be under the comes s. larg., namely *scr. vest. s., scr. argenti,* and *scr. a miliarensibus,* were combined to form a new office which was called the βεστιάριον.   The minting departments of the argentum and *a miliarensibus* are represented in the new officium by the ἄρχων τῆς χαραγῆς.

The *vestiarium* or public Wardrobe must be carefully distinguished from the Emperor's private Wardrobe, the *sacra vestis,* over which a comes s. vestis (who was a cubicularius) presided (see *C. Th.* xi. 18. 1 with note of Godofredus).   These two wardrobes remained distinct in later times, though they have been confounded by Schlumberger (in his *Sigillographie*) and by other writers.   The comes s. vestis, who was under the control of the praepositus s. cub., is

---

[1] Cp. Justinian, *Nov.* 152. 15, p. 282.   The μέτρα and σταθμά supplied by Praet. Praef. and Com. larg. are to be kept in the most holy church of each city.   For a δημόσιος ζυγοστατής in Egypt A. D. 609 see B. G. U. iii. 837. 18.

represented in the ninth century by the πρωτοβεστιάριος (an office confined to eunuchs), and his wardrobe is distinguished as τὸ οἰκειακὸν βασιλικὸν βεστιάριον (περὶ ταξ. 465₁₄, ₁₇, 478₉) from the wardrobe of the Chartularius (τὸ βεστ. or τὸ βασιλικὸν βεστ. Cer. 672, 676₁₈).[1]

For the sphere of the public vestiarium cp. *C. Th.* vii. 6 *de militari veste*, and xi. 18 *de vestibus holoveris et auratis*. Duties connected with the equipment of ships seem to have been attached to the department in later times (cp. ἐξαρτιστής below, and *Cer.* 672 and 676).[2]

Two seals, which seem to belong to our period (ninth century), are published by Schlumberger[3] (*Sig.* 603) Λεοντι μαγιστρω και επι του βεστιαριου το Σκληρω, and Μιχαηλ υπατω σιλεντιαριω και χαρτουλαριω του βασιλικου βεστιαριου. Schlumberger suggests the ascription of the former to Leo Skleros, who became Stratêgos of the Peloponnesus[4] in A. D. 811.

Another of the same period is published by Panchenko, ix. 364, πατ[ρικιω] πρωτοσπα(θαριω) και [χαρ]τουλ(αριω) τ(ου) β(ασιλικου) [β]εστιαρ(ιου).

(1) This secretum has βασιλικοὶ νοτάριοι τοῦ σεκρέτου like that of the sakellion, from which it otherwise differs. These notaries (spathars, Phil. 735₂₂; inferior Takt. Usp. 127 ὁ νοτ. τοῦ βεστ.) are mentioned, *Cer.* 594₆ and 694. Cp. seal of Comnenian (?) age in Panchenko, xiii. 101 Λέων ἀσηκ[ρή]τι[ς] νοτ(άριος) τ(οῦ) [β(ασιλικοῦ) β]ε[σ]τηαρ[ίου.

(2, 3) We may conjecture that the occurrence of a κένταρχος (ὁ κ. τοῦ βεστιαρίου Phil. 738₁₀) is due to the circumstance that the supply of military uniforms was an important department of this office. But we have no evidence for his duties or those of the λεγατάριος.

(4) The ἄρχων τῆς χαραγῆς was chief of the mint (at all events for silver and bronze, see above). χαραγή is regularly used for *moneta*. Philotheos elsewhere mentions ὁ χρυσοεψητής (*auricoctor*) 736₄, 789₂, who also appears in Takt. Usp. 127. Perhaps he belonged to the οἰκειακὸν βεστιάριον.

(5, 6) ἐξαρτιστής. χαρτουλάριος. The juxtaposition suggests that this

---

[1] It is not clear which wardrobe is meant in Constantine, *Them.* 15, where it is said that ἀργυρᾶ μινσούρια (dishes) ἀνάγλυφα κεῖται ἐν τῷ βασ. βεστ. For the private wardrobe see below D, II (2).

[2] In the eleventh century the vestiarium (τὸ σεκρέτον τοῦ β.) seems to have dealt with *vacantia* : Alex. Comnenus, *Nov.* xx. 348-9.

[3] Schlumberger groups the officials of the public and the private wardrobes, and also the βεστήτορες, under the same heading.

[4] Script. Incert. 336 (Leo Gramm. ed. Bonn).

chartulary is the χαρτουλάριος τῆς λεγομένης ἐξαρτήσεως, mentioned in a synodic epistle published by Combefis (*Manipulus rerum Cplarum*), and reprinted in Mansi, xiv. 113.   (In the reign of Leo V, to which this text refers, the post was filled by one Basil, whom the Emperor sent in search of oracles and divinations.)   ἐξάρτησις (properly ἐξάρτυσις) was an arsenal or dockyard (cp. *De adm. imp.* 75₉, George Mon. ed. Bonn, 883₂₁).   We may infer that naval expenditure belonged to the department of the Vestiarium.

(7) κουράτορες.

(8) χοσβαῆται (appear along with silentiarii in *Cer.* 234₉).   The derivation is obscure, but the gloss βεστιαρίτης quoted by Ducange *s. v.* is borne out by the fact that these functionaries belonged to the Vestiarium.

(9, 10) In having μανδάτορες (we must read in the text of Phil. πρωτομανδάτωρ, μανδάτορες) this office resembles the στρατιωτικόν.

(7) ὁ πρωτοασηκρήτης.

The ἀσηκρῆται (who might have protospathar or spathar rank, Phil. 733₁, 758₁, 735₅; spathar or lower, Takt. Usp. 124, 127) descend from the older imperial notarii.   Cp. Lydus, 3. 27 ad fin. τοὺς λεγομένους ἀσηκρήτις τῆς αὐλῆς, Procop. H. A. 14, B. P. 2. 7. (cp. Procop. H. A. 16 with Theoph. 186₁₅).   Their chief, the πρωτο-ασηκρήτης (might be ἀνθ. κ. πατρικ., Phil. 729₄; protospathar, Takt. Usp. 124).   Their seals are frequent (*Sig.* 444 *sqq.*).

Asecretis, however, was not merely a new name for notarius. The schola of ἀσηκρῆται was differentiated from that of notarii, as a superior and select class, though the functions of both were similar. The protoasecretis took the place, in rank and dignity, of the *primicerius notariorum* of the Notitia; and if the direct descendant of the primicerius is, as seems probable, the πρωτονοτάριος, this office was reduced in dignity, overshadowed by the protoasecretis, to whom it was subordinate.   The growth of the term asecretis is illustrated by the passages cited from Procopius and Lydus.[1]   We meet an ἀσηκρῆτις in the reign of Phocas.[2]   Maximus, the Confessor, was πρωτοασηκρήτης under Heraclius.[3]   Two ἀσεκρέτις are mentioned in

---

[1] Cp. also Malalas 494₈ : an ἀσεκρῆτις, along with the quaestor and Prefect, takes part in a criminal investigation.   For the ἀσηκρητεῖα in the Palace cp. e.g. Gen. 20₄₁, George Mon. ed Bonn 822₄, *Cer.* 520₇.

[2] Theophyl. Sim. 8. 10. 2 (one of the βασ. ταχυγράφοι, cp. Lydus, *loc. cit.*).

[3] *Vit. Max.*, Migne, *P. G.* 90. 72 ὑπογραφέα πρῶτον τῶν βασιλικῶν ὑπομνημάτων. For ὑπογραφῆς = the Imperial notarii see Socr., *H. E.*, 7. 23 ; ' first of the Emperor's ὑπογραφῆς ' in Agath. Pref., p. 7, means primicerius notariorum.   Cp. Gen. 85₁₄ ὄντι τῶν βασιλικῶν ἐν πρώτοις ὑπογραφέων = Cont. Th. 161₂₀ φέροντι τὴν τῶν ἀσηκρήτων ἐν πρώτοις τιμήν.

the Acts of the Council of A. D. 680 (Mansi, xi. 232, 324, 329):
Paulus ὁ μεγαλοπρεπέστατος ἀσεκρέτις καὶ βασιλικὸς σεκρετάριος and
Diogenes τοῦ μεγαλοπ. ἀσεκρέτις σεκρεταρίου βασιλικοῦ. The Emperor
Artemius had been an ἀσηκρῆτις (τῆς τῶν ἀσηκρητίων σχολῆς πρότερον
γενόμενος ἐναρίθμιος, Agathon Diac. in Mansi, xii. 193; Niceph. Patr.
49₂₀). The Patriarchs Tarasius and Nicephorus had belonged to
this service (Theoph. 458, 481). It seems to have devolved upon
the protoasecretis to draw up the Imperial χρυσοβούλλια (Basil II,
Nov. 29, p. 313 ed. Zach.).

(1) Many seals of ἀσηκρῆται are extant. See Schlumberger, Sig.,
444 sqq., Mél. 264, Panchenko, xiii. 89.

(2) For seals of νοτάριοι see Sig., 551 sqq., Panchenko, ix. 356.

The πρωτονοτάριος or chief of the school of the notaries is not
mentioned here but appears along with the protoasecretis in various
ceremonies (Cer. 7₂₀, 10₂₂, 20₁₇, 123₃, 546₁₀). From the school of the
notaries were drawn the νοτάριοι βασιλικοί attached to most of the
financial bureaux. The two categories are distinguished thus, Cer.
575₁₀₋₁₂ οἱ ἀσηκρῆται καὶ οἱ νοτάριοι τῶν ἀσηκρητειῶν = the notaries
under the protoasecretis; and οἱ τῶν σεκρέτων (χαρτουλάριοι καὶ)
νοτάριοι = the notaries of the finance ministers. Cp. 693₁₃ ὁ νοτ. τῶν
ἀσηκρητειῶν. It seems impossible to say for certain whether seals
of πρωτονοτάριοι, without definition, belong here; probably some of
them do. Note the late seals with ἀσηκρῆτις καὶ πρωτονοταρίῳ (Sig.
444, 552).

(3) The δεκανός appears with the ἀσηκρῆται in the ceremony of
creating Patricians, Cer. 246₂₁. On the Emperor's military expeditions the decanus had a baggage horse εἰς τὰ βασιλικὰ χαρτία (περὶ
ταξ. 479₈). [For the decani who were under the castrensis in the
fifth and sixth centuries see the texts cited by Böcking, and Not. Dig.,
Occ. iii. 299–300.]

(8) ὁ ἐπὶ τοῦ εἰδικοῦ.

The functions of this minister, generally known as ὁ εἰδικός, have
been commonly misunderstood. The name, though always spelt with
ει, has been connected with ἰδικός, and the office thus brought into
relation with the old res privata[1] = ἡ ἰδικὴ περιουσία or the old sacrum
patrimonium = ἡ ἰδικὴ κτῆσις. There is, however, no connexion either
between the names or the offices. τὸ εἰδικόν does not mean the private
treasury, it means the special treasury, opposed to γενικόν, and its
functions have nothing in common with those of the res privata or
the patrimonium.

---

[1] So Reiske and Ducange.

The most important text we have bearing on the functions of this office is the list of supplies for the Cretan expedition of A.D. 949, in *Cer.* ii. 45. There we have an account of the διάφορα εἴδη [1] which were ἀπὸ τοῦ σεκρέτου τοῦ εἰδικοῦ ἐξοδιασθέντα (673). Compare the list, p. 671, where it is noted ὅτι ἡ ἔξοδος τῶν ἀρμένων καὶ τῶν διφθερίων ὀφείλει ἐξέρχεσθαι ἀπὸ τὸ εἰδικόν. The office had a storehouse: cp. 674$_{22}$ διφθερίων ἀπὸ τῶν ἀποκειμένων εἰς τὸ εἰδικόν.[2] Nearly all the equipments and hardstores required for the expedition seem to have been supplied by the eidikon and the vestiarion. In addition to sails, ropes, hides, axes, wax, tin, lead, casks, &c., the eidikon also furnished clothes (underclothes, leggings, &c.), 677–8. Another text bearing on the εἰδικόν is Cont. Th. 257, where we learn that Michael III deposited in its treasury gold which he had obtained by melting down works of art.

The titles of officials under the εἰδικός further show that his sphere had nothing to do with that of the old comes rei privatae. It was specially concerned with the ἐργοδόσια or factories. In the fifth century the factories, *fabricae*, of arms (scutaria, clibanaria, armamentaria, &c.) were under the control of the magister officiorum; the procuratores of other public factories were subordinate to the comes s. largitionum. We may therefore infer that when the *s. largitiones* was transformed into τὸ γενικόν, the management of the factories was constituted as a separate ministry, and termed, in contradistinction, τὸ εἰδικόν.

The εἰδικός had a treasury (probably supplied by the sale of manufactures), from which we find him disbursing three litrae to the comes stabuli (περὶ ταξ. 462$_3$), and sums to the Imperial household (*ib.* 463$_{13}$), on occasion of an Imperial expedition. On such an occasion he himself takes charge of the transport of all kinds of εἴδη, from shoes to candlesticks, with a caravan of forty-six pack-horses (*ib.* 473–4), and he, with his hebdomarioi, gives out the supplies (cp. *ib.* 481$_7$). An important item was the supply of barley for the animals; this was furnished at the several stations by the protonotary of the theme to the comes stabuli, the amount being entered in the presence of the εἰδικός, and after the expedition the accounts were made up by the protonotaries and the chartularius stabuli in the bureau of the εἰδικός (*ib.* 476$_{15}$–477$_9$).

---

[1] It would not be correct to derive τὸ εἰδικόν from εἴδη in this sense. In Egyptian papyri εἴδος frequently occurs for 'tax' but generally suggests a tax in kind, cp. Kenyon, *Pap. Brit. Mus.* iv, No. 1346.

[2] *Cer.* 180$_{13}$ ἐπὶ τὸν εἰδικόν. Does this mean the bureau of the εἰδικός, in the palace?

The earliest mention of the εἰδικός is in Takt. Usp., where he appears with the rank of protospatharios (120 ὁ πρωτοσπ. καὶ ἐπὶ τοῦ ἰδικοῦ). Under Basil I, Nicetas, son of Constantine Triphyllios, held the post (Photius, *Ep.* 130, ed Valettas ; Gen. 71). The seals published by Schlumberger (*Sig.* 518) belong to the Comnenian epoch; likewise that published by Panchenko (xiii. 98, where I disagree with his πρωτονοταρίῳ [καὶ] εἰδικ(ῷ) and would read [τοῦ] εἰδικοῦ).

(1) The Eidikos, like most of the other finance officers, had νοτάριοι βασιλικοί in his secretum. (Spathars, Phil. 735₂₃; inferior, Takt. Usp. 127.) They received a large honorarium from newly appointed officials (*Cer.* 694₁₇). Demetrius, a βασ. νοτ. τοῦ εἰδικοῦ, took part in a conspiracy against Romanus I (Cont. Th. 400₁₂). There is a seal of a πρωτονοτάριος of the Comnenian age (*Sig.* 517).

(2, 4) ἄρχοντες and μειζότεροι τῶν ἐργοδοσίων.[1] These ἄρχοντες are doubtless descended from the ἐργαστηριάρχαι καὶ ἄρχοντες of whom two seals are preserved (Schlumberger, *Mél.* 240–1, Panchenko, xiii. 114), belonging to the seventh century, probably A.D. 643–4. For the term μειζότερος = mayor, overseer, cp. Grenfell and Hunt, *Oxyrhynchus Papyri*, I. 158. 6 κόμετι μειζοτέρῳ, ib. 2 τῷ μείζονι = overseer, 156. 5 χαρτουλαρίοις καὶ μείζοσι ; VI. 922₂₁ μειζοτέρου, 943₃ ; B. G. U. ii. 368 : all documents of sixth to seventh century.

(3) The ἐβδομάριοι τοῦ εἰδικοῦ are mentioned in περὶ ταξ. 478₁₀, 487₂₂.

(9) ὁ μέγας κουράτωρ, and (10) ὁ κουράτωρ τῶν Μαγγάνων.

It was shown above (p. 79) that, in the reign of Justinian, the *divinae domus*, which had been administered by the comes r. priv., and the *divina domus per Cappadociam*, which had been under the Praepositus, seem to have been formed into a new and separate administration under a κουράτωρ τῶν οἰκιῶν, whom we meet in A. D. 566. This functionary probably appears earlier in A. D. 557, for Agathias explains that Anatolios, who then bore the title of κουράτωρ, had the charge of the Emperor's οἶκοι and κτήματα (5. 3, p. 284). We meet Aristobulos ὁ κουρ. τῶν βασιλικῶν οἴκων in the reign of Maurice (Theoph. 261₃). The various estates and properties had special curators, subordinate to the Curator : Justin II, *Nov.* 8 (p. 19) οἵ τε ἐνδοξότατοι κουράτωρες τῶν θείων οἴκων, Tiberius II, *Nov.* 12 (p. 26) τῶν ἐνδοξοτάτων ἢ μεγαλοπρεπεστάτων κουρατώρων τῶν θείων ἡμῶν ἢ τῆς εὐσεβεστάτης βασιλίδος οἴκων. We may say that the Curator has taken the place of the

---

[1] Theophanes, *A. M.* 6285 (A. D. 792) mention τὸ βασιλικὸν ἐργοδόσιον τῶν χρυσοκλαβαρίων.

Comes domorum,[1] who was under the comes r. priv.; but he has become an independent minister, and his administration has been enlarged.

The Curator was doubtless called μέγας to distinguish him from the subordinate curators.   He had in his hands a considerable part of the administration which used to fall within the province of the comes r. priv. and comes s. patrimonii.   The financial control, as we have seen, belonged to the Sakellion.   The office was called τὸ μέγα κουρατωρίκιον; it and the office of Mangana were twins (τὰ δύο κουρατωρίκια, οἱ δύο κουράτωρες, Cer. 461₁, ₃).   Philotheos says that the only difference was that there were no ξενοδόχοι under the κουρ. τ. Μαγγ.   But did the sameness consist in actual identity or in sameness of type (like the officia of the stratêgoi)?   The μειζότερος τῶν Ἐλευθερίου, majordomo of the house of Eleutherios, occurring in both officia, if Philotheos is accurate, points to actual identity.   The question is whether the παλάτια and κτήματα were divided between the two Curators, so that the subordinate κουράτωρες in the officium of each were different persons, or whether both controlled all the private estates, but for different purposes.   The latter alternative seems to be supported further by the existence of a special κουράτωρ of the κτήματα. He is designated in περὶ ταξ. 461₂ as ὁ κτημάτινος, where he is distinguished from οἱ δύο κουράτωρες, and in Phil. 788₂₁ as ὁ κ. τοῦ κτήματος.   In the list of the officium the text gives κουράτωρες τῶν κτημάτων, but the passages quoted point to the correction κουράτωρ. This official was subordinate to the two Curators.

The origin of the second Curator may be inferred from his title, κουράτωρ τῶν Μαγγάνων (cp. Cont. Th. 397₆).   The Imperial ' houses ', named Mangana[2] and New House, were founded by Basil I, and were really large agricultural estates (οἶκος like domus, in this sense), the revenues of which were destined to defray the costs of the Imperial banquets.   This is explained in Constantine's Vita Basilii (Cont. Th. 337 μὴ βουλόμενος γὰρ τὰ δημόσια χρήματα ἅπερ οἱ ἐκ τοῦ ὑπηκόου φόροι γεννῶντες αὐξάνουσιν εἰς οἰκείας καταναλίσκειν χρείας καὶ τῶν ἀνὰ πᾶν ἔτος ὑπ' αὐτοῦ κεκλημένων, καὶ τοὺς ἑτέρων πόνους τὴν τούτων τράπεζαν ἡδύνειν ἢ συγκροτεῖν, τοὺς τοιούτους οἴκους ἐπενοήσατο καὶ προσόδους ἐκ γεωργίας ἀπέταξεν ἐν αὐτοῖς ἱκανάς, ἀφ' ὧν ἡ βασιλικὴ πανδαισία αὐτοῦ τε καὶ τῶν μετ' αὐτὸν ἄφθονον καὶ δικαίαν τὴν χορηγίαν ἔμελλεν ἔχειν

---

[1] C. Th. 10. 1. 15, A. D. 396.

[2] Mangana seems to have been acquired by Basil from the Patriarch Ignatius, who, when he returned to Constantinople to resume the patriarchal throne, was provisionally lodged ἐν τοῖς γονικοῖς αὐτοῦ παλατίοις τοῖς καλουμένοις Μαγκάνοις (Vita Ignatii, Mansi, xvi. 257).   The palace had seemingly belonged to his father, Michael I.

ἀεί). This important text proves that the κουράτωρ τῶν Μαγγάνων was a new creation of Basil I. We might reasonably infer that the νέος οἶκος, established for the same purpose, was likewise under his control. But what Philotheos states about the officia seems to show, as we have seen, that he had to do with other estates and palaces, such as τὰ Ἐλευθερίου. It looks as if Constantine's account were defective, and that Basil had also allocated a portion of the revenue from other estates to the same purpose as the revenue from Mangana, and that all such portions were dealt with by the κουρ. τ. Μαγγάνων. If this were so, some (not necessarily all) of the special κουράτωρες who were subordinate to the Great Curator would be for this purpose subordinate also to the Curator of Mangana. But the whole question is very doubtful and obscure.

Schlumberger has published (*Sig.* 142) a seal (which he ascribes to the ninth century) of Leo, protospatharios, μεγάλῳ κουράτωρι τοῦ βασιλικοῦ οἴκου τῶν Μαγγάνων, which shows that the Curator of Mangana also claimed the epithet μέγας. See also the later seals (eleventh century), *ib.* 151.

(1, 2) In this officium the πρωτονοτάριος[1] is designated as well as the βασιλικοὶ νοτάριοι.

(3) κουράτωρες τῶν παλατίων. The curator τῶν Ὁρμίσδου, *Chron. Pasch.*, A. D. 602, p. 972[2]; the curator τῶν Ἀντιόχου, *Theoph. Sim.*, 3. 3. 11 (cp. *Chron. Pasch.*, p. 973). The curator in *Cer.* 374_{10} is the curator of the palace of Hiereia. The *curae palatiorum* were in early times under the castrensis s. palatii (*Not. Or.* xvii).

(4) κουράτωρες τῶν κτημάτων. Probably an error for κουράτωρ τ. κ., cp. above and Phil. 788_{21}. Perhaps, however, the plural includes both ὁ κτημάτινος κ. and also a number of subordinate local κουράτωρες. Cp. ἡ κουρατωρεία τῶν Τρυχίνων (in Lydia), περὶ ταξ. 462_{7}.

(5) The Palace of Eleutherios had a μειζότερος instead of a κουράτωρ. The Palace was built by Irene.[3] It is mentioned in Michael's *Vit. Theod. Stud.* (Migne, *P. G.* 99. 269).

(6, 7, 8) The ξενοδοχεῖα of Sangaros, Pylae, and Nicomedia were exceptionally under the Great Curator. The other ξενοδοχεῖα were under the Sakellion.

---

[1] Phil. 735_{25} οἱ σπαθ. καὶ πρωτονοτάριοι τοῦ μεγάλου κουρατωρικίου must be corrected either to the singular or, more probably, by the addition of καὶ τοῦ Μαγγάνων κουρατωρικίου. Cp. *Cer.* 461_{2} οἱ δύο πρωτονοτάριοι τῶν δύο κουρατωρικίων.

[2] Cp. Acts of Council of A. D. 680, Mansi xi. 209 Κωνσταντίνου τοῦ ἐνδοξοτ. ἀπὸ ὑπάτων πατρικίου καὶ κουράτωρος τοῦ βασιλικοῦ τῶν Ὁρμίσδου οἴκου.

[3] Πάτρια, ed. Preger, 267_{13}. It was probably no longer a palace in the thirteenth century; cp. the seal of George in *Sig.* 155. For the term μειζότερος see above under ὁ ἐπὶ τοῦ εἰδικοῦ.

(9) The ἐπισκεπτῆται were the inspectors whom the Great Curator sent to inspect the management of the palaces and estates.

11. ὁ Ὀρφανοτρόφος.

The ὀρφανοτρόφος was the Principal of the great Orphanage of Constantinople, τὸ ὀρφανοτροφεῖον, which was situated north of the Acropolis near the Porta Eugenii.[1] In the reign of Leo I, Acacius, afterwards Patriarch,[2] and Nikon, a presbyter, were successively orphanotrophoi, and in a constitution of that Emperor (*C. I.* i. 3. 34, A.D. 472) reference is made to Zotikos *qui prius huiusmodi pietatis officium inuenisse dicitur*. Theophanes records that in A.D. 571-2 (244,) Justin II began to build the Church of SS. Peter and Paul, ἐν τῷ ὀρφανοτροφείῳ. According to the Πάτρια Κωνσταντινουπόλεως, III περὶ κτίσματων, 47, p. 235, τὸν ἅγιον Παῦλον τὸ ὀρφανοτροφεῖον ἀνήγειρεν Ἰουστῖνος καὶ Σοφία· ὡσαύτως καὶ τὸν ὅσιον ⟨Ζωτικὸν τὸ Δεύτερον⟩· καὶ ἐτύπωσεν ἀναπαύεσθαι τοὺς λωβοὺς ἐκεῖ καὶ σιτηρέσια λαμβάνειν. παρίστατο δὲ Ζωτικὸς ὁ πρωτοβεστιάριος αὐτοῦ τοῖς κτίσμασιν (cp. 164, p. 267). M. Schlumberger has published a small seal, with the busts of SS. Peter and Paul on the obverse, and on the reverse a monogram surrounded by the legend ΟΡΦΑΝΟΤΡΟΦΙ΄.[3] This seal he dates from the reign of Justinian, for the same monogram appears on some bronze coins of that Emperor and has been explained as Φ ΙΟVCΤΙΝΙΑΝΟV.[4] This interpretation is, I think, erroneous. The true interpretation is, I have no doubt, Ἰουστίνου καὶ Σοφίας,[5] and we may infer that the coins, as well as the seal, were connected with the foundation of the new orphanage by Justin II and Sophia.

From this evidence it may perhaps be deduced that before the time of Leo I, and most probably in the fourth century,[6] an orphanage was founded in Cple by a certain Zotikos, whose piety was rewarded by the title of ὅσιος. Justin and Sophia founded a new orphanage, which was dedicated to SS. Peter and Paul, and restored the house of Zotikos, which was perhaps converted into a home for lepers (λωβοτροφεῖον). Both these establishments were under the

---

[1] Mordtmann, *Esquisse topographique*, 50.

[2] Theodoros Lector, i. 13 τοῦ ὀρφανοτρόφου ; Evagrius, ii. 11 τοῦ καταγωγίου τῶν ὀρφανῶν προειστήκει.

[3] *Mél.* 299 and Pl. xiv. 16 ; *Sig.* 380.

[4] Sabatier, *Description générale*, i. 86, 191.   Wroth, *Imperial Byzantine Coins*, i. 72. Φ is supposed to represent Φλανίου.

[5] Another group (Wroth, *ib.* 73) omits the κ(αί).

[6] The tradition was that he lived in the time of Constantius II, Πάτρια, ed. Preger, p. 235.

control of the ὀρφανοτρόφος, who was probably always an ecclesiastic.[1]
We do not know how he was appointed in early times, but we may
probably conjecture that he was appointed by the Emperor, at all
events since the reign of Justin II.   In the ninth century he appears
as one of the great officials who may hold Patrician rank. Cp. Takt.
Usp. 117 ὁ πατρίκιος καὶ ὀρφανοτρόφος. A letter of Theodore Studites
(i. 29, ed. Migne) is addressed Λέοντι ὀρφανοτρόφῳ, and this Leo was
a Patrician, as his wife is mentioned in the letter as τῆς κυρίας, τῆς
πατρικίας.

Judging from his officium, the Orphanotrophos does not seem to
have possessed any control over, or duties regarding, provincial or-
phanages.   Other public charitable institutions (ξενοδοχεῖα, εὐαγεῖς
οἶκοι, &c.) were subject to the administration of the Chartulary of the
Sakellion and the Great Curator.   The Orphanotrophos, therefore,
cannot be rightly described as a minister of *assistance publique*.[2]

Schlumberger has published a seal which may have belonged to
John, the famous Orphanotrophos, brother of Michael IV. The legend
is Ιω(αννη) Μοναχ(ω) και Ορφανοτροφ(ω). See *Sig.* 380, *Mél.* 299.
Another seal (tenth or eleventh century, *Sig.* 379, *Mél.* 298) has the
legend πρώτη μαθητῶν σφραγὶς ὀρφανοτρόφου. Schlumberger says that
ὀρφανοτροφίου is intended, but he has not observed that the inscription
is metrical. The seal is probably to be referred to the great Orphanotropheion. Another seal of the eleventh century bears the legend Μιχαη(λ)
Διακον(ος) Κληρικος [και] ἀνος του Ορφαν(ο)τ(ροφειον) ο Τετραπολι(της) :
Sig. 379, *Mél.* 297.   M. Sorlin-Dorigny has explained ἀνος as πρωτο-
νοσοκόμος, or chief of the hospital staff. But I very much doubt this
interpretation. There seems to be no mark of abbreviation after ἀνος,
and I do not see how it can be otherwise explained than as = ἄνθρωπος,
for which it is the normal abbreviation in MSS. This would mean
' dependent ' or ' retainer '.

(1, 2) Χαρτουλάριοι τοῦ οἴκου and χαρτουλάριοι τοῦ ὁσίου. There were
thus two distinct establishments under the Orphanotrophos, each of
which had its staff of accountants.   We may take it that these
establishments were the new Orphanotropheion ('St. Paul') founded by

---

[1] Nicetas, *Vit. Ignatii Patriarchae*, in Mansi, xvi. 275.   Nicephorus, Bishop of
Nicaea, became ὀρφανοτρόφος. A letter of Photios (186, ed. Valettas) is addressed
Γεωργίῳ διακόνῳ καὶ ὀρφανοτρόφῳ, but it is not clear that this person was *the*
orphanotrophos ; he may have been the director of some provincial orphanage.
    The most famous orphanotrophos, John (brother of Michael IV), who virtually
governed the Empire for some years, was a monk.

[2] On the general subject of *l'assistance publique* see Ducange, *Cplis. Christiana*,
B. iv, c. ix, and Schlumberger, *Mél.* 281 *sqq.* Cp. also Pargoire, *L'Église byzantine*, 80 *sqq.*, 324 *sqq.*

Justin and Sophia, and called ὁ οἶκος, and the older foundation bearing the name of ὁ ὅσιος Ζωτικός.[1]   A late seal (thirteenth century) is preserved (*Sig.* 155) of Niketas, Bishop of Ionopolis and χαρτουλαρίῳ τοῦ μεγάλου Ὀρφανοτροφείου.

(3) ἀρκάριος.   If the singular is right, both houses had a common *arca* and treasurer.   For ἀρκάριος cp. Justinian, *Nov.* 163 β', p. 353; Grenfell and Hunt, *Oxyrhynchus Papyri*, I. cxxvi. 15 (A.D. 572).

(4) κουράτωρες.   Perhaps the curators of dependent or affiliated institutions.

V. δημοκράται.

(1) ὁ δήμαρχος τῶν Βενέτων, (2) ὁ δήμαρχος τῶν Πρασίνων.

The organization of the demes (δῆμοι, μέρη) of Constantinople is a subject in itself,[2] and I do not propose to go into it here, or to discuss the functions of the officials, closely connected as they are with the hippodrome and the horse races.   It must be sufficient to observe that there were four demes, the Blues and Greens of the city, and the Blues and Greens of the Asiatic suburbs.   The city Blues, οἱ πολιτικοὶ Βένετοι, and the city Greens, οἱ πολιτικοὶ Πράσινοι, were under Demarchs ; the suburban Blues, οἱ περατικοὶ Βένετοι, and the suburban Greens, οἱ περατικοὶ Πράσινοι, were respectively under the Domestic of the Schools and the Domestic of the Excubiti, who, acting in this capacity, were called Democrats.   But the term δημοκράτης was applied in a general sense also to the Demarchs (Phil. 715₂₀).

The demarch might have the rank of ἀνθύπατος.   The ceremony of his creation is described in *Cer.* i. 55.

1. ὁ δευτερεύων.   Cp. *Cer.* 269₁₆, 798₂₀.

2. ὁ χαρτουλάριος.   The text of Philotheos is confusing ; he should have used either the plural or the singular throughout.   That each of the two demes had its chartularius is shown by *Cer.* 799₂.

3. ὁ ποιητής.   *Cer.* 272₁₇, 799₅.

4. ὁ ἄρχων.   Is this the same as ὁ μαΐστωρ (*Cer.* 272₁₃)?   In *Cer.* 269₁₆ τοῖς λοιποῖς ἄρχουσι τοῦ μέρους seems to mean the chartularius, the ποιητής, and the μελιστής.

---

[1] The explanation of Vogt (*Basile I*ʳ, 171) is impossible.   'Les chartulaires " τοῦ οἴκου " administraient probablement la partie matérielle de l'orphanotrophion tandis que les chartulaires " τοῦ ὁσίου " en avaient l'administration morale, religieuse et intellectuelle.' τοῦ ὁσίου could not possibly signify ' l'administration morale ', &c., nor would the instructors be called χαρτουλάριοι.

[2] See Uspenski, *Partii tsirka i dimy v Konstantinopolie*, Viz. Vrem. 1. 1 *sqq.* 1894.   The demes were the urban populace organized as a local militia.   For their importance in Egypt (fourth to seventh centuries) cp. M. Gelzer, *Stud. zur byz. Verw. Aegyptens*, 18, n. 2.

5. ὁ γειτονιάρχης. *Cer.* 799, 269₁₆, 271₁₀, 272₁₆.

6. ὁ μελιστής. *Cer.* 799₆, 272₁₇.

7. ὁ νοτάριος. *Cer.* 111₅, 271₅, ₁₁. As the notarius was distinct from the chartularius (cp. also Philotheos, 738₁₄), the text in *Cer.* 272₁₇ ὁ νοτάριος ἤτοι ὁ χαρτουλάριος should be corrected by the omission of ἤτοι.

8. οἱ ἡνίοχοι. I write the plural supposing that the φακτιονάριος and the μικροπανίτης are meant. Cp. *Cer.* 338₁₂, and 799₃, where, after the chartularii, are enumerated ὁ φακτιονάριος Βενέτων, ὁ φ. Πρασίνων, ὁ μικροπανίτης λευκός, ὁ μ. ῥούσιος. Cp. 337₁₇ οἱ δύο φακτ. καὶ οἱ δύο μικρ.

9. τὰ πρωτεῖα. Cp. *Cer.* 269₁₇, 337₁₉.

10. δημῶται.

The names of many other officials of the demes will be found in *Cer.* 799 (cp. 804); also 310 *sqq.*, 352, &c.

It is to be noted that there was a staff of Hippodrome officials who were not under the control of the Demarchs, ἡ τάξις τοῦ ἱπποδρομίου. Their titles will be found in *Cer.* 799–800, and 804. The chief of them was the Actuarius. In *Cer.* 341₁₄ he stands in the Kathisma of the Hippodrome. For his duties cp. *ib.* 366₅, 304₁₂. In Philotheos he is not assigned to any officium but is mentioned several times. He may be a spathar, 735₁₈ (in Takt. Usp. 127 he is of lower rank). He is entertained at Imperial banquets, 750₁₉, 758₂₀, 774₄.

VI. στρατάρχαι.

(1) ὁ ἑταιρειάρχης.

The Hetaeriarch or Great Hetaeriarch was the captain of the βασιλικὴ ἑταιρεία,[1] a body of guards, largely foreigners, who were in close personal attendance upon the Emperor. He is not mentioned in the Takt. Usp., nor in the first list of Philotheos; but he appears in the classified list; and in the Jerusalem MS. he occurs in the general list after the drungarios τῆς βίγλας. The Hetaeriarch existed in A.D. 867 (Andreas, George Mon., ed. Bonn, 817₁₈, and in A.D. 867 Artavasdos a Persian, *ib.* 838₇) and under Basil I, in whose reign we find Stylianos holding the post of μικρὸς ἑταιρειάρχης,[2] and Michael Katudares that of (μέγας) ἑταιρ.[3] Under Leo VI we meet Nikolaos, a confidant of the Emperor, holding the office of Hetaeriarch (Cont. Th. 361₇). One of the most important duties of the μέγας ἑταιρειάρχης was to protect the Emperor against plots (cp. the action of Nikolaos, *ib.*,

---

[1] To be distinguished from the ἑταιρεία of a στρατηγός.
[2] Georg. Mon. 846₁₃.
[3] *Ib.* 847₁₉.

and also Cont. Th. 470₂). Romanus I was created Hetaeriarch, with the rank of magister, before he became Basileopator; he was succeeded in the post by his son Christophoros (Cont. Th. 394-5).

From the fact that Hetaeriarchs are not mentioned either in Takt. Usp. or in the first list of Philotheos (transcribed from an older list), we may perhaps infer that they were first created in the reign of Michael III. But the ἑταιρεία was an older term. In Takt. Usp. we find πρωτομανδάτορες τῆς ἑτερίας (129). We must, I think, identify the Hetaireia with the body of troops called φοιδεράτοι in the early part of the ninth century. The evidence for the φοιδεράτοι was cited above (p. 63, in connexion with a passage in Kudâma). We saw that they were under τουρμάρχαι, who are mentioned in the Takt. Usp. We may conclude that in Michael's reign these troops were reorganized, and that the turmarchs were replaced by Hetaeriarchs.

The organization presents some difficulties. We have seen that there was a μικρὸς ἑταιρειάρχης in Basil's reign. This seems to imply a μικρὰ ἑταιρεία. We often hear of ἡ μεγάλη ἑταιρεία (Cer. 519₁, 553₁₈, &c.) and of ἡ μέση ἑταιρεία (518₁₉, 553₁₀, &c.); but never, so far as I know, of ἡ μικρὰ ἑτ. Yet the existence of the latter seems to be implied by the term μέση, which must have meant an intermediate body between the great and the little Hetaireiai. The only possible explanation seems to be that a little Hetaireia, which existed under Basil, was afterwards abolished; we do not hear of a little Hetaeriarch after his reign.[1] In the tenth century we find that the μέση or μεσαία (Cer. 576) was under the ἑταιρειάρχης as well as the μεγάλη, and ἡ ἑταιρεία, used without qualification, seems to have included both bodies. This may be inferred from Cer. ii. 1, where the daily opening of the palace is described. When the papias opens the doors in the morning, he is accompanied by the Hetaeriarch μετὰ τῶν ἀρχόντων τῆς ἑταιρείας καὶ τῶν τῆς ἑταιρείας ἑβδομαρίων. Presently the members of the ἑταιρεία break up into two parts, those of the μέση (518₁₉) and those of the μεγάλη (519₁). We find them distinguished in other passages of the Ceremonies (553, 576, 607).

From Cer. 576₃ we learn that there were Macedonians (Slavs?) in the μεγ. ἑτ. In περὶ ταξ. 478₁₄, ₁₅ we find distinguished οἱ ἐπὶ τῆς ἑταιρείας ἄνδρες σ' and οἱ ρ' ἐθνικοὶ τῶν ἐπὶ τῆς ἑταιρείας. Besides the two ἑταιρεῖαι there were attached to them, and included under the general name ἡ ἑταιρεία, two other bodies of foreign soldiers, namely, Khazars and Pharganoi. Cer. 576₈ ἡ μέγ. ἑτ., ὁμοίως καὶ ἡ μεσαία μετὰ

---

[1] Vit. Euthymii, i. 11 mentions the presence of members of the Hetaireia at the hunting expedition in which Basil I met his death; Stylianos was also present.

καὶ τῶν Φαργάνων καὶ Χαζάρων. Cont. Th. 358 Χαζάρους τῶν ἐκ τῆς ἑταιρείας τοῦ βασιλέως Λέοντος. Pharganoi as well as the Hetaireia attended Basil I in his fatal hunting expedition in A.D. 886 (Vit. Euthymii, i. 12). Among the troops sent to South Italy in A.D. 935 were thirty-one of the μεγ. ἐτ., forty-six of the μέση, forty-five Pharganoi, and forty-seven Khazars (Cer. 660). An appointment to the μεγ. ἐτ. cost a minimum of sixteen litrae, to the μέση a minimum of ten, to the Pharganoi or Khazars a minimum of seven (Cer. 692-3). Philotheos mentions (772₁₇) οἱ ἐθνικοὶ τῆς ἑταιρείας οἷον Τοῦρκοι, Χαζάρεις καὶ λοιποί. Turks means Hungarians in Byzantine writers of this period, though it would have been a perfectly proper description of the Φαργάνοι, who were Turks from Central Asia (Transoxiana and especially Ferghana, whence their name).[1]

Each division of the ἑταιρεία had its own commanders (οἱ ἄρχοντες τ. ἐτ. Cer. 518₅) ; the μεγάλη and the μέση had each its ἑβδομάριοι or παρεβδομάριοι (ib.). The μεγάλη had a logothete, Anon. Vári, 6 ὁ τῆς μεγ. ἐτ. ὁ λογοθέτης. Protomandatores of the Hetaireia are mentioned in Takt. Usp. 129.

The Hetaireia is constantly found in association with the μαγκλαβῖται,[2] who were perhaps also under the control of the Hetaeriarch. For the duties of the Hetaeriarch and Hetaireia in guarding the Imperial tent see περὶ ταξ. 481. For his appearance in ceremonies in association with the παπίας (both these officers were responsible for the safety of the palace) see Cer. 116₅, 122₅. Cp. also 442₁₅. The Hetaeriarch might be a eunuch, Phil. 784₁₄.

(2) ὁ Δρουγγάριος τοῦ πλοΐμου.

The history of the naval commands in the seventh and eighth centuries has been elucidated by Diehl and Gelzer. Before Leo III the navy was under the supreme command of a high admiral entitled στρατηγὸς

---

[1] It seems probable that there may have been Φαργάνοι among the subjects of the Caliph who deserted to the Empire in the days of Babek's rebellion, under Caliph Mamûn. This is suggested by the case of Theophanes ὁ ἐκ Φαργάνων, Georg. Mon., ed. Bonn., 815 and 821. It is suggested by Reiske (860) that the obscure ὁ βάρβαρος in Phil. 725₅ may be the Hetaeriarch, so called as commander of foreign troops, but see above, p. 93.

[2] Cp. Anon. Vári, 5₂₄ ; Cer. 9₁₆ τὸ μαγλάβιον καὶ ἡ ἑταιρεία, 7₁₉, 25₂₄, 607₁₃. We meet μαγλαβῖται who were candidati (Phil. 786₈), stratores (ib. 736₁₈), and protospathars (ib. 785₁₀). Some of them were stationed in the Lausiakon, but they are not necessarily to be included among οἱ τοῦ λαυσιακοῦ ἄρχοντες (785₁₇) ; for we find the stratores of the μαγλάβιον distinguished from the stratores of the Lausiakon (736₁₈) ; μαγλάβιον seems to have meant a stick, see Reiske, 53 sqq. It occurs in the sense of 'stripe', De adm. imp. 236₁₀ ; George Mon., ed. Bonn, 804₁₃.

τῶν Καραβισιάνων. Under him was the δρουγγάριος τῶν Κιβυραιωτῶν (a post held by Apsimar before he became Tiberius III). Leo III abolished the great naval command, and subdivided it. He raised the drungarios of the Kibyrrhaeots to the rank of stratêgos.[1] The other principal naval theme, that of Dodekanesos or the Αἰγαῖον πέλαγος was under a drungarios during the eighth century,[2] and until the reign of Michael III. For in the Taktikon Uspenski (120) the title is ὁ δρουγγάριος τοῦ Αἰγαίου πελάγους. The third naval theme, that of Samos, is not mentioned in the eighth century, nor does it appear in the Takt. Usp. It follows that it was instituted under Michael III, Basil I, or in the early years of Leo VI, as it is registered in the lists of Philotheos. According to Constantine Porphyrogennetos (*Them.* i, p. 41) Samos was formerly the capital τοῦ θέματος τῶν πλωϊζο-μένων (which must be equivalent to the θ. τῶν Καραβισιάνων). When this large naval province was broken up Samos was probably included in the drungariate of the Aegean Sea.

The provincial fleets were known as ὁ θεματικὸς στόλος.[3] Inde-pendent of them, there was always a fleet at Constantinople under the command of ὁ δρουγγάριος τοῦ πλοΐμου. It is not improbable that this commander existed already in the seventh century, subordinate to the stratêgos of the Karabisians. He is not mentioned in the eighth century, but there can be no doubt that the office existed then, and the fleet of Constantinople must have formed part of the squadron of 800 chelandia which conveyed an army to the Bulgarian coast in the reign of Constantine V.[4] ὁ δρουγγάριος ὁ τοῦ πλοΐμου appears in the Taktikon Uspenski (120), where his rank is inferior to that of all the Domestici and Chartularii. He comes immediately after the Protostrator and before the ἐκ προσώπου τῶν θεμάτων. This fact has considerable importance. It shows that in the interval between the early years of Michael III and A. D. 900 the post of the Drungarios had become considerably more distinguished and important; for in

---

[1] Theoph. 410₆.

[2] A δρουγγάριος τῆς Δωδεκανήσου meets us in A.D. 780 (Theoph 454₁₉). This record shows that Isaac, the father of Theophanes the chronographer, bore the title of drungarios and not stratêgos. For as he died when his son was a child and his son was born in A. D. 759, he must have held the post before A.D. 780. The text in the *Vita* (*ex officio festi eius diei*) is (de Boor, ii. 28) τοῦ δὲ πατρὸς τελευτήσα·τος ἐν τῇ ὑπ᾽ αὐτοῦ διεπομένῃ τῶν Αἰγαιοπελαγητῶν ἀρχῇ. Gelzer (80), ignoring this decisive passage, leaves the question open.

[3] Cont. Th. 55₁₉, 79₁₇. The three themes of the Kibyrrhaeots, the Aegean Sea, and Samos were the naval themes *par excellence*, cp. Cer. 656 διὰ τῶν πλοΐμων τῶν γ᾽ θεμάτων, &c., but it must be remembered that other themes, e. g. Hellas, Peloponnesus, Cephallenia, Paphlagonia, had small naval establishments.

[4] Theoph. 432₃₀.

Philotheos he comes immediately after or immediately before the Logothete of the Course (the order varies), and is superior to the Domestics of the Hikanatoi and Numeroi, to all the Chartularioi, and to several other officials who had formerly preceded him in rank. This change corresponds to the revival of the importance of the fleet in the ninth century—a revival which is generally set down to Basil I and his son, but which really began under Michael III. We may be confident that the Drungariate had attained its new eminence when it was filled by Nicetas Ooryphas, a Patrician, in the reign of Basil. The fleet which was commanded by the Drungarios was now distinguished (from the thematic fleets) as the Imperial fleet, τὸ βασιλικοπλόϊμον (*Cer.* 651_{18}, 664_8, &c.).[1]

In the Taktikon Uspenski (120) we meet a naval commander who does not appear elsewhere, ὁ δρουγγάριος τοῦ κόλπου. He is enumerated immediately after the drungarios of the Aegean.[2] The κόλπος, so called without closer definition, must have been in the neighbourhood of Constantinople, and we may, I think, infer that the naval establishment which was stationed at or near the capital was, in the eighth and early part of the ninth century, under two admirals, the δρ. τοῦ πλοίμου and the δρ. τοῦ κόλπου. When the naval establishment was reorganized under or before Basil I, the latter command was abolished, and the whole fleet of Constantinople was placed under the δρ. τοῦ πλοίμου, who at the same time was elevated in rank and importance. The κόλπος was hardly the inner part of the Golden Horn? (cp. Cont. Th. 58_{11} ἐν τῷ πρὸς Βλαχέρναις κόλπῳ). It was rather the Gulf of Kios?

It may be observed that the information given by Constantine Porphyrogennetos in *De adm. imp.* c. 51 concerns only the ships appropriated to the personal service of the Emperor, and not the navy. The organization of this service by Leo VI was probably subsequent to A.D. 900, as the officer who controlled the marines of the Imperial dromonia and agraria, ὁ πρωτοσπαθάριος τῆς φιάλης, is not mentioned by Philotheos.

The officium of the drungarios of the fleet corresponds to the type of the Domesticates, in (1) the τοποτηρητής (Const. *De adm. imp.* c. 51, p. 238), (2) the χαρτουλάριος (cp. Panchenko, ix. 386,   ]έοντ[ι χ]αρτου[λα]ρ(ίῳ) τοῦ [β(ασιλικοῦ) πλω]ίμ(ου), a seal of eighth or ninth century; and Niceph. presb. in Vit. MS. And. Sal. apud Ducange),

---

[1] At the time of Basil's accession Elias was ὁ περιφανέστατος τοῦ βασιλικοῦ στόλου δρουγγάριος, Nicetas, *Vit. Ign.* apud Mansi, xvi. 257.

[2] The order is ὁ δρ. ὁ τοῦ πλοίμου, ὁ ἐκ προσώπου τῶν θεμάτων, ὁ δρ. τοῦ αἰγ. πελ., ὁ δρ. τοῦ κόλπου.

(3) the πρωτομανδάτωρ (Cont. Th. 401₂₂), and (7) μανδάτορες, (4) the κόμητες,[1] and (5) κένταρχοι. But like the officium of a strategos it has (6) a κόμης τῆς ἐταιρείας (commander of foreign marines, esp. 'Ρώς or Scandinavians).

For the πρωτοκάραβοι see *De adm. imp.* 237 (cp. Cont. Th. 400₁₃).

(3) ὁ λογοθέτης τῶν ἀγελῶν.

Philotheos includes the Minister of the Flocks and Herds among the στρατάρχαι, though as a logothete one might expect him to be enumerated among the σεκρετικοί. But from his officium it appears that he had no σέκρετον, and his duties were entirely connected with the army. He controlled the management of the large tracts in Western Asia Minor where horses were reared for the supply of the army, in the μητάτα or military colonies. In the περὶ ταξ. 458–9 we find him distributing the burden of furnishing horses and mules among the various μητάτα of Asia and Phrygia, and transporting them to Malagina. (Cp. 460₂.)

His province shows that he descends from the *praepositus gregum* of the *Not. Dig.* (*Or.* xiv. 6), who was subordinate to the comes rei privatae. The *pascua* and *saltus* of the *res privata* seem to have been largely utilized for military settlements, and were designated (perhaps already in the fourth century) as' μητάτα (μιτάτα, John Malalas, 347₁₈, cp. Theoph. 72₂₁). Compare Justinian, *Nov.* 150. 9, p. 265 ; Tiberius II, *Nov.* 12. 6, p. 29 (μετάτων).

(1, 2) ὁ πρωτονοτάριος 'Ασίας, ὁ πρωτονοτάριος Φρυγίας. We can infer that the μητάτα were entirely in Western Asia Minor; cp. the passage in περὶ ταξ. referred to above.

(3) We may identify the διοικηταὶ τῶν μητάτων with the *procuratores saltuum* of the *Not. Dig.*

(4, 5) The Logothete, like the two Curators, has ἐπισκεπτῆται, inspectors, who were doubtless a check on the διοικηταί. There is no evidence for the functions of the κόμητες.

Schlumberger (*Sig.* 467) has published a late seal of a χαρτουλάριος τῶν ἀγελῶν, not mentioned by Philotheos.

(4) ὁ πρωτοσπαθάριος τῶν βασιλικῶν.

οἱ βασιλικοὶ ἄνθρωποι frequently appear in the court ceremonies (e. g. *Cer.* 20₂₀, 30₁₅, 15₇). They were divided into τάξεις of different orders : spatharocandidati, spatharioi, stratores, candidati, and mandatores. Cp. Philotheos, 769₂₀ βασιλικῶν ἀνθρώπων ἀπὸ τῆς τάξεως τῶν

---

[1] Phil. 750₆ τὸν κόμητα τοῦ πλοίμου, read τοὺς κόμητας.

σπαθαροκανδιδάτων μέχρι τῆς τάξεως τῶν στρατώρων, i. e. all the βασιλικοὶ ἄνθρωποι except the candidati and μανδάτορες (cp. 773₅). The βασιλικοὶ σπαθάριοι (Cer. 7₅; 10₁₂ where they carry the Imperial arms) or σπαθάριοι of the σπαθαρίκιον; the βασιλικοὶ κανδιδάτοι (Phil. 767₁₃, 770₅); and the βασιλικοὶ μανδάτορες (Cer. 81₂₀, Phil. 770₅) were under the control of the πρωτοσπαθάριος τῶν βασιλικῶν; the stratores were under the Protostrator (see below); as to the spatharocandidati we are not told (cp. Cer. 81₆) and we may suppose that there was no τάξις of this order distinct from those who were on duty in the Chrysotriklinos (Phil. 733₁₉), or the Lausiakos (ib. 734), or performed some other special service in the palace. The Protospatharios, as his name indicates, was originally the chief of the spatharioi, and his control was afterwards extended over the taxeis of the candidati and mandatores. For some of his ceremonial duties cp. Phil. 706.

The Protospatharios was also called ὁ κατεπάνω τῶν βασιλικῶν, cp. Cer. 20₂₀ οἱ βασ. ἄνθ. μετὰ καὶ τοῦ κατεπάνω αὐτῶν καὶ τοῦ δομεστίκου αὐτῶν (so also 6₄, 9₁₅, 568₉), and ὁ κατεπάνω simply, Phil. 709₂₄. In Anon. Vári. 6₈ the Katepano and the Domesticus are called οἱ κατεπάνω τῶν βασιλικῶν ἀνθρώπων. When the archon of Taron is introduced to the Imperial presence he is accompanied by the Katepano and the Logothete of the Course, Cer. 138₁₇.

(1) Under the Protospatharios was the Domesticus, who appears separately in the list of high officials, but without an officium of his own.[1]

(2) σπαθάριοι. The earliest Imperial spatharioi were perhaps cubicularii who had a military character and bore a sword. Cp. Theoph. 181₃₄ Kalapodios cub. and spath., 185₁₃ κουβ. καὶ σπαθ., in the reign of Justinian. In the Acta cited in Chron. Pasch. sub A. D. 532, Kalapodios is designated as σπαθαροκουβικουλάριος. This seems to show that at that time there were other spatharioi also. In Peter the Patrician (Cer. 402₉) we meet ὁ σπαθάριος τοῦ βασιλέως, and in Cass. Var. 3. 43 a spatharios of Theodoric. (Under Anastasius I the Duke of Pentapolis had a spatharios under him, Zachariä von L., S. B. of Vienna Acad., Feb. 17, 1879, p. 142; and probably other military governors and generals had military attendants known by this name. Nilus, at the beginning of the fifth century, addresses a letter Σισιννίῳ σπαθαρίῳ, i. 277, Migne, P. G. 79.) The σπαθάριοι βασιλικοί must be carefully distinguished from the σπαθάριοι of a stratêgos (cp. Pseudo-Maurice, Strat. 1. 9; Leo, Tact. 14. 81), and also from those who bore the title as an order of rank. There was a special hall in the

---

[1] Panchenko, ix. 386, has published a seal (saec. ix-x) of a πρωτοσπ. καὶ δομ. τῶν β.

Palace for the spathars, called the spatharikion (see e. g. *Cer.* 157₇ and cp. Bieliaev, ii. 238).

For seals of Imperial spatharioi see Schlumberger, *Sig.* 590–3, and note those of Theodore (No. 6) and Maurianos (No. 14) which he ascribes to the seventh century.

(3) The κανδιδάτοι are said to have been instituted by Gordian and to have been chosen for their size and strength from the scholarii, *Chron. Pasch.*, ann. 3.[1] Their original connexion with the scholarian guards seems to be borne out by the ceremony of their creation described by Peter Patricius (*Cer.* 391). Candidati are mentioned at the beginning of the fifth century in the letters of Nilus, but we hear little of them till the sixth. From the passage of Peter we learn that they had a *primicerius*, and that their insigne was (as in the ninth century) a gold chain. In Procopius, *B. G.* 3. 38 (p. 468), we meet Asbados, who ἐς τοὺς κανδιδάτους καλουμένους τελῶν ἔτυχε, and was in command of a troop of cavalry at Tzurulon. A seventh century seal of a βασιλικὸς κανδιδάτος is published by Panchenko, viii. 231, cp. xiii. 79. The seal of CARELLU(S) CANDIDATU(S) in *Sig.* 459 is probably earlier. Drosos, Chartularius of Thrace in eighth or ninth century, had the rank of candidatus, *ib.* 122. For other seals cp. *ib.* 214 (turmarch of Sicily), 197, 355, &c.

(4) We have already met μανδάτορες who acted as adjutants in the staffs of military and other functionaries (Stratêgoi, Domestics, the Logothete of the Course, &c.). Besides these there were Imperial mandatores (βασιλικοὶ μ.), one of whom acted as spokesman of Justinian in the Hippodrome on the occasion of the Nika revolt.[2] Theophylaktos, whose seal (eighth to ninth century) is published by Schlumberger, *Sig.* 536, was a dioikêtes who had belonged to the *taxis* of mandatores (βασιλικῷ μανδάτορι καὶ δινκίτι). For a few other seals see *ib.*

(5) ὁ κόμης τοῦ σταύλου.

The κόμης τῶν βασιλικῶν σταύλων appears in the sixth century. The post was held by Baduarius, brother of Justin II (Theoph. 246₁₄).[3]

---

[1] Cp. Vegetius, 2, 7, who describes them as *milites principales qui privilegiis muniuntur.*

[2] Theoph. 182 *sq.* Two mandators, with ten excubitors, were sent to bring the Abbot Maximus to Constantinople in the seventh century, see *Acta* of the examination of Maximus in Migne, xc. 109. At the Second Council of Nicaea (A. D. 787) ὁ λαμπρότατος βασ. μανδάτωρ enters the Council with a message from the Emperors, Mansi, xii. 1051.

[3] Under Michael II we meet Damianus holding this office (κόμητα τοῦ β. ἱπποστασίου) with rank of protospathar. Cont. Th. 76₁₅.

Formerly the *praepositus* or *praepositi stabulorum* stood under the comes rei privatae (*Not. Or.* xiv. 6), but they were also called *comites stabuli* (*C. Th.* 11. 17. 3, A. D. 401) and *tribuni sacri stabuli* (*C. Th.* 6. 13. 1, where *C. I.* 12. 11. 1 substitutes *comites*).

The officium has dropped out in the MS., but we have material for reconstructing it, at least partially.   In περὶ ταξ. 459₁₀ the higher officials, οἱ ἄρχοντες τοῦ στάβλου, are enumerated (cp. 480₁₅ ; Phil. 732₂₀ οἱ πρωτοσπ. καὶ ἄρχοντες τῶν στάβλων, Anon. Vári, 5₂₂ οἱ τοῦ στ. ἄρχ., Cont. Th. 231₄, though here ἄρχοντες is more general).

(1) ὁ χαρτουλάριος. Takt. Usp. 128, Phil. 737₁₀, 788₂₃ ; περὶ ταξ. 459₆, 476₁₇. He is distinguished as ὁ ἔσω χ. from ὁ χ. τῶν Μαλαγίνων, see below. Panchenko (ix. 390) has published a seal (tenth to eleventh century) in which the title seems to be χαρτουλαρίῳ καὶ ἐκ προσώπου τῶν βασιλικῶν στάβλων.

(2) ὁ ἐπείκτης. Takt. Usp. 128, Phil. 737, 789, περὶ ταξ. 459₆, 478₁₈. An occupant of the post in the reign of Leo VI is named in Cont. Th. 362. The word means an overseer who presses a work on, ἐργοδιώκτης, cp. Theoph. 442₂₃, 367, 384₉.

(3) ὁ χαρτουλάριος τῶν Μαλαγίνων (περὶ ταξ. 476₉, 479₃). Presumably the same as ὁ ἔξω. χ., 459₇. At Malagina there were important military stables.

(4) ὁ σαφραμέντάριος. The text here gives διὰ τῶν σαφραμέντων, but other passages in the same treatise, 476₁₀, 479₄, show that it must be amended : either διὰ τοῦ σαφραμενταρίου or more probably διὰ τοῦ τῶν σαφραμέντων (cp. ὁ τῆς καταστάσεως, &c.). The meaning is unknown.

(5) οἱ δ' κόμητες τῶν Μαλαγίνων (περὶ ταξ. 479₅, 459₉).

Besides these, there seem to belong here :

(6) οἱ μ' σύντροφοι τῶν σελλαρίων (περὶ ταξ. 479₂), οἱ σύντροφοι τῶν δύο στάβλων (*Cer.* 698₂₂), sc. of the city and Malagina.

(7, 8) ὁ κελλάριος and ὁ ἀποθέτης. περὶ ταξ. 478₁₈ διὰ τοῦ ἀποθέτου τοῦ κελλαρίου τοῦ β. στάβλου, cp. 479₁₉ ὁ κόμης τοῦ σ. καὶ ὁ χαρτουλάριος καὶ ὁ κελλάριος. This κελλάριος must be distinguished from ὁ οἰκειακὸς κελλάριος, *ib.* 464₁₁. See below, p. 121.

VII. Ἀξίαι εἰδικαί.

(1) ὁ βασιλεοπάτωρ.

This dignity was instituted, about six years before Philotheos wrote, by Leo VI, in order to give a pre-eminent political position to Zautzes Stylianos.   Immediately after his accession (A. D. 886) he had appointed Stylianos to be Logothete of the Course, and conferred upon him the title of magister, with rank before the other magistri—

a position designated by πρωτομάγιστρος.[1] After the death of his wife
Theophano (Nov. A. D. 893) he married Zoe (already his paramour),
the daughter of Stylianos, doubtless in 894, and at the same time [2]
conferred on Stylianos the new title of βασιλεοπάτωρ, or βασιλοπάτωρ.[3]
The general care of affairs of state was recognized as belonging
to this office.[4] The office of ' Empress's father ' [5] was one which
from its very definition could only be occasionally filled. It was
conferred upon Romanus Lekapenos when the young Emperor
Constantine VII married his daughter.

The quasi-imperial title added to the prestige and authority of
Stylianos, but probably did not increase the sphere of his political
power. As πρωτομάγιστρος he had been virtually prime minister.
For Leo had interpreted μάγιστρος in the ancient sense of Master of
Offices ; in fact, he had revived that post, with a new meaning. In
the long series of laws which are addressed to him, Stylianos is styled
τῷ ὑπερφυεστάτῳ μαγίστρῳ τῶν θείων ὀφφικίων (Leo VI, Nov. 18 et sqq.).
See above, p. 31. These laws were evidently promulgated before
A. D. 894. Stylianos died in 896.[6]

(2) ὁ 'Ραίκτωρ.

Philotheos is the earliest writer who mentions the Rector (whom
Liutprand calls Rector domus, Antap. 6. 10), and we may assume
with confidence that the post was not introduced before the latter
half of the ninth century, by Basil I or by Leo VI. Basil the Rector,
mentioned in George Mon., ed. Bonn, 837₁₁, must have held the office
in one of these reigns. The Rector's prerogative probably consisted in
exercising some authority over the Imperial household. He appears
(Cer. 23) along with the praepositi and the members of the κουβούκλειον. The ceremony of his creation (ib. 528) was probably composed
in the reign of Constantine VII and Romanos II. He is mentioned in

[1] Vita Euthymii, ii. 1 παρευθὺ Στ. πρωτομάγιστρον καθίστησιν, Georg. Mon.,
ed. Bonn. 849 = Cont. Th. 354 προεβάλετο Στ. μάγιστρον καὶ λογοθέτην τοῦ δρόμου.
See above, p. 31.
[2] Vita Euthymii, ib. μετ' οὐ πολὺ δὲ καὶ βασιλοπάτορα ἀναδείκνυσι. The chronology
is well discussed by De Boor in his comments on this passage, 95–107. He con-
cludes that Zoe was brought into the Palace, and her father created basileopator
early in 894, and that the marriage was celebrated towards the end of the same
year. Cp. Georg. Mon. 852.
[3] This form occurs three times in the text of the Vita Euthymii. Cp.
βασιλόθυρα (see Ducange).
[4] Vita Euthymii, ib. τῶν ἐπερχομένων τῇ βασιλείᾳ διοικήσεων τὴν ἐπιστασίαν καὶ
φροντίδα ὁ αὐτὸς Στ. διέπων ἐγνωρίζετο.
[5] It is commonly taken to mean ' Emperor's father '.
[6] De Boor, Vita Euthymii, 105-7.

Cer. ii. 9, which seems to date from the reign of Michael III, but the passage in question is probably an addition of Constantine VII (544₁₉). The Emperor Alexander created a cleric,[1] named Joannes, Rector (Cont. Th. 379). He was one of those who assumed the direction of affairs at the time of the death of Alexander (*Vita Euthymii*, xxi. 1 σὺν τῷ ῥαίκτωρι ᾿Ιωάννῃ); he continued to hold the office in the first years of Romanos I; and he was sent on a military expedition (Cont. Th. 399, 401, cp. 406; cp. Liutprand, *Antap.* 3. 26). The office was also held by a cleric under Constantine VII (*De adm. imp.* 241-2). The Rector occupied a prominent place in the ceremonies seen by Liutprand in the reign of Constantine VII (*Antap.* 6. 10).

Schlumberger has published a seal (eleventh century) inscribed Βασιλειω ραικτωρη (*Mél.* 243).[2] See also Konstantopulos, Nos. 139, 150, 488-9.

(3) ὁ σύγκελλος.

The position and functions of the synkellos deserve a careful examination, but as they belong to ecclesiastical organization, lie outside the scope of the present study. The important point is that the synkellos of the Patriarch of Constantinople,[3] sometimes described as the synkellos of Constantinople,[4] was an Imperial official and appointed by the Emperor.[5] We may conjecture that his chief charge was occasionally to conduct communications between the Emperor and the Patriarch, but the duties seem to have been very light.[6] Synkelloi were not infrequently elevated to the Patriarchal throne, and it may be suspected that the Emperors of the ninth

---

[1] The tenure of the office by clerics led Ducange (Gl. *s. v.*) to suppose that the office was ecclesiastical. Reiske (834) rightly denied this.

[2] In the ninth century another Basil held the office, see Georg. Mon. 837₁₁ (ed. Bonn).

[3] George, the chronographer, e. g., is described as the synkellos of Tarasios (in the title of his Chronicle) and in Theoph. 3.

[4] Theoph. 164₁₀.

[5] That the Emperor appointed is a certain inference from the fact that the post was one of the Imperial ἀξίαι conferred διὰ λόγου. The account, in the *Vita Euthymii* (c. iv), of the appointment of Euthymios illustrates this. When Stephanos (son of Basil I), who had held the post, became Patriarch, he urged Euthymios to accept the office of synkellos, which is described as a βασιλικὸν ἀξίωμα (58); and ὁ βασιλεὺς (Leo VI) συνευδόκει καὶ τὰ ὅμοια λέγων κατένευε. Moreover, Stephanos says that the synkellate was conferred on himself by his father (ἐκ πατρῴου δωρεᾶς).

[6] *Vita Euthymii, ib.* 5 καλὸν γάρ ἐστι καὶ ἀβαρὲς καὶ ἀνεπίληπτον τὸ πρᾶγμα. He was expected to be constantly in the Palace, and to take part, like other members of the σύγκλητος, in some of the ceremonies, *ib.* 9. 10.

century aimed at making this succession a regular practice, since it would secure them the unrestricted appointment of the Patriarch.[1]

(4) ὁ χαρτουλάριος τοῦ κανικλείου.

This official, generally called ὁ ἐπὶ τοῦ κανικλείου, first appears in our sources in the ninth century. Under Michael II it was held by Theoktistos, and Genesios (23_{20}) thus explains the meaning of the title : τὴν ἐπὶ τοῦ βασιλικοῦ καλάμου ἐγκεχείριστο πρόνοιαν, δι' οὗ κανίκλιος ἐδοξάζετο. His duty evidently was to be present when the Imperial pen signed state documents, and he also signed for the Emperor. A bull of Manuel Comnenus (*Nov.* 63, p. 457) was endorsed διὰ τοῦ ἐπὶ τοῦ κανικλείου καὶ δικαιοδότου Θεοδώρου τοῦ Στυπειώτου. He also prepared the codicilli of the Patricians, Phil. 710_{14}. Such duties required no officium,[2] and the post was often combined with another office. Thus Theoktistos was at the same time Logothete of the Course, and A.D. 869 the post was held by Christophoros, who was protoasecretis (Acta of Fourth Council of Cple., Mansi, xvi. 409).

The title χαρτουλάριος shows that originally this official was one of the chartularii of the σέκρετον.

(5) ὁ πρωτοστράτωρ.

The Protostrator was strictly the chief of the *taxis* of stratores, whose duty originally was to assist the Emperor in mounting his horse (cp. *Hist. Aug.* xiii. 7 *cum illum in equum strator eius levaret*) and perform the duty of grooms (ἱπποκόμοι).[3] In the sixth century we meet a *schola stratorum* in the *officium* of the Praetorian Prefect of Africa (*C. I.* 1. 27, § 33). We meet a δομέστικος τῶν στρατώρων in the time of Justinian II along with a πρωτοστράτωρ τοῦ ὀψικίου. In A.D. 765 we meet a σπαθ. καὶ βασιλικὸς πρωτοστράτωρ (*ib.* 438_{15}). See also Cont. Th. 18_9, 24_3. Basil, the Macedonian, began his career in the Imperial service as a strator and then became Protostrator (*ib.* 231). He had before been protostrator (chief groom) of Theophilitzes (*ib.* 225_{10}).

The Protostrator rides beside the Emperor, with the Comes stabuli, *Cer.* 81_{18}. At a triumph he rides close to the Emperor, with the *flamullum*, *ib.* 609_{10}, and places the Imperial spear on the necks of

---

[1] Cp. the observation of Cedrenus (Skylitzes), ii. 581.

[2] But there was a person described as ὁ σκευάζων τὸ κανίκλειον—the manufacturer or mixer of the ink (*Cer.* 798_{16}). καν. seems to have properly meant the inkbottle, cp. Ducange, *s. v.*

[3] *C. Th.* 6. 31. 1 (A.D. 365-373?) concerns stratores in the province of Nova Epirus, but it is not clear that they belong to the Emperor's personal service.

captives, 610_{19}. He may introduce foreign visitors, instead of the Protospatharios $τ. βασιλικῶν$, or the Comes stabuli, 568_{15}. In the age of Philotheos his place in the official hierarchy was not high, but in later times it grew in dignity and importance, and in the age of the Palaeologi it was one of the highest of all (Codinus, 9). Nicetas equates it with the marshal, $μαρέσχαλκος$, of the western kingdoms.

(1) $στράτωρες, τοῦ βασιλικοῦ στρατωρικίου$ Phil. 736_{19}. Cp. Cer. $81_{19, 24}$. Most of the seals of $βασιλικοὶ στράτορες$ published by Schlumberger are late, but there are two (Sig. 597) of the eighth to ninth centuries.

(2) $ἀρμοφύλακες$ (for $ἀρματοφύλακες$ cp. $ἀρματοφυλακεῖον$, see Ducange, s.v.), meaning officials in charge of the $ἄρματα = ὅπλα$, military gear in the Imperial $ἀρμαμέντον$. There is, however, a difficulty, for the $ἀρμαμέντον$, which was under the control of the Magister Officiorum (cp. Justinian, Nov. 108, §§ 1, 3),[1] was managed under Phocas (Theoph. 297) by an official named $ὁ ἐπάνω τοῦ ἀρμαμέντον$, and he survived till the tenth century at least: see Phil. $736_5 ὁ σπαθ. καὶ ἄρχων τοῦ ἀρμ.$, and 788_{21}; Cer. 673_{20} (a protospatharios, A.D. 949) and $676_{15} τοῦ κατεπάνω τοῦ ἄρματος$ (so Reiske, but the MS. has $ἄρμα^τ$, and we should unquestionably read $ἀρμαμέντον$). The difficulty is that he is not mentioned in the official lists of Philotheos. It is hardly possible to regard him as included under the $ἀρμοφύλακες$. One would expect him to be mentioned distinctly. In the Takt. Usp. he appears, $ὁ ἄρχων τοῦ ἀρμαμέντον$, immediately after $ὁ τῆς καταστάσεως$ (124). The seal of an $ἄρχων τοῦ βασιλικοῦ ἀρμαμέντον$ is published by Konstantopulos, No. 186.

(3) $σταβλοκόμητες$. They were three in number: the $σταβλοκόμης τῆς πόλεως$, and οἱ δύο $σταβλοκόμητες$ (? of Malagina), περὶ ταξ. $478_{20}, 479_1$.

(6) $ὁ ἐπὶ τῆς καταστάσεως$.

This official, generally called $ὁ τῆς καταστάσεως$, does not appear in the list of possible patricians, but may be a protospathar, in Philotheos (in Takt. Usp. he is a spathar or lower, 124, 127). The title may be rendered Master of Ceremonies. [The use of $κατάστασις$ in the sense of 'order' is illustrated by περὶ ταξ. 503 $τὴν μὲν κατάστασιν τῆς πόλεως καὶ φιλοκαλίαν ἡτοιμάσατο ὁ ἔπαρχος$.] The court ceremonial in former times was controlled by the magister officiorum, and a work on the subject, entitled περὶ τῆς καταστάσεως, was compiled in the sixth century by Peter the Patrician who held that office. Under the magister was the *scrinium dispositionum*, of which the head was the

---

[1] $τὸ θεῖον ἡμῶν ἀρμαμέντον$. It contained $δημόσια ὅπλα$.

comes dispositionum (*C. Th.* 6. 26. 10 and 18), and it devolved on him to arrange for the details of the Emperor's daily programme. ὁ ἐπὶ τῆς καταστάσεως seems to descend from this functionary (κατάστασις may represent *dispositio*).

There was a special *officium ammissionum* under the magister (*Not. Or.* xi. 17), of which the chief was the proximus ammissionum (Peter, in *Cer.* 394₂); but in the time of Justinian there was already a κόμης τῶν ἀδμηνσιόνων (Peter, *Cer.* i. 84). In one ceremony we meet a κόμης τῶν ἀδμησιόνων (i. 41. 209). The official named ὁ ἀδμηνσουνάλιος is more frequently mentioned (*Cer.* 800₈, 23₈, 239₂₁, 442₁₀), and from 269₁₅ it appears that he might be under the orders of ὁ τῆς καταστάσεως. This is what we should expect, for in the sixth century ὁ ἀμισσιωνάλιος was 'the first of the silentiaries' (Lydus, 73₁₉).[1] In *Cer.* 800₈, 802₁₇ he is mentioned along with the διαιτάριοι of the Palace, and must have been a subordinate of one of the eunuch officials (such as the παπίας or δεύτερος).

Under ὁ τῆς καταστάσεως were the τάξεις of those orders of rank which Philotheos distinguishes as senatorial from Imperial in the stricter sense, namely, the ὕπατοι, the vestetores, the silentiaries, the apoeparchontes (for all of which see above under B, p. 23 *sqq.*). Besides these συγκλητικοί are also mentioned in the officium, which, if the text is correct, points to a lower class of συγκλητικοί not belonging to those five or higher orders. It is difficult to believe that such a class existed, and it seems to me highly probable, if not certain, that συγκλητικοί is an error for στρατηλάται, who were a synklêtic order, and would naturally, along with the apoeparchontes, belong here.

We constantly find the Master of Ceremonies acting in conjunction with silentiaries, e.g. *Cer.* 81₁₅, 127₂₅, 238₄, 503₆. From Phil. 710₁₀ we learn that a newly elevated Patrician gave a fee of twelve nomismata to the Master of Ceremonies, ἄνευ τοῦ ὀψικίου, and a fee of eighty nom. to be divided among the ὀψίκιον. This is explained by the ceremony of the creation of Patricians, *Cer.* i. 47. The silentiarii act as an escort of the new Patricians ; cp. 239₁₂, 241₇₋₉.

(7) ὁ δομέστικος τῶν βασιλικῶν.

See above under ὁ πρωτοσπαθάριος τῶν βασιλικῶν (VI. 4).

---

[1] Cp. Pet. Patr. in *Cer.* 404₃, ₁₅, 405₁₅.

D. Dignities and Offices of the Eunuchs.

In the fifth century the cubicularii were the most important class of the Palace servants and were under the Praepositus. The other court servants were under the Castrensis s. palatii, so far as they were not under the Master of Offices.[1] The castrensis seems to have disappeared by the sixth century.[2] The cubicularii included the chief officials who had charge of the private wardrobe, the Imperial table and cellars, as well as the Imperial bedchamber.

The history of these domestic offices is parallel to the history of the offices of state in the principles of its development. (1) A number of the subordinate officials are elevated to independent, co-ordinate positions, and (2) titles of office are adopted as grades of rank.

The cubicularii of the bedchamber, who were specially distinguished as κοιτωνῖται,[3] are separated from the rest of the cubiculum, under their chief the Parakoimômenos, who becomes a high official. The private wardrobe becomes an independent office under the Protovestiarios, and similarly the service of the table under ὁ ἐπὶ τῆς τραπέζης.

The rest of the cubiculum (οἱ κουβικουλάριοι τοῦ κουβουκλείου, distinguished from οἱ κ. τοῦ βασιλικοῦ κοιτῶνος) seem to have remained under the Praepositus, and the primicerius s. cubiculi of the fifth century (*Not. Dig., Or.* i. 17) continued to be their chief (Phil. 721$_{21}$, Cer. 798$_{17}$).

The servants who attended to the cleaning, heating, lighting of the Palace, the porters of the gates, &c., had probably been under the control of the castrensis. In the later period we find that two have been raised to the dignity of independent officials, the Papias and the Deuteros.

In a wide sense of the term all the eunuch officials belonged to the cubiculum. They were graded in eight ranks, and of these the praepositi, protospathars, primicerii, and ostiarii are described as οἱ προεστῶτες τοῦ μυστικοῦ κουβουκλείου (Phil. 750$_{16}$).[4] ἡ τάξις τοῦ κ., Phil. 705$_{20}$, seems to be used in the wide sense.

The term οἰκειακός (privy, domestic) may be explained here. We find it used of the Parakoimômenos (Phil. 784$_5$), and of the private vestiarion (see above under ὁ χαρτ. τοῦ βεστ.). In the latter case it distinguishes the private from the public Imperial Wardrobe, and its most important significance is to limit the term βασιλικός. There

---

[1] Cp. Mommsen, 513.

[2] Mommsen, *ib.*, suggests that his place was taken by the *cura palati*.

[3] Cp. Phil., 734$_{22-23}$.

[4] Cp. *Cer.*, 551$_{16}$ τῶν πραιποσίτων τοῦ κουβουκλείου.

were many βασιλικοί, of various ranks, who were not eunuchs and did not belong to the cubiculum, but were engaged in the more personal and domestic service of the Emperor in the Palace. These (protospathars, spatharocandidates, spathars, &c.) were distinguished as οἰκειακοί. Compare *Cer.* 100₁₇ τῶν ἀρχόντων τοῦ κουβουκλείου καὶ βασιλικῶν οἰκειακῶν (and 103₁₆). So in Takt. Usp. 118 οἱ οἰκ. πρωτο-σπαθάριοι, 123 οἱ σπαθάριοι καὶ οἰκ., 128 οἱ οἰκειακοί (candidati, &c.),[1] and cp. Phil. 785₂₂. The σπαθάριοι, &c., who were under the Proto-spatharios τῶν βασιλικῶν were of course *not* οἰκειακοί, nor were the protospathars, &c., of the μαγλάβιον. On the other hand, the pro-tospathars, &c., of the Chrysotriklinos (Phil. 732₁₇, 733₁₉) probably were οἰκειακοί.

We also find the term used of κριταί, Phil. 733₂₀ οἱ σπαθαροκ. οἱ οἰκ. καὶ κριταί. But 732₁₈ οἱ πρωτοσπ. καὶ κρ., 735₂ οἱ σπαθ. καὶ κρ. These judges were doubtless those who were known later as the κριταὶ τοῦ βήλου or ἐπὶ τοῦ ἱπποδρόμου (Zachariä von L., *Geschichte des griechisch-röm. Rechts*, 358 *sqq.*). οἰκειακοί seems to be used to distinguish them from the κριταὶ τῶν ῥεγεώνων who were under the Prefect of the City.

The financial office ἐπὶ τῶν οἰκειακῶν, which was important in later times, was not instituted as early as the ninth century. The seal of Basil, a spathar who held this office, cannot be as early as Schlumberger thinks (*Sig.* 556).

I. Ἀξίαι διὰ βραβείων.

Of the eight orders by which the eunuchs of the Palace were graded, they shared two in common with *barbati*, namely, the proto-spathariate and the patriciate. The others are, as already observed, names of office which have become grades of rank.

(1) νιψιστιάριος	Insigne (βραβεῖον):	linen καμίσιον with purple embroidery.
(2) κουβικουλάριος	,,	καμίσιον edged with purple, and παραγαύδιον.
(3) σπαθαροκουβικουλάριος	,,	gold-handled sword.
(4) ὀστιάριος	,,	gold band with jewelled handle.
(5) πριμικήριος	,,	white tunic with gold broidered shoulder pieces.
(6) πρωτοσπαθάριος	,,	gold collar with jewels and pearls.
(7) πραιπόσιτος	,,	ivory tablets, not inscribed.
(8) πατρίκιος	,,	ivory inscribed tablets.

[1] The meaning of πρωτοοικειακοί, 124, is not clear. For a seal of a protosp. καὶ οἰκειακός see *Sig.* 558.

(1) νιψιστιάριοι.

The name of the νιψιστιάριοι shows that their function was to preside over the Imperial ablutions. See *Cer.* 9₁₇. The linen καμίσιον (chemise), which was their emblem of rank, was ὑποβλαττώμενον σχήματι φιαλίου, which I understand to mean, with the figure of a basin embroidered in purple.[1]

(2) κουβικουλάριοι.

The denotation of cubicularii has been explained above. When the palace staff was arranged in grades of dignity the general term κουβικουλάριοι was naturally appropriated to one of the lowest.

(3) σπαθαροκουβικουλάριοι.

We find among the cubicularii, in the sixth century, some who were also spatharii. Compare Theoph. 185₁₃ κουβικουλαρίους καὶ σπαθαρίους. Kalapodios (*ib.* 181₃₄) and Narses (*Chr. Pasch.* 626, *sub a.* 532) were such. These eunuch spathars were afterwards distinguished from other σπαθάριοι βασιλικοί by the compound σπαθαροκουβικουλάριοι[2] (cp. σπαθαροκανδιδάτοι, ἀνθυπατοπατρίκιοι). Cp. Conc. Const. IV (A. D. 869), Act 4 *init.*, Mansi, xvi. 329[3]; *Cer.* 148₂₃.

(4) ὀστιάριοι.

For the duties of the *ostiarii* (properly door-keepers) cp. *Cer.* 10₃, 172₂, &c.[4] In A.D. 787 we meet John, a βασιλικὸς ὀστιάριος, who holds the office of Logothete of the Stratiotikon (Mansi, xii. 1051). This is important, because it seems to prove that ὀστιάριος had become a title of rank as early as the eighth century. One of the ostiarii retained the original functions of the ost., see Phil. 706₄, ₈ ὁ βασιλικὸς ὀστιάριος. For seals of ostiarii, later than the ninth century, see Schlumberger, *Sig.* 560–1.

(5) πριμικήριοι.

We saw above that the old primicerius sacri cubiculi continued to exist as a distinct official. There was also a primicerius of the Empress's bedchamber: Eustathius, *Vita Eutychii*, c. 85 (Migne, *P. G.* 86. 2, p. 2372 τῷ πριμ. Αὐγούστης); a seal is preserved of Nikolaos, primicerius of the Empress Eudoxia in A.D. 1067 (*Sig.* 570).

---

[1] The Latin translation treats φιάλιον as = *cucullus*, a cowl.

[2] *Cer.* 244₁₃, the text has σπαθοκουβικουλάριοι.

[3] Gregorios σπαθαροκ. is here described as ἀπὸ τῶν τῆς συγκλήτου.

[4] There were special quarters in the Palace for the ostiarii, called the ὀστιαρίκιον, *Cer.* 802₂₂.

The domestic of the Great Palace was also called primicerius (see below under the Deuteros). The extension of the term to denote a rank is parallel to that of μάγιστρος. Ostiarii who had been raised to the grade of primicerii sometimes designated themselves by both titles: cp. the seal of a πριμ. βασιλικὸς καὶ ὀστ. καὶ ἐπὶ τῶν οἰκειακῶν in Sig. 138. This seems to be the meaning of ὀστιαροπριμικήριοι in Cer. 71₂₁ (not, as Lat. version gives, primicerii ostiariorum). For seals of primicerii see Sig. 407–8, 569–70. Cp. Cer. 259₂₄, 574₁₃.

(6) πρωτοσπαθάριοι.

The insigne of the eunuch protospathars is described as μανιάκιον, necklet, which probably differed in shape from the κλοιός, collar, of the other protospathars; the pearls which Philotheos mentions were probably a further differentiation. Moreover, the eunuch protospathars had a special dress which Philotheos describes, a white tunic adorned with gold, in the shape of a διβητήσιον, and a red doublet with gold facings. Cp. also Cer. 574₁₀.

(7) πραιπόσιτοι.

In the fifth to sixth centuries the Praepositus s. cubiculi was one of the highest officials in the Empire, following in rank the Prefects and the Magister Militum (Not. Dig., Or. 1. 9). Besides his duties in the Palace, as head of the cubicularii,[1] he was the minister in charge of the Imperial estates in Cappadocia. He exercised, doubt-less, control over the castrensis and the primicerius s. cub. (cp. Böcking, Comm. ad Not. Occ. vii a); but on account of the loss of pages in the MSS. of the Not. Dig. we are unable to determine the organization of the s. cubiculum. The three chartularii of the s. cub. (Justinian, Nov. 16, p. 114) were probably under the primicerius. The Praepositus seems (as was shown above, p. 79) to have been de-prived of his financial functions before the end of the sixth century.

There was also a praepositus of the Empress's bedchamber, cp. C. J. 12. 5. 3 and Peter Patr. (Cer. 418) οἱ δύο πραιπόσιτοι (A.D. 491).

In the seventh or eighth century πραιπόσιτος (like μάγιστρος) became an order of rank. This change was connected evidently with another. The chief officers of the cubicularii who had been under the Praepositus (protovestiarius, &c.) became independent of any higher control than the Emperor's. But the old Praepositus continued to preside over part of the cubiculum (see above, p. 120), and he had important

---

[1] Cp. Theoph. 246₁₇ πραιπόσιτος τῶν κουβικουλαρίων. He was himself considered a cubicularius, cp. Chron. Pasch. 610, sub a. 518.

ceremonial duties to perform. The ceremonial functions which had devolved in the fifth and sixth centuries on the magister officiorum [1] belonged in the ninth and tenth to the πραιπόσιτος in conjunction with the officer known as ὁ τῆς καταστάσεως. We find a second praepositus taking part in ceremonies: Cer. 245₁₄ (ὁ ἔνδον πραιπ., i.e. the *praepositus* who was in the Chrysotriklinos, cp. Bieliaev, 2. 202). The Praepositus, at the distribution of Imperial bounties, received, if he were a patrician, as much as the magistri (Phil. 784₄) and probably he was almost always a patrician (cp. 706₁₂ where ὁ πατρίκιος καὶ πρ. precedes the other eunuch patricians, who precede the ἀνθύπατοι), though not necessarily. Cp. 730₁₇ and 784₁₀ (where we should probably read τὸν πρωτοσπαθάριον καὶ πραιπόσιτον). Thus the Praepositus, although it is convenient to consider him here, more properly belongs under the higher grade of the patricians. He was sometimes distinguished from the other praepositi as ὁ πρωτοπραιπόσιτος (Cer. 527₆).[2] Schlumberger has published a seal (Sig. 568), Βασιλείῳ πραιποσίτ[ῳ], which he ascribes to the eighth or ninth century.

Under Basil I, Baanes the Praepositus was also Sakellarios. When Basil was absent on his expedition against Tephrike, Baanes acted as regent (ἀπομονεύς) in Constantinople, along with the chief Magister and the Prefect of the City: Constantine Porph. says that this used to be the customary arrangement (περὶ ταξ. 503. ὁ διέπων was another name for the ἀπομονεύς, ib. 504₄).

(8) πατρίκιοι.

The eunuch Patricians had precedence over the ἀνθύπατοι καὶ πατρίκιοι, Phil. 727₈, 730₁₃.

II. Ἀξίαι διὰ λόγου.

In his list of the offices which were appropriated to eunuchs, Philotheos names only the chiefs; he does not enumerate the subordinates. Many functionaries connected with the palace-service are mentioned in our sources, but in consequence of this omission of Philotheos it is difficult to place them.

(1) ὁ παρακοιμώμενος τοῦ δεσπότου.

Those of the κοιτωνῖται who slept adjacent to the Emperor's bed-room were called παρακοιμώμενοι: Theoph. 453₁₂ (A. D. 780), where

---

[1] In the ceremonies connected with the reception of foreign ambassadors, the Logothete of the Course took the place of the Mag. Off., and in the tenth century the Logothete replaced the Praepositus in some other ceremonies. Cp. Bieliaev, ii. 17.

[2] Photius, Ep. 122 Βαάνει πραιποσίτῳ καὶ πατρικίῳ.

three persons are designated as κουβικουλάριοι καὶ παρακοιμώμενοι. As it would always have been the duty of the chief of the κοιτωνῖται to sleep near the Emperor, he came to be called ὁ παρακοιμώμενος. The term occurs in Theoph. 285₁₇, under the reign of Maurice (A. D. 602). At that time he was subordinate to the Praepositus (Ducange is, of course, wrong s. v. in identifying him with the Praepositus). We may conjecture that Stephen, the sacellarius of Justinian II, was also the parakoimômenos ; Theoph. calls him πρωτοευνοῦχος (367). In the ninth century, the post was held by Scholastikos (an ostiarios) under Theophilus, and by Damianos (a patrician) under Michael III (*De adm. imp.* 231), who afterwards appointed Basil the Macedonian to this office, though it was supposed to be confined to eunuchs.[1] Under Basil the post was left vacant (*ib.*). Philotheos (784₅) calls the p. ὁ οἰκειακὸς παρακοιμώμενος τοῦ—βασιλέως.

The seals of Parakoimômenoi are rare, and later than the ninth century. See Schlumberger, *Sig.* 562.

(2) ὁ πρωτοβεστιάριος τοῦ δεσπότου.

The Protovestiarius descended from the old *comes sacrae vestis* of the fifth century. He presided over the private wardrobe (*sacra vestis*, οἰκειακὸν βεστιάριον) of the Emperor, to be distinguished from the public wardrobe which was under the Chartularius τοῦ βεστιαρίου (see above, p. 95).

This wardrobe was a store of much besides dress (see περὶ ταξ. 466 *sqq.*), and probably a treasury. It supplied the gratifications (ἀποκόμβια) which were given to the court officials at the Brumalia and on other occasions (cp. *Cer.* 605₁₄). There must have been a considerable staff, but we only know that the chief subordinate was ὁ πριμικήριος τοῦ βεστ. (περὶ ταξ. 466₈, cp. Leo, *Gramm.* 300₁₈).

For protovestiarii in the ninth century see Georg. Mon. 791 (Leo under Theophilus), 831 (Rentakios under Michael III), 845 (Prokopios, sent by Basil I on an expedition to Sicily), 855 (Theodosius, a patrician, under Leo VI)[2]. The second Basileus had a protovestiarius of his own (*ib.* 846), and likewise the Caesar (*ib.* 830). We also hear of a prot. of the Domestic of the Hikanatoi (*ib.* 847).

(3) ὁ ἐπὶ τῆς τραπέζης τοῦ δεσπότου.

The post of ὁ ἐπὶ τῆς τραπέζης or ὁ τῆς τ. was apparently important in the seventh century : in the *Acta Maximi*, c. 6, p. 120, we find

---

[1] See *De adm. imp.* 231₁₇ ; Cont. Th. 206₄.
[2] See also *Vita Euthymii*, ed. De Boor, i. 8, xiv. 1, viii. 10.

Sergios Eukratas ὁ ἐπὶ τῆς τ. τῆς βασιλικῆς taking part in an examination of Maximus. The full title seems to have been δομέστικος τῆς β. τραπέζης, see Mansi, xvi. 209 (A.D. 869) Λεοντίου τοῦ ἐνδοξοτάτου ἀπὸ ὑπάτων καὶ δομ. τῆς β.τ. In the reign of Leo VI we find Constantine ὁ τῆς τ. appointed to command a military expedition to South Italy (Cont. Th. 356$_{17}$).

Under this minister was probably ὁ δομέστικος τῆς ὑπουργίας (περὶ ταξ. 463$_9$, 464$_{10}$, 491$_8$, cp. Phil. 789$_1$). Cp. Theoph. 462$_{11}$ ἐξῆλθε πᾶσα ἡ βασιλικὴ ὑπουργία καὶ ἡ κόρτη ἕως Μαλαγίνων (A.D. 786) ; 390$_{16}$, 468 . ὑπουργικά=supellex, ib. 199$_{19}$, 303$_2$. We meet a νοτάριος τῆς ὑπουργίας in Leo Gramm. 303$_{18}$ (reign of Romanus I). Constantine, De adm. imp. 184, mentions Constantine, a protospathar, who was δομ. τῆς ὑπ., and afterwards became Great Hetaeriarch and ἀνθύπατος πατρίκιος.

The καστρήσιος (castrensis) probably also belongs here : Phil. 742$_{11}$, 744$_6$ ὁ τερπνὸς κ., 744$_{15}$ ὁ κλεινὸς κ.

The ἀτρικλῖναι are not to be placed here. The office seems not to have been confined to eunuchs (spatharocandidates Phil. 733$_{21}$), and they probably formed a distinct τάξις, possibly under the Praepositus.

(4) ὁ ἐπὶ τῆς τραπέζης τῆς Αὐγούστης.

This functionary among his other duties had the care of the private barques (ἀγράρια) of the Empress: De adm. imp. 235$_{19}$. Those of the Emperor were under the management of the πρωτοσπαθάριος τῆς φιάλης.

A seal is preserved of Nicetas Xylinites, who was ἐπὶ τῆς τραπέζης of Eudoxia, wife of Basil I. Suspected of an intrigue with his mistress he was tonsured (Georg. Mon. 843, ed. Bonn). He was πρωτοσπαθάριος καὶ ἐπὶ τῆς τραπέζης τῆς θεοστέπτου Αὐγούστης (Sig. 600). The incident shows that up to that time the office was not necessarily confined to eunuchs.

(5) ὁ παπίας τοῦ μεγάλου παλατίου.

The Papias [1] presided over all the service pertaining to the buildings of the Palace (the Great Palace, as distinguished from its adjuncts the Magnaura and the Daphne). He was responsible for the security of the doors and gates, and for all matters connected with cleaning, lighting, &c. The keys of the gates and doors were in his possession, and in the case of a Palace conspiracy a great deal might

---

[1] For the connexion of the name with παπᾶς, πάππας, πάππος, &c., cp. Bieliaev, i. 146, n.

depend upon his attitude.[1]   As a rule he probably held the rank of protospathar.[2]

Under the Papias were :

(1) διαιτάριοι, namely, οἱ διαιτάριοι τοῦ μεγάλου παλατίου (Cer. 800$_9$), or chamberlains-in-waiting, who had the care of the various rooms (δίαιται) in the Palace.   They served in weekly relays and were hence called ἑβδομάριοι.   Their chief was ὁ δομέστικος τοῦ μεγάλου παλατίου (Cer. 800$_{10}$; Bieliaev, i. 159).

(2) λουσταί (Phil. 724$_4$), who seem to have had the care of the baths (see Cer. 554$_{6-14}$, 555$_{18}$), and to include the βαλνιαρίτης and the πρωτεμβατάριος.

(3) κανδηλάπται (Phil. 724$_1$) had charge of the lighting of the Palace; there were special κανδηλάπται for the Lausiakos and the Triklinos of Justinian (724$_{5, 6}$).

(4) καμηνάδες (Phil. 724$_5$) had charge of the heating of the Palace, and seem to have been also called καλδάριοι (Cer. 800$_{18}$, 803$_2$).

(5) ὡρολόγοι (Phil. 724$_6$) attended to the clocks.[3]

(6) ζαράβαι (Phil. 724$_6$).   Their duties and the meaning of the word are uncertain.   Reiske (859) thinks that ζαράβης is derived from the Arabic zarrab=pulsator, and that their function was to sound a gong (σήμαντρον) to announce the hours of divine service, &c.

The Papias and his subordinates have been very fully discussed by Bieliaev, i. 145–63.

(6) ὁ δεύτερος τοῦ μεγάλου παλατίου.

The Deuteros was the assistant of the Papias, and took his place when he was ill, but was independent of him, and had subordinates ⟨ of his own.   His special province was the care of the Emperor's chairs and thrones (and probably the furniture) in the Chrysotriklinos, as well as the curtains in those apartments, and all the Imperial apparel and ornaments which were kept there.   See Phil. 724$_{11-}$.

His subordinates were :

(1) οἱ ἐπὶ τῶν ἀλλαξίμων (Phil. 724$_{13}$), the attendants who took care of the Emperor's apparel ('changes' of dress).

(2) οἱ βεστήτορες (Phil. 724$_{14}$), with their primicerii, arrayed the Emperor on ceremonial occasions (cp. Cer. 9, &c., &c.).

(3) οἱ ἐπὶ τῶν ἀξιωμάτων (Phil. 724$_{15}$), the keepers of the insignia and ceremonial dresses worn by persons who were invested with

---

[1] Compare the part he played in the overthrow of Leo V and elevation of Michael II (Georg. Mon., ed. Bonn, 678, &c.).

[2] This is suggested by the context of 784$_{14}$.

[3] Cp. Reiske, 559 ; Bieliaev, i. 162, n.   Constantine, περὶ ταξ. 472.

dignities. These σκεύη τῶν ἀξιωμάτων were kept in the Imperial wardrobes, some of them in the oratory of St. Theodore in the Chrysotriklinos (*Cer.* 640), of which the Deuteros kept the key (*Cer.* 623₇). Philotheos says (*ib.*) that these officials συνάγουσιν τὰ ἀξιώματα παρὰ τῶν λαμβανόντων τὰς ἀξίας, which is interpreted to mean that they collected the fees paid by the recipients of the orders or offices, but we should expect τὰς συνηθείας, not τὰ ἀξιώματα.

(4) οἱ διαιτάριοι. Phil. 724 ἐπέχει δὲ ὁ δεύτερος τὰ σελλία καὶ τοὺς διαιταρίους καὶ τὸν πριμικήριον αὐτῶν. Bieliaev (i. 180) thinks that these were distinct from the διαιτάριοι who were subordinate to the Papias, and this seems borne out by the words of Philotheos (724₂₁) συνάγεσθαι δὲ τοὺς ἀμφοτέρων διαιταρίους, where Bieliaev is obviously right in explaining, 'of both the Papias and the Deuteros.' But I suspect that the διαιτάριοι τοῦ μεγάλου παλατίου formed one τάξις and had one primikerios or domestic, who was at the disposal of both the Papias and Deuteros,[1] though some of the diaitarioi were appropriated to the duties over which the Deuteros specially presided. For these duties see further, *Cer.* 7₂.

For details see further, Bieliaev, i. 163–81.

(7) ὁ πιγκέρνης τοῦ δεσπότου, (8) ὁ πιγκέρνης τῆς Αὐγούστης.

The text of Philotheos has here, in the first case, ἐπιγκέρνης—a form (which occurs in other texts also, see Ducange, *s.v.* πιγκέρνης) evidently due to a false derivation from the preposition ἐπί.[2]

(9) ὁ παπίας τῆς Μανναύρας, (10) ὁ παπίας τῆς Δάφνης.

The Magnaura and the Daphne, though closely connected with the Great Palace, had each a Papias of its own. In the case of the Daphne this was an innovation made in the reign of Michael III, see Georg. Mon. 816, ed. Bonn ; and it is possible that the Magnaura, as well as the Daphne, was originally under the charge of the Papias of the Great Palace. The Domestic (of the διαιτάριοι) of Daphne, and the διαιτάριοι of Magnaura are mentioned, *Cer.* 800₁₀, ₁₇.

It is to be noticed that besides the διαιτάριοι of the Great Palace, of Magnaura, and of Daphne, there were other τάξεις of διαιτάριοι serving in various parts of the Palace : thus the δ. τοῦ κονσιστωρίου, δ. τοῦ ἁγίου Στεφάνου, δ. τῆς ὑπεραγίας Θεοτόκου, δ. τοῦ ὀστιαρικίου, δ. τοῦ στατωρικίου, δ. τῶν ιθ΄ ἀκουβίτων (*Cer.* 800).

---

[1] In Phil. 721₉, the prim. is called ὁ πριμ. αὐτοῦ, sc. τοῦ δευτέρου.

[2] The π. is mentioned in *Vita Euthymii*, x. 12.

I subjoin a list of officials mentioned by Philotheos, but not occurring in his lists of τάξεις and σέκρετα.   Most of them have already been discussed incidentally.

ὁ ἀδμηνσιονάλιος, see above under C. VII. 6.

ὁ ἀκτουάριος, see above under C. V. 1 and 2 ad fin.

ὁ ἄρχων τοῦ ἀρμαμέντου, see above under C. VII. 5 (2).

ὁ βάρβαρος, see above under C. IV. 4 ad fin.

ὁ δεκσογράφος, see above under C. III. 3.

ὁ μινσουράτωρ, 788$_{21}$.   Cer. 244$_{17}$ εἶτα λαβὼν τὸν θυμιατὸν ὁ μινσουράτωρ ἢ καὶ ὁ παπίας τοῦ παλ. τοῦ μεγάλου; again, 245$_{16}$ ὁ μ., if a eunuch, raises the curtain (cp. schol. ad loc.).   This official must be distinguished from the military μινσουράτωρες (who measured the ground for camps, computed road distances, &c.), frequently mentioned in tactical treatises (e.g. Leo, Tact. ix. 7).   He is mentioned in Gen. 125$_{22}$.

οἱ παραστάται τοῦ ἡλιακοῦ, Phil. 758$_{20}$, 774$_{5}$, cp. above under C. III. 3 (is the ἡλιακόν of the Chrysotriklinos meant?).

οἱ τοποτηρηταὶ τῶν χορῶν, Phil. 738$_{22}$.

ὁ χρυσοεψητής, see above under C. IV. 6 (4).

ΑΚΡΙΒΟΛΟΓΙΑ ΤΗΣ ΤΩΝ ΒΑΣΙΛΙΚΩΝ ΚΛΗΤΟΡΙΩΝ ΚΑΤΑ-
ΣΤΑΣΕΩΣ, ΚΑΙ ΕΚΑΣΤΟΥ ΤΩΝ ΑΞΙΩΜΑΤΩΝ ΠΡΟΣΚΛΗΣΙΣ
ΚΑΙ ΤΙΜΗ, ΣΥΝΤΑΧΘΕΙΣΑ ΕΞ ΑΡΧΑΙΩΝ ΚΛΗΤΟΡΟΛΟΓΙΩΝ
ΕΠΙ ΛΕΟΝΤΟΣ ΤΟΥ ΦΙΛΟΧΡΙΣΤΟΥ ΚΑΙ ΣΟΦΩΤΑΤΟΥ ΗΜΩΝ
ΒΑΣΙΛΕΩΣ, ΜΗΝΙ ΣΕΠΤΕΜΒΡΙΩι, ΙΝΔΙΚΤ. Γ´, ΕΤΟΥΣ ΑΠΟ
ΚΤΙΣΕΩΣ ΚΟΣΜΟΥ ͵ϚΥΗ´, ΥΠΟ ΦΙΛΟΘΕΟΥ ΒΑΣΙΛΙΚΟΥ
ΠΡΩΤΟΣΠΑΘΑΡΙΟΥ ΚΑΙ ΑΤΡΙΚΛΙΝΟΥ.

Ἐπειδήπερ ἡμᾶς προετρέψασθε, ὦ φίλων ἄριστοι, εἰς τὰ τῶν ἀρχαίων
ἐπικύμψαι συγγράμματα, κἀκεῖθεν τὸν προκείμενον νοῦν τῆς τῶν ἀξιωμάτων τάξεως σαφῆ τῷ λόγῳ ἀκριβῶς παραστήσασθαι, φέρε δὴ τῷ περὶ
ὑμᾶς ἑλκόμενοι πόθῳ, καθ᾽ ὅσον ἐφικτόν, τὰ ἐφετὰ τῆς ὑμετέρας ἀγάπης
σχετικῶς ἐκπληρώσωμεν. πολλῶν γὰρ ὄντων καὶ μεγάλων τῶν παρὰ
τοῖς ἀρχαίοις καταλειφθέντων ἀξιωμάτων, πολλή τε καὶ μεγάλη καὶ
δύσληπτος ἡ περὶ αὐτῶν ὑπάρχει σαφήνεια. καὶ γὰρ αἱ πολλαὶ τῶν
ἀξιωμάτων ἀμαυρωθεῖσαι τῷ χρόνῳ προσκλήσεις, ἀλλὰ μὴν καὶ πᾶσαι αἱ
μετ᾽ ἐκείνας ἐφευρεθεῖσαι ἀξιωμάτων διαφοραὶ σύγχυσίν τινα παρεισάγου-
σιν τῆς ἀκριβοῦς αὐτῶν καταλήψεως. καὶ ἐπειδὴ τὴν ἡμετέραν ἀμάθειαν 703
τῆς ἀκριβοῦς τούτων καταλήψεως τὴν συγγραφὴν ἐξῃτήσασθε, ὅσον τῷ
νῷ ἀμυδρῶς ἐκ τῶν πρώην ἐγκειμένων καὶ νῦν πραττομένων περιλαβεῖν
ἠδυνήθημεν, τῇ ὑμετέρᾳ φιλίᾳ περιφανῶς ἐκτιθέμεθα. εἰδέναι γὰρ ὑμᾶς
βουλόμεθα, ὦ φίλοι, ὅτι πᾶσα μὲν τεχνῶν ἐπιστήμη πρός τι εὔχρηστον
τέλος τῶν ἐν τῷ βίῳ συνέστηκεν. ἡ δὲ τῶν ἀρτικλιῶν ἐπιστήμη ἐν
οὐδενὶ ἄλλῳ τὸ εὔχρηστον δείκνυσιν, ἀλλ᾽ ἢ ἐν τῷ τάξει καὶ συστάσει καὶ
ἀκριβεῖ διαθέσει τὰς τῶν ἀξιωμάτων διαφορὰς διαστέλλειν. καὶ γὰρ πᾶσα
περιφάνεια βίου ἢ ἔνδοξος ἀξιωμάτων ἀξία ἐν οὐδενὶ ἄλλῳ τοῖς ὁρῶσιν
ἐνδείκνυται, ἀλλ᾽ ἢ ἐν τῇ κλήσει τῆς προκαθεδρίας τῆς ἐν τῇ λαμπρᾷ
τραπέζῃ καὶ περιποθήτῳ συνεστιάσει τῶν σοφωτάτων ἡμῶν βασιλέων.
εἰ δέ τις ἐκ τῆς ἡμῶν ἀπροσεξίας ἐπισφαλὴς προσγένηται σύγχυσις τοῖς
βασιλικοῖς κλητωρίοις, οὐ μόνον τὰς τῶν βασιλικῶν ἀξιωμάτων ἀρετὰς
καταριπτεῖ, ἀλλὰ καὶ ἡμᾶς αὐτοὺς καταγελάστους καὶ ἀχρείους τῆς διακονίας παρίστησιν. διὸ οὖν, ἀγαπητοί, δεῖ ἡμᾶς ἐν τῇ τοιαύτῃ λαχόντας
διακονίας προσοχῇ μελέτης καὶ ἐπιστήμης τὰς τῶν ἀξιωμάτων κυριοκλησίας ἐν τῷ οἰκείῳ νωῒ περιγράφειν, καὶ εἶθ᾽ οὕτως τὰς αὐτῶν διαιρέσεις
καὶ ὑποδιαιρέσεις καὶ ἀκριβεῖς συστάσεις ἐκφωνεῖν καὶ ἐκτίθεσθαι. ἀλλ᾽ 704

His compendiis usus sum : L = Lipsiensis, H = Hierosolymitanus, B = Bekkeri
ed. (Bonnensis), R = Reiskius.   702 1 ΚΛΗΤΩΡΙΩΝ B   3 ΚΛΗΤΩΡΟΛΟΓΙΩΝ B
6 ΚΤΗΣΕΩΣ L B : correxi   8 προετρέψασθαι L   τὰς L B   16 παρησάγουσιν L
703 22 συνέστικεν L   23 ἄλλο L   24 διαστέλει L

ἐπείπερ τὰς τῶν ἀρχαίων ἐκθέσεις οὐχὶ πάσας, ἀλλ᾽ ὅσας ὁ χρόνος ἀμαυ-
ρωθῆναι ἐποίησεν, ἑκόντι παρεδράμομεν, φέρε δὴ τὰς ἐπὶ τῶν βασιλέων
ἡμῶν, Λέοντος καὶ Ἀλεξάνδρου, γνωριζομένας τε ἅμα καὶ πραττομένας ὡς
ἐν πίνακος τάξει στιχηδὸν ὑποτάξομεν.   ποιῶμεν δὲ τοῦτο, οὐχ ὡς τὰς
τῶν ἀρχαίων συγγραφὰς ἀνατρέποντες, ἀλλὰ τὰς περὶ τούτων ἐκθέσεις ὡς
ἐν τάξει κανόνος τυπῶσαι σπουδάζοντες, ὅπως μὴ μόνον οἱ περὶ ταῦτα
ἐσχολακότες τὴν εὐχερῆ τούτων κατάληψιν ἔχωσιν, ἀλλὰ καὶ οἱ λίαν
ἀμαθεῖς τῷ μικρῷ τούτῳ κανόνι ἑπόμενοι εὐκατάληπτον καὶ σαφῆ τὴν περὶ
τὰς τάξεις εὑρίσκωσι πραγματείαν.   οὐ γὰρ δίκαιον ἐκρίναμεν τοὺς μὴ
ταῦτα ἀκριβῶς ἐξησκημένους ἐν τῇ τοιαύτῃ τετάχθαι βασιλικῇ λειτουργίᾳ,
ὅτι οὐδὲ ἀσόφῳ καὶ ἀμαθεῖ βασιλεῖ παρεστάναι ἡμεῖς εὐμοιρήσαμεν, ἀλλὰ
πάνυ γε σοφωτάτῳ καὶ λόγῳ καὶ ἔργῳ τῇ ἄνωθεν χάριτι τετιμημένῳ. διὰ
τοῦτο δὴ οὖν παρακαλῶ ὑμᾶς, ὦ φίλοι, καὶ πάντας τοὺς μέλλοντας μεθ᾽
ἡμᾶς εἰσιέναι, μὴ παρέργως καὶ ἀνωμάλως τὸ παρ᾽ ἡμῶν συγγραφὲν
ἐπισκέπτεσθαι λόγιον, ἀλλὰ προσοχῇ μελέτης τὸν ἐν αὐτῷ ἐγκείμενον
τύπον ἀκριβῶς ἀναμάττεσθαι· καὶ πρῶτον μὲν τὰς ἀκριβεῖς κυριοκλησίας
τῶν ἀξιωμάτων γνωρίζειν· δεύτερον δὲ τὰς τούτων διαιρέσεις καὶ ὑπο-
705 διαιρέσεις, αὐξήσεις τε καὶ μειώσεις, προσκλήσεις τε καὶ ὑποκλήσεις
ἀκριβῶς ποιεῖσθαι, καθὼς ὑποτέτακται.   τὰς γὰρ διὰ βραβείων διδομένας
ἀξίας κλίμακος ὑμῖν τάξει ἐξ ὀνόματος πάσας ἐκτέθεικα, εἶθ᾽ οὕτως τὰς
διὰ λόγου προσγινομένας ἐσήμανα, μετὰ δὲ ταύτας τὰς ταύταις ὑποκει-
μένας συνέταξα, τὰς μὲν κυρίας καὶ πρώτας τούτων προκρίνας τῷ λόγῳ,
τὰς δὲ ὑποτεταγμένας ἰδίως ἑκάστην ἐκτεθεικώς.   ἀλλὰ μὴν καὶ τὰς
τούτων τάξεις εὐδιαιρέτως ἐδήλωσα, καὶ ἑκάστης τὰ τούτων τὰ οἰκεῖα
πρέσβεια διὰ τοῦ τῇδε συγγράμματος σαφῶς καθιστόρησα, καὶ εὐσαφῆ
καὶ εὐκατάληπτον τὴν περὶ τούτων πραγματείαν, ὡς ἐν εἰσαγωγῆς τάξει,
τοῖς ἐντυγχάνουσι διὰ τῆς ὑποκειμένης πλινθίδος ἐγνώρισα, ἵνα οἱ ταύτην
τὴν πλινθίδα ἐπιμελῶς ἐποπτεύοντες μέμνησθε τῆς ἡμῶν μετριότητος
μηδαμῶς κατοκνήσειν.

⟨Τόμος α´.⟩

Ἀρχὴ τῆς ὑποθέσεως τοῦ λόγου.

Τῶν βασιλικῶν ἀξιωμάτων αἱ χάριτι Θεοῦ διδόμεναι δωρεαί, ὡς ἐκ
Θεοῦ τὴν ψῆφον λαμβάνουσαι, ἐπὶ τοῦ ἱεροῦ καὶ θαυμαστοῦ βασιλικοῦ
βήματος τοῦ λαμπροῦ χρυσοτρικλίνου ἐν αἰσίαις ἡμέραις παρὰ τῶν θεοπρο-
βλήτων βασιλέων τοῖς ἀξίοις βραβεύονται, δηλονότι παρεστώσης ἀπάσης
τῆς τάξεως τοῦ βασιλικοῦ κουβουκλείου καὶ αὐτῶν τῶν βραβείων προκει-
706 μένων πλησίον τῆς βασιλικῆς ἐξουσίας.   οἱ γὰρ μέλλοντες τυχεῖν τῆς
αὐτῶν ἀντιλήψεως ἤδη προευτρεπίζονται ὑπὸ τοῦ τεταγμένου βασιλικῶν
πρωτοσπαθαρίου ἔξω τοῦ βήλου ἐστολισμένοι ῥοαίοις σαγίοις.   ἐν δὲ τῇ

704 2 παρεδράμωμεν L   4 στιχηδὸν L   12 τετημημένῳ L   18 μιώσεις L
705 25 καθιστόρισα L B correxi   27, 28 πληνθίδος, -ίδα L   29 κατοκνήσειεν L
30 hic, ut conicio, supplendum ⟨τόμος α᾽⟩   35 παρεστάσις L   706 39 ἐστω-
λισμένοι L

τούτων εἰσαγωγῇ προσυνεισέρχονται τῷ βασιλικῷ ὀστιαρίῳ ὁμότιμοι τῶν
μελλόντων τυχεῖν ἀντιλήψεως ἄνδρες σπαθαροφόροι τρεῖς, καὶ τὸ σύνηθες
σέβας ποιήσαντες ἀναμένουσι πρὸς τὸ βῆλον ἑστῶτες τὴν τοῦ εἰσαγομένου
παρουσίαν, καὶ αὖθις τοῦ βήλου πετασθέντος, συνεισέρχεται τῷ βασιλικῷ
ὀστιαρίῳ ὁ τῶν βασιλικῶν πρωτοσπαθάριος εἰσάγων τὸν μέλλοντα τυχεῖν
ἀντιλήψεως, καὶ τοῦτον προτρεπόμενος τρισὶ τόποις ποιῆσαι τὴν προσκύ-
νησιν, ἵστησιν αὐτὸν κατὰ πρόσωπον τοῦ βασιλέως πρὸς τὸ ἐξ οἰκείων
χειρῶν αὐτοῦ λαβεῖν τὸ βραβεῖον τοῦ ἀξιώματος. καὶ μικρὸν αὐτὸν τὸν
τυχόντα διαστήσας ὀπισθοπόδως ὁ αὐτὸς πρωτοσπαθάριος περιβάλλει αὐτῷ
τὸ δοθὲν παρὰ τοῦ βασιλέως βραβεῖον, καὶ αὖθις αὐτὸν προσωθήσας
ἀσπάσασθαι ποιεῖ τοὺς ἱεροὺς πόδας τοῦ βασιλέως· καταχθέντος δὲ αὐτοῦ
πρὸς τοῖς κάτω, οἱ ὁμότιμοι τοῦ ἀξιώματος ἄνδρες ὡς ἰσότιμον εἰσ-
δεξάμενοι φίλον, τὸ σέβας πληροῦντες τὴν εὐχαριστείαν διὰ τῆς προσ-
κυνήσεως τῷ βασιλεῖ προσφωνοῦσι, καὶ συν⟨εξ⟩έρχεται τούτοις. ἡ δὲ
παρεστῶσα πάντων τῶν τοῦ κουβουκλείου ἀξία τὸν βασιλέα ἀξίως ἐπευ-
φημήσασα, καὶ αὐτὴ συνεξέρχεται τούτοις. εἰσάγονται δὲ πᾶσαι αἱ τῶν   707
διὰ βραβείων ἀξιωμάτων διαφοραὶ κατὰ τάξιν καὶ ἀριθμὸν τὸν ἤδη λε-
χθήσεσθαι μέλλοντα, καὶ τὰς συνηθείας παρέχειν ὀφείλοντας. καὶ γὰρ
αἱ μὲν αὐτῶν διὰ βραβείων παρέχονται, αἱ δὲ διὰ βασιλικοῦ λόγου
προσγίνονται, καὶ συνέπονται ταῖς διὰ βραβείων διδομέναις ἀξίαις, καὶ
αἱ μὲν αὐτῶν τὸ μόνιμον ἔχουσιν, αἱ δὲ ῥᾳδίως πάλιν ἀφαιρούμεναι ἐκ
προσώπων εἰς πρόσωπα διαβαίνουσιν.

Εἰσὶ δὲ πᾶσαι ὁμοῦ αἱ διὰ βραβείων διδόμεναι τὸν ἀριθμὸν ὀκτω-   Αἱ διὰ βρα-
βείων ἀξίαι
καίδεκα, αἵτινες ἅπαξ διδόμεναι οὐδαμῶς ἀναστρέφονται. διαιροῦνται δὲ   ιη′.
αὗται εἰς μέρη δύο, εἰς συγκλητικοὺς καὶ εἰς προελευσιμαίους.

Πόσαι διὰ λόγου.

Αἱ δὲ διὰ λόγου προσγινόμεναι ταύταις καὶ τὸ ἄρχειν ἐνδόξως λαμ-   αἱ διὰ λόγου
ξ′.
βάνουσαί εἰσι καὶ αὐταὶ πᾶσαι τὸν ἀριθμὸν ξ′, αἵτινες ἀφαιρούμεναι,
ὥσπερ ἔφαμεν, ἐκ προσώπων εἰς πρόσωπα βασιλικῷ λόγῳ μετέρχονται.
διαιροῦνται δὲ καὶ αὗται εἰς μέρη ἕξ, οἷον εἰς στρατηγούς, εἰς δομεστίκους,
εἰς κριτάς, εἰς σεκρετικούς, εἰς δημοκράτας, εἰς ἴδια ὀφφίκια.

Περὶ ἀξιωμάτων βασιλικῶν εἰς τοὺς προβαθμίους.   708

Τῶν δὲ κυρίως ἀξιωμάτων τῶν διὰ βραβείων παρεχομένων αἱ κυριο-
κλησίαι, εἰς ἃς καὶ ὀφείλουσιν δοῦναι συνηθείας, εἰσὶν αὗται.   κεφάλαιον
πρώτη μὲν τῶν ἄλλων ἁπάντων ὡς προβάθμιος τὴν εἰσαγωγὴν τῶν   α′
ἀξιωμάτων λαμβάνουσα ἡ τοῦ στρατηλάτου ἐπὶ θεμάτων ἀξία, ἤτοι
ἡ ἀπὸ ἐπάρχων ὀνομαζομένη, ἧς βραβεῖον, ἐγγεγραμμένος χάρτης, διὰ

---

1 προσυνησέρχοντα L   4 συρέντος coni. R   7 οἰκίων L   10 προσοθήσας L
14 συνέρχεται L : corr. R   τούτοις scripsi : τούτῳ L   707 23 αἱ ... ιή quasi
titulum in textu exhibet B   ὀκτοκαίδεκα L   25 προσελευσιμαίους L B correxi
27 αἱ ... ἕξ quasi titulum B   28 τῶν ἀριθμῶν L   708 32 hic inserit Τόμος α′ B
35 numeros in marg. non exhibet B   36 ἀξία scripsi : ἀξίων L B

βασιλικῆς χειρὸς ἐπιδίδοται. δίδωσι συνήθειαν τῷ πρωτοασήκρητις ,, κδ', τοῖς πραιποσίτοις ,, λς'.

β' δευτέρα δὲ ἡ τῶν σιλεντιαρίων, ἧς βραβεῖον, χρυσᾶ ῥάβδος, διὰ βασιλικῆς χειρὸς ἐπιδίδοται. δίδωσι συνήθειαν τῷ δευτέρῳ ,, ς', τοῖς πραιποσίτοις ,, οβ'.

γ' τρίτη ἡ τῶν βεστητόρων ἀξία, ἧς βραβεῖον, τὸ φιβλατώριον, διὰ βασιλικῆς χειρὸς ἐπιδίδοται. δίδει συνήθειαν τοῖς πραιποσίτοις ,, κδ', τῷ δευτέρῳ ,, ς'.

δ' τετάρτη ἡ τῶν βασιλικῶν μανδατόρων ἀξία, ἧς βραβεῖον, ῥάβδος ἐρυθροδανωμένη, ἐκ χειρὸς βασιλικῆς ἐπιδίδοται. δίδωσι συνήθειαν τῷ πρωτοσπαθαρίῳ τῶν βασιλικῶν ,, ς', τοῖς πραιποσίτοις ,, ς'.

ε' πέμπτη ἡ τῶν κανδιδάτων ἀξία, ἧς βραβεῖον, μανιάκιον χρυσοῦν τρίκομβον μέχρι τέρνων κεχαλασμένον, διὰ χειρὸς βασιλικῆς ἐπιδίδοται. δίδωσι συνήθειαν τῷ παπίᾳ καὶ τῷ δευτέρῳ ,, β', τῷ παπίᾳ τῆς Δάφνης ,, β', τοῖς πραιποσίτοις ,, ς'.

709 ς' ἕκτη ἡ τῶν στρατόρων ἀξία, ἧς βραβεῖον, φραγέλιον χρυσοῦν ἐκ λίθων τιμίων κεκοσμημένον, ἐκ χειρὸς βασιλέως ἐπιδίδοται. δίδωσι συνήθειαν τῷ παπίᾳ καὶ τῷ δευτέρῳ ,, β', τοῖς πραιποσίτοις ,, δ'.

ζ' ἑβδόμη ἡ τῶν ὑπάτων ἀξία, ἧς βραβεῖον, χάρτης ἐγγεγραμμένος, διὰ βασιλικῆς χειρὸς ἐπιδίδοται. δίδωσι συνήθειαν τῷ πρωτασήκρητις ,, ς', τοῖς πραιποσίτοις ,, ιβ', τῷ παπίᾳ καὶ τῷ δευτέρῳ ,, ς'.

η' ὀγδόη ἡ τῶν σπαθαρίων ἀξία, ἧς βραβεῖον, σπάθη χρυσόκανος, ἐκ βασιλικῆς χειρὸς ἐπιδίδοται. δίδωσι συνήθειαν τῷ κατεπάνω ,, ς', τῷ δομεστίκῳ τῶν βασιλικῶν δ', τοῖς σπαθαρίοις ,, ιβ', τῷ παπίᾳ καὶ τῷ δευτέρῳ ,, β'.

θ' ἐννάτη ἡ τῶν σπαθαροκανδιδάτων ἀξία, ἧς βραβεῖον, μανιάκιον χρυσοῦν κεχαλασμένον κεκοσμημένον ἐκ περιλεύκιος, ἐκ βασιλικῆς χειρὸς ἐπιδίδοται. δίδωσι συνήθειαν τῷ παπίᾳ καὶ τῷ δευτέρῳ ,, δ', τῷ τῆς καταστάσεως ,, ιβ', τῷ δομεστίκῳ τῶν βασιλικῶν ,, γ', τοῖς σπαθαροκανδιδάτοις ,, ιβ'.

ι' δεκάτη ἡ τῶν δισυπάτων ἀξία, ἧς βραβεῖον, χάρτης ἐγγεγραμμένος, ἐκ βασιλικῆς χειρὸς ἐπιδίδοται. δίδει συνήθειαν τοῖς πραιποσίτοις ,, ιβ', τῷ πρωτοασήκρητις ,, ς', τῷ παπίᾳ καὶ τῷ δευτέρῳ ,, ς'.

ια' ἑνδεκάτη ἡ τῶν πρωτοσπαθαρίων ἀξία, ἧς βραβεῖον, κλοιὸς χρυσοῦς περὶ τὸν αὐχένα ἐκ λίθων τιμίων κεκοσμημένος, διὰ χειρὸς βασιλέως ἐπισυγκλείεται. δίδωσι συνήθειαν τοῖς πρωτοσπαθαρίοις εὐνούχοις κδ', τοῖς πρωτοσπαθαρίοις βαρβάτοις ,, κδ', τῷ κατεπάνω ,, ιη', τῷ δομεστίκῳ τῶν 710 βασιλικῶν ,, ς', τῷ παπίᾳ καὶ τῷ δευτέρῳ ,, ς'. εἰ δὲ εἰς τὸν χρυσοτρίκλινον παραδοθῇ, τῷ παπίᾳ δίδωσι ,, κδ'. ἰστέον δέ, ὅτι καί, δήμαρχος εἰ τιμηθῇ ἐξ αὐτῶν τις, δίδει τοῖς πραιποσίτοις ,, οβ'. ὁμοίως καὶ ὁ τῆς καταστάσεως τοῖς αὐτοῖς πραιποσίτοις ,, οβ'.

ιβ' δωδεκάτη ἡ τῶν περιβλέπτων πατρικίων ἀξία, ἧς βραβεῖον, πλάκες

---

3 σελεντιαρίων L et sic ubique   7 δίδι L   709 23 κατεδομεστίκῳ L: corr. R
25 χρυσοῦ L   30 δίδι L   32 κλυὸς L, οι suprascr. man. rec.   710 37 τιμηθῇ L
38 δίδι L   40 πλάκαις L

ἐλεφάντιναι κεκοσμημέναι σὺν κωδικέλλοις ἐγγεγραμμένοις εἰς τύπον τοῦ
νόμου, ἐκ βασιλικῆς χειρὸς ἐπιδίδονται. παρέχει δὲ τοῖς κοιτωνίταις, εἰ
ἄρα καὶ μηνυθῇ, λίτρας β΄. εἰς δὲ τὸ ἀποκόμβιον τοῖς πραιποσίτοις σὺν
τοῦ κουβουκλείου καὶ τοῖς λοιποῖς χρυσοῦ λίτρας η΄. ταῦτα δὲ ὀφφικιάλιος
καὶ στρατηγὸς δίδωσιν. ὁ δὲ ἄπρατος δίδει λίτρας ζ΄, καὶ τῷ τῆς καταστάσεως ἄνευ τοῦ ὀψικίου ,, ιβ΄, τὸ ὀψίκιον ,, π΄, τῷ δευτέρῳ ὑπὲρ τῶν
πλακῶν ,, κδ΄, καὶ εἰς τὰ ταβλία τοῦ χλανιδίου ,, κδ΄, τῷ κανικλείῳ ὑπὲρ τοῦ
κωδικέλλου ,, ιϛ΄, εἰς τὴν ἁγίαν Σοφίαν ,, λϛ΄.

τρισκαιδεκάτη ἡ τῶν ἀνθυπάτων ἀξία, ἧς βραβεῖον, κωδίκελλοι ἀλουρ- ιγ΄
γοειδεῖς γεγραμμένοι, ἐκ βασιλικῆς χειρὸς ἐπιδίδονται. δίδωσι συνήθειαν
τὸν τοῦ κανικλείου ,, η΄, καὶ τῷ δευτέρῳ ,, δ΄, καὶ τοῖς πραιποσίτοις ,, κδ΄.

τεσσαρεσκαιδεκάτη ἡ τῶν ἐνδοξοτάτων μαγίστρων ἀξία, ἧς βραβεῖον, ιδ΄
χιτὼν λευκὸς ὢν χρυσοΰφαντος, καὶ ἐπωμὶς χρυσόταβλος, καὶ ζώνη δερ-
ματίνη κόκκινος ἐκ λίθων τιμίων κεκοσμημένη, ἥτις λέγεται βαλτίδιν, ἐπὶ
τοῦ κονσιστορίου ἐκ βασιλικῆς χειρὸς ἐπιδίδοται. δίδωσι συνήθειαν τῷ 711
τῆς καταστάσεως τὸ καμίσιν αὐτοῦ, τοῖς δὲ πραιποσίτοις καὶ μαγίστροις
συνεστιᾶται παρέχων αὐτοῖς καὶ δόματα ἱματίων. συνήθειαν δὲ τοῖς πραιποσίτοις καὶ μαγίστροις καὶ λοιποῖς τὴν τοῦ πατρικίου διπλῆν συνήθειαν
παρέχει.

πεντεκαιδεκάτη ἡ τῆς ζωστῆς πατρικίας ἀξία, ἧς βραβεῖον, πλάκες ιε΄
ἐλεφάντιναι ὁμοίως τοῖς πατρικίοις, ἐκ χειρὸς βασιλέως ἐπιδίδοται. δίδωσι
συνήθειαν τοῖς βασιλικοῖς κληρικοῖς ,, κδ΄, τῷ δευτέρῳ ,, κδ΄, τοὺς κοιτωνίτας
λίτρας γ΄, τὸ κουβούκλειον σὺν τοῖς πραιποσίτοις μόνοις χρυσοῦ λίτρας γ΄
καὶ τὸ στιχάριν αὐτῆς τῷ πραιποσίτῳ. τῷ τῆς τραπέζης τῆς αὐγούστης
μετὰ τὴν πρωτοβεστιαρίαν καὶ τὴν πριμικήρισσαν καὶ τὰς κοιτωνιτίσσας
καὶ κουβουκλαρέας λίτρας β΄.

ἑξκαιδεκάτη ἡ τοῦ κουροπαλάτου ἀξία, ἧς βραβεῖον, χιτὼν κόκκινος ιϛ΄
χρυσοποίκιλος καὶ χλαμὺς καὶ ζώνη, ἐκ χειρὸς βασιλέως ἐπὶ ναοῦ Κυρίου
λαμπρῶς ἐπιδίδοται. δίδωσι συνήθειαν τὴν τοῦ μαγίστρου διπλήν, τῷ
δευτέρῳ λίτραν α΄, παρέχων πᾶσιν ἀντιλήψεις καὶ ἀναβιβασμούς.

ἑπτακαιδεκάτη ἡ τοῦ νωβελησίμου ἀξία, ἧς βραβεῖον, χιτὼν ἐξ ιζ΄
ἀλουργίδος χρυσόθετος καὶ χλαμὺς καὶ ζώνη, ἐκ χειρὸς βασιλέως ἐπὶ ναοῦ
Κυρίου λαμπρῶς ἐπιδίδοται. δίδωσι συνήθειαν καθὼς καὶ ὁ κωροπαλάτης.

ὀκτωκαιδεκάτη ἡ τοῦ καίσαρος ἀξία, παρομοία τῆς βασιλικῆς δόξης, ἧς ιη΄ 712
βραβεῖον, στέφανος χωρὶς σταυρικοῦ τύπου, ἐπὶ ναοῦ Κυρίου ἐκ βασιλικῆς
χειρὸς ἐπὶ κορυφῆς ἐπιτίθεται. δίδωσι συνήθειαν, ὡς καὶ ὁ νωβελήσιμος.

Ὁ δὲ γεγονὼς αὐτοκράτωρ βασιλεὺς δίδωσιν εἰς τὴν ἁγίαν τοῦ   συνήθεια
Θεοῦ μεγάλην ἐκκλησίαν χρυσοῦ λίτρας ρ΄, καὶ τῇ συγκλήτῳ πάσῃ σὺν   εὐσεβείας.
                                                   ὁ αὐτοκράτωρ.

7 κανικλήῳ L   13 ἐπιμὶς L   15 χρυσοστορίου L correxit Bieliaev I 117
(cf. Cer. 232₁₅)   711 15 τῷ L   16 καμίσιον B   17 δώματα L   20 πλάκαις ἐλε-
φάντινε L   21 ἐπιδίδοται L   δίδοσι L   24 στιχάριον B   25 κοιτωνιτήσας L
29 δίδοσι L   712 37 adnotationem marginalem quasi titulum in textu exhibet B

τῷ τοῦ κουβουκλείου καὶ λοιποῖς χρυσοῦ λίτρας ρ΄, καὶ χιλιάδας διαφόρους μιλιαρησίων ἑκάστῳ τάγματι καὶ ὀφφικίων τῇ συστάσει. τοῖς δὲ πραιποσίτοις ἐν ἐξαιρέτῳ ὀφφίκια δίδωσιν καὶ ἀντιλήψεις ἀξιωμάτων εἰς ἰδίους καὶ ἀνθρώπους αὐτῶν, καὶ ἀναβιβασμοὺς αὐτῶν τῶν πραιποσίτων, καθὼς ἂν αἰτήσονται, λαμβάνουσιν.

ὁ μικρός.   ὁ δέ γε δεύτερος βασιλεὺς δίδωσι τὸ ἥμισυ τούτων.

ἐκ δὲ τῶν προλεχθέντων ἀξιωμάτων αἱ μὲν πέντε ἄξιαι τῇ συγκλήτῳ ἁρμόζονται, οἷον ἡ ἀπὸ ἐπάρχων, ἡ τῶν σιλεντιαρίων, ἡ τῶν βεστητόρων, ἡ τῶν ὑπάτων καὶ δισυπάτων. αἱ δὲ λοιπαὶ πᾶσαι ἐν τοῖς βασιλικοῖς κατατάττονται κώδιξιν.

(Dignitates per edictum lx.)

αἱ δὲ διὰ λόγου βασιλικοῦ τοῖς ἀξίοις προσγινόμεναι δόξαι καὶ εἰς τὸ ἄρχειν τῶν ὑποτεταγμένων ἀφορισθεῖσαί εἰσι καὶ αὐταὶ τὸν ἀριθμὸν ξ΄, αἵτινες, ὡς ἔφαμεν, λόγῳ βασιλέως προσγινόμεναι, πάλιν ῥᾳδίως ἀφαιροῦνται καὶ ἐκ προσώπων εἰς πρόσωπα μεθίστανται.

713   [α΄] καὶ πρώτη μὲν καὶ μεγίστη ἡ τοῦ βασιλεοπάτορος παρὰ Λέοντος τοῦ φιλοχρίστου ἡμῶν βασιλέως ἐκφωνηθεῖσα ἀξία·

β΄ ἡ τοῦ ῥαίκτωρος ἀξία·

γ΄ ἡ τοῦ συγκέλλου·

δ΄ ἡ τοῦ στρατηγοῦ τῶν Ἀνατολικῶν ἀξία·

ε΄ ἡ τοῦ δομεστίκου τῶν σχολῶν·

ϛ΄ ἡ τοῦ στρατηγοῦ τῶν Ἀρμενιάκων·

ζ΄ ἡ τοῦ στρατηγοῦ τῶν Θρακησίων·

η΄ ἡ τοῦ κόμητος τοῦ Ὀψικίου·

θ΄ ἡ τοῦ στρατηγοῦ τῶν Βουκελλαρίων·

ι΄ ἡ τοῦ στρατηγοῦ Καππαδοκίας·

ια΄ ἡ τοῦ στρατηγοῦ Χαρσιανοῦ·

ιβ΄ ἡ τοῦ στρατηγοῦ Κολωνίας·

ιγ΄ ἡ τοῦ στρατηγοῦ Παφλαγωνίας·

ιδ΄ ἡ τοῦ στρατηγοῦ τῆς Θρᾴκης·

ιε΄ ἡ τοῦ στρατηγοῦ Μακεδονίας·

ιϛ΄ ἡ τοῦ στρατηγοῦ Χαλδίας·

ιζ΄ ἡ τοῦ δομεστίκου τῶν ἐξσκουβίτων ἀξία·

ιη΄ ἡ τοῦ ἐπάρχου πόλεως ἀξία·

ιθ΄ ἡ τοῦ στρατηγοῦ Πελοποννήσου·

κ΄ ἡ τοῦ στρατηγοῦ Νικοπόλεως·

κα΄ ἡ τοῦ στρατηγοῦ τῶν Κιβυρραιωτῶν·

κβ΄ ἡ τοῦ στρατηγοῦ Ἑλλάδος·

κγ΄ ἡ τοῦ στρατηγοῦ Σικελίας·

κδ΄ ἡ τοῦ στρατηγοῦ Στρυμόνος·

2 ἑκάστο L   3 ἐξερέτω L   6 notas marginales, quae desunt in B, ex codice addidi   713 35 Πελοπονήσου L

κε΄ ἡ τοῦ στρατηγοῦ Κεφαληνίας·
κϛ΄ ἡ τοῦ στρατηγοῦ Θεσσαλονίκης·
κζ΄ ἡ τοῦ στρατηγοῦ τοῦ Δυρραχίου·
κη΄ ἡ τοῦ στρατηγοῦ τῆς Σάμου·
5 κθ΄ ἡ τοῦ στρατηγοῦ τοῦ Αἰγέου πελάγους·
λ΄ ἡ τοῦ στρατηγοῦ Δαλματίας·
λα΄ ἡ τοῦ στρατηγοῦ Χερσῶνος·
λβ΄ ἡ τοῦ σακελλαρίου·
λγ΄ ἡ τοῦ λογοθέτου τοῦ γενικοῦ·
10 λδ΄ ἡ τοῦ κυαίστωρος ἀξία·
λε΄ ἡ τοῦ λογοθέτου τοῦ στρατιωτικοῦ·
λϛ΄ ἡ τοῦ δρουγγαρίου τῆς βίγλας·
λζ΄ ἡ τοῦ λογοθέτου τοῦ δρόμου ἀξία·
λη΄ ἡ τοῦ δρουγγαρίου τῶν πλοΐμων·
15 λθ΄ ἡ τοῦ πρωτοσπαθαρίου τῶν βασιλικῶν·
μ΄ ἡ τοῦ λογοθέτου τῶν ἀγελῶν·
μα΄ ἡ τοῦ δομεστίκου τῶν ἱκανάτων·
μβ΄ ἡ τοῦ δομεστίκου τῶν νουμέρων·
μγ΄ ἡ τοῦ δομεστίκου τῶν ὀπτημάτων·
20 μδ΄ ἡ τοῦ κόμητος τῶν τειχέων·
με΄ ἡ τοῦ χαρτουλαρίου τοῦ σακελλίου·
μϛ΄ ἡ τοῦ χαρτουλαρίου τοῦ βεστιαρίου·
μζ΄ ἡ τοῦ χαρτουλαρίου τοῦ κανικλείου·
μη΄ ἡ τοῦ πρωτοστράτορος·
25 μθ΄ ἡ τοῦ πρωτοασήκρητις ἀξία·
ν΄ ἡ τοῦ ἐκ προσώπου τῶν θεμάτων·
να΄ ἡ τοῦ κόμητος τοῦ στάβλου·
νβ΄ ἡ τοῦ εἰδικοῦ·
νγ΄ ἡ τοῦ μεγάλου κουράτωρος·
30 νδ΄ ἡ τοῦ κουράτωρος τῶν Μαγγάνων·
νε΄ ἡ τῶν δεήσεων·
νϛ΄ ἡ τοῦ ὀρφανοτρόφου·
νζ΄ ἡ τοῦ δημάρχου Βενέτων·
νή ἡ τοῦ δημάρχου Πρασίνων·
35 νθ΄ ἡ τοῦ τῆς καταστάσεως·
ξ΄ ἡ τοῦ δομεστίκου τῶν βασιλικῶν.
καὶ αὗται τὰ νῦν τιμηθεῖσαι ἀξίαι ἐπὶ Λέοντος δεσπότου.

(Classes vii dignitatum supradictarum.)

διαιροῦνται οὖν αὗται πᾶσαι εἰς μέρη ἑπτά, οἷον εἰς στρατηγούς, εἰς
40 δομεστίκους, εἰς κριτάς, εἰς σεκρετικούς, εἰς δημοκράτας, εἰς στρατάρχας
καὶ εἰς εἰδικὰς μόνας ἀξίας.

5 Αἰγαίου Β

714

(I. στρατηγοί 26)

ὅσαι ἐν ταῖς τῶν στρατηγῶν κατατάττονται τάξεις εἰσὶ τὸν ἀριθμὸν κϛ'· ὁ στρατηγὸς τῶν Ἀνατολικῶν· ὁ στρατηγὸς τῶν Ἀρμενιάκων· ὁ στρατηγὸς τῶν Θρᾳκησίων· ὁ κόμης τοῦ Ὀψικίου· ὁ στρατηγὸς τῶν Βουκελλαρίων· ὁ στρατηγὸς Καππαδοκίας· ὁ στρατηγὸς Χαρσιανοῦ· ὁ στρατηγὸς Κολωνείας· ὁ στρατηγὸς Παφλαγωνίας· ὁ στρατηγὸς τῆς Θρᾴκης· ὁ στρατηγὸς Μακεδονίας· ὁ στρατηγὸς Χαλδίας. αὗται οὖν αἱ στρατηγίαι

715 τοῖς Ἀνατολικοῖς θέμασιν ⟨συν⟩αριθμοῦνται. αἱ δὲ τῆς δύσεώς εἰσιν αὗται· ὁ στρατηγὸς Πελοποννήσου· ὁ στρατηγὸς Νικοπόλεως· ὁ στρατηγὸς Κιβυρραιωτῶν· ὁ στρατηγὸς Ἑλλάδος· ὁ στρατηγὸς Σικελίας· ὁ στρατηγὸς Στρυμόνος· ὁ στρατηγὸς Κεφαληνίας· ὁ στρατηγὸς Θεσσαλονίκης· ὁ στρατηγὸς τοῦ Δυρραχίου· ὁ στρατηγὸς τῆς Σάμου· ὁ στρατηγὸς τοῦ Αἰγέου πελάγους· ὁ στρατηγὸς Δαλματίας· ὁ στρατηγὸς Χερσῶνος καὶ οἳ ἐκ προσώπου εἰσὶ τῶν θεμάτων.

(II. δομέστικοι 7)

αἱ δὲ εἰς δομεστίκους ταττόμεναί εἰσι τὸν ἀριθμὸν ζ', οἷον ὁ δομέστικος τῶν σχολῶν, ὁ δομέστικος τῶν ἐξσκουβίτων, ὁ δρουγγάριος τοῦ ἀριθμοῦ, ὁ δομέστικος τῶν ἱκανάτων, ὁ δομέστικος τῶν νουμέρων, ὁ δομέστικος τῶν ὀπτημάτων, ὁ δομέστικος τῶν τειχέων, οἳ καὶ ὀφφικιάλιοι λέγονται.

(III. κριταὶ 3)

οἱ δὲ εἰς κριτὰς λογιζόμενοί εἰσι τὸν ἀριθμὸν γ', οἷον ὁ ἔπαρχος πόλεως, ὁ κυέστωρ, ὁ τοῦ δεήσεως.

(IV. σεκρετικοί 11)

αἱ δὲ εἰς σέκρετα καθεζόμεναί εἰσι καὶ αὗται τὸν ἀριθμὸν ια', οἷον ὁ σακελλάριος, ὁ λογοθέτης τοῦ γενικοῦ, ὁ λογοθέτης τοῦ στρατιωτικοῦ, ὁ λογοθέτης τοῦ δρόμου, ὁ χαρτουλάριος τοῦ σακελλίου, ὁ χαρτουλάριος τοῦ βεστιαρίου, ὁ πρωτοασήκρητις, ὁ τοῦ εἰδικοῦ, ὁ μέγας κουράτωρ, ὁ τῶν μαγγάνων, ὁ ὀρφανοτρόφος.

(V. δημοκράται 2)

αἱ δὲ εἰς δημοκράτας εἰσὶ τὸν ἀριθμὸν δύο, οἷον ὁ δήμαρχος Βενέτων καὶ ὁ δήμαρχος Πρασίνων.

(VI. στρατάρχαι 5)

αἱ δὲ εἰς στρατάρχας εἰσὶ καὶ αὗται τὸν ἀριθμὸν ε', οἷον ὁ ἑταιρειάρχης, ὁ δρουγγάριος τοῦ πλοΐμου, ὁ λογοθέτης τῶν ἀγελῶν, ὁ πρωτοσπαθάριος τῶν βασιλικῶν, ὁ κόμης τοῦ στάβλου.

(VII. εἰδικαὶ ἀξίαι 7)

716

αἱ δὲ εἰς εἰδικὰς μόνας ἀξίας εἰσὶ καὶ αὗται τὸν ἀριθμὸν ζ', οἷον ὁ βασιλεοπάτωρ, ὁ ῥαίκτωρ, ὁ σύγκελλος, ὁ χαρτουλάριος τοῦ κανικλείου, ὁ πρωτοστράτωρ, ὁ τῆς καταστάσεως, ὁ δομέστικος τῶν βασιλικῶν.

(OFFICIA.)

Αἱ δὲ ὑποτεταγμέναι ἑκάστῃ τούτων ἀρχῇ αἱ καὶ συνεπόμεναι αὐταῖς εἰσιν ἐξ ὀνόματος αὗται.

Ὑποπέπτωκεν δὲ ἑκάστῃ τούτων ἀξιωμάτων ἀρχῇ εἴδη ἀξιωμάτων διάφορα κατὰ ἀναλογίαν καὶ τάξιν καὶ τῆς ἑκάστου προελεύσεως, ἃ καὶ αὐτὰ

714 7 ⟨συν⟩αριθμοῦνται scripsi : ἀριθμοῦνται L   715 8 πελοπονήσου L   12 Αἰγαίου B   13 οἳ scripsi (sed fort. del. εἰσὶ) : οἱ L   θεμάτων scripsi : σχολῶν L   17 ὀπτημάτων L   31 τῶν ἀριθμῶν L   716 36 αὗτα L

ὀφφίκια ὀνομάζονται.   διαιροῦνται δὲ καὶ αὐτὰ εἰς μέρη τρία· εἰς ταγ-
ματικούς, εἰς θεματικοὺς καὶ εἰς συγκλητικούς.

τῷ γὰρ στρατηγῷ τῶν Ἀνατολικῶν ὑποπίπτουσιν κατὰ βαθμὸν εἴδη 1. Strategi
ἀξιωμάτων ια′, οἷον

1 τουρμάρχαι,	7 κόμητες ὁμοίως,
2 μεριάρχης,	8 κένταρχος τῶν σπαθαρίων,
3 κόμης τῆς κόρτης,	9 κόμης τῆς ἑταιρείας,
4 χαρτουλάριος τοῦ θέματος,	10 πρωτοκαγκελλάριος,
5 δομέστικος τοῦ θέματος,	11 πρωτομανδάτωρ.
6 δρουγγάριοι τῶν βάνδων,	

Orientalium officium.

τῷ δὲ δομεστίκῳ τῶν σχολῶν ὑποπίπτουσιν κατὰ βαθμὸν εἴδη ἀξιω- 2. Domestici
μάτων ι′, οἷον   scholarum.

1 βαθμοῦ πρώτου, τοποτηρητής,	6 προτίκτορες,
2 ⟨β′⟩ δύο κόμητες τῶν σχολῶν,	7 εὐτυχοφόροι,
3 γ′ χαρτουλάριος,	8 σκηπτροφόροι,
4 δ′ δομέστικοι,	9 ἀξιωματικοί,
5 προέξημος,	10 μανδάτορες.

τῷ δὲ στρατηγῷ τῶν Ἀρμενιακῶν ὑποπίπτουσι καὶ αὐτῷ εἴδη ἀξιωμάτων 717
κατὰ βαθμόν, ὅσα καὶ τῷ στρατηγῷ τῶν Ἀνατολικῶν, καὶ καθεξῆς ταῖς 3–13, 16-28.
λοιπαῖς στρατηγίαις,   Strategorum
                                                                              thematum
πλὴν ἐν τοῖς πλοΐμοις· προστίθεται γὰρ αὐτοῖς κεντάρχοι καὶ πρωτο- reliquorum
κάραβοι.   terrestrium
                                                                              et mariti-
τῷ δὲ δομεστίκῳ τῶν ἐξσκουβίτων ὑποτέτακται εἴδη ἀξιωμάτων θ′, οἷον morum.
                                                                              14. Domestici
                                                                              Excubi-
                                                                              torum.

1 τοποτηρητής,	6 σκευοφόροι,
2 χαρτουλάριος,	7 σιγνοφόροι,
3 σκρίβονες,	8 σινάτορες, καὶ
4 πρωτομανδάτωρ,	9 μανδάτορες.
5 δρακονάριοι,	

τῷ δὲ ὑπάρχῳ τῆς πόλεως ὑποτέτακται εἴδη ἀξιωμάτων ιδ′, οἷον 15. Praefecti
                                                                 urbis.

1 σύμπονος,	8 ἔξαρχοι,
2 λογοθέτης τοῦ πραιτωρίου,	9 γειτονιάρχαι,
3 κριταὶ τῶν ῥεγεώνων,	10 νομικοί,
4 ἐπισκεπτῆται,	11 βουλωταί,
5 πρωτοκαγκελλάριοι,	12 προστάται,
6 κεντυρίων,	13 καγκελλάριοι,
7 ἐπόπται,	14 ὁ παραθαλασσίτης.

τῷ δὲ σακελλαρίῳ ὑποτέτακται τὰ ὀφφίκια πάντα διὰ τὸ ἐν ἑκάστῳ 29. Sacel-
σεκρέτῳ τὴν ἐπισκοπὴν τῶν ἐκεῖσε πραττομένων διὰ τῆς καταγραφῆς τοῦ larii.
οἰκείου νοταρίου ποιεῖσθαι.

5 τρουμάρχαι L   6 μεριάρχης scripsi : ἡμεριάρχαι L : μεριάρχαι B   10 δρουγγάριοι
scripsi : -ος L B   14 β′ scripsi : δύο L   717 24 τοποτηρητής scripsi : -ταί L
25 χαρτουλάριος scripsi : -ιοι L   27 πρωτομανδάτωρ scripsi : -ορες L   39 οἰκίου L

30. Logothe-
tae genici.

τῷ δὲ λογοθέτῃ τοῦ γενικοῦ ὑποτέτακται εἴδη ἀξιωμάτων κατὰ βαθμὸν ιβ΄, οἷον

1 χαρτουλάριοι μεγάλοι τοῦ σεκρέ-
τ ου,
2 χαρτουλάριοι τῶν ἀρκλῶν,
3 ἐπόπται τῶν θεμάτων,
4 κόμητες ὑδάτων,
5 ὁ οἰκιστικός,
6 κουμερκιάριοι,

7 ὁ τῆς κουρατωρίας,
8 ὁ κόμης τῆς λαμίας,
9 διοικηταί,   5
10 κομεντιανός,
11 πρωτοκαγκελλάριος,
12 καγκελλάριοι.

31. Quae-
storis.
718

τῷ δὲ κυέστωρι ὑποτέτακται εἴδη ἀξιωμάτων ἕξ, οἷον   10

1 ἀντιγραφεῖς,
2 σκρίβας,
3 σκέπτωρ,

4 λιβελίσιος,
5 πρωτοκαγκελλάριος,
6 καγκελλάριοι.

32. Logothe-
tae
Stratiotici.

τῷ δὲ λογοθέτῃ τοῦ στρατιωτικοῦ ὑποτέτακται εἴδη ἀξιωμάτων ζ΄, οἷον

1 χαρτουλάριοι τοῦ σεκραίτου,
2 χαρτουλάριοι τῶν θεμάτων,
3 χαρτουλάριοι τῶν ταγμάτων,
4 λεγατάριοι,

5 ὀπτίονες,   15
6 πρωτοκαγκελλάριος,
7 μανδάτορες.

33. Drungarii
arithmi.

τῷ δὲ δρουγγαρίῳ τοῦ ἀριθμοῦ ὑποτέτακται εἴδη ἀξιωμάτων ι΄, οἷον

1 τοποτηρητής,
2 χαρτουλάριος,
3 ἀκόλουθος,
4 κόμητες,
5 κένταρχοι,

6 βανδοφόροι,   20
7 λαβουρίσιοι,
8 σημειοφόροι,
9 δουκινιάτορες,
10 μανδάτορες.

34. Drungarii
classium.

τῷ δὲ δρουγγαρίῳ τῶν πλοΐμων ὑποτέτακται εἴδη ἀξιωμάτων ζ΄, οἷον   25

1 τοποτηρητής,
2 χαρτουλάριος,
3 πρωτομανδάτωρ,
4 κόμητες,

5 κένταρχοι,
6 κόμης τῆς ἑταιρείας,
7 μανδάτορες.

35. Logothe-
tae cursus.

τῷ δὲ λογοθέτῃ τοῦ δρόμου ὑποτέτακται εἴδη ἀξιωμάτων ζ΄, οἷον   30

1 πρωτονοτάριος τοῦ δρόμου,
2 χαρτουλάριοι τοῦ δρόμου,
3 ἐπισκεπτῆται,
4 ἑρμηνευταί,

5 ὁ κουράτωρτοῦ ἀποκρισιαριείου,
6 διατρέχοντες,
7 μανδάτορες.

36. Protospa-
tharii
basilicorum.

τῷ δὲ πρωτοσπαθαρίῳ τῶν βασιλικῶν ὑποτέτακται εἴδη ἀξιωμάτων δ΄, 35
οἷον

1 δομέστικος τῶν βασιλικῶν,
2 σπαθάριοι τοῦ σπαθαρικίου, ἤτοι
τοῦ ἱπποδρόμου,

3 κανδιδάτοι ὁμοίως,
4 καὶ βασιλικοὶ μανδάτορες.

3 σεκραίτου L (et saepe)   8 οἰκιστικός coni. R recte : κιστικός L B   718 20, 26 τοποτηρητής scripsi : -ηταί L   27 κόμητες τῆς ἑταιρείας B

τῷ δὲ λογοθέτῃ τῶν ἀγελῶν ὑποτέτακται εἴδη ἀξιωμάτων ⟨ε⟩, οἷον
1 ὁ πρωτονοτάριος Ἀσίας,   4 κόμητες,
2 ὁ πρωτονοτάριος Φρυγίας,   5 ἐπισκεπτῆται.
3 διοικηταὶ τῶν μητάτων,

37. Logothetae gregum.

5 τῷ δὲ δομεστίκῳ τῶν ἱκανάτων ὑποτέτακται εἴδη ἀξιωμάτων θ΄, οἷον
1 τοποτηρητής,   6 βανδοφόροι,
2 χαρτουλάριος,   7 δουκινιάτορες,
3 κόμητες,   8 σημειοφόροι,
4 πρωτομανδάτωρ,   9 μανδάτορες.
10 5 κένταρχοι,

38. Domestici hicanatorum.

719

τῷ δὲ δομεστίκῳ τῶν νουμέρων ὑποτέτακται εἴδη ἀξιωμάτων ἕξ, οἷον
1 τοποτηρητής,   4 βικάριοι,
2 χαρτουλάριος 2ᵃ τριβοῦνοι,   5 μανδάτορες,
3 πρωτομανδάτωρ,   6 πορτάριοι.

39. Domestici numerorum.

15 τῷ δὲ δομεστίκῳ τῶν ὀπτιμάτων ὑποτέτακται εἴδη ἀξιωμάτων ε΄, οἷον
1 τοποτηρητής,   4 κένταρχοι,
2 χαρτουλάριος,   5 πρωτοκαγκελλάριος.
3 κόμητες,

40. Domestici optimatorum.

τῷ δὲ δομεστίκῳ τῶν τειχέων ὑποτέτακται εἴδη ἀξιωμάτων ϛ΄, οἷον
20 1 τοποτηρητής,   4 βικάριοι,
2 χαρτουλάριος 2ᵃ τριβοῦνοι,   5 μανδάτορες,
3 πρωτομανδάτωρ,   6 πορτάριοι.

41. Domestici moenium.

τῷ δὲ χαρτουλαρίῳ τοῦ σακελλίου ὑποτέτακται εἴδη ἀξιωμάτων ι΄, οἷον
1 νοτάριοι βασιλικοὶ τοῦ σεκρέτου,   6 γηροκόμοι,
25 2 πρωτονοτάριοι τῶν θεμάτων,   7 χαρτουλάριοι τῶν οἴκων,
3 ξενοδόχοι,   8 πρωτοκαγκελλάριος,
4 ὁ ζυγοστάτης,   9 καγκελλάριοι, καὶ
5 μετρηταί,   10 ὁ δομέστικος τῆς θυμέλης.

42. Chartularii sacellii.

τῷ δὲ χαρτουλαρίῳ τοῦ βεστιαρίου ὑποτέτακται εἴδη ἀξιωμάτων ι΄, οἷον
30 1 βασιλικοὶ νοτάριοι τοῦ σεκρέτου, 6 χαρτουλάριος,
2 κένταρχος,   7 κουράτορες,
3 λεγατάριος,   8 χοσβαῆται,
4 ἄρχων τῆς χαραγῆς,   9 πρωτομανδάτ⟨ωρ⟩,
5 ἐξαρτιστής,   10 ⟨μανδάτ⟩ορες.

43. Chartularii vestiarii.

35 τῷ δὲ χαρτουλαρίῳ τοῦ κανικλείου οὐδὲν ὑποπέπτωκε διὰ τὸ καθ᾽ ἑαυτὸν
μόνον ὑπηρετεῖν.

44. Chartularii caniclei.

1 ⟨ε⟩ supplevi   6 τοποτηρητής scripsi : τοποτηριταί L   6 βαρδοφόροι L
719 9 μανδάτωρες L   12 τοποτηρητής scripsi : -ηταί L   13 et 21 χαρτουλάριοι τριβοῦνοι L B correxi   16 et 20 τοποτηρητής scripsi : τοποτηρί L : -ηταί B   28 με-
τριταί L   33, 34 πρωτομανδάτ⟨ωρ, μανδάτ⟩ορες scripsi : πρωτομανδάτορες L B

45. Protostratoris.

τῷ δὲ πρωτοστράτορι ὑποτέτακται εἴδη ἀξιωμάτων γ΄, οἷον

1 στράτωρες,   3 σταβλοκόμητες.

2 ἁρμοφύλακες, καὶ

46. Protoasecretae.

τῷ δὲ πρωτοασήκρητις ὑποπέπτωκεν εἴδη ἀξιωμάτων γ΄, οἷον

1 ἀσηκρῆται,   3 ὁ δεκανός.   5

2 νοτάριοι βασιλικοί,

720

47. Comiti stabuli.

48. Idici.

τῷ δὲ κόμητι τοῦ στάβλου ὑποτέτακται εἴδη ἀξιωμάτων ⟨. . οἷον⟩. . . .

τῷ δὲ ἐπὶ τοῦ εἰδικοῦ λόγου ὑποτέτακται εἴδη ἀξιωμάτων δ΄, οἷον

1 βασιλικοὶ νοτάριοι τοῦ σεκρέτου,   3 ἑβδομάριοι, καὶ

2 ἄρχοντες τῶν ἐργοδοσίων,   4 μειζότεροι τῶν ἐργοδοσίων.   ₁₀

49. Curatoris magni.

τῷ δὲ μεγάλῳ κουράτωρι ὑποτέτακται εἴδη ἀξιωμάτων θ΄, οἷον

1 πρωτονοτάριος,   6 ὁ ξενοδόχος Σαγγάρου,

2 βασιλικοὶ νοτάριοι,   7 ὁ ξενοδόχος Πυλῶν,

3 κουράτορες τῶν παλατίων, 8 ὁ ξενοδόχος Νικομηδείας, καὶ

4 κουράτορες τῶν κτημάτων, 9 ἐπισκεπτῆται.   ₁₅

5 μειζότερος τῶν Ἐλευθερίου,

50. Curatoris Manganorum.

51. Orphanotrophi.

τῷ δὲ κουράτορι τῶν μαγγάνων ὑποτέτακται εἴδη ἀξιωμάτων, ὅσα καὶ τῷ μεγάλῳ κουράτορι, πλὴν τῶν ξενοδόχων.

τῷ δὲ ὀρφανοτρόφῳ ὑποτέτακται εἴδη ἀξιωμάτων δ΄, οἷον

1 χαρτουλάριοι τοῦ οἴκου,   3 ἀρκάριος,   ₂₀

2 χαρτουλάριοι τοῦ ὁσίου,   4 κουράτορες.

52, 53. Demarchorum duorum.

τοῖς δὲ δυσὶ δημάρχοις ὑποτέτακται εἴδη ἀξιωμάτων ἀνὰ ζ΄, οἷον

1 δευτερεύοντες,   6 μελισταί,

2 ὁ χαρτουλάριος, καὶ   7 νοτάριοι τῶν μερῶν,

3 ὁ ποιητής,   8 ἡνίοχοι,   ₂₅

4 ἄρχοντες,   9 πρωτεῖα,

5 γειτονιάρχαι,   10 δημῶται.

54. Cerimoniarii.

τῷ δὲ ἐπὶ τῆς καταστάσεως ὑποτέτακται εἴδη ἀξιωμάτων ε΄, οἷον

1 ὕπατοι,   4 ἀποεπάρχοντες,

2 βεστήτορες,   5 συγκλητικοί.   ₃₀

3 σιλεντιάριοι,

περὶ τάξεως τῶν εὐνούχων.

Περὶ τῆς τῶν εὐνούχων τάξεως καὶ τῆς τῶν ἀξιωμάτων αὐτῶν κυριοκλησίας καὶ ποσότης τῶν συνηθειῶν αὐτῶν.

721

Αἱ δὲ τῶν εὐνούχων ἀξίαι καὶ αὗται μὲν διχῶς δίδονται. καὶ γὰρ αἱ μὲν ἐξ αὐτῶν ἔργῳ τὰς ἀξίας νομίμως λαμβάνουσιν· αἱ δὲ λόγῳ τοῖς ἀξίοις ₃₅ προσγίνονται, αἳ καὶ ῥᾳδίως ἐκ προσώπων εἰς πρόσωπα λόγῳ βασιλέως μετέρχονται.

---

3 ἀρμ⟨ατ⟩οφύλακες conicio   720 7 spatium duarum linearum in calce paginae

vacat   ὑπὸ L : corr. R   14, 15 κουράτωρες B, et infra   22 ι΄?   24 οἱ χαρτου-

λάριοι καὶ οἱ ποιηταὶ expectes   29 ἀπὸ ἐπάρχοντες LB   32 ποσότητος?

(Dignitates eunuchorum per insignia.)

εἰσὶ δὲ ὁμοῦ πᾶσαι αἱ διὰ βραβείων αὐτοῖς παρεχόμεναι τὸν ἀριθμὸν ὀκτώ.

καὶ πρώτη μὲν ἐν αὐτοῖς ἡ τῶν νιψιστιαρίων ἀξία γνωρίζεται, ἧς ᾱ βραβεῖον καμήσιον λινοῦν ὑποβλαττόμενον σχήματι φιαλίου, καὶ λόγῳ βασιλέως προσγινόμενος. δίδωσιν συνήθειαν τοῖς πραιποσίτοις ,, ιβ′, τῷ δευτέρῳ ,, γ′, τῷ πριμικηρίῳ αὐτοῦ ,, β′.

δευτέρα δὲ ἡ τοῦ κουβικουλαρίου ἀξία, ἧς βραβεῖον ἡ ἀμφίασις τοῦ β περιβλαττομένου καμισίου καὶ ἡ τοῦ λεγομένου παραγαβδίου στολή, ἣ καὶ διὰ τῆς τῶν πραιποσίτων παρουσίας γνωρίζεται· δίδωσιν συνήθειαν τοῖς πραιποσίτοις ,, ιβ′, τῷ δευτέρῳ ,, δ′, τῷ πριμικηρίῳ ,, β′.

τρίτη ἡ τοῦ σπαθαροκουβικουλαρίου ἀξία, ἧς βραβεῖον, σπαθίον γ̄ χρυσόκανον, ὁμοίως τοῖς σπαθαρίοις διὰ βασιλικῆς χειρὸς ἐπιδίδοται· δίδωσι συνήθειαν τοῖς πραιποσίτοις ,, ιη′, τῷ παπίᾳ καὶ τῷ δευτέρῳ ,, β′, τῷ πριμικηρίῳ ,, δ′.

τετάρτη ἡ τῶν ὀστιαρίων ἀξία, ἧς βραβεῖον, χρυσῆ ῥάβδος ἐκ λίθων δ̄ τιμίων περικεφαλαίαν ἔχουσα, διὰ χειρὸς βασιλέως ἐπιδίδοται. δίδει συνήθειαν τῷ παπίᾳ καὶ τῷ δευτέρῳ ,, ϛ′, τοῖς πραιποσίτοις ,, κδ′, τῷ πριμικηρίῳ τοῦ κουβουκλείου ,, δ′·

πέμπτη ἡ τῶν πριμικηρίων ἀξία, ἧς βραβεῖον, χιτὼν λευκὸς σὺν ἐπο- ε μίοις καὶ πώλοις χρυσοϋφάντοις, λαμπρῶς ἀμφιάζεται. δίδει συνήθειαν 722 τοῖς πραιποσίτοις ,, λϛ′, τῷ δευτέρῳ ,, ιβ′, ἐὰν ἄρα δώσει αὐτὸν βασιλικὸν ἱμάτιν, τῷ πριμικηρίῳ ,, ϛ′.

ἕκτη ἡ τῶν ἐν αὐτοῖς πρωτοσπαθαρίων ἀξία, ἧς βραβεῖον, χρυσοῦν ϛ̄ μανιάκιον ἐκ λίθων τιμίων καὶ μαργαριτῶν, ἐπὶ τοῦ αὐχένος διὰ χειρὸς βασιλέως ἐπισυγκλείεται. χιτὼν δὲ καὶ αὐτοῖς λευκὸς χρυσοκόλλητος διβη- τισσοειδὴς καὶ διπλόης κόκκινος σὺν ταβλίοις χρυσοϋφάντοις. δίδωσι συνή- θειαν τοῖς πραιποσίτοις καὶ πατρικίοις εὐνούχοις καὶ πρωτοσπαθαρίοις εὐνούχοις ,, οβ′, τῷ παπίᾳ καὶ τῷ δευτέρῳ ,, ϛ′.

ἑβδόμη δὲ πέφυκεν ἡ τῶν λαμπροτάτων πραιποσίτων ἀξία, ἧς ζ̄ βραβεῖον, πλάκες πατρικιότητος, ἄνευ μὲν κωδικέλλων ἐπὶ προελεύσεως χρυσοτρικλίνου χειρὶ βασιλέως ἐπιδίδονται· δίδει συνήθειαν, εἰ ἄρα τιμηθῇ πρωτοσπαθάριος ἐν τῷ ἅμα, λ. α′, καὶ τῷ δευτέρῳ ὑπὲρ τῶν πλακῶν ,, κδ′. εἰ δὲ καὶ πατρίκιος ὁ αὐτὸς ἐν ταυτῇ τιμηθῇ, δίδωσι συνήθειαν ὡς οἱ πατρίκιοι.

ὀγδόη ἡ τῶν ἐν αὐτοῖς πατρικίων ἀξία, ἧς βραβεῖον, πλάκες, ὁμοίως η̄ σὺν κωδικέλλοις ὡς πᾶσι τοῖς πατρικίοις δίδονται. οὐ διαλλάττουσι δὲ ἐν ταῖς αὐτῶν στολαῖς τῆς τῶν πρωτοσπαθαρίων ἀμφιάσεως πλὴν λώροις καὶ μόνον, εἰ ἄρα καὶ ἡ τῶν πρωτοσπαθαρίων αὐτοῖς ἐφέπεται δόξα. οὐδὲ

721 5 ὑποβλαττομένων L   λόγος LB : correxi   9 κακαμησίου L   ἧ LB : correxi
17 et 722, 21 δίδι L   22 ἐὰρ L   23 ἱμάτιν scripsi : ἡμάτην L : ἱμάτιον B   26 χει-
τὼν L : χρυσοκόλλιτος L   31 πλάκαις L   32 δίδι L   34 τιμιθῇ L   36 πλάκαις L
38 λώρις L

κωλύονται οἱ πραιπόσιτοι ἐν ὀφφικίοις διαπρέπειν, οἷον ἄν ἐστιν ὀφφίκιον,
723 τοῦ εἶναι καὶ πραιπόσιτος καὶ ὀφφικιάλιος.   παρέχουσιν δὲ συνήθειαν οἱ
πατρίκιοι εὐνοῦχοι καθὼς καὶ οἱ βαρβάτοι.

παρὰ δὲ τῶν εἰς ὀφφίκια προβαλλομένων πάντων ἐκκομιζομένου τοῦ
πραιποσίτου, ὡς ἐκ προσώπου τοῦ βασιλέως, τὴν ἀπόκρισιν τῆς προβλή-
σεως, λαμβάνειν τὸν αὐτὸν πραιπόσιτον καθ᾽ ἕκαστον ὀφφικιάλιον συνήθειαν ,, κδ᾽. μηδεὶς τοίνυν παραβαινέτω τὴν τοιαύτην τάξιν τε καὶ στάσιν
τῶν ἐκτιθεμένων ἀξιωμάτων, ἢ ἄλλως πως ταύτας μετερχέσθω, πλὴν τῶν
κληρικῶν καὶ μόνον.   οὗτοι γὰρ λόγῳ μόνῳ μετέρχονται τὰς ἀξίας. ἡ δὲ
τῶν πρωτοσπαθαρίων ἀξία διὰ βασιλικῆς χειρὸς μετὰ ἐπιριπταρίου βασιλικοῦ ἐπισυγκλείεται.   ταύτας δὲ τὰς συναγομένας συνηθείας τῶν ἀξιωμάτων παρὰ τοῦ παπίου καὶ τοῦ δευτέρου μερίζεσθαι αὐτοῖς ἐπ᾽ ἴσης ἄνευ
τῆς συνηθείας τοῦ χρυσοτρικλίνου, ὅτι μονομερῶς τοῦ παπία ἐστίν.   τῶν
δὲ πλακῶν καὶ τῶν μαγίστρων καὶ τῶν πριμικηρίων καὶ τῶν κουβικουλαρίων
μονομερῶς λαμβάνει αὐτὰ ὁ δεύτερος, καθὼς ἀνωτέρω διαγορεύει.   τοῦ δὲ
τιμίου σταυροῦ τῷ Αὐγούστῳ μηνὶ ἐξέρχεται ὁ παπίας, καὶ εἴ τι ἄν ἐπισυνάξει, ἔχει αὐτά, καὶ ἐξ αὐτῶν δίδωσιν καὶ τῷ δευτέρῳ μέρος τι.   εἰ δὲ
δι᾽ ἀδυναμίαν εἴτε νόσον οὐκ ἐξέρχεται ὁ παπίας, ἐξέρχεται ὁ δεύτερος,
καὶ εἴ τι ἄν ἐπισυνάξει, μερίζονται αὐτὰ ὅ τε παπίας καὶ ὁ δεύτερος ἐξ
ἴσης.   ἐπέχει δὲ ὁ παπίας τὰς ἐξ ἑβδομάδας τοὺς διαιταρίους καὶ τὸ ἔλαιον
724 τῶν καμαρῶν τοῦ χρυσοτρικλίνου σὺν τῶν κανδηλαπτῶν.   τὸ δὲ ἔλαιον
τοῦ πολυκανδήλου τοῦ κατὰ τὸ μέσον κρεμμαμένου τοῦ χρυσοτρικλίνου καὶ
τῶν λοιπῶν πολυκανδήλων καὶ ψιαθίων, ἐπικρατοῦσιν αὐτὰ αὐτοὶ οἱ κανδηλάπται.   ἐπέχει δὲ καὶ τοὺς λούστας καὶ τοὺς καμηνάδας καὶ τοὺς
κανδηλάπτας τοῦ λαυσιακοῦ καὶ τοῦ Ἰουστινιανοῦ καὶ τοὺς ὡρολόγους καὶ
τοὺς ζαράβας, καὶ ὅστις ἐξ αὐτῶν λείψῃ, ἔχει ἐξουσίαν ποιεῖν ἀντισηκοῦντας,
καὶ λαμβάνει ρ᾽ συνήθειαν αὐτῶν, εἰς μὲν τοὺς πριμικηρίους ,, ιθ᾽, καὶ εἰς
τοὺς διαιταρίους καὶ λοιποὺς ἀνὰ ,, ς᾽, λαμβάνουσι δὲ καὶ οἱ πριμικήριοι ,, α᾽,
καὶ ὁ λαὸς ,, ε᾽.   ἐπέχει δὲ καὶ ὁ δεύτερος τὰ σελλία καὶ τοὺς διαιταρίους
καὶ τὸν πριμικήριον αὐτῶν καὶ τὰ στέμματα καὶ τὰς ἐσθῆτας τῶν βασιλέων
καὶ τὰ βῆλα τοῦ χρυσοτρικλίνου καὶ τοὺς ἐπὶ τῶν ἀλλαξίμων καὶ τοὺς
βεστήτορας σὺν τῶν πριμικηρίων αὐτῶν καὶ τὰ σκεύη τῶν ἀξιωμάτων καὶ
τοὺς ἐπὶ τῶν ἀξιωμάτων, οἳ καὶ συνάγουσιν τὰ ἀξιώματα παρὰ τῶν λαμβανόντων τὰς ἀξίας.   καὶ ὅστις ἐξ αὐτῶν λείψῃ, ἵνα παρέχῃ ὁ μέλλων
γίνεσθαι τὰς συνηθείας τῷ δευτέρῳ, καθὼς καὶ ὁ παπίας λαμβάνει.   εἰς δὲ
τὰς προελεύσεις ἵνα συνάγωνται οἱ βεστήτορες καὶ οἱ πριμικήριοι πάντες,
καὶ βαστάζουσιν τὰ κορνίκλια σὺν τοῖς στέμμασιν.   συνάγεσθαι δὲ τοὺς
725 ἀμφοτέρων διαιταρίους καὶ βαστάζειν εἰς τὰς προελεύσεις τὰ ταβλία τὰ
βασιλικὰ μετὰ τῶν ἀλλαξίμων.   ἀκολουθεῖν δὲ εἰς τὰς προελεύσεις τοὺς

---

723 12 ἐφίσσης L : ἐπ᾽ ἴσης B : fort. ἐξ ἴσης   13 μονομερὸς L   15 forte ⟨τὰ⟩
ἀνωτέρω   20 ἐδομάδας L   724 26 λίψῃ L   ἀντισικοῦντας L   27 ρ L   33 τὰ
ἀξιώματα L per errorem ut videtur.   Scribendum τὰς συνηθείας   34, 36 παρέχει…
συνάγονται LB correxi

ῥάπτας τοὺς βασιλικοὺς καὶ τοὺς χρυσοκλαβαρίους καὶ τοὺς χρυσοχοῦς, βαστάζοντε καὶ αὐτοὶ σπαθία τὰ βασιλικὰ εἰς τὰς θήκας αὐτῶν. καὶ λαμβάνειν αὐτοὺς παρὰ τοῦ βαρβάρου μαϊουμᾶν εἰς τὰ πρόκενσα. λαμβάνειν δὲ καὶ ξύλον τὸν παπίαν τὴν ἑβδομάδα πίσσαν μίαν, καὶ τὸν δεύτερον πίσσαν μίαν. ταῦτα δὲ πάντα φυλάττεσθαι, τηρεῖσθαί τε καὶ πράττεσθαι ἀπαρασάλευτα καὶ διαμένειν βέβαια, καθὼς ἡ εὐσεβὴς καὶ ἔνθεος βασιλεία ἡμῶν ἐξέθετο, ὡς καὶ ἐξ ἀρχαίων τῶν χρόνων παρὰ τῶν πρὸ ἡμῶν εὐσεβῶς βασιλευσάντων δικαίως ἐξετέθη.

(Dignitates eunuchorum per edictum.)

Ὅσαι διὰ βασιλικοῦ λόγου προσγίνονται τούτοις ἀξίαι.

Αἱ δὲ λόγῳ προσγινόμεναι τούτοις ἀξίαι εἰσὶ καὶ αὗται τὸν ἀριθμὸν κυρίως θʹ·

1 ὁ παρακοιμώμενος τοῦ δεσπότου,	6 ὁ δεύτερος τοῦ μεγάλου παλατίου,
2 ὁ πρωτοβεστιάριος τοῦ δεσπότου,	7 ὁ ἐπιγκέρνης τοῦ δεσπότου,
3 ὁ ἐπὶ τῆς τραπέζης τοῦ δεσπότου,	8 ὁ πιγκέρνης τῆς αὐγούστης,
4 ὁ ἐπὶ τῆς τραπέζης τῆς αὐγούστης,	9 ὁ παπίας τῆς μανναύρας,
5 ὁ παπίας τοῦ μεγάλου παλατίου,	10 ὁ παπίας τῆς Δάφνης.

ἀλλὰ μὴν καὶ αἱ ἄλλαι πᾶσαι, ὅσαι καὶ τοῖς βαρβάτοις προσγίνονται, πλὴν τῆς τοῦ ἐπάρχου καὶ κυέστωρος καὶ δομεστίκων ἀξίας.

Τόμος βʹ.

726
Sectio II.

Ταύτας οὖν ἀπάσας τὰς ἔργῳ καὶ λόγῳ διδομένας ἀξίας σαφεῖ καὶ ἀκριβεῖ λόγῳ παραστῆσαι σπουδάσαντες, οὐ δίκαιον ἐκρίναμεν, ὦ φίλοι, μέχρι τούτων καταπαῦσαι τὸν λόγον, ἀλλὰ καί, ὃ μάλιστα ὑμῖν ζητητέον, τῆς περὶ τῶν καθεδρῶν ἀκριβείας καθάψασθαι καὶ τὴν ὑπόθεσιν εἰς πέρας ἀγάγαι, καθὰ ἐξητήσασθε. καὶ γὰρ πάλιν ὡς ἐπαναλήψει ταῖς λεχθείσαις ἀπάσαις χρησάμενοι τὴν ἑκάστης τάξιν καὶ κλῆσιν καὶ οἰκείαν καθέδραν σαφέστερον ὑμῖν κανονῆσαι ἐπήχθημεν. δεῖ γὰρ τὸν καλέοντα ἀρτικλίνην ταύτας μὲν ἀπάσας ἀκριβῶς εἰδέναι, ὡς ἔφαμεν, καὶ τὴν τῶν ἱερῶν βασιλικῶν κλητωρίων κατάστασιν διττῶς ποιεῖσθαι εἰς κόσμησιν, καὶ τῷ μὲν λόγῳ τὴν κλῆσιν τῆς ἑκάστου ἀξίας οἰκείας ἐκφέρειν, τῇ δὲ δεξιᾷ χειρὶ διὰ τοῦ σχήματος προσδεικνύειν τὸν ἑκάστῃ ἁρμόζοντα τόπον, καὶ τὸν μὲν πρωτόκλητον φίλον πρὸς τὸ εὐώνυμον προτρέπεσθαι μέρος, ὅπως ἡ τῆς βασιλικῆς ἀξίας ἐπίδοσις εὐχερὴς τῷ πρωτοκλήτῳ γένηται φίλῳ, τὸν δὲ ἀπ᾽ αὐτοῦ δεύτερον ἐν τοῖς δεξιοῖς προσκαλεῖσθαι, καὶ λέγειν·

ὁ πατριάρχης Κωνσταντινουπόλεως,
ὁ καῖσαρ,
ὁ νωβελήσιμος,

725 4 τὴν scripsi : τῇ L   τῇ ἑβδομάδι B   726 20 Hic incipit fragmentum cod. H   23 ζητειτέον L   24 περὶ τῆς τῶν H   25 ἐζητήσασθε H   ἐπ᾽ ἀναλήψει B   30 om.   δὲ H   31 τοῦτο σχήματος H   33 ἐπίδωσις L

м 10

ὁ κουροπαλάτης,
ὁ βασιλεοπάτωρ,
ἡ ζωστὴ πατρικία.

727   εἰδέναι δὲ δεῖ, ὅτι αἱ ἐξ αὗται μόναι ἀξίαι ἐν τῇ ἀποκοπῇ τραπέζῃ
συνεστιῶνται τοῖς βασιλεῦσιν, αἱ δὲ λοιπαὶ πᾶσαι τῆς δευτέρας ὑπάρχουσι
τάξεως, οἷον

ὁ μάγιστρος, ὁ μάγιστρος

(εἰ δέ τις τούτων ὀφφίκιον τετίμηται, προκρίνεται τοῦ ἑταίρου, κἂν τάχα
ἔσχατος ᾖ).   εἶτα

ὁ ῥαίκτωρ,
ὁ σύγκελλος Ῥώμης,
ὁ σύγκελλος Κωνσταντινουπόλεως

(εἰ δὲ καὶ τῶν τῆς Ἀνατολῆς πατριαρχῶν τύχοιεν σύγκελλοι, προκρίνονται τούτων κατὰ τὰ ἴδια αὐτῶν πατριαρχία).   εἶθ' οὕτως

ὁ ἀρχιεπίσκοπος Βουλγαρίας,
πατρίκιοι εὐνοῦχοι
(ὁ δὲ ὢν ἐξ αὐτῶν ἐν ὀφφικίῳ προκρίνεται τοῦ ἑτέρου)·
ὁ ἀνθύπατος πατρίκιος καὶ στρατηγὸς τῶν Ἀνατολικῶν·
ὁ ἀνθύπατος πατρίκιος καὶ δομέστικος τῶν σχολῶν·
ὁ ἀνθύπατος πατρίκιος καὶ στρατηγὸς τῶν Ἀρμενιάκων·
ὁ ἀνθύπατος πατρίκιος καὶ στρατηγὸς τῶν Θρᾳκησίων·
ὁ ἀνθύπατος πατρίκιος καὶ κόμης τοῦ Ὀψικίου·
ὁ ἀνθύπατος πατρίκιος καὶ στρατηγὸς τῶν Βουκελλαρίων·
ὁ ἀνθύπατος πατρίκιος καὶ στρατηγὸς Καππαδοκίας·
ὁ ἀνθύπατος πατρίκιος καὶ στρατηγὸς τοῦ Χαρσιανοῦ·
ὁ ἀνθύπατος πατρίκιος καὶ στρατηγὸς Κολωνείας·
ὁ ἀνθύπατος πατρίκιος καὶ στρατηγὸς Παφλαγωνίας·
ὁ ἀνθύπατος πατρίκιος καὶ στρατηγὸς τῆς Θράκης·
ὁ ἀνθύπατος πατρίκιος καὶ στρατηγὸς Μακεδονίας·
ὁ ἀνθύπατος πατρίκιος καὶ στρατηγὸς Χαλδίας·

728   ὁ ἀνθύπατος πατρίκιος [καὶ στρατηγὸς] καὶ δομέστικος τῶν ἐξσκουβίτων·
ὁ ἀνθύπατος πατρίκιος καὶ ἔπαρχος τῆς πόλεως·
ὁ ἀνθύπατος πατρίκιος καὶ στρατηγὸς Πελοποννήσου·
ὁ ἀνθύπατος πατρίκιος καὶ στρατηγὸς Νικοπόλεως·
ὁ ἀνθύπατος πατρίκιος καὶ στρατηγὸς τῶν Κιβυρραιωτῶν·
ὁ ἀνθύπατος πατρίκιος καὶ στρατηγὸς Ἑλλάδος·
ὁ ἀνθύπατος πατρίκιος καὶ στρατηγὸς Σικελίας·

727 4 ἀποκοπῇ τραπέζης H   7 ὁ μάγιστρος semel H, bis L B   8 ὀφφικίῳ H :
ὀφφίκιον L B   ἑταίρου L : δευτέρου H   9 ἐσχάτως pro ἔσχατος ᾖ H   11-12 σύγκελος L   13 τοίχνεν L   14 τοῦτο H   18 πατρίκιος om. H et in sequentibus
22 ὁ ἀνθύπατος κόμης H   25 στρατηγὸς Χαρσιανός H   31 καὶ στρατηγὸς L B :
om. H   728 31 ἐξσκουβιτόρων B : ἐκσκουβίτων H   33 πελοπονίσου L   34 ὁ ἀνθυπ.
... Νικοπόλεως om. H   37 ὁ ἀνθύπατος καὶ στρατηγὸς Λογγιβαρδίας post Σικελίας H

ὁ ἀνθύπατος πατρίκιος καὶ στρατηγὸς Στρυμῶνος·
ὁ ἀνθύπατος πατρίκιος καὶ στρατηγὸς Κεφαληνίας·
ὁ ἀνθύπατος πατρίκιος καὶ στρατηγὸς Θεσσαλονίκης·
ὁ ἀνθύπατος πατρίκιος καὶ στρατηγὸς τοῦ Δυρραχίου·
ὁ ἀνθύπατος πατρίκιος καὶ στρατηγὸς τῆς Σάμου·
ὁ ἀνθύπατος πατρίκιος καὶ στρατηγὸς τοῦ Αἰγέου πελάγους·
ὁ ἀνθύπατος πατρίκιος καὶ στρατηγὸς Δαλματίας·
ὁ ἀνθύπατος πατρίκιος καὶ στρατηγὸς Χερσῶνος·
ὁ ἀνθύπατος πατρίκιος καὶ σακελλάριος·
ὁ ἀνθύπατος πατρίκιος καὶ γενικὸς λογοθέτης·
ὁ ἀνθύπατος πατρίκιος καὶ κυέστωρ·
ὁ ἀνθύπατος πατρίκιος καὶ λογοθέτης τοῦ στρατιωτικοῦ·
ὁ ἀνθύπατος πατρίκιος καὶ δρουγγάριος τῆς βίγλης·
ὁ ἀνθύπατος πατρίκιος καὶ δρουγγάριος τῶν πλωΐμων·
ὁ ἀνθύπατος πατρίκιος καὶ λογοθέτης τοῦ δρόμου·
ὁ ἀνθύπατος πατρίκιος καὶ λογοθέτης τῶν ἀγελῶν·
ὁ ἀνθύπατος πατρίκιος καὶ δομέστικος τῶν ἱκανάτων·
ὁ ἀνθύπατος πατρίκιος καὶ δομέστικος τῶν νουμέρων·
ὁ ἀνθύπατος πατρίκιος καὶ δομέστικος τῶν ὀπτημάτων·
ὁ ἀνθύπατος πατρίκιος καὶ κόμης τῶν τειχέων·
ὁ ἀνθύπατος πατρίκιος καὶ χαρτουλάριος τοῦ σακελλίου·   729
ὁ ἀνθύπατος πατρίκιος καὶ χαρτουλάριος τοῦ βεστιαρίου·
ὁ ἀνθύπατος πατρίκιος καὶ χαρτουλάριος τοῦ κανικλείου·
ὁ ἀνθύπατος πατρίκιος καὶ πρωτοστράτωρ·
ὁ ἀνθύπατος πατρίκιος καὶ πρωτοασηκρήτης·
ὁ ἀνθύπατος πατρίκιος καὶ κόμης τοῦ στάβλου·
ὁ ἀνθύπατος πατρίκιος καὶ ἐκ προσώπου τῶν θεμάτων·
ὁ ἀνθύπατος πατρίκιος καὶ ἐπὶ τοῦ εἰδικοῦ·
ὁ ἀνθύπατος πατρίκιος καὶ μέγας κουράτωρ·
ὁ ἀνθύπατος πατρίκιος καὶ κουράτωρ τῶν Μαγγάνων·
ὁ ἀνθύπατος πατρίκιος καὶ ἐπὶ τῶν δεήσεων·
ὁ ἀνθύπατος πατρίκιος καὶ ὀρφανοτρόφος·
ὁ ἀνθύπατος πατρίκιος καὶ δήμαρχος Βενέτων·
ὁ ἀνθύπατος πατρίκιος καὶ δήμαρχος Πρασίνων.

εἰ δὲ μὴ εἶεν πάντες ἀνθύπατοι οἱ ἐν τοῖς ὀφφικίοις τεταγμένοι, ἀλλ᾽
ἐν μόνῃ τῇ τῶν πατρικίων ἀξίᾳ τὰ στρατηγάτα ἢ τὰ δομεστικάτα ἢ τὰ
ὀφφίκια προσελάβοντο, οἱ μὲν λιτοὶ ἀνθύπατοι τῶν ἐν τοῖς ὀφφικίοις τεταγμένων πατρικίων ἐν ταῖς καθέδραις προκρίνονται, δηλονότι ἕκαστος αὐτῶν
κατὰ τὴν ἐπίδοσιν τοῦ κωδικέλλου αὐτοῦ τῷ βαθμῷ προτιμώμενος, πλὴν

6 Αἰγαίου Β   9 σακελλάρις Η   10 γενικοῦ Η   13 ὁ ἀνθύπατος καὶ μέγας
ἑτεριάρχης· ὁ ἀνθύπατος καὶ οἰκονόμος τῆς μεγάλης ἐκκλησίας post βίγλης Η   14 πλοΐμων Β   17 ὁ ἀνθύπ.... ἱκανάτων om. Η   21 ὁ ἀνθύπ.... σακελλίου om. Η
729 36 στρατηγάτα R Β: στρατηγήματα codd.   39 ἐπίδωσιν L

τοῦ στρατηγοῦ τῶν Ἀνατολικῶν καὶ τοῦ δομεστίκου τῶν σχολῶν· οὗτοι
γὰρ μόνοι, καὶ μὴ ὄντες ἀνθύπατοι, ἐν τῇ καθέδρᾳ τῶν ἀνθυπάτων ὑπερέ-
χουσιν ἅπαντας.   εἰ δέ τινες ἐξ αὐτῶν, εἴτε ἐκ τῶν ἀνθυπάτων, εἴτε ἐκ
τῶν λιτῶν πατρικίων, ἢ εἰς στρατηγάτα ἀνήχθησαν, εἴτε ἐν ἄλλῳ τῳ διὰ
730 λόγου προσγινομένῳ ἀξιώματι, ἕκαστος αὐτῶν κατὰ τὴν τοῦ ὀφφικίου
οἰκείαν δόξαν καὶ τῆς καθέδρας ἀπολαύει.   οὐ μὴν δὲ κατὰ τὴν τάξιν τοῦ
βαθμοῦ τῆς ἐπιδόσεως τοῦ κωδικέλλου κἂν τάχα τύχῃ ὁ ἔσχατος τῷ βαθμῷ
προκριθῆναι τοῦ πρώτου ἐν οἱῳδήποτε ὀφφικίῳ τῷ διὰ λόγου προσγινομένῳ.
εἰ δὲ καὶ παγανοὶ τύχοιεν χωρὶς ὀφφικίων πατρίκιοι, ὑποπίπτουσι τοῖς τὰ
ὀφφίκια ἔχουσι πατρικίοις.   εἰ δέ τις ἐκ τῶν λεχθέντων ὀφφικίων δια-
δεχθῇ, κατὰ τὸν πρῶτον βαθμὸν τῆς τάξεως τοῦ κωδικέλλου αὐτοῦ ἀνα-
στραφήσεται ἐν τῇ κλήσει.   κλητωρεύονται δὲ ἅπαντες οὕτως.

Sectio III.   Τόμος γ'.
               Τῆς τῶν διαφόρων ἀξιωμάτων καθολικῆς καθέδρας.

Ὁ μάγιστρος·
ὁ ῥαίκτωρ·
ὁ σύγκελλος·
ὁ πατρίκιος καὶ πραιπόσιτος·
οἱ πατρίκιοι οἱ εὐνοῦχοι·
οἱ ἀνθύπατοι πατρίκιοι καὶ στρατηγοὶ κατὰ τὰ στρατηγάτα ἢ τὰ ὀφφίκια
αὐτῶν·
ἀνθύπατοι πατρίκιοι λιτοὶ κατὰ τοὺς κωδικέλλους αὐτῶν·
πατρίκιοι στρατηγοὶ κατὰ τὰ στρατηγάτα αὐτῶν ἢ τὰ ὀφφίκια αὐτῶν·
ὁ πραιπόσιτος μὴ ὢν πατρίκιος·
(εἰ δὲ καὶ ἐν ὀφφικίῳ τετίμηται, προκρίνεται τοῦ ἑτέρου)
ὁ πρωτοσπαθάριος καὶ στρατηγὸς τῶν Ἀνατολικῶν·
ὁ πρωτοσπαθάριος καὶ δομέστικος τῶν σχολῶν·
οἱ πρωτοσπαθάριοι στρατηγοὶ τῶν ἀνατολικῶν θεμάτων κατὰ τὰς
731 στρατηγίας αὐτῶν·
ὁ πρωτοσπαθάριος καὶ δομέστικος τῶν ἐξκουβίτων·
ὁ πρωτοσπαθάριος καὶ ἔπαρχος τῆς πόλεως·
οἱ πρωτοσπαθάριοι καὶ στρατηγοὶ τῶν θεμάτων τῆς δύσεως κατὰ τὰ
στρατηγάτα αὐτῶν·
οἱ μητροπολῖται·
οἱ ἀρχιεπίσκοποι κατὰ τοὺς θρόνους αὐτῶν·
ὁ πρωτοσπαθάριος καὶ σακελλάριος·
οἱ ἐπίσκοποι οἱ ἐπεχόμενοι·
πριμικήριοι εὐνοῦχοι τοῦ κουβουκλείου·

4 εἰς στρατηγάτα ἀνήχθησαν L : ἐκ στρατηγάτων ἀνηνέχθησαν Η   730 6 τὴν
δόξαν Η   9 τοιαῦτα Η : τοῖς τὰ L B   17 σύγκελος L   18 πατρίκιος καὶ om. Η
19 πατρίκιοι om. Η   22 ἀνθ. καὶ λιτοὶ Η   23 πατρίκιοι ... αὐτῶν om. Η
28 καὶ στρατηγοὶ Η   Ἀνατολικῶν Β   κατὰ τὰ L   731 30 ὁ πρωτοσπαθάριος in Η
ut videtur evanuit   ἐξκουβιτόρων Β : ἐκσκουβίτων Η   32 τὰς στρατηγίας Η

(εἰ δὲ καὶ πρωτοσπαθάριοί εἰσιν, προκρίνονται τῶν λιτῶν πριμικηρίων·
εἰ δὲ καὶ ὀφφίκια προσελάβοντο, καὶ εἶθ' οὕτως προκρίνονται τῶν
λοιπῶν·)

ὁ πρωτοσπαθάριος καὶ λογοθέτης τοῦ γενικοῦ·
οἱ ὀστιάριοι τοῦ κουβουκλείου·
(εἰ δὲ καὶ ὀφφίκια ἔχοιεν, προκρίνονται τῶν ὁμοτίμων·)
ὁ κυέστωρ καὶ μὴ ὢν πρωτοσπαθάριος·
ὁ πρωτοσπαθάριος καὶ λογοθέτης τοῦ στρατιωτικοῦ·
ὁ πρωτοσπαθάριος καὶ δρουγγάριος τῆς βίγλης·
ὁ οἰκονόμος τῆς μεγάλης ἐκκλησίας, καθὰ τὰ νῦν ἐτιμήθη·
ὁ πρωτοσπαθάριος καὶ λογοθέτης τοῦ δρόμου·
ὁ πρωτοσπαθάριος καὶ δρουγγάριος τῶν πλωΐμων·
ὁ πρωτοσπαθάριος καὶ λογοθέτης τῶν ἀγελῶν·
ὁ πρωτοσπαθάριος καὶ ἐπὶ τῶν βασιλικῶν·
ὁ πρωτοσπαθάριος καὶ δομέστικος τῶν ἱκανάτων·
ὁ πρωτοσπαθάριος καὶ δομέστικος τῶν νουμέρων·
ὁ πρωτοσπαθάριος καὶ δομέστικος τῶν ὀπτημάτων·
ὁ πρωτοσπαθάριος καὶ κόμης τῶν τειχέων·
ὁ πρωτοσπαθάριος καὶ χαρτουλάριος τοῦ σακελλίου·
ὁ πρωτοσπαθάριος καὶ χαρτουλάριος τοῦ βεστιαρίου·
ὁ πρωτοσπαθάριος καὶ χαρτουλάριος τοῦ κανικλείου·
ὁ πρωτοσπαθάριος καὶ πρωτοστράτωρ·
ὁ πρωτοσπαθάριος καὶ πρωτοασηκρήτης· 732
οἱ πρωτοσπαθάριοι καὶ ἐκ προσώπου τῶν θεμάτων κατὰ τὸ ἴδιον ἑκάστου
θέμα·
ὁ πρωτοσπαθάριος καὶ κόμης τοῦ στάβλου·
ὁ πρωτοσπαθάριος καὶ ἐπὶ τοῦ εἰδικοῦ λόγου·
ὁ πρωτοσπαθάριος καὶ μέγας κουράτωρ·
ὁ πρωτοσπαθάριος καὶ κουράτωρ τῶν Μαγγάνων·
ὁ πρωτοσπαθάριος καὶ ἐπὶ τῶν δεήσεων·
ὁ πρωτοσπαθάριος καὶ ὀρφανοτρόφος·
οἱ πρωτοσπαθάριοι καὶ κλεισουράρχαι·
ὁ πρωτοσπαθάριος καὶ δήμαρχος Βενέτων·
ὁ πρωτοσπαθάριος καὶ δήμαρχος Πρασίνων·
ὁ πρωτοσπαθάριος καὶ ἐπὶ τῆς καταστάσεως·
οἱ πρωτοσπαθάριοι καὶ ἀπὸ στρατηγῶν τῶν Ἀνατολικῶν·
οἱ πρωτοσπαθάριοι καὶ ἀπὸ δομεστίκων τῶν σχολῶν·
οἱ πρωτοσπαθάριοι καὶ ἀπὸ στρατηγῶν τῶν ἀνατολικῶν θεμάτων·

7 κοιαίστωρ Η   9 ὁ πρωτοσπαθάριος καὶ μέγας ἑτεριάχης Η post βίγλης
10 καθὰ om. Η   12 πλοΐμων Β   20 ὁ πρωτ. ... βεστιαρίου om. Η
732 23 καὶ Η : om. L   26 οἱ πρωτοσπαθάριοι καὶ κόμητες τοῦ σταύλου Η   27 ἰδικοῦ Η
33 τῶν Βενέτων Β : Βαινέτων Η   34 τῶν Πρασίνων Β   36 ὁ πρωτοσπαθάριος LB
ἀποστρατηγοὶ Η : ἀπὸ στρατηγοῦ L   37 ὁ πρωτοσπαθάριος LB   ἀποδομέστικοι Η :
ἀπὸ δομεστίκου L   38 οἱ πρωτ. ... θεμάτων om. Η

οἱ πρωτοσπαθάριοι καὶ ἀπὸ δομεστίκων τῶν ἐξσκουβίτων·
οἱ πρωτοσπαθάριοι καὶ ἀπὸ ἐπάρχων·
οἱ πρωτοσπαθάριοι καὶ ἀπὸ στρατηγῶν τῆς δύσεως·
οἱ πρωτοσπαθάριοι καὶ ἀπὸ κυεστώρων·
οἱ πρωτοσπαθάριοι τοῦ χρυσοτρικλίνου (προεκρίθησαν πάλαι τῶν ἀπὸ
στρατηγῶν καὶ ἀπὸ ἐπάρχων)·
οἱ πρωτοσπαθάριοι καὶ κριταί·
οἱ πρωτοσπαθάριοι τοῦ μαγλαβίου καὶ ἀρτικλῖναι·
οἱ πρωτοσπαθάριοι καὶ ἄρχοντες τοῦ στάβλου·
οἱ πρωτοσπαθάριοι καὶ ἀπὸ ὀφφικίων κατὰ τά ποτε ὀφφίκια αὐτῶν·
οἱ πρωτοσπαθάριοι καὶ βασιλικοὶ κατὰ τὰς προβολὰς αὐτῶν·
733   οἱ πρωτοσπαθάριοι καὶ ἀσηκρῆται·
οἱ πρωτοσπαθάριοι οἱ διὰ πόλεως·
οἱ πρωτοσπαθάριοι οἱ ἐξωτικοί.

εἰ δὲ μὴ εἶεν πάντες πρωτοσπαθάριοι, καὶ τὰς διὰ λόγου προσγινομένας
ἀξίας κατέχουσιν, οἱ νῦν στρατηγοὶ τῆς τε ἀνατολῆς καὶ τῆς δύσεως οὐχ
ὑποπίπτουσιν τῆς ἤδη λαχούσης αὐτῶν τῶν θεμάτων καθέδρας διὰ τὴν
ἐλάττωσιν τοῦ βραβείου αὐτῶν, ὑπάρχοντος ἀξιώματος, ἀλλ᾿ ἐν τῇ τάξει, ᾗ
ἐτάχθησαν, κατὰ τὸ οἰκεῖον θέμα καθέζονται. ὡσαύτως οὖν καὶ ὁ ἔπαρχος
πόλεως καὶ ὁ κυαίστωρ. οἱ δὲ λοιποὶ πάντες ὀφφικιάλιοι ἐν τοῖς ὁμοτί-
μοις τῶν διὰ βραβείων διδομένων ἀξιωμάτων προτετίμηνται. ἐν δὲ τῇ
τάξει τῶν ὀφφικίων ἕκαστος αὐτῶν τὴν οἰκείαν καθέδραν λαμβάνει.

(Spatharo-
candidati.)

μετὰ δὲ τῆς τῶν πρωτοσπαθαρίων τιμῆς δευτέρα ἡ τῶν σπαθαροκανδιδάτων εἰσάγεται τάξις, οἷον
σπαθαροκανδιδάτοι καὶ ὀφφικιάλιοι κατὰ τὰ ὀφφίκια αὐτῶν·
οἱ σπαθαροκουβικουλάριοι τοῦ βασιλικοῦ κοιτῶνος·
σπαθαροκουβικουλάριοι τοῦ κουβουκλείου·
πρεσβύτεροι οἱ βασιλικοί·
οἱ πρεσβύτεροι καὶ ἡγούμενοι καὶ πρεσβύτεροι τῆς ἐκκλησίας·
οἱ σπαθαροκανδιδάτοι καὶ ἀπὸ στρατηγῶν·
οἱ σπαθαροκανδιδάτοι τοῦ χρυσοτρικλίνου·
οἱ σπαθαροκανδιδάτοι οἱ οἰκειακοὶ καὶ κριταί·
οἱ σπαθαροκανδιδάτοι καὶ μαγλαβῖται καὶ ἀρτικλῖναι·
οἱ σπαθαροκανδιδάτοι οἱ ἀπὸ ὀφφικίων·

1 ὁ πρωτοσπαθάριος LB   ἀποδομέστικοι H : ἀπὸ δομεστίκου L   ἐξσκουβιτόρων B :
ἐκσκουβίτων H   2 ἀποεπάρχοι (sic) H   3 ἀποστρατηγοὶ τῶν τῆς H   4 κυε-
στόρων B   5 καὶ ἐπὶ τοῦ H   ἐπάνω H : π̅ʹ L : πάλαι RB   6 καὶ ἀπὸ
ἐπάρχων L : παρὰ Λέοντος τοῦ φιλοχρίστου δεσπότου H   7 κρηταί L   9 τοῦ
σταύλου H : τῶν στάβλων LB   11 καὶ om. H   733 12 πρωτοασηκρῆται H
14 οἱ ante ἔξωτ. om. H   20 ὁμοτίμων αὐτῶν διὰ βραβείων διδομένων ἀξίων H
22 καθέδραν H : τάξιν LB   23 τὴν . . . τιμὴν conicio   σπαθαρίων κανδηδάτων H
26 σπαθαροκουβικουλάριοι L : σπαθαροκανδιδάτοι καὶ κουβικουλάριοι H   28 οἱ πρεσβύτεροι βασ. H   32 οἱ οἰκειακοὶ καὶ κρηταί L : om. οἱ H   33 σπαθάριοι H et infra
passim   ἀρτοκλῖναι H

οἱ σπαθαροκανδιδάτοι οἱ οἰκειακοὶ τοῦ λαυσιακοῦ·   734
οἱ σπαθαροκανδιδάτοι καὶ ἀσηκρῆται·
οἱ σπαθαροκανδιδάτοι καὶ κλεισουράρχαι·
ὁ σπαθαροκανδιδάτος καὶ τουρμάρχης τῶν φιβεράτων·
5 ὁ σπαθαροκανδιδάτος καὶ τουρμάρχης Λυκαονίας καὶ Παμφυλίας·
ὁ σπαθαροκανδιδάτος καὶ τοποτηρητὴς τῶν σχολῶν·
οἱ σπαθαροκανδιδάτοι καὶ τουρμάρχαι τῶν τῆς ἀνατολῆς θεμάτων κατὰ
τὰ θέματα αὐτῶν·
ὁ σπαθαροκανδιδάτος καὶ τοποτηρητὴς τῶν ἐξσκουβίτων·
10 οἱ σπαθαροκανδιδάτοι καὶ τουρμάρχαι τῶν θεμάτων τῆς δύσεως·
ὁ σπαθαροκανδιδάτος καὶ τοποτηρητὴς τοῦ ἀριθμοῦ·
οἱ σπαθαροκανδιδάτοι καὶ τουρμάρχαι τῶν πλοίμων·
ὁ σπαθαροκανδιδάτος καὶ τοποτηρητὴς τοῦ πλοίμου·
ὁ σπαθαροκανδιδάτος καὶ τοποτηρητὴς τῶν ἱκανάτων·
15 ὁ σπαθαροκανδιδάτος καὶ τοποτηρητὴς τῶν νουμέρων·
ὁ σπαθαροκανδιδάτος καὶ τοποτηρητὴς τῶν ὀπτημάτων·
ὁ σπαθαροκανδιδάτος καὶ τοποτηρητὴς τῶν τειχέων·
οἱ σπαθαροκανδιδάτοι οἱ διὰ πόλεως καὶ οἱ τῶν σεκρέτων·
οἱ δισύπατοι κατὰ τὰς τάξεις αὐτῶν.   (Disypati.)
20 εἰ δὲ μὴ εἶεν οὗτοι σπαθαροκανδιδάτοι, ταῖς μὲν διὰ βραβείων ἀξίαις
ὑποπιπτέτωσαν, ἐν δὲ τοῖς τοῦ βαθμοῦ αὐτῶν ὀφφικίοις ἀκολούθως τιμάσθωσαν.

εἶθ' οὕτως τῶν σπαθαρίων εἰσάγεται τάξις, οἷον   (Spatharii.)
οἱ κουβικουλάριοι τοῦ βασιλικοῦ κοιτῶνος·
25 οἱ κουβικουλάριοι τοῦ κουβουκλείου·
οἱ κουβουκλείσιοι τοῦ πατριάρχου·
ὁ οἰκονόμος τῆς μεγάλης ἐκκλησίας·
οἱ διάκονοι οἱ βασιλικοί·   735
οἱ διάκονοι τῆς ἐκκλησίας·
30 οἱ σπαθάριοι τοῦ χρυσοτρικλίνου·
οἱ σπαθάριοι καὶ κριταί·
οἱ σπαθάριοι καὶ μαγλαβῖται καὶ ἀρτικλῖναι·
οἱ σπαθάριοι οἰκειακοὶ τοῦ λαυσιακοῦ·
οἱ σπαθάριοι καὶ τουρμάρχαι κατὰ τὰ θέματα αὐτῶν·
35 οἱ σπαθάριοι καὶ τοποτηρηταὶ κατὰ τὰ τάγματα αὐτῶν·

---

1 οἱ οἰκειακοί L : om. οἱ H   λαυσάκου H   734 4 οἱ σπαθαροκανδιδάτοι καὶ τουρμάρχαι
τ. φ. B : om. H   5 οἱ σπαθάριοι καὶ τουρμάρχαι H (ut videtur), ita B (cum σπ ... ἆτοι)
6 οἱ σπαθάριοι καὶ τοποτηρηταὶ H (ut vid.), B (cum σπ ... ἆτοι)   7 ἀνατολικῆς H
9 οἱ σπαθάριοι καὶ τοποτηρηταὶ τῶν ἐκσκουβίτων H   ἐξσκουβιτόρων B   11 οἱ
σπαθάριοι καὶ τοποτηρηταὶ H   12 πλοιμάτων H   13 ὁ σπαθ. καὶ τοπ. τ. πλοίμου om. H
18 καὶ τῶν σεκρέτων H   23 οἷον ... κοιτῶνος om. H   26 κουβουκλείσιοι H
et forma contracta L : κουβικουλάριοι B   28 οἱ διάκονοι οἱ ... ἐκκλησίας om. H
735 31 κρηταί L   32 καὶ ante μαγ. om. L   ἀρτοκλῖναι H   33 οἱ σπαθάριοι
οἰκειακοῦ τοῦ λαυσιακοῦ H : om. L

οἱ σπαθάριοι καὶ ἀσηκρῆται·
⟨ὁ σπαθάριος⟩ καὶ πρωτονοτάριος τοῦ δρόμου·
οἱ σπαθάριοι τοῦ σπαθαρικίου·
ὁ σπαθάριος καὶ κόμης τῆς κόρτης τῶν Ἀνατολικῶν·
οἱ σπαθάριοι καὶ κόμητες τῶν σχολῶν· 5
οἱ σπαθάριοι καὶ κόμητες τῆς κόρτης τῶν ἀνατολικῶν θεμάτων κατὰ
τὰ θέματα αὐτῶν·
ὁ σπαθάριος καὶ σύμπονος τοῦ ἐπάρχου·
ὁ σπαθάριος καὶ λογοθέτης τῶν πραιτωρίων·
οἱ σπαθάριοι καὶ κόμητες τῆς κόρτης τῶν θεμάτων τῆς δύσεως κατὰ τὰ 10
θέματα αὐτῶν·
οἱ σπαθάριοι καὶ χαρτουλάριοι τοῦ γενικοῦ λογοθέτου·
οἱ σπαθάριοι καὶ ἀντιγραφῆς τοῦ κυαίστωρος·
οἱ σπαθάριοι καὶ χαρτουλάριοι τοῦ στρατιωτικοῦ λογοθέτου·
ὁ σπαθάριος καὶ χαρτουλάριος τοῦ θέματος τῶν Ἀνατολικῶν· 15
ὁ σπαθάριος καὶ χαρτουλάριος τοῦ τάγματος τῶν σχολῶν·
ὁ σπαθάριος καὶ ἀκτουάριος·
οἱ σπαθάριοι καὶ χαρτουλάριοι τῶν ἀνατολικῶν θεμάτων·
ὁ σπαθάριος καὶ χαρτουλάριος τῶν ἐξσκουβίτων·
οἱ σπαθάριοι καὶ χαρτουλάριοι τῶν δυτικῶν θεμάτων· 20
οἱ σπαθάριοι καὶ βασιλικοὶ νοτάριοι τῆς σακέλλης·
οἱ σπαθάριοι καὶ βασιλικοὶ νοτάριοι τοῦ βεστιαρίου·
οἱ σπαθάριοι καὶ βασιλικοὶ νοτάριοι τοῦ εἰδικοῦ·
οἱ σπαθάριοι καὶ νοτάριοι τῶν ἀρκλῶν τοῦ γενικοῦ·
ὁ σπαθάριος καὶ πρωτονοτάριος τοῦ μεγάλου κουρατωρικίου· 25
736 οἱ σπαθάριοι καὶ δευτερεύοντες τῶν δημάρχων·
ὁ σπαθάριος καὶ ἐπὶ τῆς κουρατωρίας τῶν βασιλικῶν οἴκων·
ὁ σπαθάριος καὶ δομέστικος τῆς ὑπουργίας·
ὁ σπαθάριος καὶ ζυγοστάτης·
ὁ σπαθάριος καὶ χρυσοεψητής· 30
ὁ σπαθάριος καὶ ἄρχων τοῦ ἀρμαμέντου·
οἱ σπαθάριοι καὶ ξενοδόχοι·
οἱ σπαθάριοι καὶ γηροκόμοι·
οἱ σπαθάριοι καὶ πρωτονοτάριοι τῶν θεμάτων κατὰ τὰ θέματα αὐτῶν·

---

1 ὁ σπαθάριος ἀσηκρήτης H   2 ⟨ὁ σπαθάριος⟩ καὶ scripsi: καὶ ὁ L B   4 οἱ
σπαθάριοι καὶ κόμητες L H B : correxi   6 οἱ σπ. κώμητες τ. σχ. H : οἱ σπ. καὶ κόμ.
. . . θέματα αὐτῶν om. H   9 οἱ σπαθάριοι καὶ λογοθέται πραιτωρίων H   12 λογοθεσίου H   13–14 οἱ σπ. κ. ἀντ. . . . . τ. στρ. λογοθέτου om. H   15 τοῦ om. L B
θέματος (non θεμάτων) L   ἀνατολικῶν . . . τοῦ τάγματος τῶν om. H   19 ὁ σπ. . . .
ἐξσκουβίτων om. H   21 τῆς σακέλλης L : τοῦ βεστιαρίου H   22 τοῦ βεστιαρίου L :
τῆς σακκέλλου H   24 οἱ σπ. . . . γενικοῦ om. H   25 οἱ σπαθάριοι καὶ πρωτονοτάριοι L H B : correxi   κουρατορικίου B   736 27 οἰκημάτων H   30 ὁ σπ. καὶ
χρυσ. om. H   χρυσοεψιτής L   31 οἱ σπαθάριοι καὶ ἄρχοντες H   ἀρμέντου B
33 γηροκόμοι H

ὁ σπαθάριος καὶ οἰκιστικός·
οἱ σπαθάριοι οἱ διὰ πόλεως καὶ οἱ ἐξωτικοί.

εἰ δὲ μὴ εἶεν καὶ οὗτοι σπαθάριοι, τὰς μὲν διὰ βραβείων ἀξίας ὑποπιπτέτωσαν, ἐν δὲ τοῖς αὐτῶν ὀφφικίοις κατὰ τάξιν τιμάσθωσαν.

5   μετὰ τούτους εἰσαγέσθω τετάρτη τάξις, ἡ τῶν ὑπάτων, στρατόρων,
κανδιδάτων, μανδατόρων, βεστητόρων, ἀπράτων, ταγματικῶν καὶ
θεματικῶν οὕτως.

ὕπατοι βασιλικοὶ καὶ χαρτουλάριοι καὶ νοτάριοι τῶν λεχθέντων σεκρέτων
κατὰ τοὺς βαθμοὺς τῶν ἑαυτῶν ὀφφικίων·

10   ὕπατοι παγανοὶ τῆς συγκλήτου·
κληρικοὶ τοῦ παλατίου καὶ τῆς μεγάλης ἐκκλησίας·
στράτωρες, εἰ τύχοιεν, τοῦ χρυσοτρικλίνου·
στράτωρες ὁμοίως τοῦ μαγλαβίου·
στράτωρες οἰκειακοὶ τοῦ λαυσιακοῦ καὶ ἀσηκρῆται·

15   στράτωρες τοῦ βασιλικοῦ στρατωρικίου·
στράτωρες, σκρίβωνες τῶν ἐξσκουβίτων καὶ χαρτουλάριοι τῶν θεμάτων·
δομέστικοι τοῦ τάγματος τῶν σχολῶν·
δομέστικοι τῶν θεμάτων τῆς ἀνατολῆς καὶ δύσεως κατὰ τὰ τάγματα 737
αὐτῶν καὶ τὰς ἀξίας αὐτῶν·

20   ἀσηκρῆται ἄπρατοι·
νοτάριοι τῶν ἀσηκρητειῶν ἄπρατοι·
κανδιδάτοι βασιλικοὶ τοῦ ἱπποδρόμου·
καὶ μανδάτορες, βεστήτορες, σιλεντιάριοι, δρουγγάριοι τῶν θεμάτων
ἄπρατοι κατὰ τὰ θέματα καὶ τοὺς δρόγγους αὐτῶν·

25   κόμητες τῶν θεμάτων ὁμοίως·
κόμητες τῶν ἀριθμῶν ἄπρατοι·
ὁ χαρτουλάριος τοῦ ἀριθμοῦ ὁμοίως·
κόμητες τοῦ πλοΐματος ὁμοίως·
ὁ χαρτουλάριος τοῦ πλοΐμου·

30   κόμητες τῶν ἱκανάτων ὁμοίως·
ὁ χαρτουλάριος τῶν ἱκανάτων ὁμοίως·
ὁ χαρτουλάριος τοῦ στάβλου ὁμοίως·
ὁ ἐπίκτης τοῦ στάβλου ὁμοίως·
⟨οἱ⟩ τριβοῦνοι τῶν νουμέρων·
ὁ χαρτουλάριος τῶν νουμέρων·
οἱ τριβοῦνοι τῶν τειχέων·
ὁ χαρτουλάριος τῶν τειχέων·
οἱ δευτερεύοντες τῶν δημάρχων·
οἱ κόμητες τῶν ὀπτημάτων·

τάξις δ'
(Hypati,
stratores,
candidati,
mandatores,
vestitores,
silentiarii,
ex-praefectis,
stratelatae.)

2 οἱ διὰ πόλεως L : om. οἱ H   οἱ ἐξωτικοί L : om. οἱ H   3 κατὰ μὲν τὰς H :
τὰς μὲν L   737 18 τάγμα L   34 οἱ addidi   35 locum ita scripserunt edd.,
notis correctionis in codice male intellectis : οἱ κομ. τ. ὀπτημάτων· ὁ χ. τ. ὀπτ.· ὁ χ. τ.
τειχ.· οἱ δευτ. τ. δημ.· οἱ τριβ. τ. τειχ.

ὁ χαρτουλάριος τῶν ὀπτημάτων·
ὁ προέξημος τῶν σχολῶν·
οἱ κένταρχοι τοῦ ἀριθμοῦ·
οἱ κένταρχοι τῶν ἱκανάτων·
οἱ προτίκτορες τῶν σχολῶν·   5
οἱ βικάριοι τῶν νουμέρων·
οἱ βικάριοι τῶν τειχέων·
οἱ δρακονάριοι τῶν ἐξσκουβίτων·
οἱ ἀποεπάρχοντες·
οἱ στρατηλάται·   10
ὁ ἀκόλουθος τοῦ ἀριθμοῦ·
ὁ πρωτομανδάτωρ τοῦ ἐξσκουβίτου·
ὁ πρωτομανδάτωρ τῶν ἱκανάτων·
οἱ πρωτοκάραβοι·
οἱ πρωτονοτάριοι τῶν θεμάτων καὶ τῶν ἀγελῶν οἱ ἄπρατοι·   15
οἱ βανδοφόροι τοῦ ἀριθμοῦ·
οἱ βανδοφόροι τῶν ἱκανάτων·
οἱ εὐτυχοφόροι τῶν σχολῶν·
οἱ σκευοφόροι τῶν ἐξσκουβίτων·
οἱ λαβουρήσιοι τοῦ ἀριθμοῦ·   20
738   οἱ σκηπτροφόροι τῶν σχολῶν·
οἱ σιγνοφόροι τῶν ἐξσκουβίτων·
οἱ σημειοφόροι τοῦ ἀριθμοῦ·
οἱ σημειοφόροι τῶν ἱκανάτων·
οἱ ἀξιωματικοὶ τῶν σχολῶν·   25
οἱ σινάτωρες τῶν ἐξσκουβίτων·
οἱ δουκινιάτωρες τοῦ ἀριθμοῦ·
οἱ δουκινιάτωρες τῶν ἱκανάτων·
οἱ μανδάτωρες τῶν σχολῶν·
οἱ πρωτοκαγκελλάριοι τῶν θεμάτων·   30
οἱ ὀπτίονες τῶν ταγμάτων·
ὁ πρωτοκαγκελλάριος τοῦ γενικοῦ λογοθέτου·
ὁ πρωτοκαγκελλάριος τοῦ κυαίστωρος·
ὁ πρωτομανδάτωρ τῶν νουμέρων·
ὁ πρωτομανδάτωρ τῶν τειχέων·   35
ὁ πρωτοκαγκελλάριος τοῦ σακελλίου·
ὁ κένταρχος τοῦ βεστιαρίου·
οἱ μανδάτορες καὶ λεγατάριοι τῶν ἐξσκουβίτων·
οἱ μανδάτορες καὶ λεγατάριοι τοῦ ἀριθμοῦ·
οἱ ἐξσκουβίτορες·   40
οἱ θυρωροὶ τοῦ παλατίου καὶ τῶν σεκρέτων·

16 βαντοφόροι τοῦ ἀριθμοῦ L   738 38 μανδάτορες scripsi : πρωτομανδάτορες L B

οἱ διατρέχοντες τοῦ δρόμου·
οἱ φακτιονάριοι·
οἱ γειτονιάρχαι·
οἱ νοτάριοι τῶν μερῶν·
5 οἱ χαρτουλάριοι τῶν μερῶν·
οἱ ποιηταὶ καὶ μελισταὶ τῶν δήμων·
οἱ ἡνίοχοι τῶν μερῶν·
οἱ μανδάτορες τῶν νουμέρων·
οἱ μανδάτορες τῶν τειχέων·
10 ὁ λεγατάριος τοῦ βεστιαρίου·
οἱ χοσβαῖται τοῦ μεγάλου βεστιαρίου·
οἱ κένταρχοι τῶν στρατηγῶν τῶν θεματικῶν·
οἱ μικροπανῖται·
οἱ παραφύλακες τῶν κάστρων ἄπρατοι·
15 κένταρχοι τῶν βάνδων·
οἱ δημῶται·
οἱ δρουγγάριοι τῶν πεζῶν·
οἱ καγκελλάριοι τῶν σεκρέτων·
οἱ τοποτηρηταὶ τῶν χορῶν·
20 οἱ στρατιῶται τῶν ταγμάτων·
οἱ στρατιῶται τῶν θεμάτων.

εἰ δὲ ἐκ πάντων τούτων τῶν λεχθέντων τινὲς ἔχοιεν ἀξίας τὰς διὰ βραβείου διδομένας, ἕκαστος αὐτῶν τῇ ἀξίᾳ τοῦ ὁμοτίμου τὸν βαθμὸν προτι-
μάσθω. εἰ δὲ παγανοὶ πέλοιεν, ἐν μόνοις τοῖς ὀφφικίοις τιμάσθωσαν κατὰ 739
25 τὴν ἤδη ἐκτεθεῖσαν τάξιν κλητορευόμενοι.

οἱ δὲ ἐξ ἐθνῶν εἰσερχόμενοι·πρέσβεις καὶ τῆς τιμίας συνεστιάσεως τῶν
βασιλέων ἡμῶν ἀξιούμενοι κλητορεύονται καὶ αὐτοὶ οὕτως·

Οἱ ἀπὸ Ῥώμης ἐπίσκοποι προεκρίθησαν τῶν καθ' ἡμᾶς ἐπισκόπων.

οἱ μὲν ἀπὸ Ῥώμης ἐρχόμενοι, ἐάν εἰσιν ἐπίσκοποι, προτιμῶνται τῶν
30 ἐπισκόπων τῆς καθ' ἡμᾶς ἐκκλησίας· εἰ δὲ πρεσβύτεροι εἶεν, ὡσαύτως
προκρίνονται. ὁμοίως καὶ ἐν ἕκαστον τάγμα τῆς ἱεροσύνης τὴν προτί-
μησιν ἀναδέχεται κατὰ τὴν καθέδραν τὴν ἀνωτέρως ῥηθεῖσαν. τὸ αὐτὸ
δὲ κρατείσθω καὶ ἐπὶ τῶν ἐν τῇ ἀνατολῇ ὄντων τριῶν πατριαρχῶν. ἐτιμή-
θησαν δὲ οἱ ἀπὸ Ῥώμης ἐλθόντες διὰ τὴν ἕνωσιν τῆς ἐκκλησίας ἐπὶ
35 Λέοντος τοῦ φιλοχρίστου δεσπότου, οἷον ὁ ἐπίσκοπος Νικόλαος καὶ καρδη-
νάλιος Ἰωάννης, ἐπάνω πάσης τῆς τάξεως τῶν μαγίστρων.

---

1 διατρέχοτες L   20 ταγμάτων scripsi : θεμάτων L   739 25 ταξειν L   κλητωρ. B
27 κλητωρ. B   28 οἱ . . . ἐπισκόπων quasi notam marginalem uncis inclus. R B
33 ἐτιμίθησαν L

Καὶ οἱ ἀπὸ Ἀντιοχείας καὶ Ἱεροσολύμων σύγκελλοι προεκρίθησαν παντὸς μαγίστρου.

ὡσαύτως καὶ οἱ ἀπὸ Ἀντιοχείας καὶ Ἱεροσολύμων σύγκελλοι ἐν τῇ δευτέρᾳ θέσει τῆς τραπέζης πρῶτοι ἐπάνω παντὸς μαγίστρου.

(Saraceni amici.)

οἱ δὲ ἐξ Ἀγάρων φίλοι τῇ τῶν πατρικίων καὶ στρατηγῶν ὑποπίπτουσι 5
τάξει ἐν ταῖς καθέδραις, οἱ μὲν ἀνατολικοὶ προκρινόμενοι τῶν ἑσπερίων·
740 καθέζονται δὲ ἐν τῇ εὐωνύμῳ θέσει, ἢ τέταρτοι φίλοι, ἢ πέμπτοι, πρὸς τὸ
αὐτοὺς ἐν τῷ δευτέρῳ μίνσῳ τῆς τραπέζης τυγχάνειν.

(Bulgari amici.)

οἱ δὲ ἀπὸ τῶν Νούνων, ἤτοι Βουλγάρων, εἰσερχόμενοι φίλοι ἐν μὲν τῇ 10
κλήσει τῶν κοινῶν κλητωρίων τέταρτοι ἢ πέμπτοι ἐν τῇ εὐωνύμῳ θέσει
κληθήσονται, δηλονότι ὑποπίπτοντες καὶ αὐτοὶ τῇ τῶν πατρικίων καὶ στρατηγῶν καὶ πάντων τῶν ἐν τῷ βήλῳ πατρικίων τεταγμένων ἀρχόντων,
ἀπολαύοντες καὶ αὐτοὶ τὸν δεύτερον μίνσον τῆς βασιλικῆς τραπέζης. ἐν
δὲ τοῖς ιθ´ τῶν ἑορτῶν ἀκουβίτοις κλητωρεύονται ὄγδοοι καὶ ἔννατοι, δη- 15
λονότι ὑποπίπτοντες τῇ τάξει τοῦ προλεχθέντος βήλου.

(Francorum legati.)

οἱ δὲ ἐκ Φράγγων πρέσβεις, εἰ μὲν ἔχοιεν χειροτονίας, κατὰ ταύτας
κληθήσονται· εἰ δὲ παγανοί εἰσιν, τῇ τῶν ὀφφικιαλίων ὑποπίπτουσι τάξει.

οἱ δὲ ἐκ τῶν λοιπῶν ἐθνῶν ἐρχόμενοι φίλοι τῇ τῶν σπαθαροκανδιδάτων 20
ὑποπίπτουσι πάντες ἀξίᾳ.

Sectio IV.
Τόμος τέταρτος.

Ἐπειδὴ τῆς τῶν ἀρτικλινῶν ἐπιστήμης ἰδικήν τινα πραγματείαν συγ-
γράψασθαι ἐσπουδάσαμεν, καὶ τὰς τοῦ οἰκείου πολιτεύματος ἀξίας ἐκφαν-
τορικῶς ἐν ταῖς καθέδραις ἀκριβῶς ἐξεθέμεθα, καὶ τὴν τῶν ἱερῶν βασιλικῶν 25
κλητωρίων εὐστάθειαν καὶ κατάστασιν ὑμῖν ὑπεδείξαμεν, φέρε δὴ καὶ τὰς
741 ἰδέας τῶν ἐφ᾿ ἑκάστῃ ἑορτῇ κικλησκομένων ἀξιωμάτων καὶ τὰς τούτων
πολυειδεῖς ἀμφιάσεις ὅπως δεῖ συνεισάγειν ἐν τοῖς κλητωρίοις, σαφῶς
ὑμῖν διηγήσομαι. ἄρξομαι δ᾿ ἐντεῦθεν (ὅτε) καὶ ἡ τῆς θείας χάριτος τῷ κόσμῳ
ἐπέφανεν ἀπαρχή, ἧς καὶ οἱ θεοπρόβλητοι καὶ θειότατοι ἡμῶν βασιλεῖς, 30
τὴν ἐγκόσμιον καὶ ὑπερκόσμιον ταύτην πανηγυρίζοντες χαρμονὴν κατὰ
μίμησιν τῆς Χριστοῦ πρὸς ἀνθρώπους ἐπιδημίας, κοινῇ τὴν πανδεσίαν τοῖς
πιστοῖς ἐφαπλώσαντες κοινωνοῦσι τῆς σωματικῆς ἑστιάσεως.

Ἡ γενέθλιος τοῦ Χριστοῦ ἡμέρα, ἐν ᾗ προτίθενται αἱ τῶν ιθ´ ἀκουβίτων ἐκθέσεις.

Δεῖ γὰρ ὑμᾶς, ὦ φίλοι, ἐν ταύτῃ τῇ λαμπρᾷ καὶ περιδόξῳ τῶν Χριστοῦ 35
γενεθλίων ἡμέρᾳ, ἡνίκα αἱ πολυσχεδεῖς καὶ ἐξαίσιοι τῶν ιθ´ προτίθονται

---

1 καὶ οἱ . . . προεκ. π. μαγίστρου uncis inclus. R B   1, 2 σύγκελλοι L   2 Ἀντιο-
χίας L   740 10 Νούνων, id est Οὔνων quod fortasse legendum est   22 δ´ B
741 28 συνηισάγειν L   29 ὅτε addidi   30 θειώτατοι L   34 ἐκθέσης L

ἀκουβίτων ἐκθέσεις, ἐν μὲν τῇ βασιλικῇ τραπέζῃ τοῦ κράματος τῆς μεγάλης
ἐκκλησίας καλεῖν εἰς συνεστίασιν τῶν φιλοχρίστων ἡμῶν βασιλέων με-
γιστάνας ἐκ τῆς βασιλικῆς συγκλήτου τὸν ἀριθμὸν ιβ', οἷον μαγίστρους,
πραιποσίτους, ἀνθυπάτους, πατρικίους, στρατηγούς, ὀφφικιαλίους, οὓς ἂν
5 δόξῃ τοὺς αὐτοκράτορας λαμβάνεσθαι· εἰσάγειν δὲ αὐτούς, ἄνευ μέντοι
τῶν οἰκείων χλαμύδων, ἡμφιεσμένους δὲ τὰ καμήσια καὶ μόνα. εἰ δὲ
τύχοιεν στρατηγοὶ κεκλημένοι, μετὰ τῶν οἰκείων σκαραμαγγίων εἰσαγέσθω-
σαν σὺν τῷ δρουγγαρίῳ τῆς βίγλης. ἐν δὲ τῇ τῶν ιθ' ἀκουβίτων τιμιω- 742
τάτῃ τραπέζῃ δεῖ ὑμᾶς καλεῖν μαγίστρους δύο, ἀνθυπάτους πατρικίους
10 στρατηγοὺς ἕξ, Βουλγάρους φίλους δύο, ὀφφικιαλίους ἀπὸ τῆς τοῦ στρατιωτικοῦ λογοθέτου τάξεως καὶ κατωτέρω δύο, πρὸς τὸ συνανακληθῆναι τῷ
βασιλεῖ εἰς τύπον τῆς ἀποστολικῆς δωδεκάδος, φίλους τὸν ἀριθμὸν ιβ'·
προκισεύειν δὲ αὐτοὺς δεῖ στιχηδὸν κατὰ τάξιν τῆς ἑκάστου ἀξίας, ἐνδεδυ-
μένους τὰς οἰκείας αὐτῶν χλαμύδας ἐμπροσθείῳ τῷ σχήματι, ὑποδεδεμένους
15 δὲ καὶ τὰ οἰκεῖα καμπάγια, καὶ εἰσαγαγεῖν αὐτοὺς μετὰ τὴν ἄφιξιν τῶν
μελλόντων παραστᾶναι βασιλικῶν ὑπουργῶν τε καὶ βουκαλίων, δηλονότι
λαβόντος τὸ σχῆμα τοῦ καστρησίου τῆς βασιλικῆς τραπέζης παρὰ τοῦ
ἄνωθεν παρεστῶτος περιφανοῦς πραιποσίτου, καὶ συνανερχομένου αὐτοῖς
μέχρι τοῦ τριβάθμου τῆς βασιλικῆς εὐωχίας, καὶ ἱστῶντος αὐτοὺς κύκλῳ
20 τῆς τιμίας τραπέζης εἰς τὸ εἰδικῶς προσκαλεῖσθαι πλησιέστερον φίλους,
οὓς ἂν δόξῃ τῷ βασιλεῖ. ἐν δὲ τοῖς ἑκατέρων τῶν μερῶν ἀκουβίτοις δεῖ
ὑμᾶς καλεῖν ἐν ταύτῃ τῇ λαμπρᾷ καὶ περιβοήτῳ ἡμέρᾳ τὴν ὑπὸ καμπάγιν
σύγκλητον πᾶσαν, οἷον ἀσηκρήτας, χαρτουλαρίους τῶν μεγάλων σεκρέτων,
βασιλικοὺς νοταρίους τῶν λεχθέντων σεκρέτων, οἷον ἀπό τε σπαθαροκαν-
25 διδάτων καὶ κατωτέρω, ὑπάτων, δισυπάτων, κομήτων τῶν σχολῶν, σιλεντιαρίων, προτικτόρων, εὐτυχοφόρων, σκηπτροφόρων, ἀξιωματικῶν τῶν δια- 743
φόρων ταγμάτων τὸν ἀριθμὸν ρξη', Ἀγαρηνῶν τοῦ πραιτωρίου κδ', τῶν
Βουλγάρων φίλων ἀνθρώπους ιβ', καὶ πένητας ἀδελφοὺς τὸν ἀριθμὸν ιβ'·
προκισσεύειν δὲ αὐτοὺς στιχηδὸν οὕτως· τοὺς μὲν συγκλητικοὺς κατὰ τὰς
30 οἰκείας αὐτῶν ἀξίας καὶ τὰς τῶν ὀφφικίων αὐτῶν διαφορὰς διαστελλόμενος
ἔνθεν κἀκεῖθεν· τοὺς δὲ Ἀγαρηνοὺς κατέναντι τῆς ὄψεως τῶν βασιλέων
ἐπὶ τῆς ἕκτης καὶ ἑβδόμης τραπέζης· τοὺς δὲ Βουλγάρων ἀνθρώπους ἐπὶ
τῆς ἐνάτης τραπέζης τῆς αὐτῆς περιόδου· τοὺς δὲ πένητας καὶ αὐτοὺς
προσκαλεῖσθαι ἐπὶ τῆς θ' τραπέζης τῆς εὐωνύμου θέσεως, ἐν ᾗ παράστασις
35 τοῦ δρουγγαρίου τυγχάνει. εἰσάγειν δὲ δεῖ ἅπαντας μετὰ τὴν ἄφιξιν τῶν
πρωτοκλήτων φίλων τῆς βασιλικῆς τραπέζης οὕτως· τοὺς μὲν ἀξιωματικοὺς
ἅπαντας μετὰ τῶν οἰκείων ἀλλαξιμάτων, χλαμύδων τε καὶ καμπαγίων,
στιχηδὸν κατὰ τάξιν τοῦ αὐτοῦ ἀξιώματος καὶ ὀφφικίου· τοὺς δὲ Ἀγαρηνοὺς
λευκοφόρους ἀζώνους ὑποδεδεμένους, δηλονότι προπορευομένου αὐτῶν τοῦ

---

3 ιδ' L : corr. R   5 αὐτοκράτωρας L   6 καμίσια B et passim   742 13 στιχηδὸν L   15 ἄφηξιν L   16 fort. παρεστάναι   22 καμπάγιον B et passim
743 34 παράστασης   35 ἄφηξιν L   39 ἀζόνους L   προπορευομένων αὐτῶν L :
-ομένου αὐτοῖς B

καλέσαντος ἀρτικλίνου καὶ συνανερχομένου ἐφ' ἑκατέρου τῶν μερῶν διὰ
τῆς ὀπισθίου θέσεως τῶν αὐτῶν ἀκουβίτων καὶ διὰ τοῦ ἐμπροσθίου τόπου
ἐξαριθμοῦντος ἐφ' ἑκάστῳ ἀκουβίτῳ δωδεκάδα προσώπων μίαν καὶ μὴ
συγχωροῦντός τινα ἀνακληθῆναι μέχρι τῆς ἐκφωνήσεως τῶν παρεστώτων
βασιλικῶν βουκαλίων. μετὰ δὲ τὴν πάντων ἀνάκλησιν δεῖ προσέχειν τὸ 5
744 μουσικὸν μέλος, καὶ ἡνίκα τὸ ἴδιον ἀπηχήσει φθέγμα, ἐξανίστασθαι ἅπαντας
εἰς εὐφημίαν τῶν δεσποτῶν καὶ τὰς ἑαυτῶν ἀπεκδιδύσκεσθαι χλαμύδας·
ἀλλὰ μὴν καὶ ὁσάκις ἂν τὸ μουσικὸν ἀπηχήσῃ, καὶ ὁσάκις ἂν θυμελικόν
τι πρὸς τέρψιν ἐκτελεσθῇ πρᾶγμα, καὶ ἡνίκα τι βρώσιμον ἐκ τῆς βασιλικῆς
τραπέζης διὰ τοῦ τερπνοῦ καστρησίου πρὸς τοὺς δαιτυμόνας ἐξαποσταλή- 10
σεται. ἐν δὲ τῇ τούτων ἐξόδῳ δεῖ προσέχειν τοῖς ῥωμαΐζουσι βουκαλίοις
καὶ σὺν τῇ αὐτῶν ἐκφωνήσει προσέχειν τὸ σχῆμα τοῦ κλεινοῦ καστρησίου,
καὶ αὖθις ἐξανιστᾶν πάντας τοὺς κεκλημένους χλανιδοφόρους διὰ τῆς
ὀπισθίου θέσεως τῶν ἀκουβίτων, καὶ ἐπανάγειν αὐτοὺς ἐκ τῶν κάτω πρὸς
τὴν ἄνω προσωπικὴν ἔξοδον τῆς αὐτῆς περιόδου. καὶ εἶθ' οὕτως μετὰ τὴν 15
τούτων τελείαν ὑπελδυσιν† καὶ αὐτοὺς τῆς βασιλικῆς τραπέζης δαιτυμόνας
ἐξάγειν, δηλονότι προπορευομένου αὐτοῖς τοῦ κλεινοῦ καστρησίου τῆς βα-
τῶν αὐτῶν   σιλικῆς τιμίας τραπέζης. ἐπὶ δὲ τῆς δευτέρας ἡμέρας τῆς πολυσχεδοῦς
ἀκουβίτων   ταύτης καὶ λαμπρᾶς πανδεσίας δεῖ ἡμᾶς εὐτρεπίζειν εἰς πρόσκλησιν τῆς
ἡμέρα β΄   βασιλικῆς περιβλέπτου τραπέζης ὁμοίως μαγίστρους, ἀνθυπάτους, πατρι- 20
κίους, ὀφφικιαλίους, καὶ οἰκειακοὺς πρωτοσπαθαρίους, τὸν ἀριθμὸν ιβ΄,
συναριθμουμένου αὐτοῖς ἐξαιρέτως τοῦ δομεστίκου τῶν σχολῶν κατὰ τύπον·
745 εἰσάγειν δὲ αὐτοὺς πάντας ἐν τῇ αὐτῶν ἀνακλήσει χλανιδοφόρους ἐστολι-
σμένους κατὰ τὸ ἴδιον σχῆμα· τοὺς δὲ οἰκειακοὺς πρωτοσπαθαρίους μετὰ
τῶν οἰκείων σπεκίων καὶ ῥωέων σαγίων, ἐμπροσθίῳ τῷ σχήματι, καθὼς 25
ἀνωτέρω δεδήλωται. ἐν δὲ τοῖς πέριξ ἀκουβίτοις δεῖ καλεῖν ἐφ' ἑκάτερα
μέρη ἐπὶ δύο ἀκουβίτων βασιλικοὺς ἀνθρώπους ἀπὸ τῆς τῶν σπαθαροκανδιδάτων ἀξίας καὶ κατωτέρω· ἐν δὲ τοῖς λοιποῖς ἀκουβίτοις ἅπαντας τοὺς
ἄρχοντας τοῦ τάγματος τῶν σχολῶν, οἷον τοποτηρητήν, εἰ τύχοι αὐτὸν
εἶναι σπαθαροκανδιδάτον, τοὺς κόμητας τῶν σχολῶν, δομεστίκους τῶν 30
σχολῶν, τὸν προέξημον, προτήκτορας, εὐτυχοφόρους, σκηπτροφόρους, ἀξιω-
ματικούς, μανδάτορας, τὸν ἀριθμὸν σμ΄, καὶ πένητας τὸν ἀριθμὸν ιβ΄· εἰσάγειν δὲ αὐτοὺς ἐν τῇ ἀνακλήσει μετὰ τῶν οἰκείων σκαραμαγγίων, τὸν
δὲ τοποτηρητὴν καὶ χαρτουλάριον τοῦ αὐτοῦ τάγματος μετὰ καὶ σαγίων
ῥωέων, δηλονότι προπορευομένου αὐτοῖς τοῦ ἀρτικλίνου κατὰ τὸν προγρα- 35
ἡμέρα γ΄   φέντα τύπον. ἐπὶ δὲ τῆς τρίτης ἡμέρας τῶν αὐτῶν ἀκουβίτων δεῖ ἡμᾶς
εὐτρεπίζειν εἰς πρόσκλησιν, ἐν μὲν τῇ βασιλικῇ τραπέζῃ ἄρχοντας μεγι-
στᾶνας τοὺς ἀνωτέρω ἐπὶ τῆς δευτέρας ἡμέρας μνημονευθέντας τὸν ἀριθμὸν
ιβ΄, ἀφαιρουμένου μὲν τοῦ τῶν σχολῶν δομεστίκου, ἀντεισιόντος δὲ κατὰ
τύπον τοῦ δομεστίκου τῶν ἐξσκουβίτων, εἰσάγειν δὲ αὐτοὺς ἐν τῇ ἀνα- 40

744 12, 17 κλινοῦ L   16 ὑπέκδυσιν (etiam ἀπόλυσιν, ἀπήλυσιν) coni. R   17 δὲ
δηλονότι L   19 δι (pro δεῖ) L   745 27 ἀπὸ L: ἐπὶ R B   28 ἀκκουβίτοις L
39 ἀντησιόντος L

κλήσει κατὰ τὸν προδειχθέντα τύπον. ἐν δὲ τοῖς ἑκατέροις τῶν μερῶν
ἀκουβίτοις δεῖ καλεῖν ὁμοίως ἐπὶ τοῖς δυσὶν ἀκουβίτοις βασιλικοὺς ἀνθρώ- 746
πους ἐν ἀξιώμασιν· ἐν δὲ τοῖς λοιποῖς ἀκουβίτοις ἅπαντας τοὺς ἄρχοντας
τοῦ τάγματος τῶν ἐξσκουβίτων, οἷον τοποτηρητήν, σκρίβωνας, τὸν χαρτουλάριον, δρακοναρίους, σκευοφόρους, σιγνοφόρους, σενάτορας, πρωτομανδάτορα καὶ μανδάτορας τὸν ἀριθμὸν σδ′, καὶ πένητας ιβ′, εἰσάγειν δὲ αὐτοὺς
κατὰ τὸν προρρηθέντα τύπον κατὰ τὸ σχῆμα τῆς δευτέρας ἡμέρας. ἐπὶ δὲ
τῆς τετάρτης ἡμέρας τῆς περιφανοῦς ταύτης, ὡς εἰπεῖν, δεξιώσεως δεῖ ἡμᾶς ἡμέρα δ
εὐτρεπίζειν εἰς κλῆσιν τῆς βασιλικῆς τιμίας τραπέζης ἐκ τῶν ἀνωτέρω καθ᾽
ἑκάστην ἡμέραν μνημονευθέντων ἀρχόντων σὺν τῷ δρουγγαρίῳ τῆς βίγλης
κατὰ τύπον τὸν ἀριθμὸν ιβ′, εἰσάγειν δὲ ἅπαντας ἐν τῇ ἀνακλήσει μετὰ
τῶν οἰκείων ἀλλαξιμάτων, καθὼς εἴρηται· τὸν δὲ δρουγγάριον τῆς βίγλης
μετὰ τοῦ οἰκείου σκαραμαγγίου καὶ σαγίου ῥοῆς. ἐν δὲ τοῖς λοιποῖς ἀκουβίτοις δεῖ ἡμᾶς καλεῖν βασιλικοὺς ἀνθρώπους κατὰ τὸν λεχθέντα τύπον,
καὶ ἅπαντας τοὺς ἄρχοντας τοῦ τάγματος τοῦ ἀριθμοῦ, οἷον τοποτηρητήν,
τὸν χαρτουλάριον, τοὺς κόμητας, τοὺς κεντάρχους, βανδοφόρους, λαβουρη-
σίους, σημειοφόρους, δουκινιάτορας, μανδάτορας, θυρωρούς, διατρέχοντας,
τὸν ἀριθμὸν σδ′, καὶ εἰσάγειν αὐτοὺς οὕτως· τὸν μὲν τοποτηρητὴν μετὰ
ῥοέου σαγίου, τοὺς δὲ λοιποὺς μετὰ τῶν οἰκείων σκαραμαγγίων, καθὼς
ἀνωτέρω δεδήλωται. ἐπὶ δὲ τῆς πέμπτης ἡμέρας δεῖ ὑμᾶς προευτρεπίζειν 747
εἰς κλῆσιν τῆς τιμίας ὄντως βασιλικῆς τραπέζης ὁμοῦ ἐκ τῶν ἀνωτέρω ἡμέρα ε′
μνημονευθέντων ἐνδόξων μεγιστάνων σὺν τοῦ δομεστίκου τῶν ἱκανάτων,
φίλους τὸν ἀριθμὸν ιβ′, καὶ εἰσάγειν αὐτοὺς μετὰ τῶν οἰκείων ἀλλαξημάτων, καθὼς ἀνωτέρω δεδήλωται. ἐν δὲ τοῖς λοιποῖς ἀκουβίτοις δεῖ καλεῖν
ὁμοῦ βασιλικοὺς ἀνθρώπους, ὡς ἀνωτέρω εἰρήκαμεν. ἐν δὲ τοῖς κατωτέρω
τοὺς ἄρχοντας τοῦ τάγματος τῶν αὐτῶν ἱκανάτων, οἷον τοποτηρητήν, τοὺς
κόμητας, τὸν χαρτουλάριον, τοὺς κεντάρχους, βανδοφόρους, σημειοφόρους,
δουκινιάτορας καὶ μανδάτορας, σδ′ τὸν ἀριθμόν, καὶ πένητας ιβ′, εἰσάγειν
δὲ αὐτοὺς ἐν τῇ ἀνακλήσει, καθὼς καὶ ἐν τοῖς λοιποῖς τάγμασιν προεγρά-
φαμεν. σημειωτέον δὲ τοῦτο· εἰ γὰρ ἐν τῇ πρώτῃ ἡμέρᾳ τῆς ἑβδομάδος
ἡ τῶν ἐνδόξων τοῦ Χριστοῦ γενεθλίων ἐπέστη ἑορτή, καὶ ἀπὸ ταύτης ἡ
τῶν ιθ′ ἀκουβίτων δεξίωσις τὴν ἀρχὴν ἐπιδείξεται, δεῖ ἡμᾶς ἐν τῇ ἕκτῃ
ἡμέρᾳ ἐπὶ μὲν τῆς τιμίας βασιλικῆς τραπέζης συγκαλεῖν εἰς ἑστίασιν τὸν ἡμέρα ς′
ἀρχιεπίσκοπον Κωνσταντινουπόλεως μετὰ καὶ ιβ′ ἡγουμένων τῶν ἐν τῇ
περὶ ἡμᾶς τόμῳ κειμένων, εἰσάγειν δὲ αὐτοὺς ἐν τῇ ἀνακλήσει οὕτως· τὸν
μὲν πατριάρχην σὺν τῷ βασιλεῖ ἅμα τοῦ στίχου εἰς τὸ ἐπὶ δίφρου καθε-
σθῆναι· τοὺς δὲ ὁσίους ἡγουμένους στιχηδὸν κατὰ τὴν οἰκείαν τάξιν καὶ
ἁρμόζουσαν δόξαν· εἰσάγειν δὲ αὐτούς, καθὼς καὶ τοὺς πατρικίους, μετὰ 748

---

746 4 τοποτηρητὰς L B : correxi   5 πρωτομανδάτορα scripsi : -ορας L B   6 τὸν
ἀριθμὸν scripsi : τοῦ ἀριθμοῦ L B   17 δουκινάτορας L B   18 τὸ μὲν L   19 ῥωέου B
747 21 ὄντος L   23 ἀλλαξιμάτων B et passim   26 τῶν κομήτων L B : correxi
27 τῶν κεντάρχων, βανδοφόρων, σημειοφόρων, δουκινιατόρων καὶ μανδατόρων L B : correxi
30 ἢ γὰρ L   32 δεξίωσης L

τῶν οἰκείων αὐτῶν φελωνίων ἀπολελυμένῳ τῷ σχήματι, δηλονότι προπορευομένου αὐτοῖς τοῦ βασιλικοῦ καστρησίου, καὶ ὁμοίως ἱστῶντος κύκλῳ
τῆς βασιλικῆς τραπέζης εἰς τὸ προσκαλέσασθαι πλησιέστερον ἐξ αὐτῶν
οὓς ἂν δόξῃ τῷ βασιλεῖ.   ἐν δὲ τοῖς λοιποῖς ἀκουβίτοις δεῖ ὑμᾶς καλεῖν
τοὺς ἐκ διαφόρων μοναστηρίων ἀναγραφομένους ἀβάδας, ἤγουν τοὺς τὰ 5
σφραγίδια παρ᾽ ἡμῶν εἰληφότας, τὸν ἀριθμὸν σις᾽· εἰσάγειν δὲ καὶ αὐτοὺς
στιχηδόν, καθὼς καὶ τοῖς λοιποῖς, ἠμφιεσμένους τὰς οἰκείας στολὰς ὡς
πρὸς συνήθειαν· ἀνακλίνειν δὲ αὐτοὺς ἐφ᾽ ἑκάστης τραπέζης δωδεκάδα
μίαν.   μετὰ δὲ τὴν τούτων ἀνάκλησιν καὶ ἑστίασιν δεῖ ὑμᾶς προσέχειν
τὸν τοῦ ὀπτομίνσου μίνσον, καὶ ἐν τούτῳ τῷ καιρῷ εἰσάγειν πρὸς χειρονο- 10
μίαν τῶν ἀνακειμένων καὶ ψαλλόντων πατέρων τοὺς δύο μεγάλους τῆς
ἐκκλησίας δομεστίκους καὶ ἱστᾶν αὐτοὺς ἔνθεν κἀκεῖθεν τοῦ περιβλέπτου
τρικλίνου πρὸς τὸ ποιεῖσθαι, ὡς εἴρηται, τὴν χειρονομίαν ἐπὶ τὴν ψαλμῳ-
δίαν τῶν ἀνακειμένων πατέρων.   δίδοται οὖν κατὰ τύπον παρὰ τοῦ εἰδικοῦ
λόγου τοῖς μὲν ἀνακειμένοις ἐπὶ τῆς βασιλικῆς τραπέζης ιβ᾽ ἡγουμένοις εἰς 15
φιλοτιμίας ἐπίδοσιν ἀνὰ νομισμάτων δ᾽· τοῖς δὲ λοιποῖς μονάχοις ἅπασιν
ἀνὰ νομίσματος ἑνὸς καὶ μόνου· τοῖς δὲ δύο δομεστίκοις ἀνὰ νομισμάτων
β᾽ κατὰ τύπον.   δεῖ εἰδέναι, ὅτι ἐν αὐτῇ τῇ ἡμέρᾳ καὶ οἱ πένητες ἐν τῷ
749 κονσιστορίῳ ἐσθίουσιν, λαμβάνοντες τὴν κατὰ συνήθειαν εὐλογίαν.   εἰ δὲ
ἐν δ᾽ ἢ πέμπτῃ ἡμέρᾳ τῆς ἑβδομάδος ἡ Χριστοῦ γέννησις καταντήσει, καὶ 20
ἀπὸ ταύτης ἄρξηται ἡ κλῆσις τελεῖσθαι τῶν ἀκουβίτων, δεῖ ὑμᾶς ἐν τῇ
κυριακῇ τῆς περιόδου τῆς αὐτῆς ἑβδομάδος πρὸ τῆς κλήσεως τοῦ πατριάρχου
καὶ τῶν ἀβάδων ἐκτελεῖν τὸ λεγόμενον κλητώριον τὸν πολύτριχον, καὶ
εὐτρεπίζειν εἰς συνεστίασιν φίλους ἐπὶ μὲν τῆς βασιλικῆς τραπέζης μαγίστρους, ἀνθυπάτους πατρικίους στρατηγοὺς ὀκτὼ καὶ Βουλγάρους φίλους 25
δύο καὶ τοὺς δύο δημάρχους Βενέτων τε καὶ Πρασίνων· εἰσάγειν δὲ καὶ
ἐξάγειν αὐτοὺς χλανιδοφόρους, καθὰ καὶ ἀνωτέρω δεδήλωται.   ἐν δὲ τοῖς
ἑκατέρων μερῶν ἀκουβίτοις δεῖ ὑμᾶς καλεῖν βασιλικοὺς ἀνθρώπους ἐθνικοὺς
πάντας, οἷον Φαργάνους, Χαζάρους, Ἀγαρηνούς, Φράγγους καὶ ὅσοι τῆς
βασιλικῆς ἐξ αὐτῶν ἀπολαύουσι τῶν ῥογῶν προμηθείας· εἰσάγειν δὲ αὐτοὺς 30
ἅπαντας καὶ ἐξάγειν μετὰ τὸ ἐθνικὸν ἴδιον σχῆμα, οἱονεὶ τὸ παρ᾽ αὐτῶν
ἐπιλεγόμενον καβάδιν.   καὶ εἶθ᾽ οὕτως τῇ ἀπὸ ταύτης εἰσιούσῃ τῆς ἑβδομάδος τετράδῃ προσκαλεῖσθαι τὸν πατριάρχην μετὰ τῶν αὐτοῦ ἡγουμένων
ἡμέρα ζ᾽ καὶ μοναχῶν, ὡς προλέλεκται.   ἐπὶ δὲ τῆς ἑβδόμης ἡμέρας τῶν αὐτῶν
ἀκουβίτων δεῖ ὑμᾶς εὐτρεπίζειν εἰς συνεστίασιν ἐπὶ τῆς βασιλικῆς τραπέζης 35
750 ἀνθυπάτους, πατρικίους, στρατηγούς, ὀφφικιαλίους σὺν τῷ ὑπάρχῳ τῆς
πόλεως καὶ τῷ δρουγγαρίῳ τῶν πλοΐμων, φίλους δύο καὶ δέκα· εἰσάγειν δὲ
αὐτοὺς καὶ ἐξάγειν μετὰ τῶν οἰκείων ἀλλαξιμάτων, καθὰ καὶ δεδήλωται·
ἐν δὲ τοῖς λοιποῖς ἀκουβίτοις καλεῖν εἰς ἑστίασιν τὸν σύμπονον καὶ τὸν
λογοθέτην τοῦ πραιτωρίου, τὸν τοποτηρητὴν τῶν πλοΐμων, τὸν χαρτουλάριον

---

748 4 δὲ L   17 νομήσματος ἑνὸς L   19 χρυσοιστοριω L : corr. Bieliaev I 118
(cf. supra p. 135 l. 15)   749 20 τετάρτη B   21 ἄρχηται B   29 ἀγαρίνους L
30 ἐξαυτῆς L : corr. R   32 καβάδιον B

τοῦ πλοίμου, τοὺς κόμητας τοῦ πλοίμου, κεντάρχους ὁμοίως, κριτὰς τῶν
ῥεγεώνων, ἐπόπτας τῆς πόλεως, γειτονειάρχας, τὸν λεγατάριον τοῦ πραιτωρίου, τὸν κεντυρίωνα, τοὺς πρωτοκαγκελλαρίους, καγκελλαρίους, καὶ μανδάτορας τοῦ πλοίμου, τὸν ἀριθμὸν σδ'· εἰσάγειν δὲ καὶ ἐξάγειν αὐτοὺς μετὰ
τῶν οἰκείων σκαραμαγγίων, πλὴν τοῦ τοποτηρητοῦ μετὰ καὶ σαγίων ῥωέων,
καθὼς ἀνωτέρω δεδήλωται. ἐπὶ δὲ τῆς ὀγδόης ἡμέρας τῶν αὐτῶν ἀκου- ἡμέρα η'
βίτων ἐκτελεῖται τὸ βωτὸν παιζοδρόμιον, καὶ δεῖ ὑμᾶς εὐτρεπίζειν εἰς
συνεστίασιν τῶν βασιλέων τοὺς προὔχοντας τῆς τάξεως τοῦ μυστικοῦ κουβουκλείου, οἷον πραιποσίτους, πρωτοσπαθαρίους εὐνούχους, πριμικηρίους,
ὀστιαρίους, τὸν ἀριθμὸν η', τὸν χαρτουλάριον τῆς βασιλικῆς σακέλλης, τὸν
ἐπὶ τοῦ εἰδικοῦ λόγου, τὸν ἀκτουάριον καὶ τὸν τῆς καταστάσεως· εἰσάγειν
δὲ αὐτοὺς μετὰ τῶν οἰκείων ἀλλαξημάτων, οὐ καθὼς τοὺς λοιποὺς ἅπαντας
ἐν ταῖς προλεχθείσαις ἡμέραις ἐκ τῶν κάτω πρὸς τὰ ἄνω σὺν τῷ καστρησίῳ
τὴν πορίαν ποιούμενοι, ἀλλ' αὖθις σὺν τῇ ἐξόδῳ τῆς βασιλικῆς ἀνακλήσεως 751
στιχίζειν αὐτοὺς κατὰ τὸ ἴδιον ἀξίωμα κύκλῳ τῆς τιμίας βασιλικῆς τραπέζης, καὶ ἅμα τῆς ἐκφωνήσεως τῶν παρεστώτων βουκαλίων ἀνακλίνειν
αὐτοὺς ἐν τῇ λαμπροτάτῃ τραπέζῃ, ἐξάγειν δὲ αὐτοὺς πάλιν τῇ αὐτῇ ἀκο-
λουθίᾳ, ὡς εἴρηται. ἐπὶ δὲ τοῖς λοιποῖς ἀκουβίτοις πρὸ τῆς βασιλικῆς
ἀνακλήσεως προανακλίνονται πένητες οἱ τὰ σφραγίδια εἰληφότες, καὶ ἔτι
αὐτῶν ἀνακειμένων καὶ ἐσθιόντων, ἐν τῷ καιρῷ τοῦ μίνσου τῶν δουλκίων,
ἀναλαμβάνονται τὰ δοθέντα σφραγίδια ὑπὸ ἀρτικλίνου, καὶ δίδοται κατὰ
τύπον παρὰ τοῦ εἰδικοῦ λόγου ἑκάστῳ πένητι εἰς βασιλικὴν εὐλογίαν ἀποκόμβιον ἔχον ἔνδοθεν νόμισμα ἕν. ἐπὶ δὲ τῆς ἐννάτης ἡμέρας τῶν αὐτῶν (ἡμέρα θ')
ἀκουβίτων τελεῖται κλητώριον δείπνου, ὃ καὶ τρυγητικὸν καλεῖται, καὶ δεῖ
ὑμᾶς προευτρεπίζειν εἰς συνεστίασιν τοῦ δείπνου τῷ βασιλεῖ φίλους ιβ',
οἷον μαγίστρους, ἀνθυπάτους πατρικίους στρατηγοὺς ὀκτώ, φίλους Βουλγάρων δύο, καὶ τοὺς ἑκατέρων δύο δημάρχους. προσκαλοῦνται δὲ οὗτοι
παρὰ τοῦ βασιλέως διὰ τοῦ ἀρτικλίνου πρωΐας, καὶ μίνσων διδομένων
συνεισέρχονται πάντες οἱ κεκλημένοι εἰς συνεστίασιν τῷ βασιλεῖ πρὸς
ἑσπέρας, καὶ εἰσάγονται καὶ ἐξάγονται πάντες μετὰ τῶν οἰκείων ἀλλαξημάτων καὶ καμπαγίων κατὰ ἀκολουθίαν καὶ τύπον τῶν προγραφέντων ἐν
τοῖς ἄνω. ἐν δὲ τοῖς ἑκατέρων τῶν μερῶν ἀκουβίτοις δεῖ ὑμᾶς καλεῖν κατὰ
τὸν ὅρον τῆς πρώτης ἡμέρας τοὺς ὑπὸ καμπάγιω συγκλητικοὺς ἅπαντας, 752
οἷον ἀσηκρήτας, ἀπὸ τῆς τῶν σπαθαροκανδιδάτων ἀξίας καὶ κατωτέρω,
χαρτουλαρίους τοῦ γενικοῦ λογοθέτου, χαρτουλαρίους τοῦ στρατιωτικοῦ
λογοθέτου, ἀντιγραφεῖς τοῦ κυέστωρος, τὸν σύμπονον, τὸν λογοθέτην καὶ
τοὺς κριτάς, νοταρίους τοῦ σακελλίου, νοταρίους τοῦ βεστιαρίου, νοταρίους
τοῦ εἰδικοῦ, ὑπάτους, σιλεντιαρίους, βεστήτορας καὶ μικροὺς ἄρχοντας τῶν
ταγμάτων, οἷον σκηπτροφόρους, σιγνοφόρους, εὐτυχοφόρους, δρακοναρίους,

750 1 πλοίματος bis B : πλο/L τὸν κόμητα LB : correxi 2 πραί L : πραιποσίτου B : πραιτωρίου scripsi 5 τοῦ τοποτηρητοῦ scripsi : τῶν τοποτηρητῶν L B
13 καστρισίῳ L 751 19 προανακλείνονται πένηταις L 23 ἔχων L 752 35 χαρτουλαρίους bis scripsi : -άριον B 36 κυέστορος B

M 11

σινάτορας καὶ δουκινιάτορας, καὶ τοὺς ἑκατέρων μερῶν δρομεῖς ἅπαντας.
δεῖ δὲ εἰσάγειν τοὺς μὲν συγκλητικοὺς ἅπαντας μετὰ τῶν οἰκείων ἀλλαξημάτων καὶ καμπαγίων, τοὺς δὲ δρομεῖς πάντας μετὰ τῶν αὐτῶν ποδέων,
καὶ τοὺς μὲν νικητὰς ἐπὶ τῆς κρείττονος θέσεως τῶν ἀκουβίτων προσανα-
κλίνειν, τοὺς δὲ ἡττηθέντας ἐπὶ τῆς ἑτέρας θέσεως, ἐν ᾗ καὶ τοὺς πένητας· 5
μετὰ δὲ τὴν προέορτον φωταυγίαν καὶ τὴν ἐπίδοσιν τῶν φατλίων ἐξάγειν
αὐτοὺς πάντας κατὰ τὸν τύπον τὸν προγραφέντα πᾶσιν. ἐπὶ δὲ τῆς δεκάτης
τῶν αὐτῶν ἡμέρας τῶν αὐτῶν ἀκουβίτων δεῖ ὑμᾶς εὐτρεπίζειν εἰς κλῆσιν τῆς βασιλικῆς
ἀκουβίτων τραπέζης ὁμοίως ἀνθυπάτους πατρικίους ὀφφικιαλίους σὺν τῷ δομεστίκῳ
ἡμέρα ί τῶν νουμέρων καὶ τῷ κόμητι τῶν τειχέων, φίλους ιβ'· εἰσάγειν δὲ αὐτοὺς ι(
καὶ ἐξάγειν μετὰ τῶν οἰκείων ἀλλαξημάτων κατὰ τὸν δηλωθέντα τύπον.
753 ἐν δὲ τοῖς λοιποῖς ἀκουβίτοις δεῖ ὑμᾶς καλεῖν τοὺς δύο τοποτηρητὰς καὶ
χαρτουλαρίους τῶν νουμέρων καὶ τειχέων, τριβούνους, βικαρίους, λεγατα-
ρίους, μανδάτορας, ξενοδόχους, γεροκόμους, χαρτουλαρίους τῶν εὐαγῶν
οἴκων, ἀρχιατροὺς καὶ τοὺς διαιταρίους τοῦ μεγάλου παλατίου καὶ τῆς Δά- 1:
φνης, τὸν ἀριθμὸν σδ', καὶ πένητας ιβ'· προκινσεύειν δὲ τοὺς ξενοδόχους
καὶ γεροκόμους χαρτουλαρίους καὶ ἰατροὺς σὺν τῶν διαιταρίων ἐπὶ τῇ
ὀπισθείῳ θέσει τοῦ ἀκουβίτου τοῦ βασιλέως, τοὺς δὲ ἄρχοντας τῶν δύο
ταγμάτων ἐπὶ τῇ κατὰ πρόσωπον θέσει τοῦ βασιλέως· εἰσάγειν δὲ αὐτοὺς
καὶ ἐξάγειν τοὺς μὲν ξενοδόχους μετὰ τῶν οἰκείων σκαραμαγγίων καὶ ῥωέων 2(
σαγίων, τοὺς δὲ ἰατροὺς ἅπαντας μετὰ τῶν οἰκείων διβενέτων, τοὺς δὲ τῶν
ταγμάτων ἄρχοντας, τοὺς μὲν τοποτηρητὰς καὶ αὐτοὺς μετὰ ῥωέων σαγίων,
ἡμέρα ιά τοὺς δὲ λοιποὺς μετὰ σκαραμαγγίων πάντας. ἐπὶ δὲ τῆς ἐνδεκάτης ἡμέρας
ἀπείργεται μὲν ἡ τῶν ἀκουβίτων ἐκτελουμένη κλῆσις, τελεῖται δὲ τὸ κλητώριον ἑσπέρας ἐν τῷ περιβλέπτῳ τοῦ Ἰουστινιανοῦ τρικλίνῳ. προστοι- 2:
χεῖται γὰρ τὸ αὐτὸ κλητώριον παρὰ τοῦ βασιλέως διὰ τοῦ αὐτοῦ ἀρτικλίνου
πρῶτας, καὶ δεῖ ἡμᾶς προσκαλεῖσθαι εἰς κλῆσιν τοῦ αὐτοῦ δείπνου μαγίστρους, ἀνθυπάτους, πατρικίους, ὀφφικιαλίους, πραιποσίτους, πρωτοσπαθαρίους εὐνούχους, πριμικηρίους, ὀστιαρίους, μαγλαβίτας, κόμητας τοῦ
ἀριθμοῦ καὶ κεντάρχους, τὸν ἀριθμὸν κατὰ τὸ ποσὸν τῆς τραπέζης, καὶ 3:
754 μετὰ τὴν θείαν τῆς ἑσπέρας μυσταγωγίαν δεῖ τὸν καλέσαντα ἀρτικλίνην
προτρέψασθαι πάντας ἀποθέσθαι τὰ ἑαυτῶν ἀλλαξήμια καὶ ἐπενδύσασθαι
τὰ οἰκεῖα αὐτῶν σκαραμάγγια εἰς τὸ μετ' αὐτῶν συνεστιαθῆναι τῷ βασιλεῖ
ἡμέρα ιβ' τῶν κατὰ τύπον. ἡ δὲ ἁγία τῶν φώτων ἡμέρα ξένην τινὰ καὶ περίβλεπτον
ἁγίων φώτων λαμπροφορίαν εἰσάγουσα θαυμαστὴν καὶ πανάγαστον τὴν δεξίωσιν ἐκτελεῖ 3:
τῆς βασιλικῆς ἑστιάσεως. τὴν γὰρ ἕνωσιν τῶν οὐρανίων καὶ ἐπιγείων
ταγμάτων διὰ τῆς δωρεᾶς τοῦ ἁγίου βαπτίσματος μυστικῶς εἰκονίζουσα
τοὺς ἐν τάξει ἀγγέλων ἱερεῖς τῆς μεγάλης τοῦ Θεοῦ καθολικῆς ἐκκλησίας
λευχημονοῦντας εἰς συνεστίασιν τῷ βασιλεῖ συνηγάγετο. καὶ δεῖ τοὺς ἐν
ταύτῃ τῇ ἡμέρᾳ λαχόντας διακονίᾳ ἀκριβῶς ἐπίστασθαι τὴν εὐπρεπῆ κατά- 4(
στασιν τῆς περιφανοῦς αὐτῶν καὶ ἱερᾶς δεξιώσεως. ἐν γὰρ τῷ τελουμένῳ
κράματι τῆς μεγάλης τοῦ Θεοῦ ἐκκλησίας δεῖ ὑμᾶς καλεῖν ἐπὶ τῆς τιμίας

6 ἐπίδωσιν L   754 35 ἐκτελεῖν L

βασιλικῆς τραπέζης, μαγίστρους, ἀνθυπάτους, πατρικίους στρατηγούς, ὀφφικιαλίους, τὸν ἀριθμὸν ιδ'· εἰσάγειν δὲ αὐτοὺς καὶ ἐξάγειν μετὰ τῶν
οἰκείων ἀλλαξίμων, ἄνευ μέντοι τῶν ἑαυτῶν χλαμύδων. ἐν δὲ τῇ βασιλικῇ
τιμίᾳ τραπέζῃ πρό γε πάντων συνεστιᾶται ὁ πατριάρχης τῷ βασιλεῖ, καὶ
δεῖ ἡμᾶς καλεῖν τοὺς λογάδας τῆς ἐκκλησίας, οἷον μητροπολίτας σὺν τῷ
συγκέλλῳ τὸν ἀριθμὸν ιβ', προστιχίζειν δὲ αὐτοὺς ἐν τῇ αὐτῶν εἰσαγωγῇ
ἁρμοδίως κατὰ τὸν ἑκάστου θρόνον, δηλονότι ἡμφιεσμένους αὐτοὺς πάσας 755
τὰς λειτουργικὰς αὐτῶν στολὰς πλὴν τῶν ὠμοφορίων καὶ μόνον· συνεισάγειν
δὲ αὐτοὺς καὶ ἐξάγειν διὰ τοῦ βασιλικοῦ καστρησίου, καθὼς ὁ τύπος τῆς
εἰσαγωγῆς περιέχει. ἐπὶ δὲ τῶν λοιπῶν ἀκουβίτων δεῖ ὑμᾶς καλεῖν
πρεσβυτέρους τοῦ μεγάλου παλατίου ιβ', τῆς μεγάλης ἐκκλησίας κδ', διακόνους ὁμοίως τοῦ παλατίου, τῆς μεγάλης ἐκκλησίας, τῆς νέας, λϚ', ὑπο-
διακόνους ὁμοίως λϚ', ἀναγνώστας ὁμοίως κδ', ψάλτας ὁμοίως κδ' καὶ
παπάδας τοῦ σεκρέτου τοῦ πατριάρχου λϚ'· ὁμοῦ σιϚ'· εἰσάγειν δὲ αὐτοὺς
καὶ ἐξάγειν οὕτως· τοὺς μὲν ἱερωμένους ἅπαντας μετὰ τῶν οἰκείων λευκῶν
φελωνίων, τοὺς δὲ σεκρετικούς, ψάλτας τε καὶ ἀναγνώστας μετὰ οἰκεῖα
καμήσια μόνον, δηλονότι κατὰ τὴν τάξιν καὶ ἔκθεσιν τὴν ἀνωτέρω μνη-
μονευθεῖσαν. δεῖ δὲ προσέχειν ἐν τῇ αὐτῇ ἀνακλήσει καὶ τὸν καιρὸν τοῦ
μίνσου τῶν λεγομένων δουλκίων, καὶ σὺν τῇ τούτων εἰσόδῳ συνεισάγειν
τοὺς δύο τῆς μεγάλης ἐκκλησίας λαμπροὺς δομεστίκους σὺν τῶν ψαλτῶν
τε καὶ ὀρφανῶν ἁπάντων τοῦ συφραγίου, λευχημονοῦντας καὶ περιβεβλη-
μένους τὰ οἰκεῖα φελώνια· διαιρεῖν δὲ αὐτοὺς ἔνθεν κἀκεῖθεν πρὸ τῆς
εἰσόδου αὐτῶν οὕτως. τῷ μὲν ἑνὶ αὐτῶν δομεστίκῳ ἅμα τῶν ψαλτῶν 756
ἁπάντων στιχίζειν ἐπὶ τῆς δεξιᾶς θέσεως τῶν τερπνῶν ἀκουβίτων· τῷ δὲ
ἑτέρῳ δομεστίκῳ αὐτῶν σὺν ὀρφανῶν ἁπάντων, καὶ αὐτὸν ἐπὶ τοῦ εὐωνύμου
κατὰ πρόσωπον θέσεως οὔσης τῶν ἀκουβίτων στιχίζειν· εἰσάγειν δὲ
αὐτοὺς ἐφ' ἑκατέρων τῶν μερῶν ἄμφω σὺν τῇ εὐλογίᾳ τοῦ πατριάρχου,
χοροστατεῖν ἅπαντας πρὸς ἀντίφωνον μελῳδίαν. καὶ ἡνίκα τῶν γ' ἀντιφωνῶν ἡ ἐκφώνησις λήξει, ἐξάγειν αὐτοὺς ἐκεῖθεν ἅμα ὅθεν καὶ ἐληλύθασιν.
ὡρίσθη δὲ καὶ παρὰ Λέοντος τοῦ σοφωτάτου δεσπότου εἰς πλείονα δόξαν
καὶ μεγίστην εὐχαριστίαν τῆς περιοδικῆς ταύτης καὶ σεβασμίου τῶν
ἑορτῶν εὐωχίας, ἐν τῇ αὐτῇ τελευταίᾳ τῶν ἀκουβίτων ἡμέρᾳ μετὰ τὴν
περαίωσιν τῆς λεχθείσης τῶν ἀντιφωνῶν ἀρχαιοπαραδότου κοινῆς μελῳ-
δίας, συνεισάγειν ἡμᾶς ἐν τῷ καιρῷ τῶν δουλκίων τοὺς δ' τῆς μεγάλης
ἐκκλησίας περιφανεῖς δομεστίκους, δηλονότι ἡμφιεσμένους τὰ οἰκεῖα αὐτῶν
καμήσια καὶ φελώνια μόνα, καὶ ἱστᾶν αὐτοὺς ἐν τῷ μέσῳ τοῦ περιβλέπτου
τρικλίνου κατὰ διάστασιν οὕτως· τὸν μὲν α' δομέστικον τῆς ἑβδομάδος
κατὰ μέσον τῶν ἑκατέρωθεν τεσσάρων λαμπρῶν ἀκουβίτων, τὸν δὲ ἀπ'
αὐτοῦ δεύτερον δομέστικον κατὰ μέσον ὁμοίως τῶν ἀπ' αὐτῶν δ' ἑκατέρωθεν λαμπρῶν ἀκουβίτων, τὸν δὲ γ' δομέστικον πάλιν ὁμοίως κατὰ μέσον
τῶν ἀπ' αὐτῶν ἑκατέρωθεν λαμπρῶν ἀκουβίτων, τὸν δὲ δ' κατὰ μέσον καὶ 757

755 17 μνημονευθῆσαν L   19 τουλδίων L : corr. R   756 24 ἅπαντα L : corr. R
25 καὶ L : σὺν R B   31 εὐχαριστείαν L   34 συνησάγειν L

Μ 11—2

αὐτὸν τῶν ἐξ ἑκατέρων μερῶν καὶ λαμπρῶν ἀκουβίτων.   καὶ σὺν τῇ ἐπι-
νεύσει καὶ εὐλογίᾳ τοῦ ἁγιωτάτου ἡμῶν πατριάρχου ἀπάρχεσθαι αὐτοὺς
τὴν τιμίαν καὶ θεάρεστον αἴνεσιν τὴν ἐξ οἰκείων χειλέων τοῦ σοφωτάτου
καὶ θεοπροβλήτου ἡμῶν βασιλέως Λέοντος ἐξυφανθεῖσαν, καὶ ἅμα τῇ
αὐτῆς ἐκφωνήσει καὶ πολυτέχνῳ τῆς χειρονομίας κινήσει ὁμοθυμαδὸν
ἅπαντας τοὺς ἀνακειμένους ᾄδειν καὶ συμψάλλειν τὸ ῥηθὲν ἱερὸν ᾆσμα τὸ
ἐκ μελισταγῶν χειλέων σταλάξαν ἅπασι τοῖς πιστοῖς ὑπηκόοις.   μετὰ δὲ
τὴν περαίωσιν τῆς δωδεκαημέρου ταύτης τῶν ἑορτῶν εὐωχίας τελεῖται
ἄλλη μεθέορτος ἡμέρα δεξίμου, φέρουσα δεξίωσιν μετὰ σαξίμου.   τύπῳ
γὰρ τελούμενον τὸ τοῦ δεξίμου πέρας, ἰδικήν τινα κατάστασιν εἰσάγει
πάλιν.   οἱ γὰρ θεοπρόβλητοι σοφοὶ δεσπόται μετὰ τὴν ἀπόλυσιν τοῦ
τυπικοῦ δεξίμου προκαθέζονται πάλιν εἰς πολλῶν ἀντίληψιν, καὶ τελεῖται
τὸ κλητώριον ἐπὶ ἀποκοπῆς τραπέζης, ἐν τῷ λαμπροτάτῳ τρικλίνῳ Ἰουστινιανοῦ τοῦ μεγάλου, καὶ δεῖ ἡμᾶς εὐτρεπίζειν εἰς συνεστίασιν τῶν
βασιλέων φίλους τοὺς ὑπὸ καμπάγιν ἅπαντας, ἄρχοντας τῆς συγκλήτου,
ἀπό τε μαγίστρων, ἀνθυπάτων, πατρικίων, ὀφφικιαλίων, βασιλικῶν πρω-
758 τοσπαθαρίων, ἀσηκρητῶν, χαρτουλαρίων τῶν μεγάλων σεκρέτων, ὑπάτων,
ἀντιγραφέων, σιλεντιαρίων, βεστητόρων, ἀπὸ ἐπάρχων, σκηπτροφόρων,
σιγνοφόρων, σενατόρων καὶ λοιπῶν ἀρχόντων τῶν δ' ταγμάτων.   δεῖ δὲ
προστιχίζειν ἅπαντας κατὰ τὸ ποσὸν τῆς τραπέζης, καὶ εἰσάγειν αὐτοὺς
καὶ ἐξάγειν ἅπαντας μετὰ τῶν οἰκείων ἀλλαξημάτων ἠμφιεσμένους καὶ τὰς
ἑαυτῶν χλαμύδας ἐμπροσθίῳ τῷ σχήματι· καὶ δεῖ προσέχειν τὸ τοῦ ὀργάνου
φθέγμα, καὶ ἡνίκα τὴν ἀπήχησιν τοῦ φθόγγου παύσῃ, ἐξανιστᾶν ἅπαντας
εἰς εὐφημίαν τῶν δεσποτῶν, καὶ αὖθις ἐκτίθεσθαι τὰς ἑαυτῶν χλαμύδας
μέχρι τῆς ἀφίξεως τοῦ μίνσου τῶν δουλκίων, καὶ πάλιν ταύτας ἀνα-
λαμβάνεσθαι πάντας, ὅπως ἂν μετ' αὐτῶν συνεξέλθοιεν ἐν τῇ ὁμοίᾳ τάξει.
τὸ δὲ ἑπόμενον τῷ δεξίμῳ ἱππικὸν ἄθλον τελεῖται μὲν τῇ ἐπαύριον τοῦ
δεξίμου ἡμέρᾳ, καὶ μετὰ τὴν αὐτοῦ ἀπόλυσιν τελεῖται κλητώριον ἐν τῷ
τρικλίνῳ τῶν καθισμάτων.   καὶ δεῖ ἡμᾶς εὐτρεπίζειν φίλους εἰς συνεστίασιν τῶν δεσποτῶν κατὰ τὸ ποσὸν τῆς τραπέζης ἐκ τῆς συγκλήτου
πάσης, οἷον μαγίστρους, πατρικίους, πραιποσίτους, ὀφφικιαλίους, πριμικηρίους, ὀστιαρίους, βασιλικοὺς πρωτοσπαθαρίους σὺν τῷ ἀκτουαρίῳ καὶ
τῷ δεκσογράφῳ καὶ τοῖς τοῦ ἡλιακοῦ παραστάταις, ἅμα τῶν σκηπτροφόρων,
δρακοναρίων, σημειοφόρων καὶ σιγνοφόρων· εἰσάγειν δὲ αὐτοὺς ἅπαντας
759 μετὰ τῶν οἰκείων ἀλλαξημάτων χωρὶς τῶν χλανιδίων, τοὺς δὲ τοῦ ἡλιακοῦ
παραστάτας μετὰ τῶν οἰκείων σκαραμαγγίων.

Μηνὶ Φε-   Τῇ δὲ δευτέρᾳ ἡμέρᾳ τοῦ Φεβρουαρίου μηνὸς ἑορταζομένης τῆς ὑπα-
βρουαρίῳ.   παντῆς τοῦ Κυρίου ἡμῶν Ἰησοῦ Χριστοῦ ἐν Βλαχέρναις, καὶ τελουμένης
τῆς λαμπρᾶς προελεύσεως, τελεῖται τὸ βασιλικὸν κλητώριον εἰς τὸν περί-

---

757 3 θεάρετον B   χειρῶν coni. R   6 συμψάλειν L   13 τὼ κλ. L
758 22 τῷ τ. ὀ. φθέγματι R B   25 ἀφήξεως L   27 τὰ δὲ L   32 ἀκταρίω L : correxi
33 ἡλιακοῦ forma contracta L (non κλιξ ut ed. Bonn. falso adnotat)   759 35 ἡλιακοῦ
(non κλιακοῦ) L   37 μινη (marg.) L

βλεπτον τρίκλινον τὸν Ὠκεανὸν πάλαι ἐπικληθέντα ἐπὶ ἀποκοπῆς
ραπέζης, καὶ δεῖ ἡμᾶς εὐτρεπίζειν εἰς συνεστίασιν τῶν βασιλέων φίλους
κ τῶν συγκλητικῶν, τοὺς ὑπὸ καμπάγιν πάντας, οἷον μαγίστρους, ἀνθυ-
άτους, πραιποσίτους, πατρικίους, ὀφφικιαλίους, βασιλικοὺς πρωτοσπα-
αρίους, συγκλητικούς, τὸν πρωτοασήκρητις, χαρτουλάριον τῶν ἐξσκουβίτων, ὑπάτους, βεστήτορας, σιλεντιαρίους, ἀλλαξήματα ἐκ τῶν ταγμα-
ικῶν ἀρχόντων, τὸν ἀριθμὸν κατὰ τὸ ποσὸν τῆς τραπέζης· εἰσάγειν δὲ
ὐτοὺς καὶ ἐξάγειν μετὰ τῶν οἰκείων ἀλλαξιμάτων, χωρὶς τῶν χλαμύδων,
ατὰ τὴν ἑκάστῳ προσοῦσαν τῆς δόξης ἀξίαν.

Τῇ δὲ κυριακῇ τῆς τῶν κρεῶν ἀπουσίας ἐπὶ μὲν τῆς βασιλικῆς τραπέζης **Κυριακῇ τῆς**
ίλους οὐ δεῖ συγκαλεῖσθαι. τὸ γὰρ αὐτὸ κλητώριον τοῖς πένησιν ὑφ- **ἀποκρέας.**
πλοῦται ἐν τῇ ἀψῖδι, καὶ μόνος ὁ βασιλεὺς τοὺς ἑαυτοῦ οἰκείους καὶ **760**
υγγενεῖς πρὸς ἑστίασιν συγκαλεῖται. τῇ δὲ τρίτῃ τῆς τυροφάγου ἡμέρας
ροσκαλεῖται τὸν βασιλέα ἅμα τῇ περὶ αὐτὸν συγκλήτῳ ὁ ἀρχιεπίσκοπος
ωνσταντινουπόλεως ἐν τῷ εὐαγεῖ μεγάλῳ πατριαρχίῳ, καὶ τελουμένης
ῆς ἱερᾶς λειτουργίας, προτίθεται κλητώριον ἐν τῷ μεγάλῳ σεκρέτῳ τοῦ
ατριάρχου. καὶ δεῖ ἡμᾶς εὐτρεπίζειν πρὸς κλῆσιν τῆς τοιαύτης τραπέζης,
αγίστρους, πραιποσίτους, ἀνθυπάτους, πατρικίους, ὀφφικιαλίους, πρωτο-
παθαρίους, σπαθαροκανδιδάτους, σπαθαρίους, στράτορας, κανδιδάτους καὶ
ρχοντας τῶν ταγμάτων κατὰ τὸ ποσὸν τῆς τραπέζης· εἰσάγειν δὲ αὐτοὺς
αὶ ἐξάγειν μετὰ τῶν οἰκείων σκαραμαγγίων καὶ μόνον. ἀπὸ δὲ τοῦ
ουφίσματος τοῦ πρώτου μίνσου δεῖ ἡμᾶς εἰσάγειν τὸν πρωτονοτάριον
οῦ πατριάρχου μετὰ τοῦ οἰκείου αὐτοῦ ἀναλογίου τε καὶ βιβλίου καὶ
στᾶν αὐτὸν ἐπὶ τῆς εὐωνύμου θέσεως τῆς βασιλικῆς τραπέζης πρὸς τὸ
παναγνῶναι τὸν περὶ νηστείας ἁρμόζοντα λόγον. μετὰ δὲ τὴν συμ-
λήρωσιν παντὸς τοῦ λόγου καὶ τὴν εἴσοδον τῶν τυρεψιτῶν ζωμῶν δεῖ
ροσάγεσθαι τοὺς ψάλτας ἄμφω σὺν τῷ αὐτῶν δομεστίκῳ, τὸν ἀριθμὸν
β'· ὡσαύτως καὶ τοὺς ἀναγνώστας ἄμφω σὺν τῷ αὐτῶν δομεστίκῳ, τὸν
ριθμὸν ὁμοίως, καὶ ἱστᾶν αὐτοὺς ἐφ' ἑκάτερα μέρη, εἰς τὸ προσάδειν
ρὸν αἶνον κατὰ τύπον. τοῖς δὲ λοιποῖς ἅπασιν ἀνὰ ἑνὸς καὶ μόνον. τῇ **761**
ὲ πέμπτῃ τῆς αὐτῆς ἑβδομάδος συγκαλεῖται εἰς ἑστίασιν ὑπὸ τῶν πιστῶν
ασιλέων ἐν τῷ μεγάλῳ παλατίῳ ὁ ἁγιώτατος καὶ οἰκουμενικὸς πατριάρχης,
αὶ συνεισέρχονται αὐτῷ μητροπολῖται, οὓς ἂν βουληθῇ ὁ αὐτὸς πατριάρχης,
αὶ δεῖ ἡμᾶς εὐτρεπίζειν εἰς κλῆσιν τῆς τιμίας αὐτῶν συνεστιάσεως ἐξ
ὐτῶν τῶν μητροπολιτῶν, οὓς ἂν τύχῃ, καὶ πρεσβυτέρους τοῦ μεγάλου
αλατίου ἐξ καὶ ἡγουμένους τῶν βασιλικῶν μεγάλων μοναστηρίων, ὅσους
ν εἶναι τύχῃ, καὶ σεκρετικοὺς παπάδας τοῦ πατριάρχου κατὰ τὸ ὑπο-
είμενον ποσὸν τῆς τιμίας τραπέζης· εἰσάγειν δὲ αὐτοὺς καὶ ἐξάγειν μετὰ
ῶν οἰκείων στολῶν τε καὶ φελωνίων κατὰ τὸν προλεχθέντα †ἐν τῷ περὶ
οῦ Ἰουστινιανοῦ μεγάλῳ κλητωροθεσίῳ†.

Τῇ δὲ ἐπιούσῃ κυριακῇ τῆς τῶν ἁγίων εἰκόνων ὀρθοδοξίας μετὰ τὴν **Τῆς ὀρθο-**
δοξίας.

760 30 κατὰ τύπον. hic lacunam susp. R   39 ἐν τῷ τρικλίνῳ Ἰουστ. τοῦ μεγάλου
λητοροθεσίου τύπον exspectes

ὑπάντησιν τῆς ἐκ βλαχερνῶν εἰσιούσης φαεινῆς λιτανείας καὶ τὴν ἱερω-
τάτην μυσταγωγίαν ἐκτελεῖται κλητώριον ἐκ τῆς ὑπηρεσίας τοῦ μεγάλου
οἰκονομίου ἐν τῷ λαμπροτάτῳ καὶ μεγάλῳ πατριαρχικῷ σεκρέτῳ, καὶ δεῖ
ἡμᾶς εὐτρεπίζειν εἰς συνεστίασιν φίλους τῷ βασιλεῖ καὶ τῷ ἁγιωτάτῳ
πατριάρχῃ, μαγίστρους, πραιποσίτους, ἀνθυπάτους, πατρικίους, μητροπολίτας, ἀρχιεπισκόπους, ὀφφικιαλίους καὶ ἄρχοντας τῆς περιφανοῦς
762 συγκλήτου, κατὰ τὸν ἀριθμὸν τοῦ ποσοῦ τῆς τραπέζης· εἰσάγειν δὲ αὐτοὺς
ἅπαντας καὶ ἐξάγειν οὕτως· τοὺς μὲν συγκλητικοὺς μετὰ τῶν οἰκείων αὐτῶν
σκαραμαγγίων καὶ μόνον, τοὺς δὲ ἱερεῖς μετὰ τῶν οἰκείων σχημάτων.

Μὴν Μάρτιος. Τῇ δὲ κε΄ τοῦ Μαρτίου μηνὸς τελεῖται ἡ εὔσημος καὶ περιφανὴς ἑορτὴ
τοῦ εὐαγγελισμοῦ τῆς ὑπεραγίας δεσποίνης ἡμῶν Θεοτόκου καὶ ἀειπαρθένου
Μαρίας, καὶ τελουμένης τῆς τυπικῆς προελεύσεως ἐν τῷ ναῷ τῶν Χαλκο-
πρατείων εἰσέρχονται οἱ βασιλεῖς ἐν τῷ παλατίῳ μετὰ τῆς παραδόξου
πάσης συγκλήτου λαμπροφοροῦντες, καὶ μετὰ τὴν εἴσοδον ταύτην ἀπο-
τίθονται πάντες τὰς ἑαυτῶν στολὰς κατὰ τύπον, καὶ φορούντων τῶν
εὐσεβῶν ἡμῶν βασιλέων τὰ κεχρυσωμένα αὐτῶν σκαραμάγγια, συναμφιά-
ζονται πάντες ὁμοίως τὰ οἰκεῖα αὐτῶν σκαραμάγγια, καὶ τελεῖται κλητώριον τῷ βασιλεῖ ἐν τῷ περιφανεστάτῳ τρικλίνῳ τοῦ Ἰουστινιανοῦ ἐπὶ ἀποκοπτῆς τραπέζης, καὶ δεῖ ἡμᾶς εὐτρεπίζειν εἰς συνεστίασιν τῶν βασιλέων
ἐν τῇ τοιαύτῃ ἡμέρᾳ μαγίστρους, πραιποσίτους, ἀνθυπάτους, πατρικίους,
στρατηγούς, ὀφφικιαλίους, βασιλικοὺς πρωτοσπαθαρίους καὶ λοιποὺς
ἄρχοντας ἐκ τῶν βασιλικῶν ταγμάτων κατὰ τὸ ποσὸν τῆς τραπέζης·
εἰσάγειν δὲ αὐτοὺς καὶ ἐξάγειν ἐν τῇ κλήσει μετὰ τῶν οἰκείων σκαραμαγγίων καὶ μόνον. τῇ δὲ πρὸ τῆς Χριστοῦ ἀναστάσεως λαμπρᾷ κυριακῇ
763 τῶν βαΐων τελεῖται ἡ προέλευσις ἐν τῷ θεοφυλάκτῳ ἱερῷ παλατίῳ. προ-
καθεσθέντων γὰρ ἐπὶ τοῦ χρυσοτρικλίνου τῶν εὐσεβῶν ἡμῶν βασιλέων
ἐξαλλαγμένων ἅμα τῷ οἰκουμενικῷ πατριάρχῃ καὶ τοῦ κουβουκλείου παντὸς
πρὸ προσώπου αὐτῶν κατὰ τάξιν στιχηδὸν παρεστῶτος, εἰσάγονται οἱ
δ΄ δομέστικοι τῶν ταγμάτων σὺν τοῖς δυσὶ δημάρχοις καὶ τῷ χαρτουλαρίῳ
τῆς βασιλικῆς σακέλλης, καὶ σὺν τούτοις δὲ πάντες οἱ γηροκόμοι τε καὶ
ξενοδόχοι τῶν εὐαγῶν οἴκων, καὶ τῆς εἰσκομιδῆς τῶν τιμίων σταυρῶν
παρ᾽ αὐτοῖς τελουμένης, εἰσάγονται πάντες, μάγιστροι, ἀνθύπατοι, πατρίκιοι
καὶ ὀφφικιάλιοι κατὰ πρόσωπον τῶν εὐσεβῶν βασιλέων, ἐστολισμένοι
τὰς ἑαυτῶν λευκὰς χλανίδας, καὶ τῆς διανομῆς τῶν τιμίων σταυρῶν εἰς
αὐτοὺς γεναμένης, τελεῖται ἡ λιτάνιος ὑμνῳδία ἀπὸ τοῦ ναοῦ τῆς ἁγίας
Θεοτόκου τοῦ Φάρου πρὸς τὸν ναὸν τῆς ἁγίας τριάδος τῆς Δάφνης, καὶ
ἀπὸ τῆς ὑποστροφῆς ταύτης τελεῖται κλητώριον τοῖς βασιλεῦσιν ἐπὶ τοῦ
λαμπροτάτου Ἰουστινιανοῦ τρικλίνου, καὶ δεῖ ἡμᾶς εὐτρεπίζειν εἰς συνεστίασιν τῶν βασιλέων φίλους, μαγίστρους, πραιποσίτους, ἀνθυπάτους,
πατρικίους, ὀφφικιαλίους, ξενοδόχους, γηροκόμους, τοποτηρητὰς τῶν ταγμάτων κατὰ τὸν ἀριθμὸν τοῦ ποσοῦ τῆς τραπέζης, καὶ εἰσάγονται πάντες οἱ

761 3 λαμπροτάτῳ L   762 16 κεχρυσομένα L

κεκλημένοι μετὰ τῶν οἰκείων ἀλλαξίμων, πλὴν τῶν χλανιδίων, οἱ δὲ γηροκόμοι καὶ ξενοδόχοι καὶ τοποτηρηταὶ τῶν ταγμάτων μετὰ τὰ οἰκεῖα αὐτῶν
σκαραμάγγια. τῇ δὲ ἁγίᾳ καὶ ἱερᾷ πέμπτῃ τῆς λαμπρᾶς ὄντως καὶ περιφανοῦς ἑβδομάδος, ἐν ᾗ ὁ τῆς θείας μυσταγωγίας παρὰ τῆς ἄνω σοφίας 764
ἐφήπλωται δεῖπνος, τελεῖται προέλευσις παγανὴ ἐν τῷ λαμπρῷ παλατίῳ, —
καὶ προευτρεπίζεται παρ᾽ ἡμῶν ἡ τοῦ βασιλικοῦ δείπνου κλῆσις πρωΐας,
καὶ δεῖ ἡμᾶς εὐτρεπίζειν εἰς συνεστίασιν τῶν δεσποτῶν μαγίστρους, πραιποσίτους, ἀνθυπάτους, πατρικίους, ὀφφικιαλίους, πρωτοσπαθαρίους εὐνούχους, πριμικηρίους, ὀστιαρίους, μαγλαβίτας, κόμητας τοῦ ἀριθμοῦ καὶ
κεντάρχους κατὰ τὸ ποσὸν τῆς τραπέζης, καὶ τούτους προσκαλεῖσθαι ἐπὶ
τὸν τῆς ἑσπέρας δεῖπνον. ἀπολυομένης οὖν τῆς συγκλήτου πάσης καὶ
πάλιν πρὸς ὥραν θ᾽ ἐπανιούσης, συνέρχονται πάντες οἱ κεκλημένοι εἰς
τὸ τελέσαι τὴν ἱερὰν εὐωχίαν, καὶ μετὰ τὴν ἀπόλυσιν τῆς πνευματικῆς
λειτουργίας προτίθεται τὸ βασιλικὸν κλητώριον ἐπὶ τοῦ περιβλέπτου
τρικλίνου τοῦ Ἰουστινιανοῦ, καὶ προκαθεσθέντος τοῦ βασιλέως ἐπὶ τῆς
τιμίας τραπέζης, εἰσάγονται πάντες οἱ κεκλημένοι μετὰ τῶν οἰκείων σκαραμαγγίων καὶ μόνον, ἐπὶ δὲ τῇ αὐτῶν ἐξόδῳ λαβόντες παρ᾽ ἡμῶν φατλία
σὺν ἡμῖν ἐξέρχονται πάντες. τῷ δὲ ἁγίῳ καὶ τιμίῳ σαββάτῳ ἀνεῳχθέντος
τοῦ λαμπροῦ παλατίου, τελεῖται προέλευσις δημοσίᾳ πρὸς τὴν ἁγίαν
Σοφίαν, καὶ ὑπαλλαττομένης τῆς ἐνδυτῆς τῆς τιμίας καὶ ἁγίας τραπέζης,
εἰσέρχεται ὁ βασιλεὺς ἐν τῷ σκευοφυλακίῳ, καὶ τῆς διανομῆς γενομένης
τῶν νάρδων, ὑποστρέφει πάλιν ὁ βασιλεὺς μετὰ δόξης ἐν τῷ αὐτοῦ
παλατίῳ, καὶ δεῖ ἡμᾶς εὐτρεπίζειν εἰς συνεστίασιν τοῦ βασιλέως ἐν τῷ 765
ἑσπερίῳ δείπνῳ φίλους, μαγίστρους, πραιποσίτους, ἀνθυπάτους, πατρικίους,
πρωτοσπαθαρίους ὀφφικιαλίους, πρωτοσπαθαρίους εὐνούχους, πριμικηρίους,
ὀστιαρίους, μαγλαβίτας, τοποτηρητὰς καὶ ἐκ τῶν ἀρχόντων τοῦ ἀριθμοῦ
κατὰ τὸ ποσὸν τῆς τραπέζης, καὶ στοιχουμένου παρὰ τοῦ βασιλέως τοῦ
αὐτοῦ κλητωρίου, καὶ δι᾽ ἡμῶν κλητωρευομένων τῶν φίλων, ἀπολύονται
οἴκαδε πάντες. μετὰ δὲ τὴν ἐνάτην ὥραν συνάξεως γινομένης, ἐξαλλάσ-
σουσιν οἱ τῆς συγκλήτου πάντες, καὶ τῆς θείας λειτουργίας ἐν τῷ ναῷ
τοῦ Φάρου τελουμένης, μετὰ τὴν ἐκφώνησιν τοῦ μυστικοῦ ὀργάνου ἐκδι-
δύσκονται πάντες τὰς ἑαυτῶν στολάς, καὶ ἐπενδιδύσκονται τὰ οἰκεῖα σκαραμάγγια, καὶ ἵσταται τὸ κλητώριον ἐν τῷ περιφανεστάτῳ τρικλίνῳ τοῦ
Ἰουστινιανοῦ, καὶ εἰσάγονται πάντες οἱ κεκλημένοι μετὰ τῶν οἰκείων
σκαραμαγγίων καὶ μόνον· μετὰ δὲ τὴν ἐπίδοσιν τῶν φατλίων συνεξέρχονται
ἡμῖν οἱ πάντες.

Ἡ δὲ ἁγία καὶ δεδοξασμένη τῆς Χριστοῦ ἀναστάσεως περιφανὴς ἡμέρα,   'Αρχὴ τῶν
ἐν ᾗ τὸ τῆς σωτηρίας ἡμῶν οἰκονομήθη κεφάλαιον, καὶ ὁ χοϊκὸς Ἀδὰμ   κλητωρίων τοῦ
ἐκ τῆς φθορᾶς πρὸς τὴν ζωὴν ἐπανῆλθεν, λαμπράν τινα καὶ περίβλεπτον   πάσχα.
εὐωχίαν τοῖς βασιλεῦσιν ἡμῶν προεξένησεν. τὸ γὰρ ὕψος τῆς ἱερᾶς
ἀναστάσεως μυστικῶς ὑποφαίνοντες ἐκ τῶν κάτω καθεδρῶν ἑαυτοὺς συνα-

766 πάραντες πρὸς ὑψηλήν τινα καὶ πολύκυδον τοῦ βήματος θεωρίαν ἑαυτοὺς
ἐπανάγουσι, καὶ τῆς Χριστοῦ ἀληθοῦς ἀγαπήσεως τὸν ἀσπασμὸν ἐκμι-
μούμενοι τὸ ὑπήκοον ἅπαν σχετικῶς κατασπάζονται, καὶ αὖθις σὺν τῇ
λαμπρᾷ συγκλήτῳ πρὸς τὴν ἄνω Σιών, τὴν Χριστοῦ ἐκκλησίαν, ὡς
μαθηταί, μετὰ δόξης συντρέχουσι. τὴν γὰρ περίδοξον τῆς ἡμέρας χαρμο- 5
νὴν ἐνδεικνύμενοι λαμπροφοροῦσι τοῖς λώροις, εἰς τύπον τῶν ἐνταφίων
Χριστοῦ σπαργάνων ἑαυτοὺς ἐνειλίττοντες. διὸ καὶ ἐν ταῖς δεξιαῖς χερσὶν
αὐτῶν τὸ νικητικὸν τοῦ σταυροῦ κατέχοντες τρόπαιον, τὴν ἐξανάστασιν
τῆς χοϊκῆς ἡμῶν οὐσίας ἐν ταῖς εὐωνύμοις κατέχουσι, καὶ τὴν θείαν
μυσταγωγίαν τῷ Θεῷ ἀναφέροντες μετὰ τὴν τῶν ἁγίων μυστηρίων μετά- 10
ληψιν, πρὸς σεμνὸν κρᾶμα τοὺς τῆς συγκλήτου προκρίτους, ὡς κοινωνοὺς
τῆς χάριτος, ἐμφανῶς προσλαμβάνονται. καὶ δεῖ ἡμᾶς εὐτρεπίζειν ἐν τῇ
αὐτῇ κλήσει τοῦ κράματος τοῦ τελουμένου ἐν τῇ Χριστοῦ καθολικῇ ἐκκλησίᾳ εἰς συνεστίασιν τῷ βασιλεῖ φίλους ἀπὸ τῆς τάξεως τῶν μαγίστρων,
ἀνθυπάτων, πατρικίων, στρατηγῶν τε καὶ ὀφφικιαλίων, τὸν ἀριθμὸν ιδ´· 15
εἰσάγειν δὲ αὐτοὺς ἐπὶ τῆς αὐτῆς τραπέζης οὕτως· τοὺς μὲν μαγίστρους,
ἀνθυπάτους καὶ πατρικίους, τοὺς λώρους ἠμφιεσμένους μετὰ τῶν χρυσέων
αὐτῶν θωρακίων καὶ μόνον, προκρίνειν δὲ ἐν τῇ τοιαύτῃ καθέδρᾳ τοὺς τὰ
θωράκια ἠμφιεσμένους ὑπὲρ τοὺς ἄλλους πατρικίους τοὺς τὰ οἰκεῖα καμήσια
767 φοροῦντας, κἂν τάχα τύχοιεν ἐλάττονες εἶναι ἐν τῇ προβλήσει· τοὺς δὲ 20
στρατηγοὺς ἅπαντας μετὰ τῶν οἰκείων αὐτῶν σκαραμαγγίων καὶ μόνον·
τοὺς δὲ ὀφφικιαλίους καὶ αὐτοὺς μετὰ τῶν οἰκείων καμησίων, ἄνευ μέντοι
τῶν ἑαυτῶν χλαμύδων. ἐπὶ δὲ τῆς προκειμένης ἐν τῷ περιβλέπτῳ χρυσέῳ
τρικλίνῳ χρυσῆς τραπέζης, ἐν ᾧ καὶ τὸ περιφανὲς κτῆμα τοῦ χρυσοῦ
πενταπυργίου εἰς τιμὴν προετέθη, δεῖ ἡμᾶς εὐτρεπίζειν εἰς συνεστίασιν τῷ 25
βασιλεῖ φίλους ἐκ τῶν προλεχθέντων μαγίστρων, ἀνθυπάτων, πατρικίων,
στρατηγῶν, ὀφφικιαλίων σεκρετικῶν, ἀπὸ τῆς τάξεως τοῦ στρατιωτικοῦ
καὶ κατωτέρω, ἀσηκρητῶν τε ὁμοῦ καὶ κομήτων τῶν σχολῶν καὶ
σκριβώνων, σὺν τῶν δύο ἐκ Βουλγάρων φίλων, τὸν ἀριθμὸν λ´· ἐν δὲ
ταῖς περιεξῆς τέσσαρσι τῶν καμαρῶν τραπέζαις ἀπὸ τῆς τάξεως τῶν 30
βασιλικῶν κανδιδάτων, βεστητόρων τε καὶ σιλεντιαρίων, δρακοναρίων,
σκηπτροφόρων, σημειοφόρων καὶ σενατόρων τὸν ἀριθμὸν λϛ´· Ἀγαρηνοὺς
δεσμίους ἐκ τοῦ μεγάλου πραιτωρίου τὸν ἀριθμὸν ιη´, καὶ ἐκ τῶν Βουλγάρων φίλων ἀνθρώπους ιη´· εἰσάγειν δὲ αὐτοὺς καὶ προστιχίζειν πρὸ τῆς
εἰσόδου αὐτῶν, τοὺς μὲν ἐπὶ τῆς χρυσῆς βασιλικῆς τραπέζης περιφανεῖς 35
δαιτυμόνας μετὰ τῶν οἰκείων ἀλλαξημάτων καὶ χλανιδίων, προσκαλεῖσθαι
δὲ τοὺς ἀπὸ τῶν Βουλγάρων φίλους ἀπὸ τῆς τάξεως τῶν στρατηγῶν ἐν τῷ
δευτέρῳ μίνσῳ ἐπὶ τῆς εὐωνύμου θέσεως τῆς τραπέζης πρὸς τὸ ἀριθμεῖσθαι
768 αὐτοὺς πέμπτους, ἢ καὶ ἕκτους φίλους, στιχίζειν δὲ ἅπαντας ἔνθεν κἀκεῖθεν
κατὰ τὴν ἁρμόζουσαν τῆς τάξεως ἑκάστῳ δόξαν. ἀπὸ δὲ τῆς στάσεως 40

766 8 νηκητικὸν L   11 προκρήτους L   767 20 ἐλάττωνες L   24 κλῆμα L :
corr. R   25 ἐς τιμήν B   27 ὀφφικιαλίων, σεκρετικῶν B, non recte, cf. infra 784. 5
fort. τοῦ ⟨λογοθέτου τοῦ⟩ στρατιωτικοῦ sed vix necessarium   28 ἀσηκριτῶν L

τῶν λεχθέντων τούτων στιχίζειν αὖθις ἔνθεν κἀκεῖθεν τοὺς ἀπὸ τῆς τάξεως τῶν κανδιδάτων καὶ κατωτέρω πρὸς τὸ καθεσθῆναι ἐπὶ τῶν ἑκατέρων δύο προκρίτων τραπεζῶν. ἐπὶ δὲ ταῖς κατωτέραις τραπέζαις δεῖ προστιχίζειν, ἐπὶ μὲν τῆς ἐξ εὐωνύμου θέσεως τοὺς ἐξ Ἀγάρων δεσμίους, ἐπὶ δὲ τῆς ἑτέρας τραπέζης τοὺς τῶν φίλων Βουλγάρων ἀνθρώπους πάντας· εἰσάγειν δὲ αὐτοὺς ἅπαντας καὶ ἐξάγειν οὕτως· τοὺς μὲν ἀπὸ τῆς συγκλήτου πάντας καὶ τῶν ταγμάτων μετὰ τῶν οἰκείων ἀλλαξίμων, τοὺς δὲ Ἀγαρηνοὺς λευκοφόρους, ἀζώνους καὶ ὑποδεδεμένους, τοὺς δὲ Βουλγάρων ἀνθρώπους μετὰ τῶν οἰκείων αὐτῶν σχημάτων. δεῖ δὲ προσέχειν τὴν ἐκφώνησιν καὶ ἀπήχησιν τῶν μουσικῶν ὀργάνων, καὶ ἡνίκα τὸ ᾀδόμενον ᾄσῃ μέλος, ἀνιστᾶν ἅπαντας εἰς εὐφημίαν τῶν δεσποτῶν καὶ αὖθις τὰς ἑαυτῶν ἐκδιδύσκεσθαι χλαμύδας, καὶ μετὰ τῆς ἀφίξεως τοῦ μίνσου τῶν δουλκίων πάλιν ταύτας ἀναλαμβάνειν πρὸς τὸ μετ' αὐτῶν ἐκπορεύεσθαι ἐν τῇ αὐτῶν ἐξόδῳ. ἐν δὲ τῇ αὐτῇ ἀναστάσει δεῖ προσέχειν τὸ ἐκ βασιλικῆς χειρὸς διδόμενον τῆς ἐγέρσεως σχῆμα, σὺν αὐτῷ δὲ καὶ τὴν ἐκφώνησιν τοῦ παρεστῶτος ἐκεῖ κουβικουλαρίου, καὶ αὖθις ἐξανιστᾶν καὶ προπέμπειν τοὺς τῶν δ' τραπεζῶν κεκλημένους, μικρὸν εἴργοντας τοὺς ἄνω φίλους, καὶ εἶθ' οὕτως συνεξερχομένους ἅπαντας. ἐπὶ δὲ τῆς δευτέρας ἡμέρας τελεῖται μεθέορτος προέλευσις ἐν τῷ σηκῷ τῶν κορυφαίων καὶ 769 ἁγίων ἀποστόλων. καὶ πληρουμένης τῆς ἱερᾶς λειτουργίας, προτίθεται κλητώριον ἐπὶ ἀποκοπῆς τραπέζης ἐν τῷ μεγάλῳ τρικλίνῳ τῶν παλατίων, καὶ δεῖ ὑμᾶς εὐτρεπίζειν εἰς συνεστίασιν τῷ βασιλεῖ μαγίστρους, πραιποσίτους, ἀνθυπάτους, πατρικίους, στρατηγούς, μητροπολίτας, ὀφφικιαλίους, πρωτοσπαθαρίους, ἀσηκρῆτας, χαρτουλαρίους, ὑπάτους, βεστήτορας, σιλεντιαρίους καὶ ἀλλαξίμων τῶν ταγματικῶν ἀρχόντων κατὰ τὸ ποσὸν τῆς τραπέζης· εἰσάγειν δὲ αὐτοὺς καὶ ἐξάγειν μετὰ τῶν οἰκείων ἀλλαξίμων καὶ καμισίων, ἄνευ μέντοι τῶν ἑαυτῶν χλαμύδων· προσέχειν δὲ τοῖς εὐφημοῦσι δήμοις, καὶ ἡνίκα ἄρξονται ἀκτολογεῖν τοὺς δεσπότας, δεῖ ἐξανιστᾶν πάντας τοὺς κεκλημένους πρὸς τὸ καὶ αὐτοὺς πραέως συνευφημεῖν τοὺς δεσπότας. τῇ δὲ τρίτῃ ἡμέρᾳ τῆς αὐτῆς ἑβδομάδος τελεῖται παγανὴ προέλευσις μετὰ ἀλλαξιμάτων ἔνδον τοῦ παλατίου, καὶ τελεῖται κλητώριον ἐπὶ τοῦ χρυσοτρικλίνου κατὰ τὸ σχῆμα τῆς πρώτης ἡμέρας. καὶ δεῖ ἡμᾶς εὐτρεπίζειν εἰς κλῆσιν ἐπὶ τῆς χρυσῆς τραπέζης ἀπὸ τῆς τάξεως τῶν μαγίστρων, πατρικίων καὶ λοιπῶν σὺν τῷ δομεστίκῳ τῶν σχολῶν καὶ βασιλικῶν ἀνθρώπων ἀπὸ τῆς τάξεως τῶν σπαθαροκανδιδάτων μέχρι τῆς τάξεως τῶν στρατώρων, κατὰ τὸ ποσὸν τῆς τραπέζης φίλους λ'· εἰσάγειν δὲ αὐτοὺς καὶ ἐξάγειν, τοὺς μὲν ὑπὸ καμπάγιν πάντας μετὰ τῶν 770 οἰκείων ἀλλαξημάτων, πλὴν καὶ χλανίδος· τοὺς δὲ πρωτοσπαθαρίους μετὰ σπεκίων καὶ ῥωέων σαγίων· τοὺς δὲ βασιλικοὺς μετὰ τῶν σκαραμαγγίων καὶ μόνον. ἐπὶ δὲ ταῖς κάτω τέσσαρσι τῶν καμάρων τραπέζαις δεῖ ἡμᾶς συγκαλεῖν βασιλικοὺς κανδιδάτους καὶ μανδάτορας καὶ μικροὺς ἄρχοντας τοῦ τάγματος τῶν σχολῶν, τὸν ἀριθμὸν οβ'· εἰσάγειν δὲ αὐτοὺς μετὰ

τῶν οἰκείων σκαραμαγγίων καὶ ἀλλαξημάτων.   τῇ δὲ τετάρτῃ ἡμέρᾳ τῆς
αὐτῆς εὐωχίας τελεῖται ὁμοίως προέλευσις παγανὴ μετὰ ἀλλαξημάτων
ἔνδον τοῦ παλατίου, καὶ εἰσάγονται τὰ φωτίσματα ὑπὸ τοῦ ὀρφανοτρόφου,
καὶ τελεῖται τὸ κλητώριον ἐν τῷ αὐτῷ χρυσοτρικλίνῳ ἐπὶ τῆς χρυσῆς
τραπέζης. καὶ δεῖ ἡμᾶς εὐτρεπίζειν εἰς συνεστίασιν τῶν βασιλέων φίλους, 5
ἀπὸ τῆς τάξεως τῶν μαγίστρων, πατρικίων σὺν τοῦ δομεστίκου τῶν
ἐξσκουβίτων καὶ τῶν αὐτοῦ σκριβώνων κατὰ τὸν προλεχθέντα τύπον, καὶ
εἰσάγειν αὐτοὺς καὶ ἐξάγειν, καθὰ εἴρηται. ἐπὶ δὲ ταῖς κατὰ τῶν καμαρῶν τραπέζαις δεῖ ἡμᾶς συγκαλεῖν ἐκ τῶν λεχθέντων βασιλικῶν ἀνθρώπων
καὶ τῶν μικρῶν ἀρχόντων τοῦ ἐξσκουβίτου τὸν ἀριθμὸν οβ', καὶ εἰσάγειν 10
αὐτοὺς κατὰ τὸν προλεχθέντα τύπον. τῇ δὲ πέμπτῃ ἡμέρᾳ τῆς αὐτῆς
πανδεσίας εἰσέρχεται ὁ πατριάρχης μετὰ τῶν αὐτοῦ μητροπολιτῶν δοῦναι
771 ἀγάπην τῷ βασιλεῖ, καὶ τελεῖται προέλευσις παγανὴ δι' ἀλλαξίμων ἔνδον
τοῦ παλατίου, καὶ συγκαθέζεται τῷ βασιλεῖ εἰς συνεστίασιν ὁ πατριάρχης
ἐπὶ τῆς ἀποκοπῆς χρυσῆς τραπέζης ἐν τῷ χρυσέῳ τρικλίνῳ, καὶ δεῖ ἡμᾶς 15
εὐτρεπίζειν ἐπὶ μὲν τῆς χρυσῆς τραπέζης φίλους ἀπὸ μὲν τῶν μητροπολιτῶν ι', καὶ ἀπὸ τῶν βασιλικῶν πρεσβυτέρων τοῦ παλατίου ἕξ, καὶ
ἡγουμένους τῶν βασιλικῶν μοναστηρίων ιβ', εἰσάγειν δὲ αὐτοὺς καὶ ἐξάγειν
οὕτως· τοὺς μὲν μητροπολίτας μετὰ τῶν οἰκείων ἀλλαξημάτων, πλὴν τῶν
ὠμοφορίων, τοὺς δὲ πρεσβυτέρους μετὰ τῶν λευκῶν φελωνίων, τοὺς δὲ 20
ἡγουμένους καὶ αὐτοὺς μετὰ τῶν οἰκείων αὐτῶν φελωνίων. ἐπὶ δὲ τῶν
κάτω τραπεζῶν δεῖ ἡμᾶς συγκαλεῖν ἀπὸ τῶν βασιλικῶν κληρικῶν ἀπὸ
τῆς τάξεως τῶν διακόνων καὶ κατωτέρω καὶ ἀπὸ τοῦ σεκραίτου τοῦ
πατριάρχου παπάδας, τὸν ἀριθμόν. . . . εἰσάγειν δὲ καὶ ἐξάγειν αὐτοὺς
μετὰ τῶν οἰκείων αὐτῶν καμησίων καὶ μόνον. τῇ δὲ ἕκτῃ ἡμέρᾳ τῆς 25
αὐτῆς περιόδου τελεῖται προέλευσις παγανὴ μετὰ ἀλλαξιμάτων ἔνδον τοῦ
παλατίου, καὶ εἰσάγονται οἱ ἐκ Βουλγάρων φίλοι μετὰ τῶν ἐκ Βουλγάρων
δώρων. καὶ τελεῖται κλητώριον ἐν τῷ αὐτῷ περιβλέπτῳ τρικλίνῳ ἐπὶ
τῆς αὐτῆς χρυσῆς τραπέζης, καὶ δεῖ ἡμᾶς εὐτρεπίζειν εἰς συνεστίασιν τοῦ
βασιλέως φίλους ἀπὸ τῆς τάξεως τῶν μαγίστρων, ἀνθυπάτων καὶ λοιποὺς 30
σὺν τῶν ἐκ Βουλγάρων φίλων καὶ τῷ δρουγγαρίῳ τῆς βίγλης καὶ τῷ δομεστίκῳ τῶν ἱκανάτων, τὸν ἀριθμὸν λ'· στιχίζειν δὲ αὐτοὺς καὶ εἰσάγειν
772 κατὰ τὸν λεχθέντα τύπον τῆς πρώτης ἡμέρας. ἐπὶ δὲ τῶν κάτω τραπεζῶν
δεῖ συγκαλεῖν ἀπό τε κομήτων καὶ κεντάρχων τοῦ ἀριθμοῦ καὶ τῶν ἱκανάτων ἄνδρας νδ', καὶ ἐκ τῶν Βουλγάρων φίλων ἀνθρώπους ιη'· στιχίζειν 35
δὲ δεῖ τοὺς Βουλγάρων ἀνθρώπους ἐπὶ τῆς κάτω τελευταίας μιᾶς τραπέζης
μόνους· εἰσάγειν δὲ αὐτοὺς καὶ ἐξάγειν μετὰ τῶν οἰκείων αὐτῶν σκαραμαγγίων. τῇ δὲ ἑβδόμῃ ἡμέρᾳ τῆς αὐτῆς δεξιώσεως τελεῖται ὡσαύτως
παγανὴ προέλευσις ἔνδον τοῦ παλατίου, καὶ γίνεται κλητώριον ἐν τῷ αὐτῷ
τρικλίνῳ ἐπὶ τῆς αὐτῆς τραπέζης, καὶ συγκαλοῦνται εἰς ἑστίασιν τῷ 40
βασιλεῖ ὁμοίως ἀπὸ τῆς τάξεως τῶν μαγίστρων καὶ πατρικίων σὺν τῷ
ὑπάρχῳ τῆς πόλεως καὶ τοῖς δυσὶ δομεστίκοις, νουμέρων τε καὶ τειχέων,

καὶ τῶν αὐτῶν τοποτηρητῶν σὺν τῷ λογοθέτῃ τοῦ πραιτωρίου καὶ τῷ
συμπόνῳ τὸν ἀριθμὸν λ'. εἰσάγονται δὲ καὶ ἐξάγονται μετὰ τῶν οἰκείων
αὐτῶν ἀλλαξιμάτων καὶ χλανιδίων. ἐν δὲ ταῖς κάτω τραπέζαις συγκαλοῦνται τριβοῦνοι, βικάριοι, οἱ ἐθνικοὶ τῆς ἑταιρείας, οἷον Τοῦρκοι, Χαζάρεις
5 καὶ λοιποί, τὸν ἀριθμὸν νδ'. ἐπὶ δὲ τῆς τιμίας τραπέζης συγκαλοῦνται
οἱ δώδεκα γειτονιάρχαι, οἱ δ' ἐπόπται καὶ οἱ δύο πρωτοκαγκελλάριοι τοῦ
ἐπάρχου. εἰσάγονται δὲ μετὰ τῶν οἰκείων καμισίων καὶ μόνον, οἱ δὲ
ἐθνικοὶ μ τὰ ιῶν αὐτῶν καβαδίων. δίδοται δὲ τοῖς γειτονιάρχαις καὶ
λοιποῖς ἀνὰ νομίσματος ἑνός. ἐπὶ δὲ τῶν προλαβόντων χρόνων συνεκα-
10 λοῦντο ἀντὶ τούτων οἱ τοῦ σκευοφυλακίου τῆς ἁγίας Σοφίας χαρτουλάριοι,
λαμβάνοντες τὴν αὐτὴν εὐλογίαν. τῇ δὲ νέᾳ κυριακῇ, τῇ μεθεόρτῳ τοῦ 773
πάσχα, ἐκτελεῖται προέλευσις λαμπροφόρος ἐν τῷ σεβασμίῳ ναῷ τῶν
ἁγίων ἀποστόλων· καὶ τελουμένης τῆς ἱερᾶς λειτουργίας, προτίθεται κλητώριον ἐν τῷ λεχθέντι τρικλίνῳ ἐπὶ τῆς δευτέρας ἡμέρας, καὶ συνεστιᾶται
15 τῷ βασιλεῖ ὁ ἁγιώτατος ἡμῶν πατριάρχης ἐπὶ ἀποκοπῆς τραπέζης, καὶ
συγκαλοῦνται εἰς ἑστίασιν σὺν τῷ βασιλεῖ φίλοι κατὰ τύπον τῆς δευτέρας
ἡμέρας τῇ ἐπαύριον τοῦ ἱεροῦ πάσχα. τῇ δὲ ἐπαύριον τῆς νέας κυριακῆς
ἡμέρᾳ ἐκτελεῖται δεξίωσις δεξίμου ἄνευ σαξίμου, καὶ καθέζεται ὁ βασιλεὺς
ἐπὶ ἀποκοπῆς τραπέζης μετὰ τοῦ οἰκείου δηβητισίου ἐπὶ τοῦ Ἰουστινιανοῦ
20 τρικλίνου. καὶ δεῖ ἡμᾶς συγκαλεῖν εἰς ἑστίασιν ἀπὸ τῆς τάξεως τῶν
μαγίστρων, πραιποσίτων, ἀνθυπάτων, πατρικίων, ὀφφικιαλίων καὶ λοιπῶν
τῶν ὑπὸ καμπάγιν πάντων κατὰ τὸ ποσὸν τῆς τραπέζης· εἰσάγειν δὲ καὶ
ἐξάγειν πάντας μετὰ τῶν οἰκείων αὐτῶν ἀλλαξιμάτων τε καὶ χλανιδίων·
προσέχειν δὲ καὶ τὸ μουσικὸν μέλος καὶ ἐξανιστᾶν τοὺς κεκλημένους ἐν
25 τῷ προδηλωθέντι χρόνῳ εἰς εὐφημίαν τῶν δεσποτῶν. τῇ δὲ ἐπαύριον τοῦ
αὐτοῦ δεξίμου τελεῖται ἐπόμενον ἱππικὸν ἀπολύσιμον, καὶ ἐξαποστέλλονται
πρὸς τὰ οἰκεῖα οἱ ἀπὸ Βουλγάρων φίλοι, καὶ προτίθεται κλητώριον ἐν τῷ 774
περιβλέπτῳ τρικλίνῳ τῶν καθισμάτων, καὶ συνεσθίουσι τῷ βασιλεῖ οἱ
πραιπόσιτοι, πατρίκιοι, ὀφφικιάλιοι, πρωτοσπαθάριοι, χαρτουλάριοι, ὕπατοι,
30 βεστήτορες, σιλεντιάριοι, ὁ ἀκτουάριος καὶ οἱ τοῦ ἡλιακοῦ σὺν τῷ δεκσωγράφῳ, τὸν ἀριθμὸν κατὰ τὸ ποσὸν τῆς τραπέζης. εἰσάγονται δὲ καὶ
ἐξάγονται κατὰ τὸν ἀνωτέρω λεχθέντα τρόπον. μεσούσης δὲ τῆς ἑορτῆς
τοῦ πάσχα τελεῖται προέλευσις δημοσία, καὶ προέρχονται οἱ βασιλεῖς
ἐμπράττως εἰς τὸν ναὸν τοῦ ἁγίου Μωκίου, καὶ τελουμένης τῆς ἱερᾶς
35 λειτουργίας προτίθεται κλητώριον τῷ βασιλεῖ ἐπὶ ἀποκοπῆς τραπέζης ἐν
τοῖς ἐκεῖσε τρικλίνοις, καὶ συνεστιᾶται ὁ πατριάρχης τῷ βασιλεῖ, καὶ δεῖ
ἡμᾶς εὐτρεπίζειν εἰς συνεστίασιν αὐτῶν φίλους ἀπὸ τῆς τάξεως τῶν
μαγίστρων, ἀνθυπάτων, πατρικίων, μητροπολίτας, ὀφφικιαλίους καὶ ταγμα-
τικούς, καὶ τῶν ἐκ τῆς συγκλήτου (ὑπὸ) καμπάγιν (ὄν)των κατὰ τὸ ποσὸν
40 τῆς τραπέζης· εἰσάγειν δὲ αὐτοὺς καὶ ἐξάγειν μετὰ τῶν οἰκείων ἀλλα-

772 9 νομήσματος L   773 11 θεόρτω L   774 29 καὶ χαρτ. Β   30 δεησσο-
γράφῳ Β   39 (ὑπὸ) καμπάγιν ὄντων scripsi: καμπαγίων τῶν L : καμπαγίων R B
40 ἐξάγιν L   ἀλλαξίμων Β

ξίμων χωρὶς τῶν χλανιδίων· ἐν δὲ τῷ προλεχθέντι τῆς ἀκτολογίας τῶν δήμων χρόνῳ ἐξανιστᾶν ἅπαντας τοὺς κεκλημένους εἰς εὐφημίαν τῶν δεσπο-

ἡ ἀνάληψις. τῶν. ἐπὶ δὲ τῆς θείας καὶ ἱερᾶς μετὰ σαρκὸς εἰς οὐρανοὺς ἀναλήψεως τοῦ Κυρίου ἡμῶν Ἰησοῦ Χριστοῦ θαυμαστῆς ἡμέρας τελεῖται δημοσία προέλευσις παρὰ τῶν βασιλέων ἡμῶν τῶν ἁγίων ἐν τῷ πανσέπτῳ καὶ 5 775 σεβασμίῳ ναῷ τῆς ὑπεραγίας δεσποίνης ἡμῶν Θεοτόκου τῆς πηγῆς, καὶ τελουμένης τῆς ἱερᾶς λειτουργίας, προτίθεται κλητώριον τῷ βασιλεῖ ἐπὶ ἀποκοπτῆς τραπέζης, καὶ συνεστιᾶται ὁ πατριάρχης τῷ βασιλεῖ, καὶ συγκαλοῦνται εἰς συνεστίασιν αὐτῷ φίλοι ἀπὸ τῆς τάξεως τῶν μαγίστρων καὶ κατωτέρω κατὰ τὴν ἔκθεσιν καὶ τὸ σχῆμα τῶν προλεχθεισῶν περιφανῶν 10 προελεύσεων.

Η πεντη- Τῇ δὲ ἁγίᾳ τῆς πεντηκοστῆς ἡμέρᾳ τελεῖται προέλευσις κατὰ τὸν κοστή. τύπον τῆς τοῦ σεβασμίου πάσχα ἐν τῇ ἁγίᾳ τοῦ Θεοῦ καθολικῇ καὶ ἀπο- στολικῇ ἐκκλησίᾳ, καὶ προτίθεται κρᾶμα ἐκεῖσε τοῖς βασιλεῦσιν, καὶ προσκαλοῦνται οἱ ἀνωτέρω λεχθέντες φίλοι. καὶ ὑποστροφῆς τῶν βασι- 15 λέων ἐν τῷ μεγάλῳ παλατίῳ μετὰ προελεύσεως γενομένης, προτίθεται τὸ βασιλικὸν κλητώριον ἐπὶ ἀποκοπτῆς τραπέζης ἐν τῷ περιβλέπτῳ Ἰου- στινιανοῦ τρικλίνῳ, καὶ συνεστιῶνται τῷ βασιλεῖ οἱ κατὰ τύπον ἀνωτέρω λεχθέντες φίλοι, εἰσαγόμενοι καὶ ἐξαγόμενοι μετὰ τῶν οἰκείων ἀλλαξι- μάτων χωρὶς χλανιδίων. μετὰ δὲ τὴν ἁγίαν τῆς πεντηκοστῆς ἡμέραν 20 ἐκτελεῖται τὸ στέψιμον τοῦ δεσπότου. τῇ δὲ πρώτῃ τοῦ Μαΐου μηνὸς

τὰ ἐγκαίνια ἐκτελοῦνται τὰ ἐγκαίνια τῆς νέας ἐκκλησίας, καὶ λιτανίου προελεύσεως τῆς νέας. γινομένης ἀπὸ τοῦ ναοῦ τῆς ἁγίας Θεοτόκου τοῦ Φάρου, τελεῖται ἡ θεία 776 λειτουργία, καὶ προτίθεται κλητώριον τοῖς βασιλεῦσιν ἐν τῷ τερπνῷ χρυ- σοτρικλίνῳ, καὶ συνεστιᾶται τῷ βασιλεῖ ὁ πατριάρχης, καὶ συγκαλοῦνται 25 εἰς συνεστίασιν αὐτοῦ ἀπὸ τῆς τάξεως τῶν μαγίστρων, πραιποσίτων, πατρικίων καὶ λοιπῶν βασιλικῶν ἀνθρώπων σὺν τῶν μητροπολιτῶν κατὰ τὸ ποσὸν τῆς τραπέζης. τῇ δὲ ιαʹ τοῦ αὐτοῦ Μαΐου μηνὸς τελεῖται τὸ γενέθλιον τῆς πόλεως ταύτης, καὶ ἐκτελεῖται δεξίωσις δεξίμου χωρὶς σαξίμου καὶ ἱππικὸν ἱπποδρόμιον, καὶ τελεῖται κλητώριον κατὰ τὸν 30 λεχθέντα τύπον. τῇ δὲ ὀγδόῃ τοῦ αὐτοῦ Μαΐου μηνὸς τελεῖται προέ- λευσις τῆς μνήμης τοῦ Θεολόγου ἐν τῷ Ἑβδόμῳ, καὶ τελουμένης τῆς λει- τουργίας, προτίθεται κλητώριον, καὶ συγκαλοῦνται κατὰ τύπον οἱ τῆς συγκλήτου πάντες κατὰ τὸ ποσὸν τῆς τραπέζης. τῇ δὲ κʹ τοῦ Ἰουλίου μηνὸς ἐκτελεῖται διὰ λιτανίου προελεύσεως ἔνδον τοῦ παλατίου ἡ μνήμη 35 Ἡλιοῦ τοῦ προφήτου, καὶ δι᾽ αὐτῆς ἡ ἀνάκλησις τῆς περιορήσεως τοῦ εὐσεβοῦς ἡμῶν βασιλέως. προεκτελεῖται δὲ πρὸ αὐτῆς τῆς ἡμέρας ἐν τῇ παραμονῇ ἑσπερινὸν ἐν τῷ Φάρῳ, καὶ ᾄδεται παρὰ πάντων ἀπολύσιμον ᾆσμα ἰσόμελον τοῦ ʽσυνταφέντεςʼ, καὶ δίδοται τοῖς μαγίστροις, πραι- ποσίτοις, ἀνθυπάτοις, πατρικίοις καὶ ὀφφικιαλίοις εἰς τύπον παρὰ τοῦ 40 βασιλέως σταυρίτζια ἀργυρᾶ. τῇ δὲ ἐπαύριον ἡμέρᾳ, ἐν ᾗ τὴν ἑορτὴν ἐκτελοῦμεν, προκαθέζεται ὁ βασιλεὺς μετὰ ἀλλαξιμάτων ἐπὶ τοῦ ἐνδόξου

775 10 προλεχθησῶν L   12 πεντικοστῆς L   776 28 μηνὸς om. B

χρυσοτρικλίνου, καὶ παρεστῶτος τοῦ μυστικοῦ κουβουκλείου, εἰσάγονται 777
ὅ,τε τοῦ σακελλίου καὶ οἱ ξενοδόχοι καὶ γηροκόμοι, προσάγοντες σταυροὺς
χρυσοστοιβάστους κατὰ μίμησιν τῆς ἑορτῆς τῶν βαΐων, καὶ λαμπρο-
φορούντων πάντων, εἰσάγεται ἡ τάξις τῶν μαγίστρων, ἀνθυπάτων, πατρι-
5 κίων καὶ ὀφφικιαλίων ἔμπροσθεν τοῦ δεσπότου, καὶ διανομῆς τῶν λεχθέντων
σταυρίων ὑπὸ τοῦ βασιλέως γενομένης, τελεῖται, ὡς ἔφαμεν, δημοσία
λιτάνιος προέλευσις ἀπὸ τοῦ ναοῦ τῆς ἁγίας Θεοτόκου τοῦ Φάρου ἐπὶ τὸν
περίβλεπτον ναὸν τῆς μεγάλης νέας ἐκκλησίας, καὶ τελουμένης τῆς ἱερᾶς
λειτουργίας, προτίθεται κλητώριον τῷ βασιλεῖ ἐπὶ τοῦ χρυσοτρικλίνου,
10 καὶ συνεστιᾶται τοῖς βασιλεῦσιν ὅ,τε πατριάρχης καὶ οἱ μητροπολῖται,
μάγιστροι, πραιπόσιτοι, ἀνθύπατοι, πατρίκιοι, ὀφφικιάλιοι καὶ λοιποὶ
βασιλικοὶ κατὰ τὸ ποσὸν τῆς τραπέζης. προκαθέζεται δὲ ὁ βασιλεὺς
μετὰ τοῦ οἰκείου διβητησίου, καὶ δεῖ ἡμᾶς εἰσάγειν καὶ ἐξάγειν πάντας
τοὺς κεκλημένους μετὰ τῶν οἰκείων αὐτῶν ἀλλαξιμάτων χωρὶς τῶν χλανι-
15 δίων. τῇ δὲ ἐπαύριον τελεῖται δεξίωσις δεξίμου καὶ μεγάλου σαξίμου,
καὶ προτεθέντος βασιλικοῦ κλητωρίου ἐπὶ ἀποκοπῆς τραπέζης ἐν τῷ
Ἰουστινιανοῦ τρικλίνῳ, προκαθέζεται ὁ βασιλεὺς μετὰ τοῦ οἰκείου διβητησίου, καὶ δεῖ ἡμᾶς εὐτρεπίζειν εἰς συνεστίασιν αὐτοῦ ἀπὸ τῆς τάξεως
πραιποσίτων, πατρικίων, ὀφφικιαλίων καὶ ἀπὸ τῶν σεκρετικῶν τῶν ὑπὸ
20 καμπάγιν πάντων κατὰ τὸ ποσὸν τῆς τραπέζης· εἰσάγειν δὲ αὐτοὺς καὶ
ἐξάγειν μετὰ τῶν οἰκείων ἀλλαξιμάτων τε καὶ χλανιδίων. τοὺς δὲ λοιποὺς 778
μαγίστρους, ἀνθυπάτους, πατρικίους καὶ ἅπαντας τοὺς βασιλικοὺς ἀνθρώπους ταμιεύειν αὐτοὺς μετὰ θωρακίων καὶ κονδομανίκων εἰς τὸ σάξιμον
τῆς τραπέζης, χορευόντων δὲ πάντων πέριξ τῆς βασιλικῆς τραπέζης καὶ
25 τὴν ἀνάρρυσιν εὐφημούντων τοῦ σοφωτάτου δεσπότου, δίδοται παρ' αὐτοῦ
τούτοις εἰς φιλοτιμίας ἐπίδοσιν ἀποκόμβιον ἔχον χρυσοῦ λίτρας γ'· προσέχειν δὲ δεῖ τὴν ἀκτολογίαν τοῦ δήμου, καὶ ἐξανιστᾶν ἅπαντας τοὺς
κεκλημένους πρὸς εὐφημίαν τοῦ δεσπότου κατὰ τὸν προγραφέντα τύπον.
ἐφεξῆς δὲ ταύτης τῆς ἡμέρας τελεῖται πεζοδρόμιον βωτὸν τῶν πολιτῶν
30 τυπωθὲν ἐπὶ Λέοντος τοῦ φιλοχρίστου δεσπότου, καὶ δίδονται σφραγίδια
ὡς κατὰ τύπον τοῦ βωτοῦ πεζοδρομίου, καὶ προτίθεται κλητώριον τῷ
βασιλεῖ ἐπὶ ἀποκοπῆς τραπέζης κατὰ τὴν μέσην θέσιν τοῦ περιφανοῦς
τρικλίνου τῶν ιθ' τερπνῶν ἀκουβίτων, καὶ συνεστιῶνται τῷ βασιλεῖ οἱ
πραιπόσιτοι σὺν τοῖς εὐνούχοις πρωτοσπαθαρίοις καὶ πριμικηρίοις, τὸν
35 ἀριθμὸν ἕξ, ὡσαύτως καὶ πάντες οἱ πένητες οἱ τὰ σφραγίδια τοῦ βασιλέως
διὰ χειρὸς τῶν μεγιστάνων λαβόντες, καὶ δίδοται αὐτοῖς ἀποκόμβιν ἀνὰ
νομίσματος α γ'. καὶ μεθ' ἡμέρας δύο τελεῖται ἱππικὸν ἱπποδρόμιον, καὶ
προτίθεται κλητώριον ἐπὶ τοῦ τρικλίνου τοῦ καθίσματος, καὶ δεῖ ἡμᾶς
εὐτρεπίζειν εἰς συνεστίασιν τῷ βασιλεῖ φίλους κατὰ τὸν ἐν τοῖς ἱππο-
40 δρομικοῖς κλητωρίοις λεχθέντα τύπον. ἐπὶ δὲ τῆς ς' τοῦ Αὐγούστου 779
μηνὸς ἡμέρας ἐκτελεῖται ἡ προέλευσις μετὰ ἀλλαξίματος ἐν τῇ μεγάλῃ

---

777 3 μίμησιν L   773 26 ἔχων L   29 πεζοδρώμιον L   32 μέσιν L   36 ἀποκόμβιον B

τοῦ Θεοῦ καθολικῇ ἐκκλησίᾳ, καὶ τελουμένης τῆς ἱερᾶς λειτουργίας, συνεστιῶνται τῷ βασιλεῖ οἱ πολλάκις ἐπὶ τοῦ κράματος μνημονευθέντες φίλοι, καὶ ὑποστρέφει ὁ βασιλεὺς ἐπὶ τὸ παλάτιον ἐμπράτως, καὶ προτίθεται κλητώριον τῷ βασιλεῖ ἐπὶ ἀποκοπῆς τραπέζης ἐν τῷ Ἰουστινιανοῦ τρικλίνῳ, καὶ δεῖ ἡμᾶς εὐτρεπίζειν εἰς συνεστίασιν τῷ βασιλεῖ φίλους ἀπὸ 5 τῆς τάξεως τῶν μαγίστρων, ἀνθυπάτων, πατρικίων, ὀφφικιαλίων, πρωτοσπαθαρίων καὶ λοιπῶν συγκλητικῶν τῶν ὑπὸ καμπάγιν ὄντων κατὰ τὸ
780 ποσὸν τῆς τραπέζης· εἰσάγειν δὲ αὐτοὺς καὶ ἐξάγειν μετὰ τῶν οἰκείων ἀλλαξιμάτων χωρὶς τῶν χλανιδίων διὰ τὸ καὶ τὸν βασιλέα μετὰ τοῦ οἰκείου διβητισίου προκαθεσθῆναι. τῇ δὲ ιε′ τοῦ αὐτοῦ μηνὸς ἡμέρᾳ τελεῖται 10 δημοσία προέλευσις τῆς κοιμήσεως τῆς ὑπεραγίας δεσποίνης ἡμῶν Θεοτόκου ἐν τῷ πανσέπτῳ ναῷ αὐτῆς τῷ ἐν Βλαχέρναις, καὶ τελουμένης τῆς ἱερᾶς λειτουργίας, προτίθεται κλητώριον ἐπὶ ἀποκοπῆς τραπέζης ἐν τῷ κάτω τρικλίνῳ τῷ ὄντι ἐπὶ τὰ παλάτια τῆς θαλάσσης, καὶ προκαθέζεται ὁ βασιλεὺς σὺν τῷ πατριάρχῃ μετὰ τοῦ οἰκείου αὐτοῦ διβητησίου. καὶ 15 δεῖ ἡμᾶς εὐτρεπίζειν εἰς συνεστίασιν αὐτοῦ φίλους ἀπὸ τῆς τάξεως τῶν μαγίστρων, πραιποσίτων, ἀνθυπάτων, πατρικίων, ὀφφικιαλίων, μητροπολιτῶν καὶ λοιπῶν ἀρχόντων βασιλικῶν τε καὶ ταγματικῶν κατὰ τὸ ποσὸν τῆς τραπέζης. εἰσάγονται δὲ καὶ ἐξάγονται οὕτως· οἱ μὲν μάγιστροι, πραιπόσιτοι, πατρίκιοι, ὀφφικιάλιοι καὶ οἱ ὑπὸ καμπάγιν πάντες 20 μετὰ τῶν οἰκείων ἀλλαξημάτων· οἱ δὲ λοιποὶ βασιλικοὶ μετὰ τῶν οἰκείων σκαραμαγγίων καὶ μόνον. ἐν δὲ τῇ αὐτῇ ἡμέρᾳ δείλης ἀπέρχεται ὁ βασιλεὺς εἰς τὸν ναὸν τοῦ ἁγίου Διομήδους, καὶ τῇ ἐπαύριον τελουμένης τῆς λειτουργίας, προτίθεται κλητώριον κατὰ τύπον, καὶ συνεσθίουσι τῷ βασιλεῖ ὁμοίως οἱ ἐκ τῆς συγκλήτου πάντες. τῇ δὲ κθ′ τοῦ αὐτοῦ μηνὸς ἡμέρᾳ 25 ἐκτελεῖται ἡ μνήμη τοῦ ἁγίου καὶ ὀρθοδόξου μεγάλου βασιλέως ἡμῶν Βασιλείου, καὶ προέρχονται μετὰ σκαραμαγγίων ἐν τῷ ναῷ τῶν ἁγίων ἀποστόλων οἱ βασιλεῖς ἐμπράττως, καὶ τελουμένης τῆς ἱερᾶς λειτουργίας, ὑποστρέφουσιν ὁμοίως οἴκαδε μετὰ δόξης, καὶ προτίθεται κλητώριον ἐν τῷ Ἰουστινιανοῦ τρικλίνῳ, καὶ δεῖ ἡμᾶς εὐτρεπίζειν εἰς συνεστίασιν τοῖς 30 βασιλεῦσι φίλους ἀπὸ τῆς τάξεως τῶν μαγίστρων, τῶν συγκλητικῶν βασιλικῶν ἀνθρώπων, κατὰ τὸ ποσὸν τῆς τραπέζης· εἰσάγειν δὲ αὐτοὺς καὶ ἐξάγειν μετὰ τῶν οἰκείων σκαραμαγγίων καὶ μόνον διὰ τὸ καὶ τοὺς βασιλεῖς ἐν τῷ τοιούτῳ σχήματι ἀκουμβίζειν. τῇ δὲ ἐπαύριον ἐκτελεῖται διὰ δεξίμου ἡ ἐν Χριστῷ αὐτοκρατορία τῶν πιστῶν βασιλέων, Λέοντος 35 καὶ Ἀλεξάνδρου, καὶ τελουμένου αἰσίως τοῦ δεξίμου, προκαθέζονται πάλιν οἱ εὐσεβεῖς δεσπόται εἰς πολλῶν ἀντίληψιν ἐπὶ τοῦ θρόνου, καὶ αὖθις
781 στοιχεῖται τὸ κλητώριον τοῦ δεσπότου, καὶ δεῖ ἡμᾶς εὐτρεπίζειν εἰς συνεστίασιν τῶν βασιλέων ἀπὸ τῆς τάξεως τῶν μαγίστρων, πραιποσίτων, ἀνθυπάτων, πατρικίων, ὀφφικιαλίων, πλὴν τῶν εὐνούχων, τοὺς ἡμίσους 40 ἁπάντων, καὶ ἀπὸ τῆς τάξεως τῆς ὑπὸ καμπάγιν συγκλήτου, καὶ τῶν

ταγματικῶν ἀλλαξιμάτων κατὰ τὸ ποσὸν τῆς τραπέζης, καὶ εἰσάγειν μετὰ
τῶν οἰκείων ἀλλαξημάτων καὶ χλανιδίων, τοὺς δὲ λοιποὺς ἅπαντας
ταμιεύειν εἰς χόρευσιν τῆς χαρᾶς τοῦ δεσπότου. κύκλῳ γὰρ χορεύοντες
μετὰ χρυσῶν θωρακίων τοὺς ἐπαίνους πλέκουσι τῶν εὐσεβῶν δεσποτῶν,
5 καὶ δίδοται πᾶσιν φιλοτιμίας δῶρον, χρυσοῦ λίτραι ιϛ΄, καὶ διανέμεται
πᾶσι παρὰ τοῦ πρωτομαγίστρου καὶ τοῦ βασιλικοῦ ἀρτοκλίνου κατὰ τύπον
τῶν καθ' ἡμᾶς κονδακίων. τῇ δὲ ἐπιούσῃ ἡμέρᾳ τελεῖται ἑπομένως
ἱππικὸν ἱπποδρόμιον, καὶ προτίθεται τὸ κλητώριον ἐπὶ τοῦ τρικλίνου τῶν
καθισμάτων, καὶ συγκαλοῦνται εἰς συνεστίασιν τῷ βασιλεῖ φίλοι κατὰ
10 τὸν ἐν τοῖς ἱπποδρομικοῖς κλητωρίοις γραφέντα τύπον. τῇ δὲ ὀγδόῃ τοῦ
Σεπτεμβρίου μηνὸς ἡμέρᾳ τελεῖται προέλευσις τῶν γενεθλίων τῆς ὑπεραγίας δεσποίνης ἡμῶν Θεοτόκου καὶ ἀειπαρθένου Μαρίας, καὶ προέρχονται
οἱ βασιλεῖς ἐμπράτως μετὰ πάσης τῆς συγκλήτου ἐν τῷ ναῷ τῆς ἁγίας
Θεοτόκου τῶν Χαλκοπρατίων, καὶ τελουμένης τῆς ἱερᾶς λειτουργίας, ὑπο-
15 στρέφει ὁ βασιλεὺς ἔφιππος μετὰ χρυσοῦ σκαραμαγγίου ἐμπράτως, καὶ 782
προτίθεται κλητώριον ἐπὶ ἀποκοπῆς τραπέζης ἐν τῷ Ἰουστινιανοῦ τρικλίνῳ, καὶ συνεστιῶνται τῷ βασιλεῖ οἱ ἀπὸ τῆς συγκλήτου πάντες.
εἰσάγονται δὲ μετὰ τῶν οἰκείων σκαραμαγγίων καὶ μόνον. τῇ δὲ τεσσαρισ-
καιδεκάτῃ τοῦ αὐτοῦ μηνὸς τελεῖται ἡ ὕψωσις καὶ ἐμφάνια τοῦ τιμίου
20 καὶ ζωοποιοῦ σταυροῦ, καὶ ἀνέρχονται οἱ βασιλεῖς ὄρθρου βαθέως ἐν τῷ
ναῷ τῆς ἁγίας Σοφίας, ποτὲ δὲ καὶ ἀπὸ ἑσπέρας· καὶ τελουμένης τῆς
τρίτης ὑψώσεως τοῦ παναγίου ξύλου, κατέρχονται πάλιν οἴκαδε διὰ τῶν
διαβατικῶν ἐν πρώτοις, καὶ τελουμένης παγανῆς προελεύσεως ἔνδον τοῦ
παλατίου, προτίθεται κλητώριον ἐν τῷ Ἰουστινιανοῦ τρικλίνῳ, καὶ δεῖ
25 ἡμᾶς συγκαλέσασθαι εἰς συνεστίασιν τῶν βασιλέων φίλους κατὰ τὸν ἤδη
τῶν κλητωρίων λεχθέντα τύπον· εἰσάγειν δὲ πάντας μετὰ τῶν οἰκείων
σκαραμαγγίων καὶ μόνον. ἐπὶ δὲ τοῦ μηνὸς Νοεμβρίου τελοῦνται τὰ
βρουμάλια τῶν δεσποτῶν, καὶ τελουμένου ἐφ' ἑκάστου κλήσει τοῦ ἑσπερίου
φωτοφανοῦς σαξίμου δίδονται ἀποκόμβια τάδε· ἐπὶ μὲν τοῦ βρουμαλίου
30 Λέοντος τοῦ φιλοχρίστου δεσπότου χρυσοῦ λίτραι κ΄· ἐπὶ δὲ τοῦ εὐτυχοῦς
Ἀλεξάνδρου αὐγούστου χρυσοῦ λίτραι ι΄· ἐπὶ δὲ τῆς εὐσεβοῦς Ζώης
αὐγούστης χρυσοῦ λίτραι η΄· ἃ καὶ διανέμονται ὑπὸ τοῦ μεγάλου πρωτομαγίστρου καὶ τοῦ κλεινοῦ ἀρτικλίνου τοῦ βασιλικοῦ κατὰ τὸν περιεχόμενον 783
τύπον τοῦ καθ' ἡμᾶς κονδακίου. αὗται οὖν πᾶσαι αἱ τυπικαὶ περιοδικῶς
35 ἐρχόμεναι τῷ χρόνῳ κλήσεις εἰδικήν τινα εἰσάγουσιν, ὡς ἔφαμεν, τῶν
κλητωρίων τάξιν. διὸ καὶ ταύτας εἰς ὑπόμνησιν τῶν καθ' ἡμᾶς τελου-
μένων ἐμφανῶς προθέμενοι ἀπταίστῳ λόγῳ αἴτησιν προσάγομεν προσέχειν
ταύταις εἰς ἡμῶν συντήρησιν καὶ κλέους δόξαν.

781 3 χώρευσιν L : χορεύοντες L   5 χροισοῦ χ̅ (sc. χρυσοῦ) L   7 κωνδ. L B
ἐπιούσι L   782 19 -κεδεκάτη L   20 βαθέως L B   33 κλινοῦ L   783 38 συντήρησιν κλέους καὶ δόξαν coni. R : fortasse καὶ τοῦ βασιλέως δόξαν

Περὶ διανομῶν τῶν εὐσεβιῶν τοῦ βασιλέως ἔν τε τοῖς βρουμαλίοις καὶ στεψίμοις καὶ
αὐτοκρατορίαις.

Ἐπειδή τινες τῶν ἐν ἀξιώμασι διαπρεπόντων, ληχνοτέραν τὴν ἔφεσιν τῶν
χρημάτων ἔχοντες, ἀμφισβητήσεις καὶ λόγους ἐγείρουσι περὶ τῆς διανομῆς
τῶν διδομένων χρημάτων καὶ τὴν ἐξ ἀρχαίων τῶν χρόνων παρακολουθή- 5
σασαν συνήθειαν ἀνατρέπειν σπουδάζουσι· φέρε δὴ καθὼς ἐκ τῶν πρὸ
ἡμῶν ἐγγράφως παρελάβομεν τύπον, καὶ ὑμῖν παραδώσωμεν.   πᾶν γὰρ τὸ
ἀρχαιότητι διαφέρον αἰδέσιμον, οὔτε προσθήκην τῶν πάλαι διανομῶν καιν-
ουργεῖν σπεύδοντες, οὔτε ἐλάττωσιν τῶν προπραχθέντων ποιούμενοι.   δεῖ
γὰρ τὸν διανομέα τῶν τοιούτων ἀρτικλίνην πρό γε πάντων τὸ ποσὸν τῆς 10
δωρεᾶς ἐκμανθάνειν, καὶ εἶθ᾽ οὕτως ἀκριβολογεῖν τὰς τῶν ἀξιωμάτων δια-
784 φοράς, καὶ ἑκάστῃ ἀξιωμάτων τάξει συγκαταριθμεῖν τοὺς αὐτῆς μετόχους,
κἂν ἐλάττονες τῶν ἀξιωμάτων τυγχάνουσι· καὶ τοῖς μὲν μαγίστροις συγ-
καταλέγειν τόν τε ραίκτορα καὶ τὴν ζωστὴν πατρικίαν, τὸν σύγκελλον καὶ
τοὺς ἀπὸ μαγίστρων μοναδικοὺς καὶ τὸν πραιπόσιτον, ἅμα δὲ καὶ τῷ οἰκειακῷ 15
παρακοιμωμένῳ τοῦ μεγάλου ἡμῶν βασιλέως· εἰς δὲ τὴν τῶν ἀνθυπάτων
τάξιν συναριθμεῖν τοὺς εὐνούχους πατρικίους· ἐν δὲ τῇ τάξει τῶν λοιπῶν
πατρικίων συγκατατάττειν τοὺς ἐν τῷ βήλῳ τῶν πατρικίων τεταγμένους
ὀφφικιαλίους, ἤγουν τοὺς πρωτοσπαθαρίους καὶ στρατηγούς, τοὺς πρωτοσπαθαρίους καὶ πραιποσίτους, τὸν δομέστικον τῶν σχολῶν, τὸν ἐξσκούβιτον, 20
τὸν ὕπαρχον, τὸν γενικόν, τὸν σακελλάριον, τὸν κυέστωρα, τὸν δρουγγάριον
τῆς βίγλης, τὸν πρωτοβεστιάριον τοῦ δεσπότου, τὸν τῆς τραπέζης, καί, εἰ
τύχοιεν, παπίας μέγας καὶ ἑταιρειάρχης πρωτοσπαθάριος εὐνοῦχος· ἐν δὲ
τῇ τάξει τῶν σεκρετικῶν ὀφφικιαλίων συγκαταριθμεῖν τοὺς εὐνούχους πρωτοσπαθαρίους ⟨καὶ⟩ πριμικηρίους καὶ ὀστιαρίους καὶ τοὺς ἐμπράτους κριτὰς 25
καὶ μόνον.   ἐκ δὲ τῆς τάξεως τῶν πρωτοσπαθαρίων δεῖ διαστέλλειν τοὺς
τοῦ χρυσοτρικλίνου καὶ μαγλαβίτας καὶ ἀρτικλίνας, ἤγουν μικρὸν πλέον
προτιμᾶσθαι.   τοὺς δὲ σπαθαροκανδιδάτους . . . συναριθμεῖν τοῖς σπα-
θαροκουβικουλαρίοις ⟨τοὺς δὲ κουβικουλαρίους⟩ μετὰ τῶν σπαθαρίων καὶ
στρατώρων καὶ ἀπ᾽ αὐτῶν τοὺς κανδιδάτους ⟨καὶ⟩ μανδάτωρας συγκατα- 30
785 λέγειν, δηλονότι τῶν σεκρετικῶν νοταρίων ὑπεξαιρουμένων ἐκ πάντων τῶν
τοῦ λαυσιακοῦ ἀρχόντων.   καὶ ἡνίκα ἑκάστη ἁρμοζόντως τάξει τοὺς συμ-
μετόχους ἐξαριθμήσῃ, κατὰ τὸ ποσὸν τοῦ δώρου τῆς εὐεργεσίας ποιεῖσθαι
τὸν συλλογισμόν, ὡς λεχθήσεται.   ἡνίκα γὰρ ὁ μάγιστρος ἄτομον τυχὸν
λάβῃ μύραν, οἱονεὶ „ κ᾽, ὀφείλει λαμβάνειν ὁ ἀνθύπατος τὸ ἥμισυ τούτου, 35
νομίσματα ι᾽.   ὁ δὲ πατρίκιος ὀφείλει ὑποπίπτειν τῷ ἀνθυπάτῳ „ α᾽, καὶ
λαμβάνειν νομίσμ. θ᾽, ὁ δὲ ὀφφικιάλιος τὸ δίμοιρον τοῦ πατρικίου νομίσμ.
ϛ᾽, οἱ δὲ πρωτοσπαθάριοι λιτοὶ τὸ ἥμισυ τοῦ πατρικίου νομίσμ. δ᾽ ι.   προτι-

---

4 ἀμφισβητήσις L   6 ἀνατρέπιν L   8 διαφέρων L   784 14 σύγκελον L
21 κυέστορα B   25 ⟨καὶ⟩ addidi   27 ἤγουν erui : lacunam exhibet B   28 duo
seu tres litt. oblitt.: fort. καὶ   29 ⟨τοὺς δὲ κουβικουλαρίους⟩ addidi   30 στρατόρων B   ⟨καὶ⟩ addidi   μανδάτορας B   31 ὑφεξ. L   785 32 ἁρμοζόντως
35 οἱονὶ L   37 ὁ δὲ ⟨πρωτοσπαθάριος καὶ⟩ ὀφφ. conicio   δημοίρω L   38 δ᾽ B sed L
Δι (4½) recte habet   προτιμόνται L

μῶνται δὲ οἱ τοῦ χρυσοτρικλίνου καὶ οἱ τοῦ μαγλαβίου πρωτοσπαθάριοι καὶ
οἱ ἀρτικλῖνοι ὑπὲρ τοὺς λιτοὺς πρωτοσπαθαρίους νομίσμ. γ΄, οἱ δὲ σπαθαροκουβικουλάριοι καὶ σπαθαροκανδιδάτοι τὸ δίμοιρον τοῦ πρωτοσπαθαρίου
,, γ΄. οἱ δὲ κουβικουλάριοι καὶ σπαθάριοι καὶ στράτωρες λαμβάνουσι τὸ
ἥμισυ τοῦ πρωτοσπαθαρίου ,, βδ΄· οἱ δὲ κανδιδάτοι μαγλαβῖται ἀνὰ ,, ϛ΄.
οἱ δὲ σεκρετικοὶ χαρτουλάριοι καὶ νοτάριοι ὑποπίπτουσι τοῖς τοῦ λαυσιακοῦ
ἄρχουσιν, ἕκαστος κατὰ τὸ ἴδιον ἀξίωμα, τρίτον. οἱ δὲ ἄρχοντες τοῦ βασιλικοῦ βεστιαρίου ὑποπίπτουσι καὶ αὐτοὶ κατὰ τὰς οἰκείας ἀξίας ἀπὸ τῶν
βασιλικῶν τοῦ λαυσιακοῦ κατὰ τὸ δίμοιρον μέρος τοῦ πρωτοτύπου, οἷον οἱ
πρωτοσπαθάριοι ἀπὸ τῶν οἰκειακῶν λιτῶν πρωτοσπαθαρίων, τὸ δίμοιρον ,, γ΄,
καὶ οἱ σπαθαροκανδιδάτοι τῶν τριῶν τὸ δίμοιρον ,, β΄, καὶ οἱ σπαθάριοι καὶ 786
στράτωρες τῶν δύο τὸ δίμοιρον αγ΄, οἱ δὲ κανδιδάτοι ϛγ΄, φολ. κ΄, οἱ δὲ λιτοὶ
καὶ ἑβδομάριοι ἀπὸ ϛ΄, οἱ δὲ ὑπουργοὶ τῆς τραπέζης τοῦ βασιλέως καὶ τῆς
αὐγούστης ἀπὸ ϛ΄() πάντες. οἱ δὲ διὰ πόλεως πρωτοσπαθάριοι ἀπὸ νομίσμ.
α΄, οἱ δὲ σπαθαροκανδιδάτοι ἀπὸ ϛϛ΄ [οἱ δὲ σπαθάριοι στράτωρες λαμβάνουσι τὸ ἥμισυ τοῦ πρωτοσπαθαρίου ,, βδ΄, οἱ δὲ κανδιδάτοι μαγλαβῖται ἀνὰ ,,
ϛ΄, οἱ δὲ σεκρετικοὶ χαρτουλάριοι καὶ νοτάριοι ὑποπίπτουσι τοῖς τοῦ λαυσιακοῦ ἄρχουσιν, ἕκαστος κατὰ τὸ ἴδιον ἀξίωμα ,, γ΄. οἱ δὲ ἄρχοντες τοῦ
βασιλικοῦ βεστιαρίου ὑποπίπτουσι καὶ αὐτοὶ κατὰ τὰς οἰκείας ἀξίας ἀπὸ
τῶν βασιλικῶν τοῦ λαυσιακοῦ κατὰ τὸ δίμοιρον μέρος τοῦ πρωτοτύπου], οἱ
δὲ σπαθάριοι, στράτωρες, ὕπατοι ἀπὸ ϛ΄(), οἱ δὲ κανδιδάτοι βεστήτορες ἀπὸ γ΄.
δίδοται δὲ καὶ ἔξω τούτου ἐκ τῆς αὐτῆς ποσότητος τῷ μὲν πρωτοβεστιαρίῳ
⟨τοῦ δε⟩σπότου κατὰ τὴν ποσότητα τῶν λιτρῶν τῇ λίτρῃ ,, α΄, τῷ δὲ τῆς καταστάσεως ,, κ΄ καὶ τῷ ὀστιαρίῳ ,, κ΄, τῷ μέρει Βενέτων ⟨ ,, δ΄ καὶ τῷ⟩ μέρει Πρασίνων ,, δ΄, τῷ ὀρχιστῇ ,, β΄, τοῖς θυρ⟨ωροῖς ,, γ΄, τοῖς⟩ διατρέχουσι ,, γ΄, τοῖς
μανδάτορσι τοῦ λογοθέτου ,, γ΄, ⟨τοῖς . . . . .⟩ φύλαξι ,, γ΄, καὶ τῷ ἀρτικλίνῃ
τῷ διανέμοντι . . . . ιβ΄. . . . . . . μὲν ἐπὶ τῆς τῶν βρουμαλίων δωρεῶν
διανομῆς· ἐν δὲ τοῖς στεψίμοις τῶν βασιλέων καὶ ταῖς αὐτοκρατορίαις ὑπεξ- 787
αιροῦνται πάντες οἱ τῶν σεκρέτων χαρτουλάριοι καὶ νοτάριοι καὶ τὰ βεστία
καὶ ὑπουργίαι καὶ οἱ διὰ πόλεως πάντες. καὶ γίνεται ἡ διανομὴ εἰς μόνους
τοὺς ἄρχοντας τοῦ λαυσιακοῦ, οἷον εἰς μαγίστρους, πραιποσίτους, ἀνθυπάτους, πατρικίους, πρωτοσπαθαρίους (σὺν τοῖς εὐνούχοις πρωτοσπαθαρίοις
καὶ μόνον)· σπαθαροκανδιδάτοις, σπαθαρίοις, καὶ στράτωρες καὶ κανδιδά-
τοις, καὶ εἰς τοὺς λεχθέντας ἐξώβρεμα τῶν ἀποκομβίων. οἱ γὰρ τοῦ κουβουκλείου πάντες ἰδιαζόντως τὰ ἀποκόμβια λαμβάνουσιν.

3 δίμοιρον L et passim   4 στράτορες B   5 βδ΄ i.e. 2 nom. et 3 miliaresia
786 12 ⟨γ΄ B : ⟨υ L   14 fort. (δ΄)   15 οἱ δὲ... 20 πρωτοτύπου (=4-9 supra) uncis
inclusi   15 et 21 στράτορες B   21 fort. (δ΄)   cum γ΄ sc. ⟨   23 . . . . σπότου
lego, om. B   ,, om. B   24 ,, δ΄ (post Βενέτων) in cod. oblitt. recte restituit B ;
quod cum lacunam vix impleat καὶ inserui.   25 τοῖς θυρ⟨ωροῖς γ΄, τοῖς⟩ ita restitui ex
vestigiis in loco oblitterato : ὀρχιστῇ . . . διατρέχουσιν B   26 τοῦ λογό ,, γ lego : τοῦ
λογοθέτου B   τοῖς νομοφύλαξι B, non verisimile : fort. τοῖς ἀρμοφύλαξι, cf. Cer. 801₄
27 διανέμοντι τὸ ἀποκόμβιον.   καὶ ταῦτα μὲν B : διανέμοντι . . . ιβ΄ α . . . . . μὲν lego
787 28 ὑφεξ. L   33 στράτορσι legendum   34 ἐξώβρεματῶν B

Περὶ συνηθείας τῶν ἀρτικλινῶν.

Ἐπεὶ δὲ τὰς διὰ τῶν βραβείων καὶ διὰ λόγων προσγινομένων ἀξιῶν
διαιρέσεις καὶ ὑποδιαιρέσεις, αὔξεις τε καὶ μειώσεις, προσκλήσεις τε καὶ
ὑποκλήσεις, εἰς τοὐμφανὲς ἐποιήσαμεν, φέρε δὴ καὶ τὰς ἔκπαλαι τοὺς ἀρτικλίνας παρὰ τῶν βασιλέων ἐκτυπωθείσας συνηθείας, καὶ ἐκ τίνων προσώ-   5
πων ταύτας διδόναι αὐτοῖς ἠφορίσθη, ἐκ τῶν ἀρχαιοτέρων ἐρανισάμενοι
τῇδε τῇ γραφῇ παραδοίημεν.   προβαλλομένης γὰρ ζωστῆς ἢ μαγίστρου,
δίδοται αὐτοῖς ἐξ ἑκάστου αὐτῶν καθάπαξ ,, κδ'.   τιμωμένου δὲ συγκέλλου,
δίδοται αὐτοῖς συνήθεια παρ' αὐτοῦ καθάπαξ ,, ιβ'.   ἀναγομένου δὲ εὐνούχου
788 ἢ βαρβάτου εἰς πατρικιότητα, ἢ ἀνθυπάτου γενομένου τινός, δίδοται αὐτοῖς   1
ἐξ ἑκάστου αὐτῶν ,, ιβ'· ὁμοίως καὶ ἐκ τῆς διανομῆς τοῦ κομβίου τοῦ διδο-
μένου παρὰ τοῦ τιμωμένου πατρικίου λαμβάνουσιν νομίσμ. ιβ'.   οἱ δὲ χειρο-
τονούμενοι στρατηγοὶ ἔν τε τῇ ἀνατολῇ καὶ τῇ δύσει παρέχουσιν αὐτοῖς
ἀνὰ νομίσμ. ιβ'.   εἰ δὲ καὶ ἐπιμένωσι στρατηγοί, ὁσάκις ἂν ῥογευθῶσιν,
οἱ μὲν ἀνατολικοὶ ἀνὰ νομίσμ. ιβ', κἂν τάχα τύχοιεν εἰς τὸ ἴδιον θέμα,   1
τὴν ῥόγαν αὐτῶν ἀποσταλῆναι.   οἱ δὲ τῆς δύσεως καὶ μὴ ῥογευόμενοι,
ὁσάκις ἂν ἐν τῇ βασιλευούσῃ τῶν πόλεων ἐπανέλθωσι, παρέχουσιν αὐτοῖς
ἀνὰ νομισμ. ιβ'.   προβαλλομένου δὲ ἐκ προσώπου στρατηγοῦ ἢ κλεισ-
ουράρχου ἢ κατεπάνω Παφλαγωνίας, δίδοται αὐτοῖς ἐξ ἑκάστου αὐτῶν ἀνὰ
νομίσμ. η', καὶ ὁσάκις εἰσελθόντες ῥογευθῶσι, πάλιν τὴν αὐτὴν ποσότητα   2
παρέχουσιν αὐτοῖς.   οἱ δὲ ὀφφικιάλιοι, κἄν τε τῇ τῶν πρωτοσπαθαρίων
τετίμηνται ἀξίᾳ, κἄν τε καὶ μή, ἀπό τε τοῦ πραιποσίτου καὶ τοῦ δομεστίκου
τῶν σχολῶν μέχρι τῆς τοῦ πρωτοσπαθαρίου τῶν βασιλικῶν, δίδουσι καὶ
αὐτοὶ ἅπαξ ἀνὰ ,, ιβ'· οἱ δὲ λοιποὶ πάντες ὀφφικιάλιοι μέχρι τοῦ δομεστικον
τῶν βασιλικῶν ἀνὰ ,, η'.   εἰ δέ τις εὐνοῦχος πρωτοσπαθάριος γένηται, δί-   2
δωσιν αὐτοῖς ἅπαξ ,, η'· πριμικήριος ἢ ὀστιάριος ἀνὰ ,, ϛ'· ὡσαύτως ὁ ἄρχων
τοῦ ἀρμαμέντου, ὁ μινσουράτωρ, ὁ κουράτωρ τοῦ κτήματος, οἱ χαρτουλάριοι
τοῦ ὀξέου δρόμου, ὁ ἀκτουάριος, ὁ πρωτονοτάριος τοῦ δρόμου, ὁ χαρτου-
789 λάριος τοῦ σταύλου, ὁ ἐπίκτης καὶ ὁ τῆς ὑπουργίας δομέστικος, ὁ ζυγοστάτης, ὁ οἰκιστικὸς καὶ ὁ χρυσοεψητής.   ἐπὶ προβολῇ δὲ παντὸς πρωτο-   3
σπαθαρίου ἀπό τε μαγλαβιτῶν καὶ τῶν ἐν τῷ οἰκειακῷ βασιλικῷ βεστιαρίῳ
καταλεγομένων, καὶ τῶν εἰς τοὺς βασιλικοὺς ἀνθρώπους συντεταγμένων,
καὶ τῶν ἐπὶ τῆς βασιλικῆς τραπέζης παρισταμένων, καὶ τῶν διὰ πόλεως
σὺν τῶν ἐξωτικῶν τιμωμένων, δίδοται αὐτοῖς ἅπαξ ἀνὰ νομίσμ. η', οἱ δὲ
τῇ τῶν σπαθαροκανδιδάτων ἢ σπαθαρίων τιμώμενοι ἀξίᾳ ἀνὰ ,, ϛ', οἱ δὲ τῇ   35
τῶν στρατώρων ἢ ὑπάτων, ἢ κανδιδάτων ἢ μανδατόρων, ἢ βεστητόρων, ἢ
σιλεντιαρίων, ἢ ἀπὸ ἐπάρχων τιμώμενοι ἀξίᾳ, παρέχουσι καὶ αὐτοὶ νομίσμ.
⟨δ'⟩ ὡσαύτως καὶ ἐπὶ τῶν σεκρετικῶν ἤγουν συγκλητικοῦ τιμωμένου αὐτοῦ
ἐν ἀξιώμασιν, δίδοται ἐξ ἑκάστου αὐτῶν κατὰ τὸ οἰκεῖον ἀξίωμα, οἱ μὲν

4 τοῖς ἀρτικλίναις legendum videtur   5 τινῶν L   8 συγκέλου L   788 11 δι-
δωμένου L   14 ὡσάκις L   ῥογευθῶσιν L   17 βασιλευούσι L   23 δίδοσι L
25 δίδοσιν L   789 30 χρυσεψητής L : correxi   38 numerum scriba non legere
potuit. ⟨δ'⟩ supplevi ; cf. infra

τῇ τῶν πρωτοσπαθαρίων ἀνὰ „ η', οἱ δὲ τῇ τῶν σπαθαροκανδιδάτων ἢ σπαθαρίων ἀνὰ „ ϛ', οἱ δὲ τῇ τῶν στρατώρων ἢ ὑπάτων ἢ κανδιδάτων ἢ μανδατόρων ἢ βεστητόρων ἢ σιλεντιαρίων ἀνὰ νομισμ. δ', ἀπράτων δὲ σεκρετικῶν γενομένων, ἀνὰ „ γ', οἱ δὲ τῶν ταγμάτων καὶ τῶν πλοΐμων καὶ τῶν
5 νουμέρων καὶ τειχέων τοποτηρηταὶ ἅμα τοῖς χαρτουλαρίοις αὐτῶν ἀνὰ „ ϛ'.
οἱ δὲ λοιποὶ πάντες ἄρχοντες ἅμα τοῖς τριβούνοις καὶ βικαρίοις ἀνὰ νομίσματος ἑνός.   τούτων τοίνυν ἀνέκαθεν πλατικώτερον εἰσεινηνεγμένων, νυνὶ
δὲ ὡς οἷόν τε ἦν σαφῶς καὶ εὐσυνόπτως ἐν ἐπιτόμῳ συνειλεγμένων, χρὴ 790
τοῖς, ὅσοι τὴν περὶ τούτων φροντίδα καὶ ὑπηρεσίαν πεποίηνται κατὰ τὴν
10 προκειμένην διδασκαλίαν, καὶ περὶ τῶν βασιλικῶν κλητωρίων, καὶ περὶ τῶν
διανομῶν, ἐκ τοῦδέ τοῦ τακτικοῦ παραγγέλματος ὡς ἀπὸ κανόνος, ἢ, τό γε
ἀληθέστερον, ὡς ἐκ τοῦ βασιλικοῦ θεσπίσματος, ἀναμφισβήτως ἐνεργεῖν.
ἔδει μὲν ἡμᾶς τοῖς συνταχθεῖσιν περὶ καθεδρῶν λόγοις καὶ τήνδε τὴν τῶν
ἱερατικῶν ἐπισυνάψαι τάξιν, ὡς ἅτε μᾶλλον τὰ πρέσβεια τῆς πρωτοκλησίας
15 φέρουσαν,   ἀλλ' ἵνα μή τις κόρος λόγου τοῖς ἀναγινώσκουσιν περιστῇ,
καὶ ἡ συγκλητικὴ τάξις σὺν τῇ ἱερατικῇ συναφθεῖσα ἀσάφειαν τοῖς εἰσαγο-
μένοις διὰ τῶν ὀνομάτων ποιήσῃ, ταύτην τυπικῶς μὲν ἤδη ἀπὸ τῆς τάξεως
τῶν μαγίστρων, πατρικίων, πραιποσίτων καὶ στρατηγῶν προεσημάναμεν.
νυνὶ δὲ τῆς περὶ τούτων κυριοκλησίας καὶ πρωτοκαθεδρίας τῶν τε ἐπαρχιῶν
20 καὶ μητροπολιτῶν, ἀρχιεπισκόπων αὐτοκεφάλων καὶ ἐπισκόπων ὑποτεταγμένων τὴν ἁρμόζουσαν τάξιν εἰδικῶς ἐμφανῆσαι βουλόμενοι, εἰδικήν τινα
καὶ τὴν πραγματείαν συγγράψαι προεθυμήθημεν.   τὰ γὰρ εἰδικῶς ὄντως
λεγόμενα σαφῆ τὴν διδασκαλίαν παρέχει· τὰ δέ πως ἐν συζυγίαις πεπλε-
γμένα ἀσάφειαν πολλάκις τοῖς ἐντυγχάνουσι προξενεῖ.   διὸ καθ' εἱρμὸν
25 ἑκάστης ἐπαρχίας τὰς μητροπόλεις ἐκθέμενοι, τῷ ἑκάστῳ μητροπολίτῃ 791
ἁρμόζοντι τόπῳ τῆς καθέδρας διεστιχήσαμεν, καὶ εἶθ' οὕτως τὰς τῶν αὐτοκεφάλων ἀρχιεπισκόπων κατὰ τάξιν δευτέραν οὖσαν ἀπὸ τῶν μητροπολιτῶν
ἐξεθέμεθα, μετὰ δὲ τούτοις τῇ ἑκάστῃ ἐπαρχίᾳ καὶ μητροπόλει ὑποτεταγμένας πόλεις καὶ ἐπισκοπὰς ἐδηλώσαμεν, οὐκ ἐκ τῶν καθ' ἡμᾶς κλητορο-
30 λογίων μόνον τὰς ἀφορμὰς ἐκλαβόμενοι, ἀλλά γε καὶ ἐκ τῶν τοῦ θεσπεσίου
Ἐπιφανίου τοῦ ἀρχιεπισκόπου Κύπρου συγγραφῆς τὰ πλεῖστα ἀναλεξά-
μενοι, ἵν' ὑμεῖς ἐν τῇ τοιαύτῃ διακονίᾳ τῶν ἀρτοκλιῶν τυγχάνοντες τεταγμένοι, μὴ δὲ ἐν τούτῳ τῷ μέρει τι διαμάρτητε, ἀλλὰ καὶ ἐν φωσάτοις μὴ
παρόντος τοῦ οἰκουμενικοῦ πατριάρχου, τύχῃ καὶ ἐν ἑτέρῳ τόπῳ, τὴν πεῖραν
35 τῶν καθεδρῶν διὰ τοῦ συγγράμματος ἔχοντα ἄπταιστα καὶ ἀμώμητα τὰ τίμια
κλητώρια τῶν βασιλέων ἡμῶν τῶν ἁγίων εἰσάγετε.

6 νομήσματος L   790 13 συνταχθῆσιν L   15 φερούσης L : corr. R   16 συγκλι-
τικὴ L   εἰσαγωμένοις L   17 ποιήσει LB : correxi   τοπηκὸς μὲν εἴδη L : corr. R
ἀπὸ L : ἐπὶ B   23 σαφεῖ L   πῶς LB : correxi   24 διὰ καθηρμὸν L B : correxi
791 26 ἁρμόζωντι L   διεστηχήσαμεν L   29 κλητωρολ. B   32 ἦν ὑμεῖς L : corr. R
ἀρτοκλίνων L   35 ἄπτεστα L   36 εἰσάγεται L : εἰσάγετε B : εἰσάγητε scripsi

CPSIA information can be obtained at www.ICGtesting.com
Printed in the USA
BVOW01s1430240913

332009BV00012B/303/P